# MEMORIES

# &

# RECORDS

## THE LORD FISHER OMNIBUS

Autobiographical Essays by The Father of the *Dreadnought*

REPUBLISHED BY NIMBLE BOOKS LLC

Nimble Books LLC

1521 Martha Avenue

Ann Arbor, MI, USA 48103

http://www.NimbleBooks.com

wfz@nimblebooks.com

+1.734-330-2593

Version 1.0; last saved 2011-05-16.

Printed in the United States of America

ISBN-13: 978-1-60888-163-5

The paper used in this publication meets the minimum requirements of the American National Standard for Information Sciences—Permanence of Paper for Printed Library Materials, ANSI Z39.48-1992. The paper is acid-free and lignin-free.

[Portrait by J. C. Beresford.

LORD FISHER, 1917.
Admiral of the Fleet.

# MEMORIES

BY

ADMIRAL OF THE FLEET
## LORD FISHER

Fisher, John Arbuthnot Fisher

HODDER AND STOUGHTON

LONDON    NEW YORK    TORONTO
MCMXIX

Readers of this book will quickly observe that Admiral of the Fleet Lord Fisher has small faith in the printed word ; and those who have enjoyed the privilege of having " his fist shaken in their faces " will readily admit that the printed word, though faithfully taken down from his dictation, must lack a large measure of the power—the " aroma," as he calls it—which his personality lends to his spoken word.

Had Lord Fisher been allowed his own way, there would have been no Book. Not for the first time in his career, the need of serving his country and his country's Navy has over-ridden his personal feeling. These " Memories," therefore, must be regarded as a compromise (" the beastliest word in the English language "—see " The Times " of September 9th, 1919) between the No-Book of Lord Fisher's inclination and the orderly, complete Autobiography which the public wishes to possess.

The book consists in the main of the author's ipsissima verba, dictated during the month of September, 1919. One or two chapters have been put together from fugitive writings which Lord Fisher had collected and printed (in noble and eloquently various type) as a gift to his friends after his death. The discreeter passages of the letters which he wrote to Lord Esher between 1903 and 1912 illustrate some portions of the life's work which—caring little for the past and much for the future,[1] much for the idea and little for the fact—Lord Fisher has successfully declined to describe in his own words.

" This one thing I do, forgetting those things which are behind, and reaching forth unto those things which are before, I press toward the mark."—Phil. iii, 13, 14.

# *Preamble*

THERE is no plan nor sequence! Just as the thoughts have arisen so have they been written or dictated! The spoken word has not been amended— better the fragrance of the fresh picked flower than trying to get more scent out of it by adding hot water afterwards! Also it is more life-like to have the first impulse of the heart than vainly to endeavour after studied phrases! Perhaps the only curiosity is that I begin my life backwards and leave my birth and being weaned till the end!

## *"The last shall be first"* is good for Autobiography!

I think a text is a good thing! So I adopt the following (from R. L. Stevenson) as being nice for the young ones to read what follows:—

> To be honest, to be kind, to earn a little and to spend a little less, to make upon the whole a family happier for his presence, to renounce when that shall be necessary, and not be embittered, to keep a few friends *but those without capitulation*, above all on the same grim condition to keep friends with himself, here is a task for all that a man has of fortitude and delicacy.

# PREFACE

Not long ago a gentleman enclosed me the manuscript of his book, and asked me for a preface. I had never heard of him. He reminded me of Mark Twain in a similar case—the gentleman in a postscript asked Mr. Twain if he found fish good for the brain ; he had been recommended it, he said. Twain replied, Yes ! and he suggested his correspondent having whales for breakfast !

One gentleman sent me a cheque for two thousand guineas, and asked me to let him have a short article, on any subject. I returned the cheque—I had never heard of him either. I have had some most generous offers from publishers.

Sir George Reid said to me : " Never write an Autobiography. You only know one view of yourself—others see you all round." But I don't see any harm in such " Memories " as I now indite ! In regard to Sir G. Reid's observation, there's one side no one else can see, and that's " *the inside !* "

Nothing in this Volume in the least approaches the idea of a Biography. Facts illumined by letters, and the life divided into sections, to be filled in with the struggles of the ascent, seems the ideal sort of representation of a man's life. A friend once wrote me the requisites of a biographer. Three qualifications were :

(*a*) Plenty of time for the job.
(*b*) A keen appreciation of the work done.
(*c*) A devotion to the Hero.

And, as if it didn't so much matter, he added—the biographer should possess a high standard of literary ability.

But yet I believe that the vindication of a man's lifework is almost an impossible task for even the most intimate of friends or the most assiduous and talented of Biographers, simply because they cannot possibly appreciate how great deeds have been belittled and ravaged by small contemporary men. These yelping curs made the most noise, as the empty barrels do! and it's only long afterwards that the truth emerges out of the mist of obloquy and becomes history.

Remember it's only in this century that Nelson has come into his own.

FISHER.

---

"Sworn to no Party—Of no Sect am I!
I can't be silent and I will not lie!"

---

"Time and the Ocean and some Guiding Star
In High Cabal have made us what we are!"

# CONTENTS

# CONTENTS

# CONTENTS

## CHAPTER XV

## CHAPTER XVI

# LIST OF ILLUSTRATIONS

xvi LIST OF ILLUSTRATIONS

*Facing page*

AMERICA AND THE BLOCKADE . . . . . . 224

SIR JOHN FISHER AT THE HAGUE PEACE CONFERENCE,
MAY, 1899 . . . . . . . . . 256

COMMANDER-IN-CHIEF OF THE MEDITERRANEAN FLEET,
1899–1902 . . . . . . . . . . 273

# MEMORIES

## CHAPTER I

### KING EDWARD VII

KING EDWARD had faith in me, and so supported me always that it is only natural I should begin this book with the remarks about him which I privately printed long since for use at my death ; but events have occurred to alter that decision and induce me to publish this book.

There are more intimate touches than those related here, which I forbear to publish. There is a limit to those peculiar and pregnant little exhibitions of a kind heart's purpose being put in print. They lose their aroma.

In the *Dictionary of National Biography* there is a Marginal Heading in the Life of King Edward as follows :

*"HIS FAITH IN LORD FISHER."*

It is the only personal marginal note ! I now descant upon it, not to be egotistical, but to exemplify one of the finest traits in King Edward's noble character— without doubt I personally could not be of the very least service to him in any way, and yet in his belief of my being right in the vast and drastic reforms in the Navy he gave me his unfaltering support right through unswervingly, though every sycophantic effort was exhausted in the endeavour to alienate him from his support of me. He quite enjoyed the numberless communications he got, and the more outrageous the calumnies the more he revelled in my reputed wickedness! I can't very well put some of them on paper, but the Minotaur wasn't in it with me! Also I was a Malay! I was the son of a Cingalese Princess—hence my wicked cunning and duplicity! I had formed a syndicate and bought all the land round Rosyth before the Government fixed on it as a Naval Base—hence my wealth! How the King enjoyed my showing him my private income as given to the Income Tax Commissioners was £382 6s. 11d. after the legal charges for income tax, annuities, etc., were subtracted from the total private income of £750![1]

But King Edward's abiding characteristic was his unfailing intuition in doing the right thing and saying the right thing at the right time. I once heard him on the spur of the moment make a quite impromptu and totally unexpected speech to the notabilities of Malta which was simply superb! Elsewhere I have related his visit to Russia when I accompanied him. As Prince Orloff said to me, swept away by King Edward's elo-quence, " *Your King has changed the atmosphere!* "

[1] Sir Julian Corbett, the author of the wonderful " Seven Years' War," wrote to me in past vituperative years as follows :
" Yesterday I was asked if it were *really* true that you (Sir John Fisher) had sold the country to Germany! I was able to assure the questioner that the report was at least exaggerated. It is often my fortune to be able to quiet minds that have been seriously disturbed by the unprecedented slanders that have been the reward of your unpre-cedented work."

King Edward, besides his wonderful likeness to King Henry the Eighth, had that great King's remarkable attributes of combining autocracy with almost a socialistic tie with the masses. I said to His Majesty once : " Sir, that was a real low form of cunning on your Majesty's part sending to ask after Keir Hardie's stomach-ache ! " By Jove, he went for me like a mad bull ! and replied : " You don't understand me ! I am the King of *ALL* the People ! No one has got me in their pockets, as some of them think they have ! " and he proceeded with names I can't quote !

Acting on Sir Francis Knollys's example and advice I burnt all his letters to me, except one or two purely personal in their delightful adherence to Right and Justice ! but even these I won't publish ever—they were not meant to be seen by others. What anointed cads are those who sell Nelson's letters to Lady Hamilton ! letters written out of the abundance of his heart and the thankfulness of an emotional nature full of heartfelt gratitude to the sympathising woman who dressed his wounds, his torn-off scalp after the Nile, and his never-ceasing calamity of what is now called neuritis, which was for ever wasting his frail body with pain and anguish of spirit as it so unfitted him for exertion.

Here is a letter to King Edward, dated March 14th, 1908 :

" With Sir John Fisher's humble duty to your Majesty and in accordance with your Majesty's orders, I saw Mr. Blank as to the contents of the secret paper sent your Majesty, but I did not disclose what makes it so valuable—that it came from a Minister of Foreign Affairs, whose testimony is absolutely reliable.

" I told Mr. Blank and asked him to forgive my presumption in saying it, that we were making a hideous mistake in our half measures, which pleased no one and thus we perpetuate the fable of ' Perfidious Albion,' and that we ought to have thrown in our lot with Russia and completely allowed her to fortify the Aland Islands as against Sweden and Germany.

" For a Naval War against Germany we want Russia with us, and we want the Aland Islands fortified.

" Germany has got Sweden in her pocket, and they will divide Denmark between them in a War against Russia and England, and unless our Offensive is quick and overwhelming Germany will close the Baltic just as effectually as Turkey locks up the Black Sea with the possession of the Dardanelles.

" *Russia and Turkey are the two Powers, and the only two Powers, that matter to us as against Germany, and that we have eventually to fight Germany is just as sure as anything can be, solely because she can't expand commercially without it.*

" I humbly trust your Majesty will forgive my presumption in thus talking Politics, but I know I am right, and I only look at it because if we fight we want Russia and Turkey on our side against Germany.

" With my grateful thanks for your Majesty's letter,
" I am your Majesty's humble servant,
" J. A. FISHER."

" *March 14th*, 1908.

*Note.*—This letter to King Edward followed on a previous long secret conversation with his Majesty in which I urged that we should " Copenhagen " the German Fleet at Kiel *à la* Nelson, and I lamented that we possessed neither a Pitt nor a Bismarck to give the order. I have alluded to this matter in my account of Mr. Beit's interview with the German Emperor, and the

# KING EDWARD VII

German Emperor's indignation with Lord Esher as signified in the German Emperor's letter to Lord Tweedmouth that Sir John Fisher was the most dreaded man in Germany from the Emperor downwards.

It must be emphasized that at this moment we had a mass of effective Submarines and Germany only had three, and we had seven Dreadnoughts fit to fight and Germany had none!

This proposal of mine having been discarded, all that then remained for our inevitable war with Germany was to continue the concentration of our whole Naval strength in the Decisive Theatre of the War, in Northern Waters, which was so unostentatiously carried out that it was only Admiral Mahan's article in *The Scientific American* that drew attention to the fact, when he said that 88 per cent. of England's guns were pointed at Germany.

I mention another excellent illustration of King Edward's fine and magnanimous character though it's to my own detriment. He used to say to me often at Big Functions : " Have I missed out anyone, do you think ? " for he would go round in a most careful way to speak to all he should. Just then a certain Admiral approached —perhaps the biggest ass I ever met. The King shook hands with him and said something I thought quite unnecessarily loving to him : when he had gone he turned on me like a tiger and said : " You ought to be ashamed of yourself ! " I humbly said, " What for ? " " Why ! " he replied, " when that man came up to me your face was perfectly demoniacal ! Everyone saw it ! and the poor fellow couldn't kick you back ! You're First Sea Lord and he's a ruined man ! You've no business to show your hate ! " and the lovely thing was that then a man came up I knew the King did perfectly hate, and I'm blessed if he didn't smile on him and cuddle him as if he was his long-lost brother, and then he turned to me afterwards and said with joyful revenge, " *Well! did you see that?* " Isn't that a Great Heart? and is it to be wondered at that he was so Popular?

An Australian wrote a book of his first visit to England. He was on a horse omnibus sitting alongside the 'Bus Driver—suddenly he pulled up the horses with a jerk! The Australian said to him, " What's up? " The Driver said, " Don't you see? " pointing to a single mounted policeman riding in front of a one-horse brougham. The Australian said, " What is it? " The 'Bus Driver said, " It's the King! " The Australian said, " Where's the escort? " thinking of cavalry and outriders and equerries that he had read of! The 'Bus Driver turned and looked on the Australian with a contemptuous regard and said : " Hescourt? 'e wants no Hescourt! Nobody will touch a 'air of 'is 'ead! " The Australian writes that fixed him up as regards King Edward!

His astounding memory served King Edward beautifully. Once he beckoned me up to him, having finished his tour round the room, to talk about something and I said : " Sir, the new Japanese Ambassador is just behind you and I don't believe your Majesty has spoken to His Excellency." The King instantly turned round and said these very words straight off. I remember them exactly; he took my breath away: " My dear Ambassador, do let me shake you by the hand and congratulate you warmly on the splendid achievement yesterday of your wonderful country in launching a ' Dreadnought' so completely home-produced in every way, guns, armour engines, and steel, etc. Kindly convey my admiration of this splendid achievement ! "

I remembered then that in the yesterday's paper there had been an account of the great rejoicings in Japan on the launch of this " Dreadnought." The sequel is good. The Japanese Ambassador sought me later in the evening and said : " Sir John ! it was kind of you to remind the King about the ' Dreadnought' as it enables me to send a much coveted recognition to Japan in the King's words ! " I said : " My dear Ambassador, I never said a word to the King, and I am truly and heartily ashamed that as First Sea Lord it never occurred to me to congratulate you on what the King has truly designated as a splendid feat ! "

I expect the Ambassador spent a young fortune in sending out a telegram to Japan, and do you wonder that King Edward was a Cosmopolitan Idol ?

Another occasion to illustrate his saying out of his heart always the right thing at the right time. I was journeying with His Majesty from Biarritz to Toulon— I was alone with him in his railway carriage, there was a railway time table before him. The train began unexpectedly to slow down, and he said " Hulloa ! why are we stopping ? " I said, " Perhaps, your Majesty, the engine wants a drink ! " so we stopped at a big station we were to have passed through—the masses of people

shouted not " Vive le Roi ! " but " EDOUARD ! "
(As the Governor of the Bank of France said to a friend
of mine, " If he stays in France much longer we shall
have him as our King ! When's he going ? "). Sir Stanley
Clarke I saw get out and fetch the Prefect and the General
in Command to the King—the King got out, said something sweet to the Prefect and then turned to the General
and said with quite unaffected delight, " Oh, Mon
Général ! How delightful to meet you again ! how
glorious was that splendid regiment of yours, the —th
Regiment of Infantry, which I inspected 20 years ago ! "
If I ever saw Heaven in a man's face, that General had
it ! He was certainly a most splendid looking man and
not to be forgotten, but yet it was striking the King
coming out with his immediate remembrance of him.
Well ! that incident you may be sure went through the
French Army, and being a conscript nation, it went into
every village of France ! Do you wonder he was loved
in France ? And yet the King had the simplicity and
even the weaknesses of a child, and sometimes the petu-
lance thereof. He gave me a lovely box of all sizes of
rosettes of the Legion of Honour adapted to each kind of
uniform coat, and he added, " Always wear this in France
—I find it aids me very much in getting about ! " As if
he wasn't as well known in all France as the Town Pump !

These are the sweet incidents that illustrate his nature !

He went to a lunch at Marienbad with some great
swells who were there who had invited His Majesty to
meet a party of the King's friends from Carlsbad, where
I was—I wasn't asked—being an arranged snub ! A

looker-on described the scene to me. The King came in and said " How d'ye do " all round and then said to the Host, " Where's the Admiral ? " My absence was apologised for—lunch was ready and announced. The King said, " Excuse me a moment, I must write him a letter to say how sorry I am at the oversight," so he left them stewing in their own juice, and His Majesty's letter to me was lovely—I've kept that one. He began by d——ing the pen and then the blotting paper !—there were big blots and smudges ! He came back and gave the letter to my friend and said, " See he gets it directly you get back to Carlsbad to-night."

Once at a very dull lunch party given in his honour I sat next King Edward and said to His Majesty : " Pretty dull, Sir, this—hadn't I better give them a song ? " He was delighted ! (*he always did enjoy everything !*) so I recited (but, of course, I can't repeat the delicious Cockney tune in writing, so it loses all its aroma !). Two tramps had been camping out (as was their usual custom) in Trafalgar Square. They appear on the stage leaning against each other for support !—too much beer ! They look upwards at Nelson on his monument, and in an inimitable and " beery " voice they each sing :

" We live in Trafalgar Square, with four Lions to guard us,
 Fountains and statues all over the place !
 The ' Metropole ' staring us right in the face !
We own it's a trifle draughty—but we don't want to make no fuss !
What's *good e-nough* for Nelson is *good e-nough* for us ! "

On another occasion I was driving with him alone, and utterly carried away by my feelings, I suddenly stood up in the carriage and waved to a very beautiful woman who I thought was in America! The King was awfully angry, but I made it much worse by saying I had forgotten all about him! But he added, " Well! find out where she lives and let me know," and he gave her little child a sovereign and asked her to dinner, to my intense joy!

On a classic occasion at Balmoral, when staying with King Edward, I unfolded a plan, much to his delight (now that masts and sails are extinct), of fusing the Army into the Navy—an " Army and Navy co-operative society." And my favourite illustration has always been the magnificent help of our splendid soldiers at the Battle of Cape St. Vincent, where a Sergeant of the 69th Regiment was the first to board the Spanish three-decker, " San Josef," and he turned then round to help Lord Nelson, who, with his one arm, found it difficult to get through the stern port of the " San Josef " again. In Lord Howe's victory two Regiments participated— the Queen's Royal West Surrey Regiment (formerly the 2nd Foot) and the Worcestershire Regiment (formerly the 29th and 36th Regiment). Let us hope that the Future will bring us back to that good old practice! This was the occasion when I was so carried away by the subject that I found myself shaking my fist in the King's face!

Lord Denbigh, in a lecture he gave at the Royal Colonial Institute, related an incident which he quite correctly stated had hitherto been a piece of diplomatic secret history, and it is how I got the Grand Cordon of the Legion of Honour, associated with a lovely episode with King Edward of blessed memory.

In 1906, at Madeira, the Germans first took an hotel ; then they wanted a Convalescent Home ; and finally put forth the desire to establish certain vested interests. They imperiously demanded certain concessions from Portugal. The most significant of these amounted to a coaling station isolated and fortified. The German Ambassador at Lisbon called on the Portuguese Prime Minister at 10 o'clock one Saturday night and said that if he didn't get his answer by 10 o'clock the next night he should leave. The Portuguese sent us a telegram. That night we ordered the British Fleet to move. The next morning the German Ambassador told the Portuguese Prime Minister that he had made a mistake in the cipher, and he was awfully sorry but he wasn't going ; it was all his fault, he said, and he had been reprimanded by his Government. (As if any German had ever yet made a mistake with a telegram !)

To resume about the Grand Cordon of the Legion of Honour. The French Official statement when conveying to me the felicitations of the President of the French Republic was that I had the distinction of being at that time the only living Englishman who had received this honour, but the disaster that had been averted by the timely action of the British Fleet deserved it. So that evening, on meeting King Edward, I told His Majesty of the quite unexpected honour that I had received, and that I had been informed that I was the only Englishman that had got it, on which the King said : " Excuse me I've got it ! " Then, alas, I made a *faux pas* and said " Kings don't count ! " And no more do they ! He got it because certainly they all loved him in the first place, and secondly, President Loubet couldn't help it, while if it hadn't been for the British Fleet on this occasion the Germans would have been in Paris in a week, and if the Germans had known as much as they do now they would have been !

I don't mean to urge that King Edward was in any way a clever man. I'm not sure that he could do the rule of three, *but he had the Heavenly gift of Proportion and Perspective !* Brains never yet moved the Masses—but Emotion and Earnestness will not only move the Masses, but they will remove Mountains ! As I told Queen Alexandra on seeing his dear face (dead) for the last time, his epitaph is the great words of Pascal in the " Pensées " (Chapter ix, 19) :

> " Le cœur a ses raisons
> Que la raison ne connaît point."

(" The heart has reasons that reason knows nothing about " !)

He was a noble man and every inch a King ! God Bless Him ! I don't either say he was a Saint ! I know lots of cabbages that are saints !—they couldn't sin if they wanted to !

### Postscript.

It suddenly occurred to me to send these notes on King Edward to Lord Esher as he had peculiar opportunities of realizing King Edward's special qualities as a King, and realized how much there was in him of the

Tudor gift of being an autocrat and yet being loved of the people !

*Lord Esher to Lord Fisher*

ROMAN CAMP,
CALLANDER, N.B.
*July* 30, 1918.

MY DEAR ADMIRAL,

The pages are wonderful, because they are *you*.
Not a square inch of pose about them.
Tears ! that was the result of reading what you have to say about King Edward. But do you recollect our talk with him on board the Royal Yacht about France and Germany ? Surely that was worth recording.
I have kept many of his letters. They show him to have been one of the " cleverest " of men. He had never depended upon book-learning—why should he ?
He read, not books—but men and women—and jolly good reading too !
But he knew everything that it was requisite a King should know—unless Learning prepares a man for action, it is not of much value in this work-a-day world : and no Sovereign since the Tudors was so brave and wise in action as this King !
Your anecdotes of him are splendid. Add to them all that you can remember.
It was a pleasure to be scolded by the King for the sake of the smile you subsequently got.
The most awful time I ever had with him was at Balmoral when I refused to be Secretary of State for War. But I beat him on that, thank God !

Ever yours,

My beloved Admiral,

ESHER.

13

# MEMORIES

*Letter from Lord Redesdale*

1 Kensington Court, W.
*May 24, 1915.*

MY DEAR FISHER,

Do me the favour of accepting this little attempt to render justice to the best friend you ever had. (King Edward the Seventh.)

You and he were worthy of one another. Your old and very affectionate friend,

REDESDALE.

The following letter, written in 1907, would never have been penned but for the kindly intimacy and confidence placed and reposed in me by King Edward ; it therefore rightly comes in these remarks about him ; and so does the subsequent explanatory note on " Nelson and Copenhagen."

### EXTRACT FROM A LETTER FROM SIR JOHN FISHER TO KING EDWARD

I have just received Reich's book. It is one unmitigated mass of misrepresentations.

In March this year, 1907, it is an absolute fact that Germany had not laid down a single " Dreadnought," nor had she commenced building a single Battleship or Big Cruiser for eighteen months.

*Germany has been paralysed by the " Dreadnought."*

The more the German Admiralty looked into her qualities the more convinced they became that they must

14

follow suit, and the more convinced they were that the whole of their existing Battle Fleet was utterly useless because utterly wanting in gun power! For instance, half of the whole German Battle Fleet is only about equal to the English Armoured Cruisers.

The German Admiralty wrestled with the " Dreadnought " problem for eighteen months, and did nothing. Why? Because it meant their spending twelve and a half million sterling on widening and deepening the Kiel Canal, and in dredging all their harbours and all the approaches to their harbours, because if they did not do so it would be no use building German " Dreadnoughts " because they could not float! But there was another reason never yet made public. It is this : Our Battleships draw too much water to get close into the German Coast and harbours (we have to build ours big to go all over the world with great fuel endurance). But the German Admiralty is going, is indeed obliged, to spend twelve and a half million sterling in dredging so as to allow these existing ships of ours to go and fight them in their own waters when before they could not do so. It was, indeed, a Machiavellian interference of Providence on our behalf that brought about the evolution of the " Dreadnought."

To return to Mr. Reich. He makes the flesh of the British public creep at page 78 *et seq.*, by saying what the Germans are going to do. He does not say what they have done and what we have done.

Now this is the truth : England has seven " Dreadnoughts " and three " Dreadnought " Battle Cruisers (which last three ships are, in my opinion, far better than " Dreadnoughts ") ; total, ten " Dreadnoughts " built and building, while Germany, in March last, had not begun even one " Dreadnought." It is doubtful if, even so late as May last, a German " Dreadnought " had been commenced. It will therefore be seen, from this one fact, what a liar Mr. Reich is.

Again, at page 86, he makes out the Germans are stronger than we are in torpedo craft, and states that England has only 24 fully commissioned Destroyers.

Again, what are the real facts ? As stated in an Admiralty official document, dated August 22nd, 1907 : "We have 123 Destroyers and 40 Submarines. The Germans have 48 Destroyers and 1 Submarine."

The whole of our Destroyers and Submarines are absolutely efficient and ready for instant battle and are fully manned, except a portion of the Destroyers, which have four-fifths of their crew on board. Quite enough for instant service, and can be filled up under an hour to full crew. And they are all of them constantly being exercised.

There is one more piece of information I have to give : Admiral Tirpitz, the German Minister of Marine, has just stated, in a secret official document, that the English Navy is now four times stronger than the German Navy. Yes, that is so, and we are going to keep the British Navy at that strength, *vide* ten "Dreadnoughts" built and building, and not one German "Dreadnought" commenced last May. But we don't want to parade all this to the world at large. Also we might have Parliamentary trouble. A hundred and fifty members of the House of Commons have just prepared one of the best papers I have ever read, shewing convincingly that we don't want to lay down any new ships at all because we are so strong. My answer is : We can't be too strong. Sir Charles Dilke, in the *United Service Magazine* for this month, says : "Sir George Clarke points out that the Navy is now, in October, 1907, stronger than at any previous time in all History," and he adds that Sir George Clarke, in making this printed statement, makes it with the full knowledge of all the secrets of the Government, because, as Secretary of the Committee of Imperial Defence, he, Sir George Clarke, has access to every bit

KING EDWARD VII. (WHO DIED MAY 6TH, 1910)
SAYING GOOD-BYE TO LORD FISHER, FIRST SEA
LORD, 1910.

(Lord Fisher 69, so also the King.)

N.B.—The King thought the 1841 vintage very
good. Certainly good men were born that year!

of information that exists in regard to our own and foreign Naval strength.

In conclusion, a letter in *The Times* of September 17th, 1907, should be read. The writer of the letter under-states the case, as the British Home Fleet is twenty per cent. stronger than he puts it.

As regards Mr. Reich's Naval statements, they are a *réchauffé* of the mendacious drivel of a certain English newspaper. I got a letter last night from a trustworthy person *à propos* of these virulent and persistent news-paper attacks as to the weakness of the Navy, stating that the recent inspection of the Fleet by Your Majesty has knocked the bottom out of the case against the Admiralty.

I don't mean to say that we are not now menaced by Germany. Her diplomacy is, and always has been, and always will be, infinitely superior to ours. Observe our treatment of the Sultan as compared with Germany. The Sultan is the most important personage in the whole world for England. He lifts his finger, and Egypt and India are in a blaze of religious disaffection. That great American, Mr. Choate, swore to me before going to the Hague Conference that he would side with England over submarine mines and other Naval matters, but Germany has diplomatically collared the United States absolutely at The Hague.

*The only thing in the world that England has to fear is Germany, and none else.*

We have no idea, at the Foreign Office, of coping with the German propaganda in America. Our Naval Attaché in the United States tells me that the German Emperor is unceasing in his efforts to win over the American Official authorities, and that the German Embassy at Washington is far and away in the ascendant with the American Government.

I hope I shall not be considered presumptuous in

saying all this. I humbly confess I am neither a diplomatist nor a politician. I thank God I am neither. The former are senile, and the latter are liars. But it all does seem such simple common sense to me that for our Army we require mobile troops as against sedentary garrisons, and that our military intervention in any very great Continental struggle is unwise, remembering what Napoleon said on that point with such emphasis and such sure conception of war, and that great combined Naval and Military expeditions should be our *rôle*. In the splendid words of Sir Edward Grey : " The British Army should be a projectile to be fired by the British Navy."

The foundation of our policy is that the communications of the Empire must be kept open by a predominant Fleet, and *ipso facto* such a Fleet will suffice to allay the fears of the " old women of both sexes " in regard to the invasion of England or the invasion of her Colonies.

### NELSON'S COPENHAGEN

In May, 1907, England had seven " Dreadnoughts " ready for battle, and Germany had not one. And England had flotillas of submarines peculiarly adapted to the shallower German waters when Germany had none.

Even in 1908 Germany only had four submarines. At that time, in the above letter I wrote to King Edward, I approached His Majesty, and quoted certain apposite sayings of Mr. Pitt about dealing with the probable enemy before he got too strong. It is admitted that it was not quite a gentlemanly sort of thing for Nelson to go and destroy the Danish Fleet at Copenhagen without notice, but " la raison du plus fort est toujours la meilleure."

Therefore, in view of the known steadfast German

purpose, as always unmitigatedly set forth by the German High Authority that it was Germany's set intention to make even England's mighty Navy hesitate at sea, it seemed to me simply a sagacious act on England's part to seize the German Fleet when it was so very easy of accomplishment in the manner I sketched out to His Majesty, and probably without bloodshed. But, alas! even the very whisper of it excited exasperation against the supposed bellicose, but really peaceful, First Sea Lord, and the project was damned. At that time, Germany was peculiarly open to this " peaceful penetration." A new Kiel Canal, at the cost of many, many millions, had been rendered necessary by the advent of the " Dreadnought " ; but worse still for the Germans, it was necessary for them to spend further vast millions in deepening not only the approaches to the German Harbours, but the Harbours themselves, to allow the German " Dreadnoughts," when built, to be able to float. In doing this, the Germans were thus forced to arrange that thirty-three British pre-" Dreadnoughts " should be capable of attacking their shores, which shallow water had previously denied them. Such, therefore, was the time of stress and unreadiness in Germany that made it peculiarly timely to repeat Nelson's Copenhagen. Alas! we had no Pitt, no Bismarck, no Gambetta! And consequently came those terrible years of War, with millions massacred and maimed and many millions more of their kith and kin with pierc̀d hearts and bereft of all that was mortal for their joy.

# MEMORIES

QUEEN ALEXANDRA, LORD KNOLLYS, and SIR DIGHTON PROBYN.

At the end of these short and much too scant memories of him whom Lord Redesdale rightly calls in the letter I printed above

*" The best friend you ever had,"*

I can't but allude to a Trio forming so great a part of his Glory. Not to name them here would be " King Edward —an Unreality." I could not ask Queen Alexandra for permission either to print her Letters or her Words, but I am justified in printing how her steadfast love, and faith, and wonderful loyalty and fidelity to her husband have proved how just is the judgment of Her Majesty by the Common People—" the most loved Woman in the whole Nation."

And then Lord Knollys and Sir Dighton Probyn, those two Great Pillars of Wisdom and Judgment, who so reminded me, as they used to sit side by side in the Royal Chapel, of those two who on either side held up the arms of Moses in fighting the Amalekites :

" And Aaron and Hur stayed up his hands,
The one on the one side, and the other on the other side ;
And his hands were steady until the going down of the sun."

Yes ! King Edward's hands were held steady till the setting of his sun on May 6th, 1910, and so did he " discomfit his enemies by their aid."

For over forty years Lord Knollys played that great part in great affairs which will occupy his Biographer with Admiration of his Self-Effacement and unerring Judgment. Myself I owe him gratitude inexpressible.

For myself, those Great Three ever live in my heart and ever will.

There are no such that I know of who are left to us to rise in their place

## CHAPTER II

"THE MOON SWAYS OCEANS AND PROVOKES THE HOUND."

THE hound keeps baying at the moon but gets no answer from her, and she continues silently her mighty influence in causing the tides of the earth, such a mighty influence as I have seen in the Bay of Fundy, and on the coast of Arcadia where the tide rises some 40 feet—you see it like a high wall rolling in towards you on the beach ! It exalts one, and the base things of earth vanish from one's thoughts.   So also may the contents of this book be like-minded by a mighty silence against baying hounds ! I hope to name no living name except for praise, and even against envy I hope I may be silent.   Envy caused the first murder.   It was the biggest and nastiest of all Cæsar's wounds :

"See what a rent the *envious* Casca made."

My impenetrable armour is Contempt and Fortitude.

Well, yesterday September 7th, 1919, we completed our conversations for the six articles in *The Times*, and to-day we begin this book with similar talks.

My reluctance to this book being published before my death is increasingly definite ; but I have put my hand to the plough, because of the overbearing argument that I cannot resist, that I shall be helping to

(*a*) Avoid national bankruptcy.

(*b*) Avert the insanity and wickedness of building a Navy against the United States.

(*c*) Establish a union with America, as advocated by John Bright and Mr. Roosevelt.

(*d*) Enable the United States and British Navies to say to all other Navies " If you build more, we will fight you, here and now. We'll ' Copenhagen ' you, without remorse."

This is why I have consented, with such extreme reluctance, to write letters to *The Times* and dictate six articles ; and having thus entered into the fight, I follow the advice of Polonius—*Vestigia nulla retrorsum*. And so, to-day, I will begin this book—not an autobiography, but a collection of memories of a life-long war against limpets, parasites, sycophants, and jelly-fish—at one time there were 19½ millions sterling of 'em. At times they stung ; but that only made me more relent-less, ruthless and remorseless.

Why I so hate a book, and those articles in *The Times*, and even the letters, is that the printed word never can convey the virtue of the soul. The *aroma* is not there—it evaporates when printed—a scentless product, flat and stale like a bad bottle of champagne. It is like an embalmed corpse. Personality, which is the soul of man, is absent from the reader. It is a man's personality that is the living thing, and in the other world that is the thing you will meet. I have often asked ecclesiastics—" What period of life will the resurrected body represent ? " It has always been a poser for them ! There will not be any bodies, thank God ! we have had quite enough trouble with them down below here. St. Paul distinctly says that it is a spiritual body in the Resurrection. It is our Personalities that will talk to each other in Heaven. I don't care at what age of a man's life, even when toothless and decrepit and indistinguishable as he may then be, yet like another Rip Van Winkle, when he speaks you know him. However, that's a digression.

What I want to rub in is this : The man who reads this in his arm-chair in the Athenæum Club would take it all quite differently if I could walk up and down in front of him and shake my fist in his face.

(It was a lovely episode this recalls to my mind. King Edward—God bless him !—said to me once in one of my moments of wild enthusiasm : " Would you kindly leave off shaking your fist in my face ? ")

I tried once, so as to make the dead print more lifelike, using different kinds of type—big Roman block letters for the " fist-shaking," large italics for the cajoling, small italics for the facts, and ordinary print for the fool. The printer's price was ruinous, and the effect ludicrous. But I made this compromise and he agreed to it—whenever the following words occurred they were to be printed in large capitals : " Fool," " Ass," " Congenital Idiot." Myself, I don't know that I am singular, but I seldom read a book. I look at the pages as you look at a picture, and grasp it that way. Of course, I know what the skunks

24

will say when they read this—" Didn't I tell you he was
superficial ? and here he is judged out of his own mouth."
I do confess to having only one idea at a time, and King
Edward found fault with me and said it would be my
ruin ; so I replied : " Anyhow, I am stopping a fortnight
with you at Balmoral, and I never expected that when I
entered the Navy, penniless, friendless, and forlorn ! "
Besides, didn't Solomon and Mr. Disraeli both say that
whatever you did you were to do it with all your might ?
You can't do more than one thing at a time with all your
might—that's Euclid.  Mr. Disraeli added something to
Solomon—he said " there was nothing you couldn't have
if only you wanted it enough."  And such is my only
excuse for whatever success I have had.  I have only
had one idea at a time. *Longo intervallo*, I have been a
humble, and I endeavoured to be an unostentatious,
follower of our Immortal Hero.  Some venomous reptile
(his name has disappeared—I tried in vain to get hold of
it at Mr. Maggs's bookshop only the other day) called
Nelson " vain and egotistical."  Good God ! if he
seemed so, how could he help it ?  Some nip-cheese
clerk at the Admiralty wrote to him for a statement of
his services, to justify his being given a pension for his
wounds.  His arm off, his eye out, his scalp torn off at
the Nile—that clerk must have known that quite well
but it elicited a gem.  Let us thank God for that clerk !
How this shows one the wonderful working of the
Almighty Providence, and no doubt whatever that fools
are an essential feature in the great scheme of creation.
Why !—didn't some geese cackling save Rome ?  Nelson

25

told this clerk he had been in a hundred fights and he enumerated his wounds ; and his letter lives to illumine his fame.

The Almighty has a place for nip-cheese clerks as much as for the sweetest wild flower that perishes in a day.

It is really astounding that Nelson's life has not yet been properly written. All that has been written is utterly unrepresentative of him. The key-notes of his being were imagination, audacity, tenderness.

He never flogged a man. (One of my first Captains flogged every man in the ship and was tried for cruelty, but being the scion of a noble house he was promoted to a bigger ship instead of being shot.) It oozed out of Nelson that he felt in himself the certainty of effecting what to other men seemed rash and even maniacal rashness ; and this involved his seeming vain and egotistical. Like Napoleon's presence on the field of battle that meant 40,000 men, so did the advent of Nelson in a fleet (this is a fact) make every common sailor in that fleet as sure of victory as he was breathing. I have somewhere a conversation of two sailors that was overheard and taken down after the battle of Trafalgar, which illustrates what I have been saying. Great odds against 'em—but going into action the odds were not even thought of, they were not dreamt of, by these common men. Nelson's presence was victory. However, I must add here that he hated the word Victory. What he wanted was Annihilation. That Crowning Mercy (as Cromwell would have called it), the battle of the Nile, deserves the wonderful pen of Lord Rosebery, but he won't do it. Warburton in "The Crescent and the Cross" gives a faint inkling of what the glorious chronicle should be. For two years, that frail body of his daily tormented with pain (he was a martyr to what they now call neuritis—I believe they called it then "*tic douloureux*"), he never put his foot outside his ship, watching off Toulon. The Lord Mayor and Citizens of London sent him a gold casket for keeping the hostile fleet locked up in Toulon. He wrote back to say he would take the casket, but he never wanted to keep the French Fleet in harbour; he wanted them to come out. But he did keep close in to Toulon for fear of missing them coming out in darkness or in a fog.

In his two years off Toulon Nelson only made £6,000 of prize money, while it was a common thing for the Captain of a single man-of-war off the Straits of Gibraltar to make a haul of £20,000, and Prize-Money Admirals in crowds basked in Bath enriched beyond the dreams of avarice. Nelson practically died a pauper.

Now this is another big digression which I must apologise for, but that's the damnable part of a book. If one could walk up and down and talk to someone, it never strikes them as incongruous having a digression.

I wind up this chapter, as I began it, with the fervent intention of avoiding any reference to those who have assailed me. I will only print their affectionate letters to me, for which I still retain the most affectionate

MEMORIES

feelings towards them.   I regret now that on one occasion
I did so far lose my self-control as to tell a specific Judas
to take back his thirty pieces of silver and go and hang
himself.  However, eventually he did get hanged, so
it was all right.

# CHAPTER III

YESTERDAY, September 8th, 1919 (I must put this date down because yesterday in a telegram I called von Tirpitz a liar) I got an enquiry whether it was correct that in 1909, as stated by Admiral von Tirpitz, I, as First Sea Lord of the Admiralty, engineered a German Naval Scare in England in order to get bigger British Naval estimates—and that I had said this to the German Naval Attaché. I replied " Tell Tirpitz— using the immortal words of Dr. Johnson—' you lie Sir, and you know it ! ' " Now, first of all, could I possibly have told the German Naval Attaché such a thing if I possessed the Machiavellian nature which is inferred by Tirpitz ?

Secondly, there was a vast multitude of acute domestic enemies too closely watching me to permit any such manœuvre.

This affords an opportunity of telling you some very interesting facts about Tirpitz. They came to be known through the widow of Admiral von Pohl (who had been at the German Admiralty and commanded the German

High Sea Fleet) interviewing a man who had been a prisoner at Ruhleben. He relates a conversation with Frau von Pohl, and he mentions her being an intimate friend of the German ex-Crown Princess, and as being extremely intelligent. Frau von Pohl had been reading Lord Jellicoe's book, and said to the ex-Ruhleben prisoner : " How strange is the parallel between Germany and Britain, that in both Navies the Admirals were in a stew as to the failings of their respective fleets." So much so on the German side, she said, that the German Fleet did not consider itself ready to fight till two months before the battle of Jutland, and the Germans till then lived in a constant fever of trepidation. These were the questions she heard. " ' Why do the English not attack ? Will the English attack to-morrow ? ' [1] These questions we asked ourselves hourly. We felt like crabs in the process of changing their shells. Apparently our secret never oozed out." She put the inefficiency of the German Fleet all down to Tirpitz, and said that if any man deserved hanging it was he. Admiral von Pohl was supposed to have committed suicide through dejection. If all this be true, how it does once more illuminate that great Nelsonic maxim of an immediate Offensive in war ! Presumably Frau von Pohl had good information ; and she added : " The only reason Tirpitz was not dismissed sooner was lest the British should suspect from his fall something serious was the matter, and attack at once."[2] Part of her interview

[1] See letters at end of this chapter.
[2] On hearing of von Tirpitz's dismissal I perpetrated the following letter, which a newspaper contrived to print in one of its editions.

# VON POHL AND VON TIRPITZ

is of special interest, as it so reminded me of my deciding on Scapa Flow as the base for the fleet. For as Frau von Pohl states, its speciality was that the German Destroyers could not get to Scapa Flow and back at full speed. Their fuel arrangements were inadequate for such a distance. " My husband," she said, " was called out by the Emperor to put things right, but was in a constant state of trepidation." Alas ! trepidation was on our side also, for in a book written by a Naval Lieutenant he says how a German submarine was supposed to have got inside Scapa.[1] As a matter of fact, it was subsequently discovered that a torpedo had rolled out of its tube aboard one of our Destroyers and passed close to H.M.S. " Leda," who quite properly reported " a torpedo has passed under my stern." This caused all the excitement.

I can't say why, but it didn't appear any more, nor was it copied by any other paper !

DEAR OLD TIRPS,

We are both in the same boat ! What a time we've been colleagues, old boy ! However, we did you in the eye over the Battle Cruisers and I know you've said you'll never forgive me for it when bang went the " Blucher " and von Spee and all his host !

Cheer up, old chap ! Say " Resurgam " ! You're the one German sailor who understands War ! Kill your enemy without being killed yourself. *I don't blame you for the submarine business.* I'd have done the same myself, only our idiots in England wouldn't believe it when I told 'em !

Well ! So long !

Yours till hell freezes,

FISHER.

29/3/16.

I say ! Are you sure if you had tripped out with your whole High Sea Fleet before the Russian ice thawed and brought over those half-a-million soldiers from Hamburg to frighten our old women that you could have got back un-Jellicoed ?

R.S.V.P.

[1] "A Naval Lieutenant, 1914-1918," by Etienne, 1919, pp. 48 *et seq.*

# MEMORIES

Admiral von Pohl succeeded Admiral von Ingenohl as Commander-in-Chief of the German High Sea Fleet. It has not much bearing on what I have been saying, but it is interesting that Frau von Pohl said that the wife of the German Minister of the Interior had told her that her husband, on November 6th, five days before the Armistice, had talked to the Emperor of the truth as to the German inferiority. The Emperor listened, first with amazement, and then with incredulity, and ultimately in a passion of rage called him a madman and an arrogant fool, and turned him out in fury from his presence. This is not quite on all fours with Ludendorff, but Ludendorff may have been confining himself strictly to the fighting condition of the Army ; and without doubt he was right there, for General Plumer told me himself he had the opportunity of bearing personal testimony to the complete efficiency of the German Army at the moment of the Armistice. Plumer was, it may be observed, rightly accorded the honour of leading the British Army into Cologne.

The man who contemplates all the things that may be somewhat at fault and adds up his own war deficiencies with that curious failure of judgment to realise that his enemy has got as many if not more, has neither the Napoleonic nor the Nelsonic gift of Imagination and Audacity. We know, now, how very near—within almost a few minutes of total destruction (at the time the battle-cruiser " Blucher " was sunk)—was the loss to the Germans of several even more powerful ships than the " Blucher," more particularly the " Seydlitz." Alas! there

Sir John Fisher in "Renown," 1897.

was a fatal doubt which prevented the continuance of the onslaught, and it was indeed too grievous that we missed by so little so great a " Might Have Been ! " Well, anyhow, we won the war and it is all over. But I for one simply abominate the saying " Let bygones be bygones." I should shoot 'em now ! And seek another Voltaire.

I get the following from Lord Esher :—" In January, 1906, King Edward sent me to see Mr. Beit, who had been recently received by the German Emperor at Potsdam. The Emperor said to Beit that ' England wanted war : not the King—not, perhaps, the Government ; but influential people like Sir John Fisher.' He said Fisher held that because the British Fleet was in perfect order, and the German Fleet was not ready; England should provoke war. Beit said he had met Fisher at Carlsbad, and had long talks with him, and that what he said to him did not convey at all the impression gathered by His Imperial Majesty. The Emperor replied : ' He thinks it is the hour for an attack, and I am not blaming him. I quite understand his point of view ; but we, too, are prepared, and if it comes to war the result will depend upon the weight you carry into action—namely, a good conscience, and I have that. . . . Fisher can, no doubt, land 100,000 men in Schleswig-Holstein—it would not be difficult—and the British Navy has reconnoitred the coast of Denmark with this object during the cruise of the Fleet. But Fisher forgets that it will be for me to deal with the 100,000 men when they are landed.' "

D

MEMORIES

The German Emperor told another friend of mine
the real spot. It was not Schleswig-Holstein—that was
only a feint to be turned into a reality against the Kiel
Canal if things went well. No, the real spot was the
Pomeranian Coast, under a hundred miles from Berlin,
where the Russian Army landed in the time of Frederick
the Great. Frederick felt it was the end and sent for
a bottle of poison, but he didn't take it, as the Russian
Empress died that night and peace came.

Long before I heard from Lord Esher, I had written
the following note about Beit :—

A mutual friend at Carlsbad introduced me to Mr.
Beit, the great South African millionaire. He adored
Cecil Rhodes, and so did I. Beit, so I was told, had
got it into his head that I somewhat resembled his dead
friend, and he talked to me on one occasion about Rhodes
until 3 a.m. after dining together. Beit begged me to
come and see him on my return to London at his house
in Park Lane, just then finished, but I never did for I
was vastly busy then. I was troubled on all sides,
like St. Paul.

" Without were fightings, and within were fears."
Fighting outside the Admiralty, and fears inside it.

He really was a dear man, was Beit.

Of course I don't know anything about his business
character. Apparently there is a character a man puts
on in business, just as a man does in politics, and it may
be quite different from his character as a gentleman.

Beit every year made a pilgrimage to Hamburg, to see
his old mother, who lived there, and it much touched me,
his devotion to her. But our bond of affection was our
affection for Rhodes.

The German Emperor sent for Beit, for I gathered
that Beit saw how peace was threatened. I don't know

34

if this was the reason of the interview. In this Imperial conversation my name turned up as Lord Esher had made a statement that by all from the German Emperor downwards I was the most hated man in Germany. The German Emperor did say to Beit that I was dangerous, and that he knew of my ideas as regards the Baltic being Germany's vulnerable spot, and he had heard of my idea for the " Copenhagening " of the German Fleet. But this last I much doubt. He only said it because he knew it was what we ought to have done.

With regard to saying anything more of that interview I prefer to keep silent. In an Italian book, printed at Brescia in A.D. 1594, occur these words of Steven Guazzo ;

" They should know," says Anniball, " that it is no lesse admirable to know how to holde one's peace than to know how to speake. For, as wordes well uttered shewe eloquance and learning, so silence well kept sheweth prudence and gravitie ! "

I wish Beit could have read Stead's splendid appreciation of Cecil Rhodes, who describes him as a Titan of intrinsic nobility and sincerity, of innate excellence of heart, and immense vitality of genius, and describes the splendid impulsiveness of his generous nature. I am told that Rhodes's favourite quotation was from Marcus Aurelius :

" Take care always to remember you are a Roman, and let every action be done with perfect and unaffected gravity, humanity, freedom and justice."

Stead's opinion was that Rhodes was a practical mystic of the Cromwell type. Stead was right. Rhodes was a Cromwell. He was Cromwellian in thoroughness, he was Napoleonic in audactiy, and he was Nelsonic in execution.

> " Let us praise famous men."
> (*Ecclesiasticus*, chapter 44, verse 1).

# MEMORIES

36, BERKELEY SQUARE.

MY DEAR FRIEND,

I was asked yesterday : Could I end the War ?

I said : " Yes, by one decisive stroke ! "

" What's the stroke ? " I was asked.

I replied : " Never prescribe till you are called in."

But I said this : " Winston once told me, ' You can see Visions ! That's why you should come back.' "

For instance, even Jellicoe was against me in sending the Battle Cruisers to gobble up von Spee at the Falkland Islands ! (All were against me !) Yes ! and all were against me in 1904 ! when the Navy was turned inside out —ships, officers and men. " A New Heaven and a New Earth ! " 160 ships put on the scrap heap because they could neither fight nor run away ! *Vide* Mr. Balfour's speech at Manchester about this " Courageous stroke of the pen ! "

We now want another Courageous Stroke ! And the Stroke is ready ! It's the British Navy waiting to strike ! And it would end the War !

This project of mine sounds an impossibility ! but so did von Spee's annihilation ! Pitt said " I walk on Impossibilities." All the old women of both sexes would squirm at it ! They equally squirmed when I did away with 19½ millions sterling of parasites in ships, officers and men, between 1904 and 1910 ! They squirmed when, at one big plunge, we introduced the Turbine in the Dreadnought (the Turbine only before having been in a penny steamboat). They squirmed at my introduction of the water tube Boiler, when I put the fire where the water used to be and the water where the fire used to be ! And now 82 per cent. of the Horse Power of the whole world is Turbine propulsion actuated by water tube Boilers !

They squirmed when I concentrated 88 per cent. of

the British Fleet in the North Sea, and this concentration was only found out by accident, and so published to the ignorant world, by Admiral Mahan in an article in *The Scientific American!*

And they squirm now when I say at one stroke the War could be ended.  It could be!

Yours, etc.

(Signed) FISHER.

*Lord Fisher to a Privy Councillor*

36, BERKELEY SQUARE,<br>LONDON,<br>*Dec.* 27, 1916.

MY DEAR FRIEND,

You've sent me a very charming letter, though I begged you not to trouble yourself to write, but as you have written and said things I am constrained to reply, lest you should be under false impressions.  I have an immense regard for Jellicoe. . . . Callaghan I got where he was—he was a great friend of mine—but Jellicoe was better ; and Jellicoe, in spite of mutinous threats, was appointed Admiralissimo on the eve of war.  I just mention all this to show what I've done for Jellicoe because I knew him to be a born Commander of a Fleet !  Like poets, Fleet Admirals are born, not made !  *Nascitur non fit !*  Jellicoe is incomparable as the Commander of a Fleet, but to prop up an effete Administration he allowed himself to be cajoled away from his great post of duty.  I enclose my letter to him.

I need hardly say how private all this is, but you are so closely associated with all the wonders we effected from October 21, 1904, onwards, that I feel bound to take you into my inmost confidence.  Jellicoe retorted I had praised Beatty—*so I had* !  See my reply thereon.

37

# MEMORIES

I told the Dardanelles Commission (why they asked me I don't know !) that Jellicoe had all the Nelsonic attributes except *one*—he is totally wanting in the great gift of Insubordination. Nelson's greatest achievements were all solely due to his disobeying orders ! But that's another story, as Mr. Kipling would say. Wait till we meet, and I'll astonish you on this subject ! Any fool can obey orders ! But it required a Nelson to disobey Sir John Jervis at the Battle of Cape St. Vincent, to disregard the order to retire at Copenhagen, to go into the Battle of the Nile by night with no charts against orders, and, to crown all, to enter into the Battle of Trafalgar in a battle formation contrary to all the Sea orders of the time ! BLESS HIM ! Alas ! Jellicoe is saturated with Discipline ! He is THE ONE MAN to command the Fleet, BUT he is not the man to stand up against a pack of lawyers clothed with Cabinet garments, and possessed with tongues that have put them where they are !

David was nodding when he said in the Psalms : " A man full of words shall not prosper on the Earth." *They are the very ones that* DO *prosper* ! For War, my dead Friend, you want a totally differently constituted mind to that of a statesman and politician ! There are great exemplars of immense minds being utter fools ! They weigh everything in the Balance ! I know great men who never came to a prompt decision—men who could talk a bird out of a tree !

War is Big Conceptions and Quick Decisions. Think in Oceans. Shoot at Sight ! The essence of War is Violence. Moderation in War is Imbecility. All we have done this war is to imitate the Germans ! We have neither been Napoleonic in Audacity nor Cromwellian in Thoroughness nor Nelsonic in execution. Always, always, always " TOO LATE " !

I could finish this present German submarine menace in a few weeks, but I must have POWER ! My plans

38

would be emasculated if I handed them in. I must be able to say to the men I employ : " *If you don't do what I tell you, I'll make your wife a widow and your house a dunghill ! ! !* (*and they know I would !*)

Don't prescribe till you're called in ! Someone else might put something else in the pill !

Heaven bless you !

When people come and sympathise with me, I always reply, with those old Romans 2,000 years ago expelled :

> " Non fugimus :
> Nos fugamur."
> " We are not Deserters,
> We are Outcasts."

Yours, etc.

(Signed) FISHER.

*From a Privy Councillor to Lord Fisher*

*Jan. 8th,* 1917.

MY DEAR FISHER,

I have always thought Jellicoe one of those rare exceptions to the general rule that no great commander is ever a good administrator. I knew you had picked him out long ago to command the Grand Fleet if war came, and it is in my mind that you had told me years ago your opinion of him as a Sea Commander so that it was what I was expecting and hoping for at the time, though I was sorry for Jellicoe superseding Callaghan when the war broke out, but I remembered your old saying, " Some day the Empire will go down because it is Buggins's turn " ! At the same time, I'm not sure that any man can stand the strain of active command under present conditions for more than $2\frac{1}{2}$ years. I see no sign of tiredness about Jellicoe now, but it must be almost impossible to keep at high tension so long without losing some of the spring and dash, and it did

39

look as if a stronger man than Jackson was wanted as First Sea Lord at the Admiralty. Of course when you were First Sea Lord and Jellicoe with the Grand Fleet it was absolutely the right combination, but as they haven't brought you back to the Admiralty I feel Jellicoe is the man to be where he is, provided his successor is the right man too. I don't know Beatty, so can only go by what I hear of him. I can only pray that when his day of trial comes he will come up to your high standard.

I largely agree with all you say about the politicians. No doubt our great handicap in this war is that nearly all the party leaders get their positions through qualities which serve them admirably in peace time, but are fatal in war. The great art in politics in recent years has always seemed to me to be to pretend to lead, when you are really following the public bent of the moment. All sense of right and wrong is blunted, and no one stands up for what he honestly believes in but which may not at the moment be popular. If he does, he is regarded as a fool, and a " waster," and may get out. A habit of mind is thus formed which is wholly wanting in initiative, and in war the initiative is everything. I agree with you absolutely :—" *Make up your mind, and strike ! and strike hard and without mercy.*" We have thrown away chance upon chance, and nothing saves us but the splendid fighting material at our disposal. I doubt whether the recent changes will bring about any great change. I trust they may, but, whatever happens, neither side can go on indefinitely. Everything points to Germany's economic condition being very bad, and there may come a crash, *but meantime the submarine warfare is most serious, and no complete answer to it is yet available.*

Yours very sincerely,

# CHAPTER IV

## ECONOMY IS VICTORY

MR. GLADSTONE stood by me last night. Mr.
McKenna was by his side. I am not inventing this
dream. It is a true story. (It is Godly sincerity that
wins—not fleshly wisdom!)

A gentleman, such as you, was by way of interviewing
Mr. Gladstone. Mr. Gladstone was castigating me. I
was a Public Department. He said to you, who were
interviewing him, that he was helpless against all the
Public Departments, for he was fighting for Economy,
and he gave a case to you worse than either Chepstow
or Slough. I am sorry to say it was the War Office he
was illustrating, as I am devoted to Mr. Churchill and
would not hurt him for the world—even in a dream.
It is too puerile to describe in print, but what Mr.
Gladstone pointed to I have told you in conversation.

Now, the above is an Allegory.

Imagine! nearly a year after the Armistice and yet
we are spending two millions sterling a day beyond an
absolutely fabulous income—beyond any income ever
yet produced by any Empire or any Nation!

*Sweep them out!*

# MEMORIES

Dr. Macnamara, a few days since, in his *apologia pro vita sua* excuses his Department to the public by saying that on the very day of the Armistice the Board of Admiralty sat on Economy! *So they did!* They *sat* on it!

Economy! To send Squadrons all over the globe that were not there before! The globe did without them during the War—why not now? " Oh my Sacred Aunt! " (as the French say when in an extremity). " Showing the flag," I suppose, for that was the cry of the " baying hounds " in 1905 when we brought home some 160 vessels of war that could neither fight nor run away—and whose Officers were shooting pheasants up Chinese rivers and giving tea parties to British Consuls. How those Consuls did write! And how agitated was the Foreign Office! I must produce some of these communications directly " DORA " is abolished. Well, that's what " showing the flag " means.

*Sweep 'em out!*

Gladstone was hopeless against Departments—so is now the Nation.

Dr. Macnamara may not know it, but Mr. Herbert Samuel was to have had his place. I did not know either of them, but I said to the Prime Minister " Let's have the ' Two Macs ' ! " Mind, I don't class him with the Music Hall artist. (*Tempus :* Death of Campbell-Bannerman)—that epoch—I cannot forget Mr. Asquith's kindness to me. He had telephoned to me from Bordeaux after seeing the King at Biarritz, asking me to meet him on his arrival home next night at 8.30 p.m.

at 40 Cavendish Square. His motor car was leaving the door as I arrived. He told me he had seen the King, and had proposed Mr. McKenna as First Lord of the Admiralty. The King seemed to have some suspicion that I should not think Mr. McKenna a congenial spirit. I made no objection—I thought to myself that if Mr. McKenna were hostile then *Tempus edax rerum*. I don't think Jonathan and David were " in it," when Mr. McKenna and I parted on January 25th, 1910—my selected day to go and plant roses in Norfolk. I blush to quote the Latin inscription on the beautiful vase he gave me ;

Joanni Fisher
Baroni Kilverstonæ
Navarchorum Principi, Ensis, Linguæ,
Stili Valde Perito,
Vel in Concilio vel in Praelio insigni,
Nihil Timenti,
Inflexibili, Indomitabili, Invincibili,[1]
Pignus Amicitiae Sempiternae,
Dederunt Reginaldus et Pamela McKenna.

To
John
Lord Fisher of Kilverstone
First of Admirals
Skilled of Sword, Tongue & Pen
Brilliant in Council and Battle
Dreading Nought
Inflexible, Indomitable, Invincible [1]
This Token of Enduring Friendship
a Gift from
Reginald & Pamela McKenna

And, even now, when time and absence might have deadened those feelings of affection, he casts himself into

[1] *Note.*—These are the names of the three first great Battle Cruisers of the Dreadnought type.

43

the burning fiery furnace, bound with me in a trusteeship of a huge estate with only 3s. 4d. in the £ left—all that the spendthrifts leave us. "Showing the flag" and presumably resuscitating the same old game of multitudinous dockyards to minister to the ships that are "showing the flag"; and so more Chepstows and more Sloughs! And these multitudes of ship-wrights superfluous in Government Dockyards who ought to be in day and night shifts making good at Private Yards the seven millions sterling of merchant vessels that Dr. Macnamara's Government associates supinely allowed to be sent to the bottom! Those political and professional associates, who, instead of using the unparalleled British Navy of the moment as a colossal weapon for landing Russian Armies in Pomerania and Schleswig-Holstein, aided by the calm and tideless waters of the Baltic, were led astray to follow the road that led to conscription and an army of Four Million Soldiers, while the Navy was described in the House of Commons as "a subsidiary service." How Napoleon must now be chortling at his prognostication coming true, that he put forth at St. Helena, as described on page 177 of Lord Rosebery's "Last Phase," that the day we left the sea would be our downfall!

But this chapter is on "Economy"; and I have to tell a story here about my dear friend McKenna. He was Secretary of the Treasury; he, and an almost equal friend of mine—Mr. Runciman—were, as we all know, extremely cunning at figures. Lots of people were then looking after me—Kind friends! For instance, I remember my good friend John Burns at one Cabinet Committee meeting instructing me on a piece of blotting paper how to deal with a hostile fleet. I don't mean to say that John Burns would not have been a first-class Admiral. To be a good Admiral, a man does not need to be a good sailor. That's a common mistake. He wants good sailors under him. He is the Conceptionist. However, to resume. At that time I was " Pooh-Bah " at the Admiralty ; the First Lord was in a trance, and the Financial Secretary had locomotor ataxy. I was First Sea Lord, and I acted for both the Financial Secretary and the First Lord in their absence. I wasn't justified, but I did it. So I was the *tria juncta in uno* ; and I referred, as First Sea Lord, a matter to the Financial Secretary for his urgent and favourable consideration, and he favourably commended it to the First Lord, who invariably cordially approved. It was all over in about a minute. *Business buzzed !*

(I'm doubtful whether this ought to come out before Dora's abolished. That's why I wanted these papers to be edited in the United States by some indiscreet woman, where no action for libel lies. Colonel House did ask me to go to America when I saw him in Paris last May. There is a great temptation, for the climate goes from the Equator to the Pole, and a dear American Admiral friend of mine expatiated to me on the joy of laying hold of the hand of the summer girl at Palm Beach in Florida and never letting it go until you get to Bar Harbour in the State of Maine. I have had endless invitations and most hearty words from Florida to Maine, and from Passedena to Boston, and I have as many American dear friends as I have English.)

Well! the Treasury could not make out how all those submarines were being built—where the devil the money was coming from; so these ferrets came over. I led a dog's life, or rather a rabbit's life, chased from hole to hole. Nothing came of it; and as an outcome of that time I left the Admiralty with 61 good submarines and 13 building. The Germans, thank God! had gone to the bottom with their first submarine, which never came up again, and the few more they had at that time were not much use.

I must tell a story now. Mind! I don't want to run down the Treasury. The Treasury is an absolutely necessary affliction.

There was once a good Parsee ship-owner with a good Captain. But this Captain *would* charge his owner with the cost of his carriage from his ship to the office. Not being far, the old Parsee thought the Captain ought to walk, and if he didn't walk then he ought to pay for the cab himself. They call the carriages " buggies " at Bombay. However, when the old Parsee had to pay the bill next month—there it was : " Buggy —so many rupees." He told his Captain he would pay that once but never again ; and not finding it in the items of the bill presented the following month he gave the Captain his cheque. As the Captain put it in his pocket he said : " Buggy's there ! " That's what happened to the Treasury and the submarines.

I had a friend in the Accountant-General's Department

called " The Mole." He taught me how to hide the
money. I may observe I was called a " Mole." It
wasn't a bad name. I was not seen or heard, but I was
recognised by upheavals—" There is that damned fellow
Fisher again, I will swear to it ! " But, as David said,
" Let us be abundantly satisfied " that we have such
among us as McKennas and Runcimans. I should like
to let those ferrets loose now. However, " Out of Evil
Good comes." Now comes a pardonable digression, I
think.

Here's a letter I got yesterday, September 9th, 1919,
coming from Russia. Now suppose we had not made
the very damnedest mess of Russia ever made in this
world—with Lord Milner first going there and then
Mr. Henderson, the head of the Labour Party, ambassa-
doring (as least, he says so) and this nation in every
possible conceivable way alienating the Russian people
—then I never could have had this magnificent letter
from Russia to give you. Just observing, before I quote
it : Supposing a French Army landed at Dover to help
us subjugate Ireland ? I guess we should all forget
whether we were Tories or Carsons or Smillies, and unite
to get this French army out of our Archangel, and
the Entente Cordial would be " in the cart," as the
vulgar say. Well, this is the letter which does my heart
good. It is from a young lad in an English man-of-war,
now off St. Petersburg. He is writing of the recent
defeat of the Russian fleet there :—

" There has been such a fight. I was only a looker-on.
I was furious. Kronstadt was attacked by our motor

boats each carrying two torpedoes " [by the way, I was vilified for introducing motor boats] " and seaplanes with destroyers backing them up " [isn't it awful ! I introduced destroyers also]. " Two Russian battleships, a Depôt ship and a Destroyer Leader were torpedoed.

" Our motor boats were MAGNIFICENT !

" I nearly cried with pride at belonging to the same Race.

" There has been nothing like it in the whole War.

" I would rather take part in a thing like that than be Prime Minister of England. You would have been so proud if you could have seen them."

The letter is to the boy's mother. On it is written, by him who sends it me, " The Nelson touch, I think ! "

[*By kind permission of "The Westminster Gazette."*]

NATIONAL SERVICE OR THE NAVY?

SIR JOHN FISHER AND LORD ROBERTS, 1906.

# CHAPTER V

THE DARDANELLES

"UNTIL THIS DAY REMAINETH THE SAME VAIL UNTAKEN
AWAY "
2 Corinthians, iii, 14.

I COMPARED this morning early what I had formerly
written on the subject of Personalities with what I said
to you yesterday on the same subject in my peripatetic
dictation—I can't recognise what is in type for the same
as what I spoke.

This morning I get a letter from Lord Rosebery.
Lord Rosebery is, I think, in a way attached to me.
In fact he must be, or I should not have drunk so much
of his splendid champagne! Now *you* don't call me
"frisky" when I walk up and down talking to you;
and although he reads the actual living words I say to
you, yet when he sees the beastly thing in print he calls
me "frisky"! I keep on saying this *ad nauseam*, to
keep on hammering it not only into you but into the
public at large who happen to read these words—that
no printed effusion can ever represent what, when face
to face, cannot help conveying conviction to the hearer.
And so we come to the same old story, that the written

word is an inanimate corpse. You want to have the Soul of the Man pouring out to you his personality.

And here again, when I contrasted the notes which I spoke from with what I said, again I find I don't recognise them—Well! enough of that!

Now if anyone thinks that in this chapter they are going to see Sport and that I am going to trounce Mr. Winston Churchill and abuse Mr. Asquith and put it all upon poor Kitchener they are woefully mistaken. It was a Miasma that brought about the Dardanelles Adventure. A Miasma like the invisible, scentless, poisonous—*deadly* poisonous—gas with which my dear friend Brock, of imperishable memory and Victoria Cross bravery, wickedly massacred at Zeebrugge, was going (in unison with a plan I had) to polish off not alone every human soul in Heligoland and its surrounding fleet sheltered under its guns from the Grand Fleet, but every rabbit. It was much the same gas the German put into the " Inflexible " (which I commanded), in 1882 to light the engine-room. When it escaped it was scentless ; instead of going up, as it ought to have done, it went down, and permeated the double-bottom, and we kept hauling up unconscious men like poisoned miners out of a coalpit. Gas catastrophe—Yes! Brock was lost to us at the massacre of Zeebrugge—lost uselessly ; for no such folly was ever devised by fools as such an operation as that of Zeebrugge divorced from military co-operation on land. What were the bravest of the brave massacred for? Was it glory? Is the British Navy a young Navy requiring glory? When 25 per

# THE DARDANELLES

cent. of our Officers were killed a few days since, sinking two Bolshevik battleships, etc., and heroic on their own element, the sea, we all thank God, as we should do, that Nelson, looking down on us in Trafalgar Square, feels his spirit is still with us. But for sailors to go on shore and attack forts, which Nelson said no sailor but a lunatic would do, without those on shore of the military persuasion to keep what you have stormed, is not only silly but it's murder and it's criminal. Also by the time Zeebrugge was attacked, the German submarine had got far beyond a fighting radius that required this base near the English coast. As Dean Inge says: "We must hope that in the Paradise of brave men the knowledge is mercifully hid from them that they died in vain."

Again, this is a digression—but such must be the nature of this book when speaking *ore rotundo* and from the fulness of a disgusted heart, that such Lions should be led by such Asses. The book can't convey my feelings, however carefully my good friend the typewriter is taking it down. All the quill drivers, the ink spillers, and the Junius-aping journalists will jeer at you as the Editor, and say, "Why didn't you stop him? Where's the argument? Where's the lucid exposition? Where's the subtle dialectician who will talk a bird out of a tree? Where is this wonderful personality I'm told of, who fooled King Edward, and ravished virgins, and preached the Gospel (so he says)? Like Gaul, he is divided into three parts; we don't see one of them."

We'll get along with the Dardanelles now. All this

51

will make pulp for paper for the *National Review*.

> " Imperial Cæsar dead and turned to clay
> Now stops a hole to keep the wind away."

Well, I left off at the " Miasma " that, imperceptibly to each of them in the War Council, floated down on them with rare subtle dialectical skill, and proved so incontestably to them that cutting off the enemy's big toe in the East was better than stabbing him to the heart in the West ; and that the Dardanelles was better than the Baltic, and that Gallipoli knocked spots off the Kiel Canal, or a Russian Army landed by the British Fleet on the Baltic shore of Schleswig-Holstein.

Without any doubt, the " beseechings " of the Grand Duke Nicholas in the Caucasus on January 2nd, 1915,[1] addressed to Kitchener in such soldierly terms, moved that great man's heart ; for say what you will, Kitchener was a great man. But he was a great deception, all the same, inasmuch as he couldn't do what a lot of people thought he could do. Like Moses, he was a great Commissariat Officer, but he was not a Napoleon or a Moltke ; he was a Carnot *in excelsis*, and he was the facile dupe of his own failings. But " Speak well of those who treat you well." I went to him one evening at 5 p.m., with Mr. Churchill's knowledge, and said to him as First Sea Lord of the Admiralty that if his

[1] On January 2, 1915, Russia asked for a demonstration against the Turks in order to relieve the pressure they were putting on the Russian forces in the Caucasus. Next day the War Office cabled a promise, through the Foreign Office, that this should be done. Before he sent the cable Lord Kitchener wrote to Mr. Churchill : " The only place that a demonstration might have some effect in stopping reinforcements going East would be the Dardanelles."

myrmidons did not cease that same night from seducing men from the private shipyards to become " Cannon-fodder " I was going to resign at 6 p.m. I explained to him the egregious folly of not pressing on our ship-building to its utmost limits. He admitted the soft impeachment as to the seduction ; and there, while I waited, he wrote the telegram calling off the seducers. If only that had been stuck to after I left the Admiralty, we shouldn't be rationed now in sugar nearly a year after the Armistice, nor should we be bidding fair to become a second Carthage. We left our element, the sea, to make ourselves into a conscript nation fighting on the Continent with four million soldiers out of a population of forty millions. More than all the other nations' was our Army.

The last words of Mr. A. G. Gardiner's article about him who is now dictating are these : " He is fighting his last great battle. And his foe is the veteran of the rival service. For in his struggle to establish con-scription Lord Roberts's most formidable antagonist is the author of the ' Dreadnought.' "

Well, once more resuming the Dardanelles story. These side-lights really illuminate the situation. These Armies we were raising incited us to these wild-cat expeditions. I haven't reckoned them up, but there must have been a Baker's Dozen of 'em going on. Now, do endeavour to get this vital fact into your mind. We are an Island. Every soldier that wants to go anywhere out of England—a sailor has got to carry him there on his back.

# MEMORIES

Consequently, every soldier that you raise or enlist, or recruit, or whatever the proper word is, unless he is absolutely part of a Lord Lieutenant's Army, never to go out of England and only recruited, like the Militia—that splendid force !—to be called up only in case of invasion—as I say, every soldier that is recruited on any other basis means so much tonnage in shipping that has to be provided, not only to take him to the Continent ; but it's got to be kept ready to bring him back, in case of his being wounded, and all the time to take him provisions, ammunition, stores.  Those vessels again have to have other vessels to carry out coal for those vessels, and those colliers have again to be supplemented by other colliers to take the place of those removed from the normal trade, and the coal mines themselves necessitate more miners or the miners' working beyond the hours of fatigue to bring forth the extra coal ; or else the commercial work of the nation gets diminished and your economic resources get crippled, and that of itself carried *in extremis* means finishing the war.  As a matter of fact, it *has* nearly finished the English Nation—the crippling of our economic resources by endeavouring to swell ourselves out like the Frog in Æsop's Fables, and become a great continental Power—forgetting the Heaven-sent gift of an incomparable Navy dating from the time of Alfred the Great, and God's providing a breakwater 600 miles long (the British Islands) in front of the German Coast to stop the German access to the ocean, and thus by easy blockade killing him from the sea as he was killed eventually.  Alas ! what happened ?  In the House of Commons the British Navy is called a subsidiary Service. And then Lord Rosebery doesn't like my " frisking" ; and cartoons represent that I want a job ; and fossil Admirals call me immodest !

Mr. Churchill was behind no one both in his enthusiasm for the Baltic project, and also in his belief that the decisive theatre of the war was beyond doubt in Northern waters ; and both he and Mr. Lloyd George, the Chancellor of the Exchequer, magnificently responded to the idea of constructing a great Armada of 612 vessels, to be rapidly built—mostly in a few weeks and only a few extending over a few months—to carry out the great purpose ; and I prepared my own self with my own hands alone, to preserve secrecy, all the arrangements for landing three great armies at different places—two of them being feints that could be turned into a reality. Also I made all the preparations, shortly before these expeditions were to start, to practise them embarking at Southampton and disembarking at Stokes Bay, so that those who were going to work the Russian Armies would be practised in the art, having seen the experiment conducted on a scale of twelve inches to the foot with 50,000 men.

(We once embarked 8,000 soldiers on board the Mediterranean Fleet in nineteen minutes, and the fleet steamed out and landed them at similar speed. Old Abdul Hamid, the Sultan, heard of it, and he complimented me on there being such a Navy. That was the occasion when a red-haired, short, fat Major, livid with rage, complained to me on the beach that a bluejacket had shoved him into the boat and said to him " Hurry up, you bloody lobster, or I'll be 'ung ! " I explained to the Major that the man *would* have been hanged ; he was responsible for getting the boat filled and shoved off in so many seconds.)

I remember that at the War Council held on January 28th, 1915, at 11.30 a.m., Mr. Churchill announced that the real purpose of the Navy was to obtain access to the Baltic, and he illustrated that there were three naval phases. The first phase was the clearing of the outer seas ; and that had been accomplished. The second phase was the clearing of the North Sea. And the third phase was the clearing of the Baltic. Mr. Churchill laid stress on the importance of this latter operation, because Germany always had been and still was very much afraid of being attacked in the Baltic. For this purpose special vessels were needed and the First Sea Lord, Lord Fisher, had designed cruisers, etc., etc., meaning the Armada. Mr. Lloyd George said to me at another meeting of the War Council, with all listening : "How many battleships shall we lose in the Dardanelles?" " A dozen ! " said I, " but I prefer to lose them else-where." In dictating this account I can't represent his face when I said this.

Here I insert a letter on the subject which I wrote to Lord Cromer in October, 1916 :—

36, BERKELEY SQUARE,
*October 11th*, 1916.

DEAR LORD CROMER,

To-day Sir F. Cawley asked me to to reconcile Kitch-ener's statement of May 14th at the War Council that the Admiralty proposed the Dardanelles enterprise with my assertion that he (Kitchener) did it. Please see question No. 1119. Mr. Churchill is speaking, and Lord Kitchener said to him " *could we not for instance make a demonstration at the Dardanelles ?* "

I repeat that before Kitchener's letter of Jan. 2nd to Mr. Churchill there was no Dardanelles ! Mr. Churchill had been rightly wrapped up in the splendid project of the British Army sweeping along the sea in association with the British Fleet. See Mr. Churchill at Question No. 1179.

" The advance of the (British) Army along the Coast was *an attractive operation, but we could not get it settled.* Sir John French wanted very much to do it, but it fell through."

See Lord Fisher, *War Council of Jan. 13th !* Sir John French then present—(3 *times he came over about it*)— " Lord Fisher demurred to any attempt to attack Zeebrugge without the co-operation of the British Army along the coast."

As to the *Queen Elizabeth*, Mr. Churchill is right in saying there was great tension between Kitchener and myself. He came over to the Admiralty and when I said " *if the ' Queen Elizabeth' didn't leave the Dardanelles that night I should !* " he got up from the table and he left ! and wrote an unpleasant letter about me to the Prime Minister ! *Lucky she did leave ! !* The German submarine prowling around for a fortnight looking for her (*and neglecting all the other battleships*) blew up her duplicate wooden image.

Yours, etc.,

(Signed)  FISHER.

Mr. Churchill is quite correct. I backed him up till I resigned. *I would do the same again !* He had courage and imagination ! He was a War Man !

If you doubt my dictum that the Cabinet Ministers

only were members of the War Council and the rest of us voice tubes to convey information and advice, ask Hankey to come before you again and state the status !

Otherwise the experts would be the Government ! Kindly read what Mr. Asquith said on Nov. 2nd, 1915, in Parliament. (See p. 70.)

(We had constructed a fleet of dummy battleships to draw off the German submarines. This squadron appeared with effect in the Atlantic and much confused the enemy.)

Mr. Asquith also was miasma-ed ; and it's not allowable to describe the discussion that he, I, and Mr. Churchill had in the Prime Minister's private room, except so far as to observe that Mr. Churchill had been strongly in favour of military co-operation with the fleet on the Belgian Coast, and Sir John French, on three different visits to the War Council, had assented to carrying out the operation, provided he had another Division added to his Force. This project—so fruitful as it would have been in its results at the early stage of the war—was, I understand, prevented by three deterrents : (1) Lord Kitchener's disinclination ; (2) The French didn't want the British Army to get into Belgium ; (3) The Dardanelles came along.

I objected to any Naval action on the Belgian Coast without such military co-operation. Those flat shores of the Belgian coast, enfiladed by the guns of the accompanying British Fleet, rendered that enterprise feasible, encouraging and, beyond doubt, deadly to the enemy's sea flank. Besides preventing Zeebrugge from being fortified and the Belgian Coast being made use of as a jumping-off place for the air raids on London and elsewhere, with guns capable of ranging such an enormous distance as those mounted in the Monitors, we could have enfiladed with great effect all attacks by the Germans.

When we got to the Council table—the members having been kept waiting a considerable time—the Prime Minister gave the decision that the Dardanelles project must proceed ; and as I rose from the Council table Kitchener followed me, and was so earnest and even emotional[1] that I should return that I said to myself after some delay : " Well, we can withdraw the ships at any moment, so long as the Military don't land," and I succumbed. I was mad on that Armada of 612 vessels, so generously fostered by Mr. Lloyd George and Mr. Churchill and sustained by the Prime Minister. They were of all sorts and sizes—but alas ! as they reached completion they began to be gradually perverted and diverted to purposes for which they were unfitted and employed in waters to which they were unsuited. Nevertheless they made (some of them) the Germans flee for their lives,

[1] " The dramatic scene which followed may one day furnish material for the greatest historical picture of the war. Lord Fisher sat and listened to the men who knew nothing about it and heard one after another pass opinion in favour of a venture to which he was opposed. He rose abruptly from the table and made as if to leave the room.

" The tall figure of Lord Kitchener rose and followed him. The two stood by the window for some time in conversation and then both took their seats again. In Lord Fisher's own words : ' I reluctantly gave in to Lord Kitchener and resumed my seat.'

" Mr. Asquith saw that drama enacted, and Mr. Asquith knew that it arose out of Lord Fisher's opposition to the scheme under discussion. But he allowed his colleagues on the Council to reach their conclusions without drawing from the expert his opinion for their guidance. The monstrous decision was therefore taken without it. But they all knew it—such a scene could not occur without everyone knowing the cause."

and with such a one as the gallant Arbuthnot or the splendid Hood, who gave their lives for nothing at Jutland, we might have had another Quiberon.

To resume: I gave Lord Cromer, the Chairman of the Dardanelles Commission a précis of the Dardanelles case. It doesn't appear in the Report of the Dardanelles Commission. I forgive him that, because, when in his prime, he did me a good deed. It is worth relating. I entreated him to cut a channel into Alexandria Harbour deep enough for a Dreadnought; and he did it, though it cost a million sterling, and thus gave us a base of incalculable advantage in certain contingencies.

I will now shortly pass in review the Dardanelles statement that I gave Lord Cromer. Those who will read this book won't want to be fooled with figures. I give a figurative synopsis. Of course, as I told the Dardanelles Commission (Cromer thought it judicious to omit my comment, I believe), the continuation of the Dardanelles adventure beyond the first operations, confined solely to the ships of the fleet which could be withdrawn at any moment and the matter ended—the continuation, I explained to the Dardanelles Commission, was largely due to champion liars. It must ever be so in these matters. I presume that's how it came about that two Cabinet Ministers—no doubt so fully fed up with the voice tube, as it has been described—told the nation that we were within a few yards of victory at the Dardanelles, and so justified and encouraged a continuance of that deplorable massacre. However, no politician regards truth from the same point of view as a gentleman. He puts on the spectacles of his Party. The *suppressio veri* and the *suggestio falsi* flourish in politics like the green baize tree.

> Sworn to no Party—of no Sect am I :
> I can't be silent and I will not lie.

Before the insertion of the following narrative prepared by me at the time of the Dardanelles Commission I wish to interject this remark : When sailors get round a Council Board they are almost invariably mute. The Politicians who are round that Board are not mute; they never would have got there if they had been mute. That's why for the life of me I can't understand what on earth made David say in the Psalms " A man full of words shall not prosper on the Earth." They are the very ones who do prosper ! It shows what a wonderful fellow St. Paul was ; he was a bad talker and yet he got on. He gives a bit of autobiography, and tells us that his bodily presence was weak and his speech contemptible, though his letters were weighty and powerful. However, in that case, another Gospel was being preached, where the worldly wise were confounded by the worldly foolish.

While my evidence was being taken before the Dardanelles Commission, the Secretary (Mears) was splendid in his kindness to me, and my everlasting gratitude is with the " Dauntless Three " who broke away from their colleagues and made an independent report. They were Mr. Fisher—formerly Prime Minister of Australia, (a fellow labourer), Sir Thomas

Mackenzie (High Commissioner for New Zealand), and Mr. Roch, M.P. Their Report was my life-buoy; a précis of their Report, so far as it affects me and which I consider unanswerable, establishes that it is the duty of any Officer, however highly placed, to subordinate his views to that of the Government, unless he considers such a course so vitally antagonistic to his Country's interests as to compel him to resign. I know of no line of action so criminally outrageous and subversive of all discipline as that of public wrangling between a subordinate and his superior, or the Board of Admiralty and an Admiral afloat, or the War Office and their Commander-in-Chief in the Field.

This Dardanelles Commission reminds me of another "cloudy and dark day," as Ezekiel would describe it, when five Cabinet Ministers, at the instigation of an Admiral recently serving, held an enquiry absolutely technical and professional on matters about which not one of them could give an authoritative opinion but only an opinion which regarded political opportunism—an enquiry neither more nor less than of my professional capacity as First Sea Lord of the Admiralty. The trained mind of Mr. McKenna only just succeeded in saving me from being thrown to the wolves of the hustings. But it has inflicted a mortal wound on the discipline of the Navy. Hereafter no mutinous Admiral need despair (only provided he has political and social influence) of obtaining countenance for an onslaught against his superiors; and we may yet lose the decisive battle of the world in consequence.

# THE DARDANELLES

The following is my narrative of my connexion with the Dardanelles Operations.

" The position will not be clear and, indeed, will be incomprehensible, if it be not first explained how very close an official intimacy existed between Mr. Winston Churchill and Lord Fisher for very many years previous to the Dardanelles episode, and how Lord Fisher thus formed the conviction that Mr. Churchill's audacity, courage, and imagination specially fitted him to be a War Minister.

" When, in the autumn of 1911, Mr. Winston Churchill became First Lord of the Admiralty, Lord Fisher had retired from the position of First Sea Lord which he had occupied from October 21st, 1904, to January 25th, 1910, amidst great turmoil all the time. During Lord Fisher's tenure of office as First Lord, vast Naval reforms were carried out, including the scrapping of some 160 ships of no fighting value, and great naval economies were effected, and all this time (except for one unhappy lapse when Mr. Churchill resisted the additional ' Dreadnought ' building programme) Mr. Winston Churchill was in close association with these drastic reforms, and gave Lord Fisher all his sympathy when hostile criticism was both malignant and perilous. For this reason, on Mr. Churchill's advent as First Lord of the Admiralty in the autumn of 1911, Lord Fisher most gladly complied with his request to return home from Italy to help him to proceed with that great task that had previously occupied Lord Fisher for six years as First Sea Lord, namely, the preparation for a German War which Lord

Fisher had predicted in 1905 would certainly occur in August, 1914, in a written memorandum, and afterwards also personally to Sir M. Hankey, the Secretary of the Committee of Imperial Defence, necessitating that drastic revolution in all things Naval which brought 88 per cent. of the British Fleet into close proximity with Germany and *made its future battle ground in the North Sea its drill ground*, weeding out of the Navy inefficiency in ships, officers, and men, and obtaining absolute fighting sea supremacy by an unparalleled advance in types of fighting vessels.

" Mr. Churchill then at Lord Fisher's request did a fine thing in so disposing his patronage as First Lord as to develop Sir John Jellicoe into his Nelsonic position. So that when the day of war came Sir John Jellicoe became admiralissimo in spite of great professional opposition. . . .

" This increased Lord Fisher's regard for Mr. Churchill, and on July 30th, 1914, at his request, Lord Fisher spent hours with him on that fifth day before war was declared and by his wish saw Mr. Balfour to explain to him the Naval situation. This is just mentioned to show the close official intimacy existing between Mr. Churchill and Lord Fisher, and when, on October 20th, 1914, Mr. Churchill asked Lord Fisher to become First Sea Lord he gladly assented to co-operating with him in using the great weapon Lord Fisher had helped to forge.

" Mr. Churchill and Lord Fisher worked in absolute accord until it came to the question of the Dardanelles,

.

### THE KINGFISHER.

" This bird has a somewhat long bill and is equipped with a brilliant
blue back and tail; the latter not of sufficient length to be in the
way. Its usual cry is much like the typical cry of the family, but
besides this it gives a low, hoarse croak from time to time when
seated in the shadows. Although exclusively a water bird, it is not
unfrequently found at some distance from any water. It is very
wary, keeping a good look-out, and defends its breeding place with
great courage and daring."—*Zoological Studies.*

when Lord Fisher's instinct absolutely forbade him to give it any welcome. But finding himself the one solitary person dissenting from the project in the War Council, and knowing it to be of vital importance that he should personally see to the completion of the great shipbuilding programme of 612 vessels initiated on his recent advent to the Admiralty as First Sea Lord, also being confident that all these vessels could only be finished rapidly if he remained, Lord Fisher allowed himself to be persuaded by Lord Kitchener on January 28th, 1915, to continue as First Sea Lord. That point now remains to be related in somewhat greater detail.

" To begin with :—When exactly 10 years previously Lord Fisher became First Sea Lord, on October 20th, 1904, that very day occurred the Dogger Bank incident with Russia, and the Prime Minister made a speech at Southampton that seemed to make war with Russia a certainty ; so Lord Fisher, as First Sea Lord, immediately looked into the Forcing of the Dardanelles in the event of Russia's movements necessitating British action in the Dardanelles. He then satisfied himself that, even with military co-operation, it was mighty hazardous, and he so represented it at that time. The proceedings of the Committee of Imperial Defence, however, will furnish full details respecting the Dardanelles, especially Field-Marshal Lord Nicholson's remarks when Director of Military Operations, and also those of Sir N. Lyttelton when Chief of the General Staff.

" But Lord Fisher had had the great advantage of commanding a battleship under Admiral Sir Geoffrey Phipps

Hornby when, during the Russo-Turkish War, that celebrated Flag Officer lay with the British Fleet near Constantinople, and Lord Fisher listened at the feet of that Naval Gamaliel when he supported Nelson's dictum that no sailor but a fool would ever attack a fort ! Nevertheless, Nelson did attack Copenhagen—was really beaten, but he bluffed the Danish Crown Prince and came out ostensibly as victor. Nelson's Commander-in-Chief, Sir Hyde Parker, knew Nelson was beaten and signalled to him to retreat, but Nelson disobeyed orders as he did at St. Vincent and the Nile, and with equal judgment.

" We might have done the same bluff with the Turks, had promptitude and decision directed us, but procrastination, indecision, and vacillation dogged us instead. The 29th Division oscillated for weeks between France and Turkey. (*See* below my notes of the War Council Meetings of February 19th and 24th.)

" *Note.—See* Mr. Churchill's statement at the 19th Meeting of the War Council on May 14th, 1915, that had it been known three months previously that an English army of 100,000 men would have been available for the attack on the Dardanelles, *the naval attack would never have been undertaken.*

" The War Council met on May 14th, 1915, and certain steps proposed to be taken by Mr. Churchill immediately afterwards, decided Lord Fisher that he could no longer support the Dardanelles operations. He could not go further in this project with Mr. Churchill, and was himself convinced that we should seize that moment to give up the Dardanelles operations. So Lord Fisher went.

"Lord Fisher's parting with Mr. Churchill was pathetic, but it was the only way out. When the Prime Minister read to Lord Fisher Lord Kitchener's letter to the Prime Minister attacking Lord Fisher for withdrawing the 'Queen Elizabeth' from certain destruction at the Dardanelles, Lord Fisher then realised how splendid had been Mr. Churchill's support of him as to her withdrawal. A few days afterwards the German submarine that had been hovering round the British Fleet for a fortnight blew up the wooden image of the super-Dreadnought we had sent out there as a bait for the German submarines, showing how the Germans realised the 'Queen Elizabeth's' value in letting all the other older battleships alone for about a fortnight till they thought they really had the 'Queen Elizabeth' in this wooden prototype !

"It must be emphasised on Mr. Churchill's behalf that he had the whole Naval opinion at the Admiralty as well as the Naval opinion at the Dardanelles with him—Lord Fisher was the only dissentient.

"It must be again repeated that though Lord Fisher was so decidedly against the Dardanelles operations from the very first, yet he was very largely influenced to remain because he was convinced it was of vital importance to the nation to carry out the large building programme initiated by him, which was to enable the Navy to deal such a decisive blow in the decisive theatre (in Northern Waters) as would shorten the war—by the great projects

alluded to by Mr. Churchill at the 9th meeting of the
War Council on January 28th, 1915, when he described
the Three Naval phases of the War, leading to our occupation of the Baltic as being the supreme end to be attained.

" Had Lord Fisher maintained his resignation on 28th
January, 1915, the Dardanelles enterprise would certainly
still have gone on, because it was considered a matter of
vital political expediency (*see* Mr. Balfour's memorandum
of 24th February, 1915), but those 612 new vessels would
not have been built, or they would have been so delayed
as to be useless. As it was, by Lord Fisher's leaving the
Admiralty even so late as May 22nd, 1915, there was
great delay in the completion of the five fast Battle
Cruisers and in the laying down of further Destroyers
and Submarines, and, in fact, four large Monitors
(some of which had been advanced one thousand tons)
that had been considerably advanced were stopped
altogether for a time and the further building of fast
Battle Cruisers was given up. Lord Fisher had prepared
a design for a very fast Battle Cruiser carrying six 20-inch
guns, and the model was completed. She was of exceptionally light draught of water and of exceptionally high
speed. He had arranged for the manufacture of these
20-inch guns.

" It has also to be emphasised that that programme of
new vessels owed its inception to a great plan, sketched
out in secret memoranda, which it can be confidently
asserted would have produced such great military results
as would certainly have ended the war in 1915.

" These plans were in addition to that concurred in by

Sir John French in his three visits to the War Council in November, 1914, for joint action of the British Army and the British Fleet on the Belgian Coast.

"*Note.—See* Note to 8th meeting of the War Council on January 13th, 1915, where Lord Fisher demurs to any Naval action without the co-operation of the British Army along the coast."

I quote here a report of the opinion of Mr. Andrew Fisher, the High Commissioner of Australia, and formerly Prime Minister of Australia ; a member of the Dardanelles Commission, on the duty of departmental advisers :—

" I am of opinion it would seal the fate of responsible government if servants of the State were to share the responsibility of Ministers to Parliament and to the people on matters of public policy. The Minister has command of the opinions and views of all officers of the department he administers on matters of public policy. Good stewardship demands from Ministers of the Crown frank, fair, full statements of all opinions of trusted experienced officials to colleagues when they have direct reference to matters of high policy." *I give prominence to this because Ministers, and Ministers only, must be responsible to the democracy.*

If they find themselves in conflict with their expert advisers *they should sack the advisers or themselves resign.* An official, whether a Sea Lord or a junior clerk—having been asked a question by his immediate chief and given his answer and the chief acts contrary to advice—should not be subjected to reprimand for not stating to the board of directors that he disagrees with his chief or that he has given a reluctant consent. *If there is blame it rests with the Minister and not with his subordinates.*

" *I dissent in the strongest terms,*" *says Mr. Fisher in his Minority Report, " from any suggestion that the Depart-*

*mental Adviser of a Minister in his company at a Council meeting should express any views at all other than to the Minister and through him unless specifically invited to do so."*

Sir Thomas Mackenzie expresses exactly the same view.

Mr. Asquith, in the House of Commons on November 2, 1915, said :—

" It is the duty of the Government—of any Government—to rely very largely upon the advice of its military and naval counsellors ; but in the long run, a Government which is worthy of the name, which is adequate in the discharge of the trust which the nation reposes in it, must bring all these things into some kind of proportion one to the other, and sometimes it is not only expedient, but necessary, to run risks and to encounter dangers which pure naval or military policy would warn you against."

The Government and the War Council knew my opinion—as I told the Dardanelles Commission, it was known to all. It was known even to the charwomen at the Admiralty. It was my duty to acquiesce cheerfully and do my best, but when the moment came that there was jeopardy to the Nation I resigned.

Such is the stupidity of the General Public—and such was the stupidity of Lord Cromer—that it was not realized there would be an end of Parliamentary Government and of the People's will, therefore, being followed, if experts were able to override a Government Policy. Sea Lords are the servants of the Government. Having given their advice, then it's their duty to carry out the commands of the political party in power until the moment comes when they feel they can no longer support a policy which they are convinced is disastrous.

# THE DARDANELLES

Here follows a summary for the Chairman of the Dardanelles Commission of my evidence (handed to Lord Cromer, but not circulated by him or printed in the Report of the Commission):—

"Mr. Churchill and I worked in absolute accord at the Admiralty until it came to the question of the Dardanelles.

"I was absolutely unable to give the Dardanelles proposal any welcome, for there was the Nelsonic dictum that 'any sailor who attacked a fort was a fool.'

"My direct personal knowledge of the Dardanelles problem dates back many years. I had had the great advantage of commanding a battleship under Admiral Sir Geoffrey Phipps Hornby when, during the Russo-Turkish War, that celebrated flag officer took the Fleet through the Dardanelles.

"I had again knowledge of the subject as Commander-in-Chief of the Mediterranean Fleet for three years during the Boer War, when for a long period the Fleet under my command lay at Lemnos off the mouth of the Dardanelles, thus affording me means of close study of the feasibility of forcing the Straits.

"When I became First Sea Lord on October 20th, 1904, there arrived that very day the news of the Dogger Bank incident with Russia.

"In my official capacity, in view of the possibility of a war with Russia, I immediately examined the question of the forcing of the Dardanelles, and I satisfied myself at that time that even with military co-operation the operation was mighty hazardous.

"Basing myself on the experience gained over so many years, when the project was mooted in the present War my opinion was that the attempt to force the Dardanelles would not succeed.

"I was the only member of the War Council who dissented from the project, but I did not carry my dissent to the point of resignation because I understood that there were overwhelming political reasons why the attempt at least should be made.

" Moreover, I felt it to be of vital importance that I should personally see to the completion of the great shipbuilding programme which was then under construction, which had been initiated by me on my advent to the Admiralty, and which included no less than 612 vessels.

" The change in my opinion as to the relative importance of the probable failure in the Dardanelles began when the ever-increasing drain upon the Fleet, as the result of the prosecution of the Dardanelles undertaking, reached a point at which in my opinion it destroyed the possibility of other naval operations which I had in view, and even approached to jeopardising our naval supremacy in the decisive theatre of the War.

" I may be pressed with the question why did I not carry my objections to the point of resignation when the decision was first reached to attack the Dardanelles with naval forces.

" In my judgment it is not the business of the chief technical advisers of the Government to resign because their advice is not accepted, unless they are of opinion that the operation proposed must lead to disastrous results.

" The attempt to force the Dardanelles, though a failure, would not have been disastrous so long as the ships employed could be withdrawn at any moment, and only such vessels were engaged, as in the beginning of the operations was in fact the case, as could be spared without detriment to the general service of the Fleet.

" I may next be asked whether I made any protest at the War Council when the First Lord proposed the Dardanelles enterprise, or at any later date.

" Mr. Churchill knew my opinion. I did not think it would tend towards good relations between the First Lord and myself nor to the smooth working of the Board of Admiralty to raise objections in the War Council's discussions. My opinion being known to Mr. Churchill in what I regarded as the proper constitutional way, I preferred thereafter to remain silent.

"When the operation was undertaken my duty from that time onwards was confined to seeing that the Government plan was carried out as successfully as possible with the available means.

"I did everything I could to secure its success, and I only resigned when the drain it was making on the resources of the Navy became so great as to jeopardise the major operations of the Fleet.

"On May 14th, 1915, the War Council made it clear to me that the great projects in Northern waters which I had in view in laying down the Armada of new vessels were at an end, and the further drain on our naval resources foreshadowed that evening convinced me that I could no longer countenance the Dardanelles operations, and the next day I resigned.

"It seemed to me that I was faced at last by a progressive frustration of my main scheme of naval strategy.

"Gradually the crowning work of war construction was being diverted and perverted from its original aim. The Monitors, for instance, planned for the banks and shallows of Northern waters, were sent off to the Mediterranean where they had never been meant to operate.

"I felt I was right in remaining in office until this situation, never contemplated at first by anyone, was accepted by the War Council. I felt right in resigning on this decision.

"My conduct and the interpretation of my responsibility I respectfully submit to the judgment of the Committee. Perhaps I may be allowed to say that as regards the opinion I held I was right.

FISHER,
*October 7th, 1916."*

73

# MEMORIES

This is a letter which I wrote to Colonel Sir Maurice Hankey, Secretary of the War Council :—

*September 1st,* 1916.

DEAR HANKEY,

IN reply to your letter in which you propose to give only one extract concerning my hostility to the Dardanelles enterprise, do you not think that the following words in the official Print of Proceedings of War Council should be inserted in your report in justice to me ?

" *19th Meeting of the War Council, May 14th,* 1915.— Lord Fisher reminded the War Council that he had been no party to the Dardanelles operations. When the matter was first under consideration he had stated his opinion to the Prime Minister at a private interview."

The reason I abstained from any further pronouncement was stated.

Yours, etc.,

(Signed)   FISHER.

I note you will kindly testify to the accuracy of my statement that I left the Council table with the intention of resigning, but yielded to Kitchener's entreaty to return.

Have you the letter I wrote on January 28th, 1915, to Mr. Asquith, beginning :—

" I am giving this note to Colonel Hankey to hand to you . . . . . . ," because in it occur these following words :—" At any moment the great crisis may occur in the North Sea, for the German High Sea Fleet may be driven to fight by the German Military Headquarters, as part of some great German military operation."

It looks as if Hindenburg might try such a coup now.

I heard from Jellicoe a few days since that the Zeppelins now made the German submarines very formidable, and by way of example he pointed out that the " Falmouth "

74

was torpedoed even when at a speed of 25 knots and zigzagging every five minutes.

In some notes compiled on this matter I find it recorded that I was present at the meeting on the 13th January, when the plan was first proposed and approved in principle, and was also present at the meeting on the evening of the 28th January, when Mr. Churchill announced that the Admiralty had decided to push on with the project. On the morning of the 28th January I said that I had understood that this question would not be raised to-day, and that the Prime Minister was well aware of my own views in regard to it.

After the failure of the naval attack on the Narrows on the 18th March, I remarked at the meeting on the 19th March that I had always said that a loss of 12 battleships must be expected before the Dardanelles could be forced by the Navy alone, and that I still adhered to this view.

Also, at the meeting held on the 14th May, I reminded the War Council that I had been no party to the Dardanelles operations. When the matter was under consideration I had stated my opinion to the Prime Minister at a private interview.

Some light is perhaps thrown on my general attitude towards naval attacks by the following remark, made at the meeting held on the 13th January, which related, not to the Dardanelles project, but to a proposed naval attack on Zeebrugge :—

I said that the Navy had only a limited number of battleships to lose, and would probably sustain losses in an attack on Zeebrugge. I demurred to any attempt to attack Zeebrugge *without the co-operation of the Army along the coast*.

This note is here inserted because the Dardanelles operation interfered with the project of certain action in the Decisive Theatre of the War explained in a Memorandum given to the Prime Minister on January 25th, 1915, but it has been decided to be too secret for publication even now, so it is not included in these papers.

A Memorandum was also submitted by me on General Naval Policy, deprecating the use of Naval Force in Coast Operations unsupported by Military Force and emphasising the supreme importance of maintaining the unchallengeable strength of the Grand Fleet in the Decisive Theatre.

LORD FISHER TO COLONEL SIR MAURICE HANKEY

*September 6th, 1916.*

DEAR HANKEY,

I HAVE only just this very moment received your letter, dated September 4th, and its enclosure, for I had suddenly to leave the address you wrote to on important official business. . . .

The Prime Minister and Kitchener knew from me on January 7th or January 8th that I objected to the Dardanelles enterprise, but I admit this does not come under your official cognisance as Secretary of the War Council, consequently I cannot press you in the matter.

If I ever am allowed hereafter to see what you have prepared for Lord Cromer's Committee of Inquiry I shall be better able to judge of its personal application to myself.

I was told yesterday by an influential Parliamentary friend that the likelihood was that *all* would emerge from the Dardanelles Inquiry as free from blame, except one person only—Lord Fisher! That really would be comic! considering that I was the only sufferer by it, by loss of office and of an immense certainty in my mind of Big Things in the North Sea and Baltic by the unparalleled Armada we were building so marvellously quickly, *e.g.*, submarines in five months instead of 14, and destroyers in nine months instead of 18! and immense fast Battle Cruisers with 18-inch and 15-inch guns in 11 months instead of two years! *Why, it was the desolation of my life to leave the Admiralty at that moment!* Knowing that once out I should never get back! The " wherefore " you know!

Yours, etc.,

(Signed)  FISHER,

*6th September*, 1916.

LORD FISHER TO THE RIGHT HON. WINSTON CHURCHILL.

" *The Baltic a German Lake.*"

MY DEAR WINSTON,

I AM here for a few days longer before rejoining my " Wise men " at Victory House—

" The World forgetting,
By the World forgot! "

but some Headlines in the newspapers have utterly upset me! Terrible!!

" The German Fleet to assist the Land operations in the Baltic."

" Landing the German Army South of Reval."

We are five times stronger at Sea than our enemies and here is a small Fleet that we could gobble up in a few minutes playing the great vital Sea part of landing an Army in the enemies' rear and probably capturing the Russian Capital by Sea!

This is " Holding the ring " with a vengeance!

Are we really incapable of a big Enterprise?

I hear that a new order of Knighthood is on the tapis

77

—O.M.G. (Oh ! My God !)—Shower it on the Admiralty ! !

> Yours,
>
> FISHER.
>
> 9/9/17.

P.S.—In War, you want—" SURPRISE."
To beget " SURPRISE " you want
" IMAGINATION " to go to bed with
" AUDACITY."

Admiral von Spee's first words at the Falkland Islands when he saw the British Battle Cruisers were

" Oh, what a surprise " !

And he went to the bottom with 3,000 men and 11 ships, and not one man killed or wounded on board the " Invincible."

LORD FISHER'S NOTES OF HIS OWN SPECIAL INTERVEN-
TIONS AT WAR COUNCIL MEETINGS

*Notes.— The first two meetings of the War Committee took place on August 5th and August 6th, 1914.*

*Lord Fisher was appointed First Sea Lord on October 30th, 1914.*

*The third meeting of the War Council (being the first after Lord Fisher's appointment) took place on November 25th, 1914.*

*3rd Meeting of the War Council, November 25th, 1914.*

Lord Fisher asked whether Greece might not attack Gallipoli in conjunction with Bulgaria.

It was pointed out Bulgaria blocked the way.

(*Note.*—From his experience of three years as Commander-in-Chief of the Mediterranean Fleet, Lord Fisher had formed the conviction that Bulgaria was the key of the situation, and this he had pointed out to Lord Kitchener personally at the War Office.)

*4th Meeting of War Council, December 1st, 1914.*

Lord Fisher pressed for the adoption of the Offensive.
The Defensive attitude of the Fleet was bad for its morale, and was no real protection from enemy submarines.

The suggestion of seizing an island off the German coast was adjourned.

*7th Meeting of War Council, January 8th, 1915.*

### ZEEBRUGGE.

Asked whether the bombardment of Zeebrugge would materially lessen the risks to transports and other ships in the English Channel, Lord Fisher replied that he thought not. In his opinion the danger involved in the operation (in loss of ships) would outweigh the results.

*8th Meeting of War Council, January 13th, 1915.*

### ZEEBRUGGE.

Lord Fisher said that the Navy had not unlimited battleships to lose, and there would probably be losses in any attack on Zeebrugge. He objected to any attack on Zeebrugge *without the co-operation of the Army along the coast.*

The Dardanelles was mentioned, Mr. Churchill stating that he had exchanged telegrams with Admiral Carden as to the possibilities of a naval attack on the Dardanelles. He had taken this step because Lord Kitchener, in a letter to him, dated January 3rd, had urged instant naval action at the Dardanelles to relieve the pressure on the Grand Duke Nicholas in the Caucasus.

*9th Meeting of War Council, January 28th, 1915,*
11.30 *a.m.*

(*Note.*—Before this meeting the Prime Minister discussed with Mr. Churchill and Lord Fisher the proposed Dardanelles operations and decided in favour of considering the project in opposition to Lord Fisher's opinion.)

## THE DARDANELLES.

Mr. Churchill asked if the War Council attached importance to the proposed Dardanelles operations, which undoubtedly involved risks.

Lord Fisher said that he had understood that this question was not to be raised at this meeting. The Prime Minister knew his (Lord Fisher's) views on the subject.

The Prime Minister said that, in view of what had already been done, the question could not be left in abeyance.

(*Note.*—Thereupon Lord Fisher left the Council table. He was followed by Lord Kitchener, who asked him what he intended to do. Lord Fisher replied to Lord Kitchener that he would not return to the Council table, and would resign his office as First Sea Lord. Lord Kitchener then pointed out to Lord Fisher that he (Lord Fisher) was the only dissentient, and that the Dardanelles operations had been decided upon by the Prime Minister ; and he urged on Lord Fisher that his duty to his country was to go on carrying out the duties of First Sea Lord. After further talk Lord Fisher reluctantly gave in to Lord Kitchener and went back to the Council table.[1])

[1] It must be emphasised here, as well as in regard to Lord Kitchener's statement to the War Council dated May 14th, 1915, that Lord Fisher considered that it would be both improper and unseemly for him to enter into an altercation either at the War Council or elsewhere with his chief Mr. Churchill, the First Lord. Silence or resignation was the right course.

THE FIRST SEA LORD. By William Nicholson.

Mr. Churchill stated *that the ultimate object of the Navy was to obtain access to the Baltic*. There were, he said, three Naval phases :—

> 1st phase.—The clearing of the outer seas (this had been accomplished).
> 2nd phase.—The clearing of the North Sea.
> 3rd phase.—*The clearing of the Baltic.*

*Mr. Churchill laid stress on the importance of the third phase and said this latter operation was of great importance, as Germany always had been, and still was, very nervous of an attack from the Baltic.* For this purpose special vessels were required, and the First Sea Lord (Lord Fisher) had designed cruisers, &c., &c.[1] The meeting was adjourned to 6.30 the same evening.

### 10th Meeting of War Council (same day), January 28th, 1915, at 6.30 p.m.

The plan of a naval attack on Zeebrugge was abandoned and the Dardanelles operations were decided upon.

### 11th Meeting of War Council, February 9th, 1915.

Mr. Churchill reported that the Naval attack on the Dardanelles would take place on February 15th. (This was afterwards postponed until February 19th.)

### 12th Meeting of War Council, February 16th, 1915.

Agreed that the 29th Division should be sent to the Dardanelles and other arrangements made to support the Naval attack on the Dardanelles.

The Admiralty were authorised and pressed to build or obtain special craft for landing 50,000 men wherever a landing might be required.

[1] This was the Armada of 612 vessels authorised by Mr. Lloyd George as Chancellor of the Exchequer.

*13th Meeting of War Council, February 19th, 1915.*

Transports ordered to be got ready :—

1. To convey troops from Egypt to the Dardanelles ;
2. To convey the 29th Division from England to the Dardanelles,
*but no final decision to be taken as to 29th Division.*

*14th Meeting of War Council, February 24th, 1915.*

General Birdwood selected to join Admiral Carden before the Dardanelles.
*The decision as to sending 29th Division postponed.*

*15th Meeting of War Council, February 26th, 1915.*

Mr. Churchill said he could not offer any assurance of success in the Dardanelles attack.

*16th Meeting of War Council, March 3rd, 1915.*

The future of Constantinople was discussed, and what should be the next step after the Dardanelles. Lord Lansdowne and Mr. Bonar Law, besides Mr. Balfour, were present.

*17th Meeting of War Council, March 10th, 1915.*

The War Office was directed to prepare a memorandum on the strategical advantages of Alexandretta.

*18th Meeting of War Council, March 19th, 1915.*

The sinking of the battleships " Irresistible," " Ocean," and " Bouvet," the running ashore of " Gaulois " and the disablement of " Inflexible," were discussed.

The continuance of naval operations against Dardanelles was authorised if the Admiral at the Dardanelles agreed.

Lord Fisher said that it was impossible to explain away the sinking of four battleships. *He had always said that a loss of 12 battleships must be expected before the Dardanelles could be forced by the Navy alone.* He still adhered to this view.

*Note.*—There was no meeting of the War Council from March 19th to May 14th.

### 19th Meeting of War Council, May 14th, 1915.

Mr. Churchill reported that one, or perhaps two, German submarines had arrived in the Eastern Mediterranean, *and that the attack on the Dardanelles had now become primarily a military rather than a naval operation.* It had been decided to recall the " Queen Elizabeth." Mr. Churchill stated that if it had been known three months ago that an army of from 80,000 to 100,000 men would now be available for the attack on the Dardanelles the naval attack would never have been undertaken.

*Lord Fisher reminded the War Council that he had been no party to the Dardanelles operations. When the matter was first under consideration he had stated his opinion to the Prime Minister at a private interview.*

*Conclusion.*—Lord Kitchener to send a telegram to Sir Ian Hamilton asking what military force he would require in order to ensure success at the Dardanelles.

*Note.*— On the evening of this day Mr. Churchill drafted orders for further naval reinforcements for the Dardanelles, a course to which Lord Fisher could not assent.

(This led to Lord Fisher leaving the Admiralty.)

*A Note on the Dardanelles Operations.*

Major-General Sir Chas. Caldwell, K.C.B., was Director of Military Operations at the War Office during the whole period of the inception, incubation and execution of the Dardanelles adventure, and in an article in the " Nineteenth Century " for March, 1919, he completely disposes of the criticisms of Mr. G. A. Schreiner in his book " From Berlin to Bagdad," and of those of Mr. H. Morgenthau, the late United States Ambassador at Constantinople, in his recent book, " The Secrets of the Bosphorus." Both these works convey the impression that the general attack by the Fleet upon the Defences of the Narrows on March 18th, 1915, very nearly succeeded. This verdict is not justified by the facts as certified by Sir C. Caldwell. He proves incontestably that, even in the very unlikely case of indirect bombardment really effecting its object in putting the batteries out of action, there would still be the movable armament of the Turks left to worry and defeat the mine-sweepers, and there would still be the drifting mines and possibly the torpedoes fired from the shore to imperil the battleships. When peace did come it occupied the British Admiral a very long time to sweep up the mines. The damaging effect of Naval Bombardment was over-estimated—the extent to which the enemy's movable armament would interfere with mine-sweeping was not realised, and the extent and efficiency of the minefields were unknown and unheeded. Sir Charles Caldwell says :

" The whole thing was a mistake, quite apart from the disastrous influence which the premature and unsuccessful operation exerted over the subsequent land campaign."

It is also most true what Sir C. Caldwell says that " the idea at the back of the sailors' minds (who so reluctantly assented to the *political* desire of getting possession of the Straits) was that it was an experiment which could always be instantly stopped if the undertaking were to be found too difficult." But alas ! " *the*

*view of the War Council came to be that they could not now
abandon the adventure."*

Marshal Liman von Sanders, who had charge of the
defence of the Dardanelles, said :

" The attack on the Straits by the Navy alone I don't
think could ever have succeeded.   I proposed to flood the
Straits broadcast with mines, and it was my view that
these were the main defences of the Dardanelles, and
that the function of the guns of the forts was simply to
protect the minefields from interference."

The evidence given by Captain (now Rear-Admiral
Sir) William Reginald Hall, R.N., Director of Naval
Intelligence, at the Dardanelles Inquiry, conflicts with
the facts as afterwards made known to us ; and no
doubt this led to such official speeches as were made of
our being so near victory at the Dardanelles—speeches
which caused the further great sacrifice of life which took
place after General Sir Charles Munro, the present
Commander-in-Chief in India, had definitely and
without any equivocation officially reported that the
Evacuation of the Gallipoli Peninsula should immediately
take place.

Field Marshal Lord Nicholson asked Captain Hall,
R.N., how far the Gallipoli Peninsula was under
German control ; and his answer was that it was known
that the defences had been inspected by a German and
that many Germans were arriving there, whereas it is a
matter of fact stated by General Liman von Sanders
and confirmed from other sources that the Germans
were in complete control ; and it took the British Admiral
many weeks after the Armistice, helped by the Turks, to
clear a way through the mines for his Flagship to take
him to Constantinople.   At question 4930 Captain Hall
stated his spies made him convinced that he could have
pushed through with only the loss of one or more ships
and got to Constantinople on March 18th.

# MEMORIES

## An Episode of the War.

A friend asking me yesterday (this was written in 1917) about the replacement of Tonnage destroyed by the German Submarines, and telling me how quite ineffectual had been the course pursued up to the present when really we are in measurable distance of starvation or else an ignoble peace, I ventured to send him the enclosed account (*written at the time*) of how 612 Vessels were hustled ! As in all other War matters, it is Personality that is required, even more than Brains !

## Statement of new Shipbuilding Inaugurated by Lord Fisher.

*Note.—* The following Memoranda are inserted as vital to the explanation of Lord Fisher's reluctance to resign on the Dardanelles question. It will be seen that Mr. Churchill had given him sole charge of the creation of this armada of new ships, *intended for great projects in the Baltic and North Sea.*

### Tuesday, November 3rd, 1914.

(*Note.—* Lord Fisher had joined the Admiralty as First Sea Lord four days before this meeting.)
    The First Sea Lord (Lord Fisher) presided at a Conference this day at the Admiralty.

### *Present* :

Second Sea Lord.
Third Sea Lord.
Additional Civil Lord.
Parliamentary and Financial Secretary.
Secretary.

Naval Secretary to First Lord.
Engineer-in-Chief.
Assistant Director of Torpedoes and another representative of the Director of Naval Ordnance.
Commodore (S) and Assistant.
Naval Assistant to First Sea Lord.
Director of Naval Construction and an Assistant.
Superintendent of Contract Work.
Superintending Electrical Engineer.
Director of Dockyard Work.
Director of Naval Contracts and an Assistant.

Lord Fisher explained to those present that this Conference had been summoned with the approval of Mr. Churchill, primarily with the object of expediting the delivery of 20 submarines which were to be at once commenced,

*but in the second place a big further building programme for a special purpose had been decided on.*

The question of placing orders for submarines had been under consideration for some time past. The First Lord, however, had assented to the cancellation of all existing papers on this subject, *and a fresh start was to be made immediately on the lines of a special war routine.* All red-tape methods—very proper in time of peace—were now to be abandoned, and *everything must be entirely subordinated to rapidity of construction.* It was desired to impress upon all present the necessity of avoiding " paper" work, and of proceeding in the manner indicated in the secret memorandum which would be circulated next day in regard to the matter. Arrangements would be made in due course to obtain additional vessels of other types in a similar manner.

*Note.*—After this, a meeting of all the shipbuilding firms of the United Kingdom took place at the Admiralty under the presidency of Lord Fisher, and the programme mentioned above in italics was parcelled out there and then.

BUILDING PROGRAMME.

*Meeting on November 3rd, 1914, four days after Lord Fisher became First Sea Lord.*

5 Battle Cruisers of 33 knots speed of light draught.
2 Light Cruisers.
5 Flotilla Leaders.
56 Destroyers.
64 Submarines.
37 Monitors.
24 River Light Gunboats.
19 Whaling Steamers.
24 Submarine Destroyers.
50 Seagoing Patrol Boats.
200 Motor Barges, oil engines.
90 Smaller Barges.
36 Sloops.
___

612 Total.
___

MEMORANDUM BY LORD FISHER, DATED NOVEMBER 3RD, 1914, ON LAYING DOWN FURTHER NUMBERS OF SUBMARINES.

There is no doubt that at this moment the supply of additional submarine boats in the shortest time possible is a matter of urgent national importance. They will not be obtained unless the whole engineering and ship-building resources of the country are enlisted in the effort, and the whole of the peace paraphernalia of red-tape routine and consequent delay are brushed on one side. I have carefully studied the submarine question during my retirement and have had many opportunities of keeping in touch with the present position and future possibilities, and am convinced that 20 submarines can be commenced at once, and that the first batch of these should be delivered in nine months, and the remainder at short intervals, completing the lot in 11 or 12 months.

NOTE.—*A dozen more were actually delivered in five months, and made the voyage alone from America to the Dardanelles.*

To do this, however, cheapness must be entirely subordinated to rapidity of construction, and the technical departments must have a free hand to take whatever steps are necessary to secure this end without any paper work whatever. Apparently this matter has been under consideration at the Admiralty already for a considerable time, but

*nothing has yet been ordered,*

and the First Lord has concurred that a fresh start be made independently of former papers,

*and the matter placed under my sole supervision, without any other officers or departments intervening between me and the professional officers.*

I will give instructions as to the work, and direct that

*if any difficulties are met with, they be brought to me instantly to be overcome.*

The professional officers' reports as to acceptances of tenders or allocation of work must be immediately carried out by the branches.

Only in this way can we get the boats we require. To ensure the completion of the 20 boats, steps to be immediately taken to order the parts for the engines for 25 boats. We know from experience that it is in the machinery parts that defects and failures occur in manufacture of castings, forgings, etc., causing great delay. The parts for the extra five sets of engines will be available for these replacements, and eventually the five extra sets can be fitted in five further hulls. I propose to review the progress being made once a fortnight in the hope that it may be feasible to order still further submarines beyond these 20 now to be commenced at once.

*The training of sufficient officers and men for manning these extra boats must obviously be proceeded with forthwith, and those responsible must see to it that the officers and crews are ready.*

FISHER.

*November 3rd*, 1914.

*NOTE by Lord Fisher.*—I gave personal orders on this day to the Director of Mobilization to enter officers, men, and boys to the utmost limit regardless of present or supposed prospective wants, so when he left the Admiralty last week to be Captain of the *Renown* he wrote me we wanted for nothing in the way of personnel!

FISHER.

*August 15th*, 1916.

# CHAPTER VI

## ABDUL HAMID AND THE POPE

Be to my virtues very kind,
Be to my faults a little blind.

Two great Personalities came across my path when
I commanded the Mediterranean Fleet for three years
—the Sultan Abdul Hamid and Pope Leo XIII. They
each greatly admired the astuteness of the other.
Wily as Abdul was, the Pope was the subtler of the two.
I did not have the interviews with the Pope which I
might have had. There was no real occasion for it,
as was the case with Abdul Hamid ; and also, though by
the accident of birth I was of the Church of England
(nearly everybody's religion is the accident of his birth),
yet by taste and conviction I was a Covenanter, and
therefore dead against the Pope. I would have loved
to participate in the fight against Claverhouse at the
battle of Drumclog.

I happen to be looking at the battlefield of Drumclog
now, and I hope to be buried in Drumclog Church—
that is, if I die here ; or in the nearest Church to my
death bed. I am particular to say this, as it avoids so
much trouble ; and I don't have any more feeling for a

cast-off body than for a cast-off suit of clothes. The body, after he's left it at death, is not the man himself, any more than his cast-off clothes. The only thing I ask for is a white marble tablet made by Mr. Bridgman of Lichfield (if he's still alive), with the inscription on it to be found in Croxall Church as written of herself by my sainted Godmother, of whom Byron wrote so beautifully : " She walks in beauty like the night." She deserved his poem.

That was a big digression ; but being dictated, as it is, this is a conversation book and not a classic. Classics are dry. Conversation, taking no account of grammar or sequence, is more interesting. However, that's a matter of opinion. To talk is easy, but to write is terrific. Even Job thought so, that patient man.

To resume Abdul Hamid and the Pope.

Neither rats nor Jews can exist at Malta. The Maltese are too much for either. A Maltese can't get a living in the Levant. The Levantine is too much for the Maltese. No Levantine has ever been seen in Armenia. His late Majesty, Abdul Hamid, was an Armenian. He massacred more Armenians than had ever been massacred before. I've no doubt that can be explained. It is supposed that the Armenian coachman of the previous Sultan was his father. He certainly was not a bit like his presumed father, the Sultan. When I dined several times with the Sultan, his father's picture hung behind him and he used to ask people if they traced the likeness —there wasn't even a resemblance.

The Sultan paid me a very special honour in sending

his most distinguished Admiral with his Staff down to the British Fleet lying at Lemnos, to escort me up to Constantinople. This Admiral was known to me ; and it afforded me an opportunity, in the passage up the Dardanelles, of making a thorough inspection of the Forts and all the particulars connected with the defence of the Dardanelles. Nothing was kept back from me ; and incidentally it was through this inspection I became on such terms with the Pashas that a most amicable arrangement was reached between us as to our ever having to work in common. A very striking incident occurred illustrating Kiamil Pasha's remark to me of how every Turk in the Turkish Empire trusted the English when they trusted no one else. Kiamil's argument was that such trust was only natural after the Crimean War, and after the war with Russia—when Russia was at the gates of Constantinople, and the British Fleet, coming up under Admiral Hornby in a blinding snowstorm, encountering great risks and not knowing but what the Forts, bribed by Russia, might open fire—that British Fleet, by its opportune arrival, hardly a minute too soon, effectually banged, barred and bolted the gates of Constantinople against the Russians and produced peace. And Kiamil's emphasis was that, notwithstanding all these wonderful things that England had done for Turkey, England never asked for the very smallest favour or concession in return, whereas other nations were all of them notoriously always grabbing ; and I told Kiamil Pasha that I felt very proud indeed, as a British Admiral, that England had this noble character and deserved it. The incident I referred to was this : Upon an observation being made to the Turkish Commander-in-Chief in the Dardanelles as to whether some written document wouldn't be satisfactory to him, he replied he wanted no such document—if a British Midshipman brought him a message, the word of a British Midshipman was enough for him.

The views I formed at that period of the impregnability of the Dardanelles stood me in good stead when the Dogger Bank incident became known on Trafalgar Day, 1904—the very day I assumed the position of First Sea Lord of the Admiralty. We were within an ace of war with Russia ; the Prime Minister's speech at Southampton, if consulted, will show that to be the case ; and I then drew up a secret memorandum with respect to the Dardanelles, which I alluded to at the War Council when the attack on the Dardanelles was being discussed, also in my official memorandum to Lord Cromer, the Chairman of the Dardanelles Commission, and in my evidence before the Commission.

Personally I had a great regard for Abdul Hamid. Our Ambassadors had not. One who knew of these matters considered Abdul Hamid the greatest diplomat in Europe. I have mentioned elsewhere how greatly he resented Lord Salisbury throwing over the traditional English Alliance with Turkey and Lord Salisbury saying in a memorable speech that in making that alliance in past years we had backed the wrong horse. For were not (was Abdul Hamid's argument) England and Turkey the two greatest Mahomedan nations on Earth—

England being somewhat the greater ? Kiamil—the Grand Old Man of Turkey—told me the same. He had been many times Grand Vizier, and I went especially with the Mediterranean Fleet to Smyrna to do him honour. He was the Vali there. His nickname in Turkey was " The Englishman "; he was so devoted to us. He lamented to me that England had had only one diplomatist of ability at Constantinople since the days of Sir Stratford Canning, whom he knew. His exception was a Sir William White, who had been a Consul somewhere in the Balkan States. No other English Ambassador had ever been able to cope with the Germans. I remonstrated with Kiamil by saying that Ambassadors now were only telegraph instruments—they only conveyed messages, and quite probably from some quite young man at the Foreign Office who had charge of that Department. I venture to remark here in passing what I have very frequently urged to those in authority— that the United States system is infinitely better than ours. Their diplomatic representatives are all fresh from home, with each change of President; ours live all their lives abroad and practically cease to be Englishmen, and very often, like Solomon, marry foreign wives. Another thing I've urged on Authority is that some Great Personage should annually make a tour of inspection of all the Diplomatic and Consular Agents (exactly as the big Banks have a travelling Inspector), who would ask how much he had increased the trade of the great British Commonwealth of Nations; and if it weren't more than five per cent. would give him the sack. This Great Travelling Personage must be a man independent in means and station of any Government connexion and undertake the duty as Sir Edward (now Lord) Grey goes to Washington. The German Ambassador at Constantinople used to go round selling beetroot sugar by the pound ! The English Ambassador said to me at a Garden Party he gave by those lovely sweet waters of the Bosphorus : " You see that fellow there with a white hat on ? He's the President of the British Chamber of Commerce ; he's an awful nuisance. He's always bothering me about some peddling commercial business ! "

Abdul Hamid was exceeding kind to me and invited me to Constantinople, and he descanted (the Boer War then being on) what a risk there was of a big coalition against England. Curiously enough, his colleague the Pope had the same feeling. It is very deplorable, not only in the late War but also in the Boer War especially, how utterly our spies and our Intelligence Departments failed us. I was so impressed with what the Sultan told me that I set to work on my own account ; and through the patriotism of several magnificent Englishmen who occupied high commercial positions on the shores of the Mediterranean, I got a central forwarding station for information fixed up privately in Switzerland ; and it so happened, through a most Providential state of circumstances, that I was thus able to obtain all the cypher messages passing from the various Foreign Embassies, Consulates and Legations through a certain central focus, and I also obtained a key to their respective cyphers.

ADMIRAL OF THE FLEET LORD FISHER, G.C.B., O.M., ETC., 1917.

## ABDUL HAMID AND THE POPE

The Chief man who did it for me was not in Government employ ; and I'm glad to think that he is now in a great position—though not rewarded as he should have been. No one is. But as to any information from an official source reaching me, who was so vastly interested in the matter, in the event of war where the Fleet should strike first—all our Diplomats and Consuls and Intelligence Departments might have been dead and buried. And how striking the case in the late War—the Prime Minister not knowing at the Guildhall Banquet on November 9th, 1918, that the most humiliating armistice ever known would be accepted by the Germans within thirty-six hours, and one of our principal Cabinet Ministers saying the Sunday before that the Allies were at their last gasp. And read now Ludendorff, Tirpitz, Falkenhayn, Liman von Sanders, and others—they knew exactly what the Allies' condition was and what their own was. And if the Dardanelles evidence is ever published, it will be found absolutely ludicrous how the official spokesmen gravely give evidence that the Turks had come to their last round of ammunition and that the roofs of the houses in Constantinople were crowded with people looking for the advent of the approaching British Fleet. Why ! it took our Admiral, on the conclusion of the Armistice, with the help of the Turks and all his own Fleet, several weeks to clear a passage through the mines, on which Marshal Liman von Sanders so accurately based his reliance against any likelihood of the Dardanelles being forced.

# CHAPTER VII

## A JEU D'ESPRIT

### BOWS AND ARROWS—SNAILS AND TORTOISES— FACILE DUPES AND SERVILE COPYISTS

" Not the wise find salvation."—*St. Paul.*

ONE of the charms of the Christian religion is that the Foolish confound the Wise. The Atheists are all brainy men. Myself, I hate a brainy man. All the brainy men said it was impossible to have aeroplanes. No brainy man ever sees that speed is armour. Directly the brainy men got a chance they clapped masses of armour on the " Hush-Hush " ships. They couldn't understand speed being armour, and said to themselves : " Didn't she draw so little water she could stand having weight put on her ? Shove on armour ! " and so bang went the speed, and the " Hush-Hush " ships, whose fabulous beauty was their forty shoregoing miles an hour, were slowed down by these brainy men. Don't jockeys have to carry weights ? Isn't it called handicapping ? Isn't it the object to beat the favourite—the real winner ? There really is comfort in the 27th verse of the 1st chapter of 1 Corinthians, where the Foolish are wiser than the Wise.

## A JEU D'ESPRIT

What !—A battle cruiser called the " Furious " going 40 shore-going miles an hour with 18-inch guns reaching 26 miles ! " Take the damn guns out and make it into an aeroplane ship ! " (And I'm not sure they could ever get the aeroplanes to land on her, owing to the heat of the funnels causing what they call " Air pockets " above the stern of the ship.)

Yes ! and we still have ancient Admirals who believe in bows and arrows. There's a good deal to be said for bows and arrows. Our ancestors insisted on all church-yards being planted with yew trees to make bows. There you are ! It's a home product ! Not like those damn fools who get their oil from abroad ! And I have now the Memorandum with me delivered to me when I was Controller of the Navy by a member of the Board of Admiralty desiring to build 16 sailing ships ! Again, didn't the Board of Admiralty issue a solemn Board Minute that wood floated and iron sank ? So what a damnable thing to build iron ships ! Wasn't there another solemn Board Minute that steam was damnable and fatal to the supremacy of the British Navy ? Haven't we had Admirals writing very brainy articles in magazines to prove that there was nothing like a tortoise ? You could stand on the tortoise's back ; you weren't rushed by the tortoise, whereas these " Hush-Hush " ships, they were flimsy, and speed was worshipped as a god. One mighty man of valour (only " he was a leper " as regards sea fighting) told me at his luncheon table that when one of these " Hush-Hush " ships encountered at her full strength of nearly a hundred thousand horse power a gale of wind in a mountainous sea she was actually strained! It's all really too lovely; but of course the humour of it can't be properly appreciated by the ordinary shore-going person. Yes, the brainy men, as I said before, crabbed the " Hush-Hush " ships; they couldn't understand that speed was armour when associated with big guns because the speed enabled you to put your ship at such a distance that she couldn't be hit by the enemy, so it was the equivalent of impenetrable armour although you had none of it, and you hit the enemy every round for the simple reason that your guns reached him when his could not reach you. Q.E.D. as Euclid says. What these splendid armour bearers say is " Give me a strong ship which no silly ass of a Captain can hurt." Of course this implies that if it's Buggins's turn to be Captain of a ship he gets it; it's his turn, even if he is a silly ass. The phase of mind they have is this : " None of your highly strung racehorses for me, give me a good old cart-horse ! " So we build huge costly warships which will last a hundred years, but become obsolete in five.

It all really is very funny—if it wasn't disastrous and ruinous ! And they are such a motley crew, these discontented ones who come together in John Bright's cave of Adullam ; and the Poor Dear Public read an interview in a newspaper with some Commander Knowall; and then a magazine article by Admiral Retrograde ; and some old " cup of tea " writes to *The Times* (wonderful paper *The Times* —" Equal Opportunity for All ") and there you are !

# A JEU D'ESPRIT

Lord Fisher is a damned fool ; and if he isn't a damned fool he's a maniac. Oh ! very well then, if he isn't a maniac, then he's a traitor. Wasn't Sir Julian Corbett very seriously asked if he (Sir John Fisher) hadn't sold his country to Germany ? Sir Julian thought the report was exaggerated, and that satisfied the Searcher after Truth. But I ask my listeners, however should we get on without these people ? How dull life would be without their dialectical subtleties and " reasoned statements " (I think they call them) and " considered judgments " !

My splendid dear old friend, who could hardly write his name, the Chief Engineer of the first ironclad, the "Warrior," told me, when I was Gunnery Lieutenant of her in 1861, that he had arranged for his monument at death being of " malleable " iron. No cast iron for him, he said ! It played you such pranks. So it is with these carbonised cranks who wield the pen, actuated by the wrong kind of grey matter of their brain, and, their tongues acidulated with lies, sway listening Senates and control our wars. It requires a Mr. Disraeli to deal with these victims of their own verbosity, who are the facile dupes of their vacuous imaginations and the servile copyists of the Billingsgatean line of argument !

# CHAPTER VIII

" A wise old owl lived in an oak ;
   The more he heard, the less he spoke ;
   The less he spoke, the more he heard ;
   Why can't we be like that wise old bird ? "

LORD HALDANE with his " art of clear thinking "
elaborated the Imperial War Staff to its present magnificent dimensions. If any man wants a thing advertised, let him take it over there to the Secret Department. Only Sir Arthur Wilson and myself, when I
was First Sea Lord of the Admiralty, knew the Naval
plan of war. He was the man, so head-and-shoulders
above all his fellows, who in his time was our undoubted,
indeed our incomparable, Sea Leader. No one touched
him ; and I am not sure that even now, though getting
on for Dandolo's age, he would not still achieve old
Dandolo's great deeds. What splendid lines they are
from Byron :

" Oh for one hour of blind old Dandolo,
   Th' Octogenarian Chief, Byzantium's Conquering Foe ! "

I loved Sir Arthur Wilson's reported reply to the maniacs
who think the Navy is the same as the Army. If it is
not true it is *ben trovato*. He said the Naval War Staff

at the Admiralty consisted of himself—assisted by every soul inside the Admiralty, and he added, " including the charwomen "—they emptied the waste-paper baskets full of the plans of the amateur strategists—Cabinet and otherwise.

No such rubbish has ever been talked as about the Navy War Staff and also, in connexion therewith, the Admiralty clerks who are supposed to have wrecked its first inception in the period long ago when my great friend the late Admiral W. H. Hall was introduced into the Admiralty to form a Department of Naval Intelligence. I give my experience. I have been fifteen or more years in the Admiralty—Director of Ordnance and Torpedoes, Controller of the Navy, Second Sea Lord and First Sea Lord. Inside the Admiralty, for conducting administrative work, the Civil Service clerk is incomparably superior to the Naval Officer. The Naval Officer makes a very bad clerk. He hasn't been brought up to it. He can't write a letter, and, as you can see from my dictation, he is both verbose and diffuse. The Clerk is terse and incisive.

I'll go to instances. My Secretary, W. F. Nicholson, C.B., was really just as capable of being First Sea Lord as I was, when associated with my Naval Assistant. I often used to say that the First Sea Lord was in commission, and that I was the facile dupe of these two ; and I was blessed with a succession of Naval Assistants who knew so exactly their limitations as regards Admiralty work as allowed the Admiralty machine to be, as was officially stated, the best, most efficient, and most effective of all the Government Departments of the State. I have a note of this, made by the highest authority in the Civil Service. I would like here to name my Naval Assistants, because they were out and away without precedent the most able men in the Navy : Admirals Sir Reginald Bacon, Sir Charles Madden, Sir Henry Oliver, Sir Horace Hood, Sir Charles de Bartolomé, Captain Richmond and Captain Crease—I'll back that set of names against the world.

I was the originator of the Naval War College at Portsmouth—that's quite a different thing from an Imperial General Staff at the War Office. The vulgar error of Lord Haldane and others, who are always talking about " Clear thinking " and such-like twaddle, is that they do not realise that the Army is so absolutely different from the Navy. Every condition in them both is different. The Navy is always at war, because it is always fighting winds and waves and fog. The Navy is ready for an absolute instant blow ; it has nothing to do with strategic railways, lines of communication, or bridging rivers, or crossing mountains, or the time of the year, when the Balkans may be snowed under, and mountain passes may be impassable. No ! the ocean is limitless and unobstructed ; and the fleet, each ship manned, gunned, provisioned and fuelled, ready to fight within five minutes. The Army not only has to mobilize, but—thank God ! this being an island—it has to be carried somewhere by the Navy, no matter where it acts. I observe here that when Lord Kitchener went to Australia to inaugurate the scheme of

Defence, he forgot Australia was an island. What Australia wants to make it impregnable is not Conscription—it's Submarines. However, I fancy Kitchener was sent there to get him out of the way. They wanted me to go to Australia, but I didn't.[1] Jellicoe has gone there. But then, Jellicoe hasn't always sufficient foresight ; *exempli gratia*, he was persuaded to take the deplorable step of giving up command of the Grand Fleet and going as First Sea Lord of the Admiralty. Never was anything so regrettable. I told the War Council that I am very glad Nelson never went to the Admiralty, and that Nelson would have made an awful hash of it. Nelson was a fighter, not an administrator and a snake charmer—that's what a First Sea Lord has to be.

Gross von Schwartzhoff told me on the sands of Scheveningen :—

" Your Navy can strike in thirteen hours ;
Our Army can't under thirteen days."

Frau von Pohl tells us the Germans did expect us so to strike, but Nelson was in heaven (Dear Reader, look again at what Frau von Pohl said, you'll find it in Chapter III.). On one occasion I got into a most unpleasant atmosphere. I arrived at a country house late at night, and at breakfast in the morning, I not knowing who the guests were, a Cabinet Minister enunciated the proposition that sea and land war were both in principle and practice alike. At once getting up from the breakfast

[1] At my entreaty a far better man went, Admiral Sir Reginald Henderson, G.C.B. He is a splendid seaman and he devised a splendid scheme.

# MEMORIES

table, in the heat of the moment, and not knowing that distinguished military officers were there, I said, " Any silly ass could be a General." I graphically illustrated my meaning. I gave the contrast between a sea and a land battle. The General is somewhere behind the fighting line, or he ought to be. The Admiral has got to be *in* the fighting line, or he ought to be. The Admiral is indeed like the young Subaltern, he is often the first " Over the top." The General, at a telescopic distance from the battle scene and surrounded by his Kitcheners, and his Ludendorffs, and his Gross von Schwartzhoffs, has plenty of time for the " Clear thinking " *à la* Lord Haldane ; and then, acting on the advice of those surrounding him, he takes his measures. So far as I can make out from the Ludendorff extracts in *The Times*, Hindenburg, the Generalissimo, was clearly not in it. He was " the silly ass " ! Ludendorff did it all as Chief of the Staff.

Now what's the corresponding case at sea ? The smoke of the enemy, not even the tops of his funnels, can be seen on the horizon. (I proved this myself with the great Mediterranean fleet divided into two portions.) Within twenty minutes the action is decided ! Realise this—it takes some minutes for the Admiral to get his breeches on, to get on deck and take in the situation ; and it takes a good many more minutes to deploy the Fleet from its Cruising Disposition into its Fighting Disposition. In the Cruising Disposition his guns are masked, one ship interfering with the fire of another. The Fleet for Battle has to be so disposed that all the guns, or as many as possible, can concentrate on one or a portion of the enemy's fleet. Each fleet pushes on at its utmost speed *to meet the other*, hoping to catch the other undeployed. Every telescope in the fleet (and there are myriads) is looking at the Admiral as he goes to the topmost and best vantage spot on board his flag ship to see the enemy, and sees him alone outlined against the sky—neither time nor room for a staff around him, and if there were they'd say, " It's not the Admiral who is doing it," and be demoralized accordingly—fatal to victory. In the fleet the Admiral's got to be like Nelson —" the personal touch " so that " *any silly ass can't be an Admiral* " ; and the people of the Fleet watch him with unutterable suspense to see what signal goes up to alter the formation of the fleet—a formation on which depends Victory or Defeat. So it was that Togo won that second Trafalgar ; he did what is technically known as " crossing the T," which means he got the guns of his fleet all to bear, all free to fire, while those of the enemy were masked by his own ships. One by one Rozhdest-vensky's ships went to the bottom, under the concerted action of concentrated fire. What does it ? Speed. And what actuates it ? One mind, and one mind only. Goschen was right (when First Lord of the Admiralty) ; he quoted that old Athenian Admiral who, when asked what governed a sea battle, replied, " Providence," and then with emphasis he added : " and a *good Admiral*." Which reminds me too of Cromwell—a pious man, we all know ; when asked a somewhat similar question as to what ruled the world, he replied " The Fear of the

Lord," and he added with an emphasis equal to that of the Athenian Admiral—" And a broomstick." No one votes more for the Sermon on the Mount than I do ; but I say to a blithering fool " *Begone !* "

A Naval War Staff at the Admiralty is a very excellent organisation for cutting out and arranging foreign newspaper clippings in such an intelligent disposition as will enable the First Sea Lord to take in at a glance who is likely amongst the foreigners to be the biggest fool or the greatest poltroon, who will be opposed to his own trusted and personally selected Nelson who commands the British Fleet. The First Sea Lord and the Chief Admiral afloat have got to be Siamese twins. And when the war comes, the Naval War Staff at the Admiralty, listening every moment to the enemy's wireless messages (if he dare use it), enables the First Sea Lord to let his twin at sea know exactly what is going on. He takes in the wireless, and not necessarily the Admiral afloat, on account of the far greater power of reception in a land installation as compared with that on a ship. When you see that spider's web of lines of wire on the top of the Admiralty, then thank God this is more or less a free country, as it got put up by a cloud of bluejackets before a rat was smelt ! An intercepted German Naval letter at the time gave me personally great delight, for it truly divined that wireless was the weapon of the strong Navy. For the development of the wireless has been such that now you can get the direction of one who speaks and go for him ; so the German daren't open his mouth. But if he does, of course the message is in cypher ; and it's the elucidation of that cypher which is one of the crowning glories of the Admiralty work in the late war. In my time they never failed once in that elucidation. Yes, wireless is the weapon of the strong. So also is the Submarine—that is if they are sufficiently developed and diversified and properly applied, but you must have quantities and multiplicity of species.

What you want to do is to fight the enemy's fleet, make him come out from under the shelter of his forts, where his ships are hiding like rabbits in a hole—put in the ferrets and out come the rabbits, or they kill 'em where they are. Nelson blockading Toulon, as he told the Lord Mayor of London in one of his most characteristic letters, didn't want to keep the French fleet in ; he wanted them to come out and fight. But he kept close in for fear they should evade him in darkness or in fog.

But the mischief of a Naval War Staff is peculiar to the Navy. I understand it is quite different in the Army—I don't know. The mischief to the Navy is that the very ablest of our Officers, both young and old, get attracted by the brainy work and by the shore-going appointment. I asked a splendid specimen once whatever made him go in for being a Marine Officer. He said he wanted to be with his wife ! Well, it's natural. I know a case of a Sea Officer whose long absence caused his children not to recognise him when he came home from China and, indeed, they were frightened of him. The land is a shocking bad training ground for the sea. I once heard one bluejacket say to another the reason *he* believed in the Bible was that in heaven there is " no more sea." I didn't realise it at the time, but I looked up " Revelations " and found it was so. A shallower spirit observed : " Britannia rules the waves, but the mistake was she didn't rule them straight." A very distinguished soldier who came to see me when I was Port Admiral at Portsmouth said that the Army, as compared with the Navy, was at a great disadvantage. In the Army, or even in the country, he said, anyone who had handled a rifle laid down the law as if he were a General ; but the Navy, he said, was " A huge mystery hedged in by sea-sickness."

So far as the Navy is concerned, the tendency of these " Thinking Establishments " on shore is to convert splendid Sea Officers into very indifferent Clerks. The Admiralty is filled with Sea Officers now who ought to be afloat ; and the splendid civilian element—incomparable in its talent and in its efficiency—is swamped. Before the war, when I was First Sea Lord, when I left the Admiralty at 8 p.m., prior to some approaching Grand Manœuvres, I left it to my friend Flint, one of the Higher Division Clerks, to mobilize the fleet by a wireless message from the roof of the Admiralty ; and the deciding circumstances having arisen, he did it off his own bat at 2 a.m. A weaker vessel, knowing of the telephone at my bedside, might have rung me up ; but Flint didn't. Good old Flint ! Always one of the Clerks was on watch, all the year round, night and day ; and that obtained in the Admiralty long before any other Department adopted it.

Now for such work as I have described you don't want

sea art ; you want the Craven scholar, and I had him. A Sea Officer can never be an efficient clerk— his life unfits him. He can't be an orator ; he's always had to hold his tongue. He can't argue ; he's never been allowed. Only a few great spirits like Nelson are gifted with the splendid idiosyncrasy of insubordination ; but it's given to a few great souls. I assure you that long study has convinced me that Nelson was nothing if not insubordinate. This is hardly the place to describe his magnificent lapses from discipline, which ever led to Victory. It's only due on my part, who have had more experience than anyone living of the civilian clerks at the Admiralty, to vouch for the fact that Sir Evan Macgregor, the ablest Secretary of the Admiralty since Samuel Pepys, Sir Graham Greene, Sir Oswyn Murray, Sir Charles Walker and my friends V. W. Baddeley, C.B., and J. W. S. Anderson, C.B., W. G. Perrin, J. F. Phillips, and many others have done work which has never been exceeded as regards its incomparable efficiency. I can't recall a single lapse.

The outcome of this expanded Naval War Staff beyond its real requirements, such as I have indicated, and which were provided for while I was First Sea Lord, was that a Chief of the Staff, in imitation of him at the War Office, was planked into the Admiralty and indirectly supplanted the First Sea Lord. I won't enlarge on this further. It's many years before another war can possibly take place, and it's now a waste of educated labour to discuss it further. All I would ask is for anyone to take up the last issue of the Navy List and see the endless pages of

Naval Officers at the Admiralty or holding shore appointments. There has never been anything approaching these numbers in all our Sea History ! It is deplorable !

The Naval War College, which I established at Portsmouth, is absolutely a different affair. There it can be arranged that all the Officers go to sea daily and work as if with the fleet, with flotillas of Destroyers that are there available in quantities. These Destroyers would represent all the items of the fleet ; and the formations of war and the meetings of hostile fleets could be practised and so constitute the Naval War College a real gem in war efficiency.

AGED 14. MIDSHIPMAN.
H.M.S. "Highflyer," China.

# CHAPTER IX

## RECAPITULATION OF DEEDS AND IDEAS

" Friends, Romans, Countrymen, lend me your ears ! "

WE have arranged that in this book you (to whom I am dictating) are to insert a *réchauffé* of my fugitive writings and certain extracts from the three bulky volumes of my letters to Lord Esher, which he has so very kindly sent me.

All, then, that I have to say in this chapter will be a summing up of all that is in my opinion worth saying, and you are going to be responsible for the rest. My judgment is that the British Public will be sick of it all long before you come to the end of your part. One can have too much jam. Nor do you seem inclined to put in all the " bites." For instance, it was told King Edward, who warned me of what was being said, that my moral character was shocking. No woman will ever appear against me at the Day of Judgment. One dear friend of mine attributed all his life's disasters to kissing the wrong girl. I never even did that. However, there is no credit in my morality and early piety. For I ever had to work from 12 years old for my daily bread, and work hard, so the Devil never had a " look in." I love Dr. Watts, he is so practical.

> " And Satan finds some mischief still.
> For idle hands to do."

Bishop Jeremy Taylor, who wrote that Classic, " Holy Living and Dying," who had a nagging wife who made him flee from home and youthful lusts, said " That no idle rich healthy man could possibly go to Heaven." No doubt it is difficult for such a one. You will remember the Saviour told us that the Camel getting through the eye of a needle is more likely. Usually, earthly judgments on heavenly subjects are wrong. Observe Mary Magdalene, and the most beautiful Collect for her Saint's Day which was in our First Prayer Book of 1540. This was later expunged by the sacerdotal, pharisaic, self-righteous mandarins of that period. The judgments of this world are worse than the judgments of God. When David was offered three forms of punishment—Famine or the Sword or Pestilence —he chose the pestilence, saying, " Let us now fall into the hands of the Lord ; for his mercies are great ; and let me not fall into the hand of man." At the moment of making this note of which I am speaking I am looking at two very beautiful old engravings I rescued from the room here allotted to the Presbyterian Minister ! One of them is the " Woman Taken in Adultery " and the other is " Potiphar's Wife " ! My host tells me it was a pure accident that these pictures came to be in the Minister's room ; but such events happen to Saints.

Wasn't there "The Scarlet Letter"—that wonderful book by Hawthorne?

I observe in passing how wonderfully well these Presbyterians do preach. Our hosts have a beautiful Chapel in the house, and they have got a delightful custom of selecting one from the Divines of Scotland to spend the week-end here. Their sermons so exemplify what I keep on impressing on you—that the printed word is a lifeless corpse. Can you compare the man who reads a sermon to the man who listens to one saturated with holiness and enthusiasm speaking out of the abundance of the heart? No doubt there is tautology, but there's conviction. Two qualities rule the world—*emotion and earnestness*. I have said elsewhere, with them you can move far more than mountains; you can move multitudes. It's the personality of the soul of man that has this immortal influence. Printed and written stuff is but an inanimate picture—a very fine picture sometimes, no doubt, but you get no aroma out of a picture. Fancy seeing the Queen of Sheba herself, instead of only reading of her in Solomon's print! And those Almug trees—"And there came no such Almug trees, nor were seen until this day."

To a friend I was once adoring St. Peter (I love his impetuosity)—I am illustrating how earthly judgments are so inferior to heavenly wisdom. St. John, who was a very much younger man, out-ran Peter. Up comes Peter, and dashes at once into the Sepulchre. Those men in war who get there and then don't do anything— *Cui bono?* A fleet magnificent, five times bigger than the enemy, and takes no risks ! A man I heard of—his wife, separated from him, died at Florence. He was on the Stock Exchange. They telegraphed, " Shall we cremate, embalm, or bury ? " " Do all three," he replied, " take no risks ! " Some of our great warriors want the bird so arranged as to be able to put the salt on its tail. But I was speaking of my praising St. Peter. What did my friend retort (the judgment of this world, mind you !) ? " Peter, Sir ! he would be turned out of every Club in London ! " So he would ! Thank God, we have a God, so that when our turn comes we shall be forgiven much because we loved much.

From this Christian homily I return to what I rather vainly hope is my concluding interview.

Before beginning—one of my critics writes to *The Times* saying I am not modest—I never said I was. However, next day, Sir Alfred Yarrow mentions perhaps the most momentous thing I ever did—that is the introduction of the Destroyer ; and the day following Sir Marcus Samuel writes that I am the God-father of Oil—and Oil is going to be the fuel of the world. Sir George Beilby is going to turn coal into Oil. He has done it. Thank God ! we are going to have a smokeless England in consequence, and no more fortified coaling stations and peripatetic coal mines, or what coal mines were. And then, I was going to give some more instances, but that's enough " *to point the moral and adorn the tale.*"

# RECAPITULATIONS

" Seekest Thou Great Things for Thyself ? Seek
them not ! " (The Prophet Jeremiah.)

You have given me a list of subjects which you think
require elucidation in regard to my past years—a *résumé*
especially of the incidents which claim peculiar notice
between 1902 and 1910 ; and you ask me to add thereto
such episodes from the past as will enlighten the reader
as to how it came about that those big events between
1902 and 1910 were put in motion.

It's a big order, in a life of some sixty years on actual
service—with but three weeks only unemployed, from the
time of entry into the Navy to the time of Admiral of
the Fleet.

I begin by being heartfelt in my thankfulness to a benign
Providence for being capable yesterday, September 13th,
1919, of enjoying suet pudding and treacle with a pleasure
equal to that which I quite well remember, of having
suet pudding and treacle on July 4th, 1854, when I went
on board H.M.S. " Victory," 101 guns, the flagship at
Trafalgar of Admiral Lord Viscount Nelson. Yes !
my thankfulness, I hope, is equal to but hardly as
wonderful as that of the almost toothless old woman who,
being commiserated with, replied : " Yes, I only 'as
two left ; *but thank God they meet !* " So I say, to
express the same thankfulness with all my heart for the
years that remain to me, though I have all my teeth—or
nearly all—notwithstanding that I have not had even one
single " thank you " for anything that I have done since
King Edward died. Nevertheless, I thank that same God

as the old woman thanked, Who don't let a sparrow fall without a purpose and without knowledge.

I have no doubt the slight has done me a lot of good !

I thought at the age of nineteen, when I was Acting Captain of H.M.S. "Coromandel," that I never could again be so great. Please look at my picture then. It's a very excellent one—rather pulled down at the corners of the mouth even then. (The child is father to the man.) And though now nearly as old as Dandolo I don't feel any greater than at 19. Dandolo after an escapade at the Dardanelles similar to mine, became conqueror of Byzantium at 80 years of age. And Justinian's two Generals, Belisarius and Narses, were over 70. Dolts don't realise that the brain improves while the body decays—provided of course that the original brain is not that of a congenital idiot, or of an effete poltroon who never will run risks.

" Risks and strife " are the bread of Life to a growing brain.

I beg the reader of this dictation to believe that, whatever he may hear to the contrary (and he probably will), though swaggering as I did just now at suet-puddening at 79 as efficiently as at nineteen, yet I do daily realise what that ancient monk wrote in the year 800, when he studied the words of Job—that " Man that is born of a woman hath but a short time " compared to eternity, and death may be always near the door ; and no words are more beautiful in connection therewith than when a parting friend at the moment of departure makes us say : " Teach us who survive in this and other like daily

118

spectacles of mortality to see how frail and uncertain our own condition is."

First of all in this Recapitulation comes back to me a prophecy I ventured at that age of 19 I have just mentioned—that the next great war that we should have at sea would be a war of young men. And how beautifully this is illustrated by the letter received only a few days ago from that boy in Russia (see Chapter IV) where two battleships were sent to the bottom and the British sailors in command were only Lieutenants. And in passing one cannot help paying a tribute to the Subalterns on shore. General Sir Henry Rawlinson said lately : " Those who really won the war were the young Company Leaders and the Subalterns," and pathetic was the usual Gazette notice of those killed :

" Second Lieutenants *unless otherwise mentioned.*"
There was little " otherwise ! " So has it been in the Navy, at Zeebrugge and elsewhere.

There is, however, a very splendid exception—when all hands, old and young, went to the bottom ; and that is in the magnificent Merchant Navy of the British Nation. Seven million tons sank under these men, and the record of so many I've seen who were saved was : " Three times torpedoed." And remember ! for them no Peerage or Westminster Abbey. They didn't even get paid for the clothes they lost, and their pay stopped the day the ship was sunk. Except in the rare cases where the shipowner was the soul of generosity, like my friend Mr. Petersen, who paid his men six months or a year to do nothing after such a catastrophe. But we go with Mr. Havelock

Wilson : " We hope to change all that." For who is going to deny, when we all stand up for them, that the Merchant Navy shall be incorporated in the Navy of the Nation and with all the rights and money and rank and uniform and widows' pensions and pensions in old age ? All this has to come ; and I am Mr. Havelock Wilson's colleague in that matter, as he was mine in that wonderful feeding and clothing of our thousands of British Merchant sailor prisoners, who didn't, for some damned red tape reason, come within the scope of the millions of money in that enormous Prince of Wales's Fund, and the Red Cross.

Somebody will have to be a martyr, perhaps it's me. And I expect I am going to be burnt at the stake for saying these things ; but in those immortal words of the past " I shall light the candle ! " Isn't it just too lovely —when Bishop Latimer, as the flames shot up around him at the stake in Oxford in A.D. 1555, cried to his brother Bishop, equally burning :

" Play the man, Master Ridley ! We shall this day light such a candle by God's Grace in England as I trust shall never be put out."

So may it be in our being burnt for the sake of the great Merchant Navy that saved our country !

———————

As regards the years 1902 to 1910, the first conceptions of these great changes stole upon me when I perceived in that great Fleet in the Mediterranean how vague were the views as to fighting essentials. For instance, in one of the lectures to the Mediterranean Fleet Officers I set forth a case of so dealing with a hostile fleet that we should ourselves first of all deliberately and in cold blood sacrifice several of our fastest cruisers. Why?

To delay the flying enemy by the wounding of his hindermost ships. Possibly a ruthless German Admiral might leave a " Blücher " to her fate ; but not so our then probable and chivalrous foe ! The most shocking description I have ever read of the horrors of war was that detailed by one of the crew of the " Blücher " as he describes Beatty's salvoes gradually approaching the " Blücher " and falling near in the water, and then the hell when these salvoes arrived, immediately extinguishing the electric light installation, till all below between decks was pitchy darkness only lighted up by the bursting shells as they penetrated and massacred the crew literally by hundreds, who, huddled up together in the " Blücher's " last moments, were hoping behind the thickest armour to escape destruction.

I saw that the plan of sacrificing vessels in the pursuit of an enemy seemed a new feature to my hearers ; and yet it was as old as the hills. And another " eye-opener " I had—in the inability to realise so obvious a fact as, alas ! was somewhat the case in the North Sea recently— that you need not be afraid of a mine field ; for where the enemy goes you can go, if you keep in his wake, that is. In close regard with this matter, I am an apostle of " End-on Fire," for to my mind broadside fire is peculiarly stupid. To be obliged to delay your pursuit by turning even one atom from your straight course on to a flying enemy is to me being the acme of an ass. And, strange to say, in connection with this I, only yesterday, September 13th, 1919, got a letter from Admiral Weymouth —a most excellent letter, delightfully elaborating with exceptional acuteness this very idea, which came along so long ago as 1900, when the first thought of the "Dreadnought" came into my brain, when I was discussing with my excellent friend, Mr. Gard, Chief Constructor of Malta Dockyard, the vision of the "Dreadnought."

I greatly enjoyed years ago overhearing a lady describe to another lady, when crossing over to Ryde, a passing Ryde passenger steamer (just built and differing very greatly from the one we were on board of) as a Battleship. And she wasn't far out as to what a battleship should be. The enterprise of the Ryde Steam Packet Company had just produced that vessel, which went just as fast astern as she did ahead. In fact, she had no stern. There was a bow at each end and a rudder at each end and screws at each end; so they never had any bother to turn round. Now when you go to Boulogne or Folkestone, I don't know how much time you don't waste fooling around to go in stern first, so as to be able to come out the right way; and having escaped sea-sickness so far, I myself have found that the last straw. Let us hope every ship now built after this Chapter will be a "Double-Ender." But in this world you are a lunatic if you go too fast.

Take now the submarines. They began by diving

head first to get below water ; and in the beginning some stuck their noses in the mud and never came up again, and in the shallow waters of the North Sea this limited the dimension of the submarine. But now there's no more diving. A lunatic hit by accident on the idea of sinking the ship horizontally ; so there is no more bother about the metricentric problems, and all the vagaries of Stabilities. No limit to size !

This sort of consideration brought into one's mind that a great " Education " was wanted ; and that we wanted " Machinery Education," both with officers and men ; and also that the education should be the education of common sense. My full idea of Osborne was, alas ! emasculated by the schoolmasters of the Nation ; but it is yet going to spread. As sure as I am now dictating to you, the practical way of teaching is " *Explanation, followed by Execution.*" Have a lecture on Optics in the morning : make a telescope in the afternoon. Tell the boys in the morning about the mariner's compass and the use of the chart ; and in the afternoon go out and navigate a Ship.

Similarly, with the selection of boys for the Navy, I didn't want any examination whatsoever, except the boy and his parents being " vetted," and then an interview with the boy to examine his personality (his *soul*, in fact) ; and not to have an article in the Navy stuffed by patent cramming schoolmasters like a Strasburg goose. A goose's liver is not the desideratum in the candidate. The desideratum was : could we put into him the four attributes of Nelson :—

# MEMORIES

I. Self reliance.

> (If you don't believe in yourself, nobody else will.)

II. Fearlessness of Responsibility.

> (If you shiver on the brink you'll catch cold, and possibly not take the plunge.)

III. Fertility of Resource.

> (If the traces break, don't give it up, get some string.)

IV. Power of initiative.

> (Disobey orders.)

## AIRCRAFT.

Somewhere about January 15th, 1915, I submitted my resignation as First Sea Lord to Mr. Churchill because of the supineness manifested by the High Authorities as regards Aircraft; and I then prophesied the raids over London in particular and all over England, that by and by caused several millions sterling of damage and an infinite fright.

I refer to my resignation on the aircraft question with some fear and trembling of denials; however, I have a copy of my letter, so it's all right. I withdrew my resignation at the request of Authority, because Authority said that the War Office and not the Admiralty were responsible and would be held responsible. The aircraft belonged to the War Office; why on earth couldn't I mind my own business? I didn't want the Admiralty building and our wireless on the roof of it to be bombed; so it *was* my business (the War Office was as safe as a church, the Germans would never bomb that establishment !).

Recently I fortuned to meet Mr. Holt Thomas, and he brought to my recollection what was quite a famous meeting at the Admiralty. Soon after I became First Sea Lord on October 31st, 1914, I had called together at the Admiralty a Great Company of all interested in the air ; for at that moment I had fully satisfied myself that small airships with a speed of fifty miles an hour would be of inestimable value against submarines and also for scouting purposes near the coast. *So they proved.*

Mr. Holt Thomas was a valued witness before the Royal Commission on Oil and Oil Engines, of which I was Chairman (a sad business for me financially—I only possessed a few hundred pounds and I put it into Oil— I had to sell them out, of course, on becoming Chairman of the Oil Commission, and what I put those few hundreds into caused a disappearance of most of those hundreds, and when I emerged from the Royal Commission the oil shares had more than quintupled in value and gone up to twenty times what they were when I first put in).

Through Mr. Holt Thomas we obtained the very important evidence of the French inventor of the Gnome engine—that wonderful engine that really made aeroplanes what they now are. His evidence was of peculiar value ; and so also was that of Mr. Holt Thomas's experience ; and the result of the Admiralty meeting on aircraft was that we obtained from Mr. Holt Thomas an airship in a few weeks, when the experience hitherto had been that it took years ; and a great number of this type of aircraft were used with immense advantage in the war. I remember so well that the very least time that could be promised with every effort and unstinted money, was three months (but Mr. Holt Thomas gave a shorter time). In three *weeks* an airship was flying over the Admiralty at 50 miles an hour ("there's nothing you can't have if you want it enough"), and now we've reached the Epoch—prodigious in its advent—when positively the Air commands and dominates both Land and Sea; and we shall witness quite shortly a combination in one Structure of the Aeroplane, the Airship, the parachute, the common balloon, and an Aerial Torpedo, which will both astound people by its simplicity and by its extra-ordinary possibilities, both in War and Commerce (the torpedo will become cargo in Commerce). The aeroplane has now to keep moving to live—but why should it? The aerial gyroscopic locomotive torpedo suspended by a parachute has a tremendous significance.

And let no one think like the ostrich that burying one's head in the sand will make Invention desist. At the first Hague Peace Conference in 1899, when I was one of the British Delegates, huge nonsense was talked about the amenities of war. War has no amenities, although Mr. Norman Angell attacked me in print for saying so. It's like two Innocents playing singlestick; they agree, when they begin, not to hit hard, but it don't last long! Like fighting using only one fist against the other man with two; the other fist damn soon comes out! The Ancient who formulated that "All's fair in love and war" enunciated a great natural principle.

# RECAPITULATIONS

*" War is the essence of violence."*
*" Moderation in War is imbecility."*
*" HIT FIRST. HIT HARD. KEEP ON HITTING."*

The following Reports and letter will illustrate this history of my efforts in this direction :—

Lord Fisher returned to the Admiralty on October 30th, 1914.
38 S.S. airships were at once ordered—single engine type. Six improved type.
Before Lord Fisher left the Admiralty, a design of a double-engine type was got out, and subsequently another 32 airships were ordered.

CIRCULAR LETTER issued by Lord Fisher in 1914 when First Sea Lord :—

Lord Fisher desires to express to all concerned his high appreciation of the service rendered by those who carried out the recent daring raid on Lake Constance.

He considers that the flight mentioned, made over 250 miles of enemy country of the worst description, is a fine feat of endurance, courage, and skill, and reflects great credit on all who took part in the raid, and through them on the Air Service to which they belong.

The following précis of correspondence is inserted because contributory to Lord Fisher's resignation. He had previously written to Mr. Churchill, resigning on the ground of the disregard of his warnings respecting the Aircraft menace :—

An Official Secret German Dispatch, obtained from a German Source, dated December 26th, 1914 :—

The General Staff of the German Army are sending aircraft to attack French fortified places. Full use to be

made of favourable weather conditions for attack of
Naval Zeppelins against the East Coast of England with
the exception of London. The attack on London will
follow later combined with the German Army Airships.

---

Précis of History of Rigid Airships of Zeppelin
Type .—

Lord Fisher, when First Sea Lord, in December, 1908,
instructed Admiral Bacon to press for the construction of
rigid airships for naval purposes at the meetings of a
Sub-Committee of the Committee of Imperial Defence,
which held its first meeting in December, 1908, after
many meetings at which Admiral Bacon presented the
naval point of view with much lucidity. The Committee
recommended on January 28th,1909, the following :—

(a) The Committee are of opinion that the dangers to
which we might be exposed by developments in aerial
navigation cannot be definitely ascertained until we
ourselves possess airships.

(b) *There are good grounds for assuming that airships
will prove of great value to the Navy for scouting and possibly
for destructive purposes.*[1] From a military point of view
they are also important.

(c) A sum of £35,000 should be included in the Naval
Estimates for the purpose of building an airship of a
rigid type. The sum alluded to should include the cost
of all preliminary and incidental expenses.

(d) A sum of £10,000 should be included in Army

---

[1] This was written in December, 1908, and our Fleet and ships were
always dogged in the war by them.

AGED 19. LIEUTENANT.
In temporary command of "Coromandel" in China.

# RECAPITULATIONS

Estimates for continuing experiments with navigable balloons of a non-rigid type, and for the purchase of complete non-rigid airships and their component parts.

*January 28th*, 1909.
Approved by Committee of Imperial Defence, *February 25th*, 1909.

And nothing more was done till I came back to Admiralty on October 30th, 1914!

Letter from Admiral Sir S. Eardley Wilmot, formerly Superintendent of Ordnance Stores, Admiralty :—

THE OLD MALT HOUSE,<br>
MARLOW,<br>
August 13th, 1916.

DEAR LORD FISHER,

Having given us splendid craft to fight on and under the sea, I wish you would take up the provision of an air fleet.   There is going to be a great development of air navigation in the future and all nations will be at it.   With our resources and wealth we can take and keep the lead if we like.

As a modest programme to start with we might aim at 100 air battleships and 400 air cruisers : all on the " lighter than air " principle.

I met a young fellow who had been in the Jutland action and asked him how the 15-inch guns did. " Splendidly," he said—" They did nearly all the real execution."   I hear the Germans have got 17-inch guns which is what I anticipated, but they won't get ahead of us in that time tho' we can't yet snuff out their Zepps, thanks to you know who.

Yours sincerely,<br>
(Signed)   S. EARDLEY WILMOT.

*Note.*—More than a year before I got this letter I had

got a 20-inch gun ready to be built for a new type of Battle Cruiser !

### THE SUBMARINE MINE

As quite a young Lieutenant, with extraordinary impudence I told the then First Sea Lord of the Admiralty that the Hertz German Submarine Mine, which I had seen a few days before in Kiel Harbour, would so far revolutionise sea warfare as possibly to prevent one fleet pursuing another, by the Fleet that was flying dropping submarine mines in its wake ; and certainly that sudden sea operations of the old Nelsonic type would seriously be interfered with. He very good humouredly sent me away as a young desperado, as he remembered that I had been a lunatic in prophesying the doom of masts and sails, which were still then magnificently supreme, and the despised engineer yet hiding his diminished head had to keep the smell of oily oakum away from the noses of the Lords of the ship.

That same Hertz mine in all its essentials remains still " The King of Mines," and if only in those years immediately preceding the war we had manufactured none else, instead of trying to improve on it, we should have bagged no end of big game. But as it was, our mines were squibs ; the enemy's ship always steamed away and got into harbour, while ours always went down plump.

The Policy of the Submarine Mine favoured us, but our authorities couldn't see it. I printed in three kinds of type :

(1) Huge capitals ; (2) Italics ; (3) big Roman block

letters the following words, submitted to the authorities very early in the war :—

" Sow the North Sea with Mines on such a huge scale that Naval Operations in it become utterly impossible."

*So you nip into the Baltic with the British Fleet.*

That British Mining Policy blocked the North Sea entrance to the Kiel Canal—that British Mining Policy dished the neutrals. When the neutrals got blown up you swore it was a German mine—it was the Germans who began laying mines ; and a mine, when it blows you up, don't hand you a ticket like a passport, saying what nationality it is. In fact, our mines were so damned bad they couldn't help believing it was a German mine. But I might add I think they would have sunk any Merchant ship, squibs though they were ; and I may add in a parenthesis this British policy of submarine mines for the North Sea would have played hell with the German submarines, not so much blowing them up but entangling their screws.

Well, at the last—*longo intervallo*—towards the close of the war, being the fifteenth " Too Late " of Mr. Lloyd George's ever memorable and absolutely true speech, the British Foreign Office did allow this policy, and the United States sent over mines in thousands upon thousands, and we're still trying to pick 'em up, in such vast numbers were they laid down !

> *We really are a very peculiar people.*
> *Lions led by Asses !*

I bought a number of magnificent and fast vessels for

laying down these mines in masses—no sooner had I left the Admiralty in May, 1915, they were so choice that they were diverted and perverted to other uses.

But perhaps the most sickening of all the events of the war was the neglect of the Humber as the jumping-off place for our great fast Battle Cruiser force, with all its attendant vessels—light Cruisers, Destroyers, and Submarines, and mine-layers, and mine-sweepers—for offensive action at any desired moment, and as a mighty and absolute deterrent to the humiliating bombardment of our coasts by that same fast German Battle Cruiser force. The Humber is the nearest spot to Heligoland ; and at enormous cost and greatly redounding to the credit of the present Hydrographer of the Navy, Admiral Learmonth (then Director of Fixed Defences), the Humber was made submarine-proof, and batteries were placed in the sea protecting the obstructions, and moorings laid down behind triple lines of defence against all possibility of hostile successful attack.

However, I had to leave the Admiralty before it was completed and the ships sent there ; and then the *mot d'ordre* was Passivity ; and when the Germans bombarded Scarborough and Yarmouth and so on, we said to them *à la Chinois*, making great grimaces and beating tom-toms ; " If you come again, look out ! " But the Germans weren't Chinese, and they came ; and the soothing words spoken to the Mayors of the bombarded East Coast towns were what Mark Twain specified as being " spoke ironical."

## RECAPITULATIONS

I conclude this Chapter with the following words, printed in the early autumn of 1914 :—

" By the half-measures we have adopted hitherto in regard to Open-Sea Mines we are enjoying neither the one advantage nor the other."

That is to say, when the Germans at the very first outbreak of war departed from the rules of the Hague Conference against the type of mine they used, we had two courses open to us : there was the moral advantage of refusing to follow the bad lead, or we could seek a physical advantage by forcing the enemies' crime to its utmost consequences. We were effete. We were pusillanimous, and we were like Jelly-fish.

*And we " Waited and See'd."*

# CHAPTER X

APOLOGIA PRO VITA SUA

WE started out on the compilation of this book on the understanding that it was not to be an Autobiography, nor a Diary, nor Meditations (à la Marcus Aurelius), but simply " MEMORIES." And now you drive me to give you a Synopsis of my life (which is an artful periphrasis), and request me to account for my past life being one continuous series of fightings—Love and Hate alternating and Strife the thread running through this mortal coil of mine. (When a coil of rope is made in a Government Dockyard a coloured worsted thread is introduced ; it runs through the centre of the rope : if the rope breaks and sends a man to " Kingdom Come," you know the Dockyard that made it and you ask questions ; if it's purloined the Detective bowls out the purloiner.) So far my rope of life has not broken and the thread is there —Strife.

Greatly daring, and " storms of obloquy " having been my portion, I produce now an *apologia pro vita mea*, though it may not pulverise as that great Cardinal pulverised with his famous Apologia (" He looked like Heaven and he fought like Hell ").

Here I would insert a note which I discovered this very afternoon sent me by an unknown friend when Admiral von Spee and all his host went to the bottom. Before that event there had been a series of disasters at sea, and a grave uneasy feeling about our Navy was spreading over the land. The three great Cruisers—"Hogue," "Cressy" and "Aboukir"—had been sunk near the German coast. What were they doing there ? Did they think they were Nelson blockading Toulon ? The "Goeben" and "Breslau" had escaped from our magnificent Battle Cruisers, then in the Mediterranean, which had actually boxed them up in the Harbour of Messina ; and they had gone unharmed to Constantinople, and like highwaymen had held a pistol at the head of the Sultan with the threat of bombarding Constantinople and his Palace and thus converted Turkey, our ancient ally, into the most formidable foe we had. For is not England the greatest Mahomedan Power in the world ? The escape of the "Goeben" and "Breslau" was an irreparable disaster almost equalled by our effete handling of Bulgaria, the key State of the Balkans ; and we didn't give her what she asked. When we offered it and more next year, she told us to go to hell. Then there was the "Pegasus," that could neither fight nor run away, massacred in cold blood at Zanzibar by a German Cruiser as superior to her as our Battle Cruisers were to von Spee. And last of all, as a climax, that sent the hearts of the British people into their boots, poor Cradock and his brave ships were sunk by Admiral von Spee. I became First Sea Lord within 24 hours of that event, and without delay the Dreadnought Battle Cruisers, "Inflexible" and "Invincible," went 7,000 miles without a hitch in their water tube boilers or their turbine machinery, and arrived at the Falkland Islands almost simultaneously with Admiral von Spee and his eleven ships. That night von Spee, like another Casabianca with his son on board, had gone to the bottom and all his ships save one —and that one also soon after—were sunk. I have to reiterate about von Spee, as to this day the veil is upon the faces of our people, and they do not realise the Salvation that came to them.

1. We should have had no munitions—our nitrate came from Chili.

2. We should have lost the Pacific—the Falkland Islands would have been another Heligoland and a submarine base.

3. Von Spee had German reservists, picked up on the Pacific Coast, on board, to man the fortifications to be erected on the Falkland Islands.

4. He would have proceeded to the Cape of Good Hope and massacred our Squadron there, as he had massacred Cradock and his Squadron.

5. General Botha and his vast fleet of transports proceeding to the conquest of German South-West Africa would have been destroyed.

6. Africa under Hertzog would have become German.

7. Von Spee, distributing his Squadron on every Ocean, would have exterminated British Trade.

That's not a bad *résumé!*

Now I give the note, for it really is first-rate. Who

wrote it I don't know, and I don't know the paper that it came from :—

" It is amusing to read the eulogies now showered on Lord Fisher. He is the same man with the same methods, the same ideas, and the same theories and practice which he had in 1905 when he was generally abused as an un-scrupulous rascal for whom the gallows were too good. Lord Fisher's silence under storms of obloquy while he was building up Sea Power was a striking evidence of his title to fame."

The writer of the paragraph quotes the above words from some other paper ; then he goes on with the fol-lowing remark :—

" We cordially endorse these observations. At the same time, not all of those who raised the ' storms of obloquy ' in 1905 and for some years subsequently are now indulging in eulogy. Many of them just maintain a more or less discreet silence, varied by an occasional insinuation either in public or in private that everything is not quite as it should be at the Admiralty, or that Lord Fisher is too old for his job, etc., etc., etc. As we have often remarked, many of the vituperators of Lord Fisher hated him for this one simple reason, that he had weighed them up and found them wanting. They had imposed on the public, but they couldn't impose on him. Some of these vituperators are now discreetly silent, but we know for a fact that their sentiments towards the First Sea Lord are not in the slightest degree changed."

To proceed with this synopsis :—

I entered the Navy, July 12th, 1854, on board Her Majesty's Ship " Victory," after being medically examined by the Doctor on board of her, and writing out from dictation The Lord's Prayer ; and I rather think I did a

Rule of Three sum. Before that time, for seven years I had a hard life. My paternal grandfather—a splendid old parson of the fox-hunting type—with whom I was to live, had died just before I reached England ; and no one else but my maternal grandfather was in a position to give me a home. He was a simple-minded man and had been fleeced out of a fortune by a foreign scoundrel —I remember him well, as also I remember the Chartist Riots of 1848 when I saw a policeman even to my little mind behaving, as I thought, brutally to passing individuals. I remember seeing a tottering old man having his two sticks taken away from him and broken across their knees by the police. On the other hand, I have to bear witness to a little phalanx of 40 splendid police (who then wore tall hats and tail coats) charging a multitude of what seemed to me to be thousands and sending them flying for their lives. They only had their truncheons—but they knew how to use them certainly. They seized the band and smashed the instruments and tore up their flags.

I share Lord Rosebery's delightful distaste ; and wild horses won't make me say more about those early years. These are Lord Rosebery's delicious words :—

" There is one initial part of a biography which is skipped by every judicious reader ; that in which the pedigree of the hero is set forth, often with warm fancy and sometimes at intolerable length."

How can it possibly interest anyone to know that my simple-minded maternal grandfather was driven through the artifices of a rogue to take in lodgers, who of their charity gave me bread thickly spread with butter—butter was a thing I otherwise never saw—and my staple food was boiled rice with brown sugar—very brown ?

Other vicissitudes of my early years—until I became Gunnery Lieutenant of the first English Ironclad, the "Warrior," at an extraordinarily early age—may be told some day; and all that your desired synopsis demands is a filling in of dates and a few details, till I became the Captain of the "Inflexible"—the "Dread-nought" of her day. I was promoted from Commander to Captain largely through a Lord of the Admiralty by chance hearing me hold forth in a Lecture to a bevy of Admirals.

H.M.S. "VIGILANT," PORTSMOUTH.
*October 3rd, 1873.*

Mr. Goschen and Milne left at 10 a.m. I stayed and went on board "Vernon," Torpedo School Ship, at 11. Had a most interesting lecture from Commander Fisher, a promising young officer, and witnessed several experiments. The result of my observations was that in my opinion the Torpedo has a great future before it *and that mechanical training will in the near future be essential for officers.* Made a note to speak to Goschen about young Fisher.

That was in 1873. More than thirty years after, "Young Fisher" was instrumental in making this principle the basis of the new system of education of all naval cadets at Osborne.

I remember so well taking a " rise " out of my exalted company of Admirals and others. The voltaic element, which all lecturers then produced with gusto as the elementary galvanic cell, was known as the " Daniell Cell." A bit of zinc, and a bit of copper stuck in sawdust saturated with diluted sulphuric acid, and there you were !

A bit of wire from the zinc to one side of a galvanometer and a bit of wire from the copper to the other side and round went the needle as if pursued by the devil.

There were endless varieties of this " Daniell Cell," which it was always considered right and proper to describe. " Now," I said, " Sirs, I will give you without any doubt whatsoever the original Daniell Cell "—at that moment disclosing to their rapt and enquiring gaze a huge drawing (occupying the whole side of the lecture room and previously shrouded by a table cloth)—the Lions with their mouths firmly shut and Daniel apparently biting his nails waiting for daylight! Anyhow, that's how Rubens represents him.

I very nearly got into trouble over that " Sell." Admirals don't like being " sold."

I should have mentioned that antecedent to this I had been Commander of the China Flagship. I wished very much for the Mediterranean Flagship ; but my life-long and good friend Lord Walter Kerr was justly preferred before me. The Pacific Flagship was also vacant ; and I think the Admiral wanted me there, but I had a wonderful good friend at the Admiralty, Sir Beauchamp Seymour, afterwards Lord Alcester, who was determined I should go to China. So to China I went ; and, as it happened, it turned out trumps, for the Admiral got softening of the brain, and I was told that when he got home and attended at the Admiralty I was the only thing in his mind ; the only thing he could say was " Fisher ! " And this luckily helped me in my promotion to Post Captain.

After starting the " Vernon " as Torpedo School of

the Navy and partaking in a mission to Fiume to arrange
for the purchase of the Whitehead Torpedo, I was sent
at an hour's notice overland to Malta, where on entering
the harbour I noticed an old tramp picking up her
anchor, and on enquiry found she was going to Constantinople, where the ship I was to command was with
the Fleet under Sir Geoffrey Hornby. I went alongside,
got up a rope ladder that was hanging over the side and
pulled up my luggage with a rope's end, when the Captain
of the Tramp came up to me and said : " Hullo ! " I
said " Hullo ! " He said " What is it you want ? " He
didn't know who I was, and I was in plain clothes, just
as I had travelled over the Continent, and I replied :
" I'm going with you to Constantinople to join my
ship " ; and he said " There ain't room ; there's only one
bunk, and when I ain't in it the mate is." I said " All
right, I don't want a bunk." And he said " Well, we
ain't got no cook." And I said " That don't matter
either." That man and I till he died were like Jonathan
and David. He was a magnificent specimen of those
splendid men who command our merchant ships—I
worshipped the ground he trod on. His mate was just
as good. They kept watch and watch, and it was a
hard life. I said to him one day " Captain, I never see
you take sights." " Well," he said, " Why should I ?
When I leaves one lamp-post I steers for the other "
(meaning lighthouses) ; " and," he says, " I trusts my
engineer. He gives me the revolutions what the engine
has made, and I know exactly where I am. And," he
says, " when you have been going twenty years on the

same road and no other road, you gets to know exactly how to do it." "Well," I said, "what do you do about your compass ? are you sure it's correct ? In the Navy, you know, we're constantly looking at the sun when it sets, and that's an easy way of seeing that the compass is right." "Well," he said, "what I does is this. I throws a cask overboard, and when it's as far off as ever I can see it, I turns the ship round on her axis. I takes the bearing of the cask at every point of the compass, I adds 'em all up, divides the total by the number of bearings, which gives me the average, and then I subtracts each point of the compass from it, and that's what the compass is wrong on each point. But," he says, " I seldom does it, because provided I make the lamp-post all right I think the compass is all right."

I found Admiral Hornby's fleet at Ismid near Constantinople, and Admiral Hornby sent a vessel to meet me at Constantinople. He had heard from Malta that I was on board the tramp. That great man was the finest Admiral afloat since Nelson. At the Admiralty he was a failure. So would Nelson have been ! With both of them their Perfection was on the Sea, not at an office desk. Admiral Hornby I simply adored. I had known him many years ; and while my cabins on board my ship were being painted, he asked me to come and live with him aboard his Flagship, which I did, and I was next ship to him always when at sea. He was astounding. He would tell you what you were going to do wrong before you did it ; and you couldn't say you weren't going to do it because you had put your helm over and the ship had begun to move the wrong way. Many years afterwards, when he was the Port Admiral at Portsmouth, I was head of the Gunnery School at Portsmouth, and, some war scare arising, he was ordered to take command of the whole Fleet at home collected at Portland. He took me with him as a sort of Captain of the Fleet, and we went to Bantry Bay, where we had exercises of inestimable value. He couldn't bear a fool, so of course he had many enemies. There never lived a more noble character or a greater seaman. He was incomparable.

———

After commanding the " Pallas " in the Mediterranean under Sir Geoffrey Hornby, I was selected by Admiral Sir Cooper Key as his Flag Captain in North America in command of the " Bellerophon " ; and I again followed Sir Cooper Key as his Flag Captain in the " Hercules " when he also was put in command of a large fleet on another war scare arising. It was in that year I began the agitation for the introduction of Lord Kelvin's compass into the Navy, and I continued that agitation with the utmost vehemence till the compass was adopted. After that I was chosen by Admiral Sir Leopold McClintock, the great Arctic Explorer, to be his Flag Captain on the North American Station, in the " Northampton," then a brand new ship. He again was a splendid man, and his kindness to me is unforgettable. He had gone through great hardships in the Arctic—once he hadn't washed for 179 days. He was like a rare old bit of mahogany ; and I was told by an admirer of his that when the thermometer was 70 degrees below zero he found the ship so stuffy that he slept outside on the ice in his sleeping bag.

I was suddenly recalled to England and left him with very deep regret in the West Indies to become Captain of the " Inflexible." I had the most trying parting from that ship's company of the " Northampton "; and not being able to stand the good-bye, I crept unseen into a shore boat and got on board the mail steamer before the crew found out that the Captain had left the ship. And the fine old Captain of the Mail Steamer—Robert Woolward by name—caught the microbe and steamed me round and round my late ship. He was a great character. Every Captain of a merchant ship I meet I seem to think better than the last (I hope I shan't forget later on to describe Commodore Haddock of the White Star Line, for if ever there was a Nelson of the Merchant Service he was). But I return to Woolward. He had been all his life in the same line of steamers, and he showed me some of his correspondence, which was lovely. He was invariably in the right and his Board of Directors were invariably in the wrong. I saw a lovely letter he had written that very day that I went on board, to his Board of Directors. He signed himself in the letter as follows :—

" Gentlemen, I am your obedient humble servant " (he was neither), " ROBERT WOOLWARD—Forty years in your employ and never did right yet."

I must, while I have the chance, say a few words about my friend Haddock. It was a splendid Captain in the

1885.   AGED 41.   POST CAPTAIN.
In command of Gunnery School at Portsmouth.

White Star steamer in which I crossed to America in 1910, and I remarked this to my Cabin Steward, as a matter of conversation. " Ah ! " he said, " you should see 'addick." Then he added " We knows him as 'addick of the ' Oceanic.' Yes," he said, " and Mr. Ismay (the Head of the White Star Line) knows him too ! " The " Oceanic " was Mr. Ismay's last feat in narrowness and length and consequent speed for crossing the Atlantic. I have heard that when he was dying he went to see her. This conversation never left my mind, although it was only the cabin steward that told me ; but he was an uncommon good steward. So when I came back to the Admiralty as First Sea Lord on October 31st, 1914, I at once got hold of Haddock, made him into a Commodore, and he commanded the finest fleet of dummy wooden " Dreadnoughts " and Battle Cruisers the world had ever looked on, and they agitated the Atlantic, and the " Queen Elizabeth " in wood got blown up by the Germans at the Dardanelles instead of the real one. The Germans left the other battleships alone chasing the " Elizabeth." If this should meet the eye of Haddock, I want to tell him that, had I remained, he would have been Sir Herbert Haddock, K.C.B., or I'd have died in the attempt.

Now you have got perhaps not all you want, but sufficient for the Notes to follow here.

### THE " WARRIOR "

I was appointed Gunnery Lieutenant of the " Warrior " our First Ironclad in 1863, when I was a little over 22

years old. I had just won the Beaufort Testimonial
(Senior Wrangler), and that, with a transcendental Certificate from Commodore Oliver Jones, who was at that
time the demon of the Navy, gave me a " leg up."

The " Warrior " was then, like the " Inflexible " in
1882 and the "Dreadnought" in 1905, the cynosure of
all eyes. She had a very famous Captain, the son of
that great seaman Lord Dundonald, and a still more
famous Commander, Sir George Tryon, who afterwards
went down in the "Victoria." She had a picked crew
of officers and men, so I was wonderfully fortunate to be
the Gunnery Lieutenant, and at so young an age I got
on very well, except for sky-larking in the ward-room,
for which I got into trouble. There was a dear old
grey-headed Paymaster, and a mature Doctor, and a still
more mature Chaplain, quite a dear old Saint. These,
with other willing spirits, of a younger phase, I organised
into a peripatetic band. The Parson used to play the
coal scuttle, the Doctor the tongs and shovel, the dear
old Paymaster used to do the cymbals with an old tin
kettle. The other instruments we made ourselves out
of brown paper, and we perambulated, doing our best.
The Captain came out of his cabin door and asked the
sentry what that noise was ? We were all struck dumb
by his voice, the skylight being open, and we were silent.
The Sentry said : " It's only Mr. Fisher, Sir ! " so he
shut the door ! The Commander, Sir George Tryon,
wasn't so nice ! He sent down a message to say the
Gunnery Lieutenant was " to stop that fooling ! "
(However, this only drove us into another kind of sport !)

We were all very happy messmates; they kindly spoilt me as if I was the Baby. I never went ashore by any chance, so all the other Lieutenants liked me because I took their duty for them. One of them was like Nelson's signal—he expected every man to do his duty! I was his bosom friend, which reminds me of another messmate I had who, the witty First Lieutenant said, always reminded him of Nelson! Not seeing the faintest resemblance, I asked him why. " Well," he said, " the last thing Nelson did was to die for his country, and that is the last thing this fellow would do!" It may be an old joke, but I'd never heard it before, and it was true.

I got on very well with the sailors, and our gunnery was supposed to be A1. They certainly did rush the guns about, so I was sent in charge of the bluejackets to a banquet given them ashore. I imagined that on our return they might have had a good lot of beer, so I appealed to their honour and affection, when we marched back to the ship in fours, to take each other's arms. They nobly did it! And I got highly complimented for the magnificent way they marched back through the streets!! And this is the episode! The galleries at the banquet were a mass of ladies, and very nice-looking ones. When the banquet was over, the Captain of the Maintop of the "Warrior," John Kiernan by name, unsolicited, stood up in his chair and said : " On behalf of his top-mates he wished to thank the Mayor and Corporation for a jolly good dinner and the best beer he'd ever tasted," He stopped there and said : " Bill, hand me up that beer again." Bill said there was no more! A pledge had been given by the Mayor that they should have only two bottles of beer each. But this episode was too much for the Mayor, and instantly in came beer by the dozen, and my beloved friend, the Captain of the Maintop, had another glass. This is how he went on (and it was a very eloquent speech in my opinion. I remember every word of it to this day) He said : " This is joy," and he looked round the galleries crowded with the lovely ladies, and said : " Here we are, British Sailors entirely surrounded by females ! ! " They waved their handkerchiefs and kissed their hands, and that urged the Captain of the Maintop into a fresh flight of eloquence. " Now," he said, " Shipmates, what was it like now coming into this 'ere harbour of Liverpool " (we had come in under sail) ; " why," he said, " this is what it was like, sailing into a haven of joy before a gale of pleasure." I then told him to shut up, because he would spoil it by anything more, and Abraham Johnson, Chief Gunner's Mate, my First Lieutenant, gave him more beer ! and so we returned.

Abraham Johnson was a wonder ! When the Admiral inspected the "Warrior," Abraham Johnson came to me and said he knew his Admiral, and would I let him have a free hand ? I said : " All right ! " When the ship was prepared for battle, the Admiral suddenly said : " I'll go down in the Magazine," and began going down the steps of the Magazine with his sword on ! Abraham was just underneath down below, and called up to the Admiral : " Beg pardon, Sir ! you can't come down here ! " " D—n the fellow ! what does he mean ? " Abraham reiterated : " You can't come down here." The Admiral said :

" Why not ? " " Because no iron instrument is allowed in the Magazine," said Abraham. " Ah ! " said the Admiral, unbuckling his sword, " that fellow knows his duty. This is a properly organised ship ! "

It is seldom appreciated—it certainly was not then appreciated on board the " Warrior " when I was her Gunnery Lieutenant—that this, our first armour-clad ship-of-war, the " Warrior," would cause a fundamental change in what had been in vogue for something like a thousand years ! For the Navy that had been founded by Alfred the Great had lasted till then without any fundamental change till came this first Ironclad Battleship. There is absolutely nothing in common between the fleets of Nelson and the Jutland Battle ! Sails have given way to steam. Oak to steel. Lofty four-decked ships with 144 guns like the " Santissima Trinidad," to low-lying hulls like that of the first "Dreadnought." Guns of one hundred tons instead of one ton ! And Torpedoes, Mines, Submarines, Aircraft. And then even coal being obsolete ! And, unlike Nelson's day, no human valour can now compensate for mechanical inferiority.

I rescue these few words by a survivor of the German Battle Cruiser " Blücher," sunk on January 24th, 1915, by the British Battle Cruisers " Lion " and " Tiger." The German Officer says :

" The British ships started to fire at us at 15 kilometres distant " (as a matter of fact it was about 11 to 12 miles). "The deadly water spouts came nearer and nearer ! The men on deck watched them with a strange fascination !

" Soon one pitched close to the ship, and a vast watery billow, a hundred yards high, fell lashing on the deck !

" The range had been found !

" The shells came thick and fast. The electric plant was destroyed, and the ship plunged into a darkness that could be felt ! You could not see your hand before your nose ! Below decks were horror and confusion, mingled with gasping shouts and moans ! At first the shells came dropping from the sky, and they bored their way even to the stokeholds !

" The coal in the bunkers was set on fire, and as the bunkers were half empty the fire burnt fiercely. In the engine-room a shell licked up the oil and sprayed it around in flames of blue and green, scarring its victims and blazing where it fell. Men huddled together in dark compartments, but the shells sought them out, and there Death had a rich harvest."

I forgot to say we had a surprise visit from Garibaldi on board the "Warrior"—Garibaldi, then at the zenith of his glory. The whole crew marched past him singing the Garibaldi Hymn. He was greatly affected. It was very fine indeed ; for we had a picked stalwart crew, and their sword bayonets glistening in the sun, and in their white hats and gaiters they looked, as they were, real fighting men ! And then, in a moment, they stripped themselves of their accoutrements and swarmed up aloft and spread every sail on the ship, including studding sails, in a few minutes. It was a dead calm, and so was feasible.

From the "Warrior" I went to the gunnery school ship, the "Excellent"; and it was during these years that some of my " manias " began to display themselves, the result being that three times I lost my promotion through them.

# APOLOGIA PRO VITA SUA

It had fortuned that in 1868, when starting the Science of Under-Water Warfare as applied to the Ocean, I met a humble-minded armourer whose name was Isaac Tall, and for many years we worked together. He devised, amongst other inventions, an electrically-steered steam vessel that could tow barges laden with 500 lb. mines which were dropped automatically at such a distance apart as absolutely to destroy all hostile mines in a sufficient area to give a passage for Battleships. Small buoys were automatically dropped as the countermines were dropped to mark the cleared passage. That invention, simplicity itself, still holds the field for clearing a passage, say, into the Baltic. Not one single man was on board the steam vessel of the Barges carrying the counter mines.

Before leaving the Admiralty, in January, 1910, I introduced the use of Trawlers, and we employed them in experimental trials, clearing away hostile mines. Our mines in those days were very inferior to the Hertz German Mine, which really remains still the efficient German Mine we have to contend with. In 1868 I took out a provisional patent for a Sympathetic Exploder, and, strange to say, it is now coming into play in a peculiar form as a most effective weapon for our use.

I have remarked elsewhere how the First Lord of that date did not believe in mines or torpedoes, and I left for China as Commander of the China flagship.

Archbishop Magee, that wonderful Prelate who asked some layman to interpret his feelings when the footman spilt the onion sauce over him, said of " Exaggerations " that they were needful ! He said you wanted a big brush to produce scenic effects ! A camel's-hair brush was, no doubt, the inestimable weapon of Memling in those masterpieces of his minute detail that were at Bruges when I was a young Post Captain, and that so entranced me there. Ah! that wonderful Madame Polsonare where we lodged ! How she did so well care for us ! The peas I used to watch her shelling ! The three repositories :

First—the old ones to be stewed.

Second—those for the Polsonare Family.

Thirdly—the youngest and sweetest of the peas for us —her lodgers !

And how most delicious they were ! And how delightful was old " Papa " Polsonare ! and the daughters so plump and opulent in their charm !

And their only son the " brave Belge ! " He was a soldier ! What has become of them now ? They cared for us as their very own, and charged us the very minimum for our board and lodging ! And having nothing but my pay then I was grateful ! And the Kindergarten so delightful ! The little children all tied together by a rope when they went out walking. Pamela was my youngest daughter. " The last straw " was her nickname ! And it was written up over the mantelpiece that it was " défendu " to kiss Pamela ! She was about three years old, I think, and went to school with a bun and her books strapped to her back, and when the Burgomaster gave away the prizes she was put on a Throne to hand them out (dressed as a Ballet Dancer !). But alas ! when the moment came she was found to be fast asleep !

I am always so surprised that so little notice is taken of Satan's dramatic appearance before the Almighty with reference to the Patriarch Job. It's so seldom that Satan in person comes before us. He usually uses someone else, and in this case of Job it's quite the most subtle innuendo I ever came across ! It so accentuates what occurs in common life !

" *Doth Job fear God for nought ?* " Well may one be thankful and prayerful when prosperity is showered on one ! Can you be so in adversity and affliction—undeserved and unexplainable ? However, Job got through all right ! But Prayer is as much misunderstood as Charity. A splendid Parson in Norfolk replied to his congregation who asked him to pray for rain that really it was useless while the wind was east ! Also it appears to me that one farmer, wanting rain for his turnips, doesn't have any feeling for the other man who is against rain because of carrying his crop of something else. Indeed the pith and marrow of prayer is that it must be absolutely unselfish, and so Dr. Chalmers accordingly acutely said the finest prayer he knew was : " Almighty God, the Fountain of all Wisdom, who knowest our necessities," etc. (*see* Collects at end of Communion Service).

Coming home from the China Station in 1872, I was Commander of the old Battleship " Ocean." She was an old wooden Line of Battleship that had armour bolted on her sides. When we got into heavy weather, the

timbers of the ship would open when she heeled over
one way, and shut together when she heeled the other,
and squirted the water inboard! And always we had
many fountains playing in the bottom of the ship from
leaks, some quite high. At Singapore the Chaplain left
us ; he couldn't face it, as we were going home round the
Cape of Good Hope at the stormy season. So I did
chaplain! When we put into Zanzibar on the East Coast
of Africa, I heard there was a sick Bishop ashore from
Central Africa who had been carried down on a shutter
with fever. I went to see him, to ask whether he could
take on next day, Sunday, and give the crew a change!
He turned out to be a splendid specimen, and had given
up a fat living in Lincolnshire to be a Missionary. I
found him eating boiled rice and a hard boiled egg on a
broken plate—we gave him a good feed when he came
on board—but I am telling the story because his Sermon
was on Prayer. He gave us no text, but began by saying
he had been wondering for the last half-hour what on
earth that thing was overhead between the beams on the
main deck where we were assembled! Of course we
knew it was one of the long pump handles for pumping
the ship out with the chain pumps (a thing of past ages)
—all the crew had to take continually to the pumps, she
was leaking so badly—and " There ! " he said, " I'm a
Bishop, and instead of saying my prayers I've been letting
my thoughts wander," and he gave us a beautiful extempore sermon on wandering thoughts on Prayer that
hit everyone in the eye !

I believe he died there in Central Africa, a polished

English gentleman, with refined tastes and delighting in the delicacies of a cultured life ! A missionary had come preaching at his Country Church and had made him ashamed of his life of ease, so he told me !

We got into a fierce gale off the Cape, and I began to envy the Chaplain we had left behind at Singapore, especially when the Captain said he thought there was nothing for it but for me, the Commander, to go aloft about the close reefed fore topsail as the men would follow no one of lower rank. My monkey jacket was literally " blown into ribbons ! " I had heard the expression before, but never had realised it could be exact !

Sir Thomas Troubridge foundered with all hands in the exact place in an old two-decker—I think it was the " Blenheim." He was Nelson's favourite, and got ashore in the " Culloden " at the Nile ; but that's another story as Mr. Kipling says !

### How I became Captain of the " Inflexible "

The " Inflexible " in 1882 was a wonder. She had the thickest armour, the biggest guns, and the largest of everything beyond any ship in the world. A man could crawl up inside the bore of one of her guns. Controversy had raged round her. The greatest Naval Architects of the time quarrelled with each other. Endless inventions were on board her, accumulated there by cranks in the long years she took building. A German put a new type of gas into the engine room, which was lovely, and no smell, so bright, so simple ! But when it chanced to escape from a leaky joint, it descended and did not rise, so it got into all the double bottoms and nearly polished off a goodly number of the crew. There were whistles in my cabin that yelled when the boiler was going to burst, or the ship was not properly steered, and so on. So to be Captain of the " Inflexible " was much sought after. As each name was discussed by the Board of Admiralty it got " butted," that is to say, it would be remarked : " Yes, he's a splendid officer and quite fit for it, but——" and then some reason was adduced why he should not be selected (he had murdered his father, or he had kissed the wrong girl !). Lord Northbrook, who was First Lord, got sick of these interminable discussions as to who should be Captain of the " Inflexible," so he unexpectedly said one morning : " Do any of you know a young Captain called Fisher ? " And they all—having no notion of what was in Lord Northbrook's mind, and I being well known to each of them—had no " buts " ! So he got up and said : " Well, that settles it. I'll appoint him Captain of the " Inflexible." I was about the Junior Captain in the biggest ship !

However, the " Inflexible " brought me to death's door, as I was suddenly struck down by dysentery when ashore in charge of Alexandria after the bombardment. I had arranged an armoured train, with which we used to reconnoitre the enemy, who were in great strength and only a few miles off. The Officer who took my place in the armoured train the day after I was disabled by dysentery was knocked over by one of the enemy shells, and so it was telegraphed home that I was killed, and Queen Victoria telegraphed back for details, and very interesting leading articles appeared as to what I might have been had I lived. Lord Northbrook telegraphed for me to be sent home immediately, kindly adding that the Admiralty could build another " Inflexible " but not another Fisher.

As I was being carried on board, in a brief moment's consciousness I heard the Doctor say : " He'll never reach Gibraltar ! " and then and there I determined I would live. When I got home, Lord Northbrook appointed me Head of the Gunnery School of the Navy. Queen Victoria asked me to stay at Osborne, and did so every year till she died ; and this in spite of the fact that she hated the Admiralty, and didn't much care for the Navy.

I kept on being ill from the effects of the dysentery for a long time, but Lord Northbrook never let go my hand. When all the doctors failed to cure me, I accidentally came across a lovely partner I used to waltz with, who begged me to go to Marienbad, in Bohemia. I did so, and in three weeks I was in robust health. It was the Pool of Bethesda, and this waltzing angel put me into it, for it really was a miracle, and I never again had a recurrence of my illness.

# CHAPTER XI

## NELSON

LORD ROSEBERY may have forgotten it, but in one of our perigrinations round and round Berkeley Square (I lived next door to him) he made a remark to me which made a deep and ineffaceable impression on me—that he felt sure one of the great reasons of Nelson being so in the hearts of his countrymen was the conviction that he had been slighted by Authority and even so after his death. Unquestionably his brother Admirals were envious. He was kept kicking his heels at Merton on half pay in momentous times, and so poor as to necessitate his getting advances from his Banker. He was cavalierly treated when he was told to haul down his flag and come home after the Battle of the Nile. I know all about the Queen of Naples and Lady Hamilton ; but what was that in comparison with his astounding genius for war and his hold on the Fleet ? And I want to draw attention to this delightful trait in his glorious character. Supposing (what I don't admit) that there was any irregularity in his attachment to Lady Hamilton, he never disguised his feeling for her, or his gratitude to her for all she did for his grievously wounded and frail body after the Nile and her splendid conduct in getting his Fleet revictualled and stored by the Neapolitans through her influence with the King and Queen, when all the Authorities were against it. He used to ask his Captains to drink her health, and said (in my opinion quite truly), that if there were more Emmas there would be more Nelsons.

Then look at the Battle of the Nile! It was an incomparable battle—but it only made Nelson into a Common or Garden Lord; when the Battle of Cape St. Vincent, which was practically won by Nelson, made Sir John Jervis into an Earl. History is so written that no end of literary gentlemen will endeavour to confute all I am saying by extracts (or, as they will call them, facts) from Contemporary Documents and Newspapers. Well now, to-day, read the *Morning Post* and *Daily News* on the same incident! (For myself I prefer the *Daily News*.) Again, Nelson died poor. That appeals. What Prize Money might he not have accumulated, had he chased dollars as he chased the enemy! Then with his dying breath, mortally wounded in the hour of the greatest of sea victories, he asks his country to provide for his friend as he could do nothing for her himself; and, whatever may have been her faults, she had nursed and tended him, not only when sorely wounded after the Nile, but afterwards when his frail body was almost continuously racked with pain. She died in penury and found a pauper's grave in a foreign land. A passing Englishman paid her funeral expenses. It makes one rise up and say " Damn ! "

159

# MEMORIES

That vivid immortal spirit, whose life was his country's, who never flogged a man ; whose heart was tender and " worn on his sleeve for daws to peck at," has to suffer even now for miscreants who published his letters to this friend of his that only her eye was meant to see. Also, Prudes nowadays forget how very different was the standard of morals at that time. Does not history tell us that Dukes were the honoured results of illicit relationships ? And we don't think any the worse of Abraham because he was the husband of more than one wife. But let that pass. I heard yesterday that a distinguished Bishop said he loved my sentiments but not my words. But fancy ! Nelson left on half-pay in War ! It's unbelievable, but yet it so happened. It was envy ; and he was no sycophant, so he couldn't be a courtier. It was so with him as with our great Exemplar : " The Common People heard him gladly." And what a " Send-off " it was on Southsea beach at Portsmouth when he embarked for Trafalgar ! What a scene it was, with these Common People surging round him—none else were there, and neither the King nor the Admiralty sent a dummy, as is customary, to represent them. But isn't it always the way ? General Booth and Doctor Barnardo weren't buried in Westminster Abbey ; but they had a more glorious funeral—millions of the " Common People" followed them to their graves, unmarshalled and unsolicited. Give me the Common People, and a fig for your State ceremonial !

Perhaps in this cursory view of Nelson one may be

1904. AGED 63. ADMIRAL.
Commander-in-Chief at Portsmouth.

permitted to seize on what appears to me the central incident of his life, which so peculiarly illustrates his extraordinary genius for War. His audacity! His imagination! His considered rashness! I think myself the Battle of the Nile is that incident—for this reason : that it has been recorded in writing what actually occurred to Lord Nelson and to the French Admiral at the very same instant of time—each having at his side the very same officer in each Fleet. It was sunset. Nelson was walking the deck with the Navigating Officer of the Fleet —the " Master of the Fleet " was his technical title. The look-out man at the mast-head reports seeing on the horizon the mast-heads of a mass of ships at anchor—it was the French Fleet in Aboukir Bay. Nelson instantly stops in his walk and orders the signal to the Fleet to make all possible sail and steer for the enemy. He is remonstrated with, both by his own officers on board and by his favourite Captain of the Fleet at going in to fight the French Fleet without any charts. If he waited till the sun rose, they would be able to see from aloft the shoal water and so steer with safety alongside the enemy. Nelson answers his favourite Captain that if that Captain's ship does get on shore, as he fears, then she'll be a buoy to show him where anyhow one shoal is. Troubridge *did* get on shore, and he *was* a buoy. Nelson went in. The French Admiral blew up at midnight in his flagship the " Orient " and Casabianca, his Captain, and his son are the theme of a great poem : " The boy stood on the burning deck."

# MEMORIES

The French Admiral was walking up and down the deck with *his* Master of the Fleet, when *his* look-out man at the mast-head reported on the horizon the topmast sails of a number of ships. The French Admiral stopped in his walk as abruptly as Nelson and at the very same instant that Nelson stopped in his walk ; but he said " It's the English Fleet, but they won't come in to-night. They have no charts ! " So he did not recall his men from the shore—and in the result his fleet was destroyed, and the one or two ships that did escape under Admiral Dumanoir were captured. And Napoleon wrote, " But for Nelson at the Nile I would have been Conqueror of the World "—or words to that effect. And yet Nelson was only made a common or garden Lord for this great battle, and spent two years on the Continent kicking his heels about to pass the time before returning to England. Imagine ! he wasn't wanted ! I think Lord Rosebery was right—Nelson being slighted has led to his greater appreciation.

Again—even a greater slight, a slight he feels more— when he looks down from his monument in Trafalgar Square, does he see anywhere those splendid Captains of his ? But let alone those Captains of his—does he see anywhere a single Admiral ? *Not one.* And yet who made England what she is ? Those splendid Sea Heroes are in very deed " *England's forgotten worthies* " ! Yes ! Nelson looks down from his isolated column, and looks in vain for Hawke, Dundonald, Howe, Hood, Rodney, Cornwallis, Benbow, " *and a great multitude which no man can number* "—all Seamen of Deathless Fame, fighting single frigate actions, cutting out the enemy's ships from under the guns of forts, sending in fire ships and burning the enemy's vessels thought to be safe in harbour under the guns of their forts—Doers of Imperishable Deeds ! [1]    Death found them fighting.    We have heaps of statues to everybody else.    Indeed such a lot of them that they reach down as far off as Knightsbridge.    But who knows about Quiberon—one of the greatest of sea fights ?  And if you mention Hawke, your friend probably thinks only of his worthy descendant—the cricketer.

An old woman eating a penny bun asked a friend of mine called Buggins, when she was passing through Trafalgar Square, " *What are them lions a-guarding of ?* " Buggins told her that her penny bun would have cost her threepence if it hadn't been for the man them lions were a-guarding of.

When I see the Duke of York's Column still allowed to rear its futile head, and scores of other fifth-rate nonentities glorified by statues, I thank God I'm a sailor —we don't want to be in that galley !

I began my sea life with the last of Nelson's Captains, through Nelson's own niece; and I fitly, I think, among my last words may ask the Nation to do justice to Nelson's Trade !  This country owes all she has to the sea, it was the sea that won the late war, and if we'd stuck to the

---

[1] There are statues of Franklin and of Robert Falconer Scott in Waterloo Place ; but neither of these displayed his heroism in naval action.   They were each peaceable seekers—but what on earth good accrues from going to the North and South Poles I never could understand—no one is going there when they can go to Monte Carlo !

# MEMORIES

sea we should not now be thinking of bankruptcy and some of us imagining Carthage! We were led away by Militarist folly to be a conscript Nation and it will take us all we know to recover from it. We shall recover, *for England never succumbs!*

# CHAPTER XII

LORD ESHER has kindly sent me three bulky volumes of letters I wrote him from 1903 onwards—I have others also. Many of them are unquotable, so blasting are they in their truth to existing reputations. It's not my business to blast reputations—so the real gems are missing.

Somebody felt in 1903 that the War Office was wrong, and so a Committee was set up with Lord Esher as President, Sir George Clarke and myself the other two members ; and that very able and not sufficiently recognised man, now General Sir C. Ellison, was Secretary. How I got there is still a mystery ; but it was a great enjoyment as Generals came to stay with me at Admiralty House, Portsmouth—I was the Port Admiral. I always explained to them I was Lord Esher's facile dupe and Sir George Clarke's servile copyist, and thereby avoided odium personally (I was getting all the odium I wanted from the Admirals !).

As usual, when we reported, the Government didn't appreciate those inestimable words " *Totus Porcus* " (No Government—anyhow no English Government—

ever yet went " the whole hog "—" Compromise " is
the British God !).[1]

1903 [*Sir John Fisher, Commander-in-Chief at
Portsmouth*].

. . . My humble idea is that "*men are everything
and material nothing*" whether it's working the War
Office or fighting a fleet ! So some day I am going to
try and entice you to read my lectures to the Officers of
the Mediterranean Fleet because the spirit intended to
be diffused by them is what I think is the one great want
in the British Army, and without it 50,000 Lord Eshers
would be no good in producing " Angel Gabriel " organisations ! The Military system is rotten to the very core !
You want to begin *ab ovo* ! The best of the Generals
are even worse than the subalterns because they are more
hardened sinners ! I fear I shocked Ellison, but
he is simply first class and I most heartily congratulate
you on your selection. . . . I really begin 'o feel I never
ought to have joined you as I have some very big jobs
on now which require incessant personal attention and
this must be my excuse for not coming up to see Girouard
this week. I have the new Civil Lord staying with me
and I have got to prevent him joining with a lot of asses
at the Admiralty, who want to throw half a million of
money in the gutter.

*Nov.* 19th, 1903.

On my return I found the first proofs of your three
papers. I have studied them with close care and interest.
There are some points of detail which puzzle me, but it
seems you are absolutely convincing on the main lines.
What I venture to emphasise is this :—We cannot reform
the Army Administration until it is laid down what it is
the Administration is going to Administer ! For instance,

[1] In the following selections, words between square brackets are not
part of the original letters.

the Citizen Army for Home Defence! Are we going to have it? If so, then you will certainly want a Member of the Board or Council to superintend it! Again, I say, the *Regular Army* (as distinguished from the Home Army and the *Indian Army*) should be regarded as a projectile to be fired by the Navy! The Navy embarks it and lands it where it can do most mischief!—Thus, the Germans are ready to land a large Military Force on the Cotentin Peninsula in case of War with France and my German Military Colleague at the Hague Conference told me this comparatively small Military Force would have the effect of demobilising half a million of men who would thus be taken away from the German Frontier—they never know where the devil the brutes are going to land! Consequently instead of our Military Manœuvres being on Salisbury Plain and its vicinity (ineffectually aping the vast Continental Armies!) we should be employing ourselves in joint Naval and Military Manœuvres embarking 50,000 men at Portsmouth and landing them at Milford Haven or Bantry Bay!—This would make the Foreigners sit up! Fancy! in the Mediterranean Fleet we disembarked 12,000 men with guns in 19 *minutes!* What do you think of that! and we should hurry up the soldiers! No doubt there would be good-natured chaff! Once we embarked 7,000 soldiers at Malta and took them round and landed them elsewhere for practice, and I remember having a complaint that the Bluejackets said " Come on, you bloody lobsters! Wake up!" However all the above *en passant*. I expect the Prime Minister must have pretty good ideas now crystallised as to how the Army should be constituted—let us ask him for this at once—if he hasn't got it, let us tell him we must have it, because as I said at starting, you can't organise an administration without clearly knowing what you are going to administer. This is a hasty bit of writing but not a hasty thought.

# MEMORIES

1903.
*Nov. 25th.*

I send you two books—a more portly volume I hesitate to send !—Also I fear without some verbal explanation you may not see the application to Military matters of these purely Naval Notes, but they do apply in the spirit if not in the letter ! For instance I had an overwhelming confidence that every Officer and man in the Mediterranean Fleet had also an overwhelming confidence that we thoroughly knew all we had to do in case of war in every conceivable eventuality ! Well ! that is the confidence you also want in an Army ! Have you got it !

*Dec. 2nd.*

Here is a letter just come from Prince Louis of Battenberg illustrating what I was saying to you this morning as to a Member of the Board of Admiralty however junior in rank being accepted as a superior controlling authority by all in rank above him. An Officer actually at the moment serving under Prince Louis in the Admiralty itself being put over Prince Louis in the Admiralty itself, and sending for him and giving him orders ! I don't know that it would be possible to have a stronger case to quote when by and by we have to defend or rather have to lay down and define the status of the Members of the New War Office Board. Inglefield, the new Naval Lord, being a Junior Captain, will be sending for *Admiral* Boys, Director of Transports, who is specially under him and who I rather think entered the service before Inglefield was born.

*Dec. 4th.*

. . . . You are right about the Submarines !
" *We strain at the gnat of perfection and swallow the camel of unreadiness,*" and that permeates every branch of Naval and Military Administration, forgetting the homely proverb that " half a loaf is better than no

168

bread ! " but please God ! " *the dauntless three* " [Sir Geo. Clarke, Lord Esher and Sir John Fisher] (as I see we are now called) will change all that ! " We'll stagger humanity " as old Kruger said !

*Dec. 7th.*

Arnold-Forster [Secretary for War] has been here three days and he is most cordially with us. I wish you had been here with him. He places implicit trust in us. He has shown me an outline of an excellent memorandum proposing an immediate reduction of 300,000 men and he will let me have a copy as soon as printed, also a memorandum of his difficulties in the War Office. . . . This is another proof of the value of the advice of my Military Nicodemus (he is one of the Sanhedrin !) that there must be an active " clear-out " of the present military gang, root and branch, lock, stock, and gunbarrel ! Sir John French and General Smith-Dorrien (lately Adjutant-General in India) are names I have suggested to Arnold-Forster as members of his new Board.

*Dec. 11th.*

. . . . Don't forget your phrase " *the biennial fortnightly picnic* " *! it's splendid ! That* will fetch the mothers of families and reconcile them to the Swiss system ! I hope you won't lose any time in talking to the Prime Minister and showing him the immense advantages that will accrue from his turning over further matters to us instead of dear Arnold-Forster " raising Cain " as he surely will do ! It would be so easy to associate Sir John French, Hildyard and Smith-Dorrien (very curious that all these three Generals were first in the Navy and got their early education there) with us for the further matters.

*Dec. 17th.*

Another Military Nicodemus came to see me yesterday. I had never met him before ! He occupies a high official position. He highly approved of you and me, "but he had never heard of the third member of the Committee. What a pity they had not put a soldier on the Committee!" (How these Christians hate one another!) But the point of his remarks was the present system of Army Promotions, which he said was as iniquitous and baleful in its influence as could be possibly conceived, and then he illustrated by cases of certain officers made Generals. My only object in writing this to you is Selborne having spoken of the Admiralty method where the first Lord has the Naval Members of the Board in consultation, but he and his Private Secretary (who is always a Naval Officer of note) have the real responsibility.

*Dec. 20th.*

—— is and always has been drastic in his ideas of military reform, and I cordially agree with him and Stead agrees with me that the British Public loves a root and branch reform. One remnant left of the old gang or the organisations and you taint the whole new scheme!

Don't fear about Arnold-Forster. He will come with us all right—you are absolutely sound on the Patronage question, but I would have the soldiers precisely on the same footing as Tyrwhitt at the Admiralty [Private Secretary. He was my Flag Captain] for detailed reasons I will give you when we meet. It is an ideal arrangement (the Private Secretary at Admiralty). He has the power, he pulls the strings, he has no position, he causes no jealousy, he talks to all the Lords as their servant, and he manipulates them all and oils the machine for his special master, the First Lord, to perpetrate a job when necessary! Make him a big-wig like an Official Military Secretary, and all this goes—he becomes too big for his boots!

*Dec. 21st.*

... I've been bombarded by Stead. I tried to boom him off but the scoundrel said if I didn't see him, he would have to invent! I pointed out to him my *métier* was that of the mole! Trace me by upheavals! When you see the Admirals rise it's that d—d fellow Jack Fisher taking the rise out of them! So I implored Stead to keep me out of the *Magazine Rifle* [this was my name for *The Review of Reviews*] or he will interfere with my professional career of crime. So please use your influence with him in the same direction. You and Clarke are the two legitimate members of the Committee to be trotted out, as you are both so well known. No sailor is ever known. The King was awfully good about this. He said " Sailors went all round the world but never went in it " ! Stead is a very keen observer, as you know. He said our Committee could do anything, and that neither the Press nor Parliament nor the Public would tolerate any Military opposition to us because the whole Military hierarchy was utterly discredited from top to bottom ; but he doubted *The Times—I don't.* Further he expressed his firm belief there would be a change of Government possibly at Easter but certainly soon—if so we ought on that ground alone to " dig out " with our Report.

1903.
(No date.)

Knollys was very much impressed by the possibilities of the Submarine when he was down here. He saw them to better advantage than you did as it was blowing half a gale of wind with a good sea on when he saw the evolutionising! and it was very striking. I am working subterraneously about the Submarines and there are already " upheavals " in consequence.

1904.
*Jan. 5th.*

. . . I yesterday sent all my plans to French for embarking the whole of his First Army Corps on Monday, June 27th (Full Moon) at Portsmouth, and he is coming here with his Chief Staff Officer, Sir F. Stopford, next week, and we'll land him like Hoche's Army in Bantry Bay ! [Sir John French commanded at Aldershot. *The War Office stopped this.*]

1904.
*Jan. 17th.*

. . . . For the reason I have given you at length in another letter I am convinced that French should be 1st Military Member and under him there should be 3 *Directors* (not Hieroglyphics such as A.Q.M.G., D.A.Q.M.G., A.Q.M.G. 2, etc., etc.).

Sir F. Stopford—Director of Intelligence and Mobilisation.
Gen. Grierson—Director of Training.
Gen. Maxwell—Director of Home Defence.

Also I still maintain that Smith-Dorrien and Plumer should be the 2nd and 3rd Military Members, and perhaps one young distinguished Indian Officer as 4th Military Lord. Haig, Inspector-General of Cavalry in India, should be brought home as the principal Director under *2nd Military Lord*. We must have youth and enthusiasm, because it is only by the agency of young and enthusiastic believers in the immense revolution which must be carried out, that our scheme can bear fruit. The first thing of all is that every one of the " old gang " must be cleared out ! " lock, stock, and gunbarrel, bob and sinker ! " The next is that every one of the new men *must be successful men*, and must be young and enthusiastic and cordial supporters of the new policy

—over every fellow's door at the War Office under the new régime has got to be written in large letters :—
" No looking back. Remember Lot's wife ! "

1904.
(No date.)

The next pressing and important matter we have to deal with is *to get the right men as Members of the new Army Council.* Either you or Clarke have made a splendid observation that a rotten system may be run effectively by good men but duffers would spoil the work of the Angel Gabriel ! . . . *If we don't get in men who will enthusiastically adopt our scheme and work with us,* LET US THROW UP AT ONCE ! as we shall only have an awful fiasco and I (for one) don't want to go down with my grey hairs to the grave sorrowing and discredited ! Therefore I suggest to you that we should agree on our men and *run them at once !* Like fighting the French Fleet ! it's half the battle gained to take the offensive, propose our men, give their advantages and ask them (our enemies) what they have to say against them and suggest every beastly thing we can against any likely competitors—Selection by Disparagement ! I put forward names in enclosed paper simply as a basis.

1st Military Member—*Sir John French,* because he never failed in Africa (the grave of Military Reputations). He is *young* and *energetic,* has commanded the 1st Army Corps so far with conspicuous success and has the *splendid gift* of choosing the right men to work with him (*vide* his Staff in S. Africa, the best Staff out there) and as 1st Military Lord it would be his special function to prepare the Army in the Field for fighting, and who therefore better to command it when war breaks out, as his functions then at the War Office would disappear and be transferred to the Commander-in-Chief at the seat of war—Further, he is an enthusiastic and out-and-out believer in joint Naval and Military operations as the proper species of manœuvres for this Nation. In this

173

# MEMORIES

belief he is almost solitary amongst all the Generals, who all want to play at the German Army. "*Plump for French and Efficiency!*" *Any vote given against French is a vote given for Kelly-Kenny instead!*

2nd Military Member.—*Smith-Dorrien*. Has been with great success in every campaign for the last 20 years, has been *Adjutant-General* in India (a much bigger billet than *Adjutant-General* in London!). *He is young and energetic* and is an extremely conciliatory and accomplished gentleman and would work the personnel of the Army (which would be his chief function as the Second Military Member) far better than some " safe " old man because he is in touch with the young generation. He took a Marine Officer of the Mediterranean Fleet as his A.D.C. when appointed a Brigadier in South Africa, because he considered him the ablest young officer in the Malta Garrison! Utterly shocking all the Military Mandarins. "*Vote for Smith-Dorrien and Progress!*"

"*Every vote given against Smith-Dorrien is a vote for* —— [*A lady who then " ran " the War Office!*]

3rd Military Member. Supplies and Transport.— *General Plumer*. The only man besides French that *never failed in anything he undertook in Africa!* They say he has " the luck of the Devil," but the fact is that " the luck of the Devil " is wholly attributable to a minute attention to anything that will ensure the success of his (Satanic Majesty's) designs, and he leaves nothing to chance! Such is Plumer! He also is young, energetic and enthusiastic.

"*Vote for Plumer and a full belly!*"

"*Every vote given against Plumer is a vote given for paper boots and no ammunition!*"

4th Military Member—*General F. G. Slade*, now Inspector General of Garrison Artillery—has served in six campaigns and always come out top : has been in the Horse, Field and Garrison Artillery and commanded at Gibraltar. He is *young and energetic and enthusiastic* and will blow the trumpet of the Board (*as well as his own !*).

"*Vote for Slade and hitting the Target !*"

"*Every vote given against Slade will be a vote given in favour of some d—d old woman.*" . . .

1904.
*Jan. 31st.*

Post Office Telegraphs. Government Despatch No. . . . .
" Await Arrival."

Lord Esher   Windsor Castle.

In reply to your telegram just received our committee manœuvres commenced at Portsmouth on December 30 beating Moses by nine days as he took 40 days before he got down from the Mount with his report but if you refer to submarine manœuvres I have last night put them off to February twenty third to last three weeks from that date stop I see we are accused of not giving credit to the good motives that have always actuated the War Office stop Why is the War Office like hell answer because it is paved with good intentions  Sir John Fisher Portsmouth.

[Not bad for an official telegram !]

1904.
*Feb. 1st.*

. . . I really think it is of extreme importance that you should be on the spot daily just now as without doubt " wire-pulling " of the " Eve " order will be going on.   When the other day I met those three ladies on the back stairs of the War Office all in picture hats and smelling of White Rose or some other beastly thing, I thought to myself " How about Capua ? " for really they were very nice looking indeed.   You know the story about them having the entrée to the War Office !

# MEMORIES

1904.
*Feb. 28th.*

Best of Chairmen ! Snatch a moment to look through enclosed . . . as I am dead gone on starting the idea of a general list of officers, and general uniform and early entry and they will all go to sea, but I don't want to mention that yet awhile ; it will come of itself when 3/5ths of every man-of-war's crew are soldiers ; that's not many years hence and will bring the income tax down to 3 pence in the pound ! Mark my words ! this will come, but it's no use giving people premature shocks, so let me keep it quiet now. My idea is to acclimatise the chosen few to it first of all and then gradually spread it about, and when Kitchener comes home he will see it through. (He shares my view, I know.)

1904.
(?) *March.*

. . . Campbell-Bannerman told me last night he intended to make a special point of the Secretary of State's responsibility and power being unduly lessened, and he would not admit that the new order of things makes him the same as the First Lord of the Admiralty ! . . . To avoid the slightest misconception that may arise as to the lessening of the parliamentary responsibility of the Secretary of State for War by the formation of the Army Council or of his supreme authority as the Cabinet Minister responsible for the Army, it's only necessary to reiterate and emphasise the statement that he is absolutely in the same position as the First Lord of the Admiralty, the patent constituting the Army Council being absolutely similar to the Admiralty Patent and no question has ever been raised nor is there any doubt whatever of the reform and present responsibility of the First Lord of the Admiralty as the Cabinet Minister responsible for the Navy.

1904.
*March 10th.*

Just back from the English Channel with the Sub-marines and am very enthusiastic ! . . . We really must arrange to get the British Army to Sea somehow or other ! Yesterday all the mice died in their cages and two of the crew fainted, but the young Lieutenant of the Submarine didn't seem to care a d—n whether they all died so long as he bagged the Battleship he was after, and he practically got her and then he came up in his Submarine to breathe ! Depend on it we shall have more " Niles " and " Trafal-gars " so long as we continue to propagate such " young bloods " as this ! But see how splendid if we could shove the same " ginger " into the young Military aspirants, and they all came from the same schools ! but the whole secret is to catch them very young and mould them while they are then so plastic and receptive to be just what you want them. Another submarine had an explosion which made the interior " *Hell* " for some seconds (as the Submarine was bottled up and diving to evade a De-stroyer who had caught her with a hook) but the Sub-marine Lieutenant saw them all d—d first before he would rise up and be caught. Another young fire-eater had his periscope smashed but bagged a battleship nevertheless by coming up stealthily to blow just like a beaver, and look round. *It really is all lovely !* but what I am writing about is—*you must embark an Army Corps every year and give them sea training.*

[" The Army and Navy Co-operative Society."

I must here interpose a few words to explain that I had submitted an elaborate method of increasing the military efficiency of officers—first by very early entry as in the Navy—having free or State education for them —hence " Equal opportunity for all " : Officers' pay of all ranks to be sufficient for them to live on—and the regimental system abolished—and the same system as in the Navy by which military officers would serve in all arms—Engineers, Artillery, Cavalry and Infantry, instead of being familiar with but one part of their profession. When the Sea Lords sit round the Board of Admiralty they can talk about anything, because they've been in every type of vessel and every branch of their Profession. Again, in a good regiment the promotion is slow because the officers stick to it. In a bad regiment the promotion is rapid because everyone wants to leave it. Then, finally, I submitted the idea of the Army and Navy being incorporated in one great Service. There is no going aloft now—a ship can be manned by soldiers with equal efficiency as by sailors. You want nucleus crews thoroughly used to the ship and always in her, knowing all her foibles. Brains—the Beef needn't be equally clever ! The military officers in the Peninsular War only 16 years old were splendid and they were numerous.]

1904.
*March 20th. Telegram.*

Suggest if Prime Minister takes no immediate action he may be asked that the Committee in self-defence be allowed to make correspondence public as already I am hearing from influential friends that we are discredited by having made exaggerated and unjustifiable statements and that besides the scandalous and disparaging words of the Secretary of State in the House of Commons that the Prime Minister has more or less disavowed us by the tenour of his remarks. . . . I venture to suggest to you that it is a great mistake for our Committee to be made a catspaw to suit Cabinet susceptibilities or parliamentary wirepulling and that we press for a full and complete publication.

1904.
*May 26th.*

. . . Arnold-Forster spent several hours here with me yesterday and he is coming again to-day discussing his difficulties. I tell him he can't expect his Council all at once to possess the attributes of the Board of Admiralty (which he so intensely admires) which began in 1619 ! They want to be educated. The individual Members are far too subservient now and do not realise they are administrative members and *not* Army Officers. They must go about in plain clothes and a tall hat, and order Field Marshals about like schoolboys ! . . .

1904.
*June 17th.*

. . . It would have been simply disastrous to have had an increased Army Vote. Has Clarke ever come to close quarters with you as to his project for getting the Army Estimates down to 23 millions ? for that is really the figure which represents the proportionate part of the total sum which I make out to be available for the fighting services, and unless some such figure can be arrived at for the Army, I do not think the British Public will face the reduction in the Navy Estimates *which I see to be possible with the increased efficiency ;* because they will rightly argue that the Navy is the 1st, 2nd, 3rd, 4th *ad infinitum* line of defence, and it is simply monstrous therefore that the bloated Army should starve the essential Navy. . . . It is this Army Vote that absolutely blocks me, because I am perfectly certain it will wreck us unless it can be brought down to some such figure as 23 millions at the outside. That N.-W. Frontier of India is the bug-bear which has possessed the whole lot of our present rulers ! and there is no " advocate of the devil " to plead the other side. So I hope you will put that mind of yours to work to make the Prime Minister see his mission to cut down the Army Vote to 23 millions and *then* we can go ahead and get that threepenny income tax we all so long for *and which we can get if we like !*

1904.

I was with the Prime Minister from 12.30 to 4 p.m. He was most pleasant and delightful but evidently didn't see his way to making the reduction in the Army Vote which is imperative. . . . He and all the rest appear stupefied by the Indian Frontier Bogey and the 100,000 men wanted. I gave him figures to show the Army had been increased 60,000 odd men in 10 years. If he would reduce them at once he would get nearly threepence off the income tax and get rid of his recruiting difficulties. The Auxiliary Forces 4½ millions—absurd—the Volunteers 2 millions—still more absurd !

1904.
*July 16th.*

A.-F.'s scheme rotten ! You have hit the nail on the head about expense. He had the remedy in the palm of his hand ! He simply had to reduce what the Army had *unnecessarily* increased in 10 years—the 60,000 officers and men—and he got 6 millions sterling (including the accessories) and solved the recruiting question ! . . . 3,700 Royal Engineers put on in 10 years and only 1/3 of them went to the war in S.A. ! the rest enjoying themselves in civilian work ! and was there ever such ineptitude as trying to make them into railway men, electric engineers and sailors for submarine mines when you have the real thing in abundance in the railway and telegraph workmen of the country and fishermen for any water work ? This is only one sample. Every blessed item of the military organisation is similarly rotten ! Why ? Because the military system of entry and education is rotten.

*1904.*
*July 28th.*

. . . We. have a new scheme for a reorganisation of the whole Admiralty and have got the Order in Council for it ! *The new scheme gives the First Sea Lord nothing to do*, except think and send for Idlers ! It also resuscitates the old titles of *Sea Lords* dating from A.D. 1613, but which some silly ass 100 years ago altered to *Naval Lords*.

*1904.*
*August 17th.*

. . . I have got 60 sheets of foolscap written with all the new Naval proposals and am pretty well prepared for the fray on October 21st.

[Sir John Fisher became First Sea Lord of the Admiralty on October 21st (Trafalgar Day), 1904 ; and the correspondence is scanty between that date and the autumn of 1907.]

*1907.*
*Sept 12th.*

. . . I really can't understand Mr. Buckle giving—— his head in this way in the columns of *The Times* ! but I suppose it " catches on " and makes the flesh creep of the " *old women of both sexes* " (as Lord St. Vincent čalled the " Invasion lot " in his day !) and his memorable saying so infinitely more true now than then. When asked his opinion of the possibility of an invasion, he replied " that if considered as a purely military operation he was loth to offer an opinion but he certainly could positively state it could never take place by sea ! "

*1907.*
*Oct. 7th.*                       MOLVENO.

. . . My unalterable conviction is that the Committee of Imperial Defence is tending rapidly to become a sort of Aulic Council and the man who talks glibly, utterly irresponsible, will usurp the functions of the *two* men who *must* be the " Masters of the War "—the First Sea Lord and the Chief of the General Staff. Make no mistake—I don't mean those two men are to be Dictators, but the Government says : " Do so and so ! " *These are the two executive Officers.* . . . In regard to the " Invasion Bogey " about which I am now writing to you, how curious it is that from the German Emperor downwards their hearts were stricken with fear that *we* were going to attack *them.* . . . Here is an interview between Beit and the German Emperor given me at first hand, immediately on Beit's return from Berlin.

*Beit* : " Your Majesty is very greatly mistaken in supposing that any feeling exists in England for war with Germany. I know both Mr. Balfour and Sir Henry Campbell-Bannerman are absolutely averse to any such action. I know this of my own personal knowledge."

*The Emperor* : " Yes, yes, but it doesn't matter whether either of them is Prime Minister or what party is in power. *Fisher remains ! that's the vital fact !* I admire Fisher. I say nothing against him. If I were in his place I should do all that he has done (in concentrating the British Navy against Germany) and I should do all that *I know* he has it in his mind to do. Isvolsky, the Russian Minister of Foreign Affairs, holds the same opinion."

And yet Mr. Leo Maxse gibbets Sir John Fisher every month in the *National Review* as a traitor to his country and a panderer to Germany, who " ought to be hung at his own yard arm ! "

1907.
*Nov. 28th.*

Can you manage to be at my room at Admiralty at 11.30 sharp to-day (Saturday) to see arrangements for swallowing the German Mercantile Marine, and other War Apparatus ? [*i.e.* " The Spider's Web "].

# LETTERS TO LORD ESHER

1907.
*Dec. 12th.*

. . . I hope the Admiralty memorandum is to your satisfaction—of course it is only the first instalment. What fascinates me is that the Committee as a whole don't seem to take the point that the whole case of Roberts rests on an absolute Naval surprise, which is really a sheer impossibility in view of our organised information.

1908.
*Jan. 1st.*

. . . I had a *tête-à-tête* lunch with Winston Churchill ; he unexpectedly came to the Admiralty and I was whirled off with him to the Ritz. I had two hours with him. He is very keen to fight on my behalf and is simply kicking with fury at —— & Co., but I've told him the watchword is " Silence." He is an enthusiastic friend certainly ! He told me he would get six men on both sides to join in *con amore*, F. E. Smith, &c., &c. I forget the other names. It was rather sweet : he said his penchant for me was that I painted with a big brush ! and was violent !—I reminded him that even " The Kingdom of Heaven suffereth violence, and the violent take it by force "—*vide* yesterday's Second Lesson.

1908.
*Jan. 17th.*

*Secret.* . . . I rather want to keep clear of Defence Committee till Morocco is settled, as I don't want to disclose my plan of campaign to *anyone*, not even C.-B. himself. The only man who knows is Sir Arthur Wilson, and he's as close as wax ! The whole success will depend upon *suddenness and unexpectedness*, and the moment I tell anyone there's an end of both ! ! ! So just please keep me clear of any Conference and personally I would sooner the Defence Committee kept *still*. I'm seeing

about the Transports. I started it about 7 weeks ago
and got 3 of my best satellites on it. . . . So you'll
think me a villain of the deepest dye !

1908.
(?) *Feb. 9th.*
. . . We want both a *re-distribution* as well as a
*re-organisation* of the Army—and the (comparatively)
small Regular Army should be based on the system of
" Nucleus Crews "—that is to say the *whole body of
Officers* are provided and 2/5ths (or the expert) part of
the crew, and the other 3/5ths of the Army you get
from the outside Army by whatever name you like to
call it—National Army, or Citizen Army, or Lord
Lieutenant's Army.

1908.
*Feb. 21st.*
. . . *Secret.* Tirpitz asked a mutual civilian friend
living in Berlin to enquire very privately of me whether
I would agree to limiting size of guns and size of ships,
as this is *vital* to the Germans, who *can't go* bigger than
the Dreadnought in guns or size. I wrote back by
return of post yesterday morning " Tell him I'll see him
d—d first ! " (*Them's the very words !*) I wonder what
Wilhelm will say to that if Tirpitz shows him the letter !

1908.
*Apr. 19th.*
. . . I got a note to say the King wanted to see me
this afternoon at 3 p.m. . . . *Private.* I got 3
letters from the King at Biarritz, all extremely cordial
and communicative and unsought by me. I mention
this to prove to you his kindly feelings and support. . . .
When I met the King on arrival he said I was to be sure
and see him as he had something serious to say to me.
I suppose I was with him more than an hour, and he was
as cordial and friendly as ever ; and this was the serious

thing—" that I was Jekyll and Hyde ! *Jekyll* in being successful at my work at the Admiralty—but *Hyde* as a failure in Society ! That I talked too freely and was reported to say (which of course is a lie) that the King would see me through anything ! That it was bad for me and bad for him as being a Constitutional Monarch ; if the Prime Minister gave me my congé, he couldn't resist it, &c., &c." . . . I told the King that if I had never mentioned His Majesty's name in my life, precisely the same thing would be said out of sheer envy of His Majesty being kindly disposed, and it could not be hid that the King had backed up the First Sea Lord against all kinds of opposition—As a matter of fact I *never* do go into Society, and only dine out when I'm worried to meet the King, and I'm not such a born idiot as to have said any such thing as has been reported to the King (it is quite likely *someone else has said it !*). Well he left that (having unburdened his mind) and smoked a cigar as big as a capstan bar for really a good hour afterwards, talking of everything from China to Peru, not excluding *The Times* article on himself. . . . Oh ! he said something of how I worked the Press, but I didn't follow that up. No one knows, except perhaps yourself, that unless I had arranged to get the whole force of public opinion to back up the Naval Revolution it would have been simply impossible to have carried it through successfully, for the vested interests against me were enormous and the whole force of Naval opinion was *dead* against me. But I did venture one humble remark to the King : " Has anyone ever been able to mention to Your Majesty one single little item that has failed in the whole multitude of reforms introduced in the last $3\frac{1}{2}$ years ? " No ! he said. No one had ! So I left it there. . . . If the Angel Gabriel were in my place he would be falsely accused. I'm only surprised that the King hasn't been told worse things—perhaps he has ! " *Let him that thinketh he standeth take heed lest he fall.*" I always have that thought, and hope the King will have a cottage somewhere in Windsor Forest or elsewhere which he will kindly give me when it happens, so that I can come over and have a yarn with you !

1908.
*May 5th.*

4.15 a.m.　The *Early* Bird ! ! . . . Yesterday, with all Sea Lords present, McKenna formally agreed to 4 Dreadnoughts *and if necessary* 6 Dreadnoughts next year (perhaps the greatest triumph ever known !) . . . He tells me Harcourt for certain will resign on it . . . and he is paring down the money with a view to Supplementary Estimates. . . . This is what I suggest to you to impress on Lloyd George : *Let there be no mistake about the two Keels to one in Dreadnoughts !* Let Lloyd George reassure McKenna and tell him to have no fear —it doesn't affect next year, as McKenna consents to 4 or even 6 ; but it does affect the year after, and the Admiralty Finance should be arranged accordingly and not deplete next year at expense of year after.　I wonder if this is all clear to you—that McKenna is going to give us the *numbers* for next year all right.　Shove in again the great fact—The Navy and Army Estimates not far different in magnitude, and yet the Army not big enough to fight Bulgaria, and the Navy can take on all the Navies of the world put together.—" *Ut veniant omnes ! ! !* "— " Let 'em all come ! " You might tell Lloyd George he can rely on my parsimony.

1908.
*Sept. 8th.*

. . . " The heart untravelled fondly turns to home." —We have no poets nowadays like Pope, Goldsmith and Gay—only damned mystical idiots like Browning and Tennyson that want a dictionary and the Differential-Calculus sort of mind to understand what they are driving at !

186

## LETTERS TO LORD ESHER

. . . I sat several times [on a recent visit abroad] between Stolypin, the Russian Prime Minister, and Isvolsky, the Foreign Secretary. I didn't begin it, but Stolypin said to me " What do you think we want most ? " He fancied I should answer " So many battleships, so many cruisers, &c., &c.," but instead I said : " Your Western Frontier is denuded of troops and your magazines are depleted. *Fill them up*, and then talk of Fleets ! " Please see enclosure from Kuropatkin's secret report : " *The foundation of Russia's safety is her Western boundary ! ! !* " . . . Have you seen Monsieur Rousseau (I think is his name) in *Le Temps* ? I had an extract of it, and put it aside to send you, but alas ! it has gone. " Procrastination is the thief of good intentions "—which is not so good as " Punctuality is the curse of comfort." But the good Frenchman (like Monsieur Hanotaux before him) is lost in admiration of what moved Mahan to his pungent saying that Garvin seized on with the inspiration of genius—" that 88 per cent. of the English guns were trained on Germany ! " . . . By the way, I've got Sir Philip Watts into a new *Indomitable* that will make your mouth water when you see it ! (and the Germans gnash their teeth !)

1908.
*Dec.*

The King has sent me a dear letter, and adds " *Don't print this !* " Isn't he a sweet ? *What wonderful friends I have !* It's a marvel ! All I do is to kick their shins.

1908.
(No date.)

. . . I am going to ask you to reconsider your supplementary paper herewith. I can't find that the Admiralty have admitted that 24,000 men would ever start off together as two raids of 12,000 each. I personally have expressed my decided opinion (I think at the 7th meeting) [of the Committee of Imperial Defence] to the contrary. Indeed, I am emphatically of opinion that no raid of any kind [that is, *landing of troops*] is feasible with all our late developments, which are developing further every day (*e.g.* we have our wireless on top of Admiralty Building and are communicating with the Scilly Islands now and shortly I hope Gibraltar and so certainly to every point of the German coast where we shall have Wireless Cruisers all over the place. (*Not a dog will wag its tail without being reported.*) So don't let us get a scare over 24,000 men coming unobserved. *One lot of* 12,000 can be put in as the limit ; but my suggestion is—*leave out numbers*, and simply say as a precautionary measure for the confidence of the country, *it's a good safe arbitrary standard to lay down that two Divisions of Regular Troops* are always to be left in the Country just in the same way as laid down at the Admiralty that the Home Fleet is not for Service abroad.

1909.
*Jan. 26th.*

. . . The Admiralty hear (by wireless every moment) what all the Admirals and Captains are saying to each other anywhere in Europe and even over to the coasts of America.

1909.
*March 15th.*

Private & Secret & *Personal.* I have just finished in these early hours a careful re-study of your paper E. 5 (which I love) and the criticisms thereon by French and the General Staff. I dismiss French's criticism as being that of a pure correct Cavalry expert and not dealing with the big questions. The General Staff criticism is on the other hand *the thin end of the insidious wedge of our taking part in Continental War as apart absolutely from Coastal Military Expeditions in pure concert with the Navy*—expeditions involving hell to the enemy because backed by an invincible Navy (the citadel of the Military

188

force). I don't desire to mention these expeditions and never will, as our military organisation is so damnably leaky ! but it so happens for two solid hours this morning I have been studying one of these of inestimable value only involving 5,000 men, and some guns, and horses about 500—a mere fleabite ! but a collection of these fleabites would make Wilhelm scratch himself with fury ! However, the point of my letter is this—Ain't we d—d fools to go on wasting our very precious moments in these abstruse disquisitions on this line and that or the passage of the Dutch German Frontier River and whether the bloody fight is to be at Rheims or Amiens, until the Cabinet have decided the great big question raised in your E. 5 : *Are we or are we not going to send a British Army to fight on the Continent as quite distinct and apart from Coastal Raids and seizures of Islands, etcetera, which the Navy dominate ?* Had not the Prime Minister better get this fixed up before we have any more discussions such as foreshadowed to-morrow ?

1909.
*March 21st.*

. . . It won't do to resign on a *hypothesis* but on a fact ! All is in train for the *8* Dreadnoughts ! and as Grey says when the day is reached to sign the contracts and *then* a veto—*then* is the day to go in a great company and not one alone ! . . . I am vehemently urged to squash my " malignant stabbers-in-the-back " by making a speech somewhere and saying as follows—but I won't— it would be an effectual cold douche to the 8 Dreadnoughts a year ! I might say

" The unswerving intention of 4 years has *now* cul- minated in *two* complete Fleets in Home Waters, *each of which* is incomparably superior to the whole German Fleet mobilised for war. Don't take my word ! Count them, see them for yourselves ! You *will* see them next June. This can't alter for years, even were we supinely

189

passive in our building ; but it won't alter because we will have 8 Dreadnoughts a year. *So sleep quiet in your beds !* "

And I might also add :—

" The Germans are not building in this feverish haste to fight you ! *No !* it's the daily dread they have of a second Copenhagen, which they know a Pitt or a Bismarck would execute on them !
" Cease building or I strike ! "

1909.
*March* 30*th.*
. . . Grey rubbed in two great points yesterday :—
(i) Lack of information as to German acceleration will be acted on as if acceleration were a fact.
(ii) The *8* this year won't affect next year.

1909.
*June* 15*th.*
. . . Yes, we made a good job of Saturday ; but the two most noticeable things of all were never noticed :—
(i) The swarm of Destroyers going 20 knots past the Dreadnought found themselves suddenly confronted by a lot of passenger steamers and yachts, which at the last moment got right in their way—the accidents might have been intense—but the young Destroyer commanders kept their nerve and their speed and scootled through the eye of the needle just grazing them all. It was splendid to see and made my heart warm ! (N.B.—A Press delegate—the *Toronto Globe*, I think, seized me by the arm and said, " *Sir, I see the glint of battle in your eye !* ")
(ii) I saw the Speaker of the House of Commons being bundled into a " char-à-banc " holding 24 other promiscuous persons by a bluejacket. Truly a democratic sight !

1909.
*July 3rd.*

. . . The latest development is that somebody has a pile of my private letters to various people—not printed or typewritten but *the original letters*, so he says, which he is going to produce unless I agree to resign in October ! Some of the letters stolen and some given (so I am told !). However " hot " they may be I don't regret a word I ever wrote, and I believe my countrymen will forgive me. *Anyhow I won't be blackmailed !* There was murder in the King's eye when I told him (but I didn't tell him all !) . . . *I am going to fight to the finish ! Heaven bless you for your help.*

1909.
*August 3rd.*

. . . The Mouse was able to help the Lion yesterday as the King got on to you in regard to vile attempts of jealousy as to your being on the Defence Committee. The King is certainly A 1 in sticking to his friends ! but you have always said this yourself to me when I have been down on my luck ! All has gone most splendidly in all ways and the King is enormously gratified at the magnificent show of the Fleet to put before the Emperor of Russia. I told the Emperor it was a fine avenue !— 18 miles of ships—the most powerful in the world and none of them more than 10 years old !

1909.
*August 27th.*

[A letter on the Beresford Report speaks of two " base innuendoes," of which the second is]

(ii) The " *suggestio falsi* " that the Admiralty had been wanting in Strategical Thought—whereas we had effected the immense advance of establishing the Naval War

College and gave evidence of practical strategy in effecting
the concentration of our Fleets instead of the previous
state of dispersion. No such redistribution of strategical
force since the days of Noah !

But worse still—Not one word of commendation for
the Admiralty for its unparalleled work in gaining fighting
efficiency and instant readiness for war by the institution
of the Nucleus Crew system—the introduction of Battle
practice—the unexampled advance in Gunnery (the
" Invincible " with her 12-inch guns hitting the target
1/14th her own size 15 *times out of* 18 *at 5 miles*, she
herself going 20 knots and the target also moving at an
unknown speed and unknown course) and getting rid of
160 vessels that could neither fight nor run away—*Not
one word of appreciation of all this by the Committee!*
and yet they had the practical result before them in the
manœuvres of 374 vessels manœuvring in fogs and shoals
without a single mishap or a single defect and 96 Submarines and Torpedo Craft on the East Coast making
Invasion ridiculous ! No—it has been a bitter disappoint-
ment—more bitter because each of the five members of
the Committee so expressive to me and to others of the
complete victory of the Admiralty. *Cowards all !* It
is the one redeeming feature that *The Times* came
down decidedly on the right side of the fence ! the one
and only paper that got at the kernel of the matter.
*Discipline !* where art thou now after this Report ?

1909.
*Sept. 13th.*

. . . What pleases me most is the King having sent
for you, and your 1½ hours' breakfast and afterwards
driving with him, because as no doubt you know,
——(and some others) started a propaganda against
you which fell absolutely flat and it's a rattling
good thing the King making much of you in this way
as it gets *about and without any question the King now
largely moulds the public will !* As to your letter in regard

THE FUNERAL OF KING EDWARD VII.
Lord Fisher as Principal Aide-de-Camp.

to myself, it of course gives me great joy that the King gives me his blessing and also dear Knollys's wonderful fidelity to me is a miracle ! (I always think of an incident long ago when he calmly ignored a furious effusion of mine to the King and put the letter in the fire without saying a word to me till long afterwards ! I all the time joyful—thinking I had done splendidly !)

[After a forecast of a coming change in the Government the letter goes on]

You will at once say : What is the First Sea Lord going to do ? Answer—Nothing ! It is the ONLY course to follow ! I have thought it all out most carefully and decided to keep absolutely dumb. When a new Admiralty patent appears in the *London Gazette* without my name in it, I pack up and walk out and settle down in the Tyrol. Temperature 70° in the shade and figs ten a penny and wear out all my white tunics and white trowsers ! McKenna, to whom I am absolutely devoted, may force my hand to help him. In view of all he has risked for me (he was practically out of the Cabinet for 24 hours at one time ! This is a fact) I am ready to go to the stake for him ; but if he is well advised he also will be dumb. . . . I am so surprised how utterly both the Cabinet and the Press have failed to see the " inwardness " of the new " Pacific Fleet " ! I had a few momentous words in private with Sir Joseph Ward (the Prime Minister of New Zealand). *He saw it !* It means *eventually* Canada, Australia, New Zealand, the Cape (that is South Africa) and India *running a complete Navy !* We manage the job in Europe. They'll manage the job . . . as occasion requires out there ! The very wonderful thing is that only dear old Lord Kelvin and the First Sea Lord at the first wanted the Battle Cruiser type alone and *not " Dreadnoughts "*; but we had a compromise, as you know, and got 3 *Indomitables* with the Dreadnoughts ; and all the world now has got " Indomitables " on the brain ! Hip ! Hip ! Hurrah !

1909.
*Dec. 25th.*

. . . Wilson and I have talked a lot about our War plan for the Navy. You know he told the Defence Committee that only he and I knew of the War Plan, which is quite true and it was the same when his fleet was joined with mine when South African War was in progress. He would sooner die than disclose it. (God bless Sir Arthur Wilson !)

1910.
*Jan. 23rd.*

Of course no question as to strategic merits of a Canal, and it ought originally to have been the scheme instead of Rosyth, but now is it possible to make the *volte-face* ? *I fear not !* I got Rosyth delayed 4 years as NOT being the right thing or the right place and hoping for our Kiel Canal ; but though I succeeded in the delay, alas ! I did not in the substitution. However, I will see Hankey as you suggest. Yes, I'm quite happy, and my cry is NOT " à Berlin ! " . . . I've got some war charts that would make your mouth water !

[Sir John Fisher left the Admiralty on his birthday, Jan. 25th, 1910, and was raised to the Peerage.]

1910.                                   KILVERSTONE HALL,
*February 2nd.*                              THETFORD.

. . . I've just got here from Cheshire, where for days running I've had Paradise. 3 lovely girls in the house, a *splendid* ball room and music always on hand ! 3 young Guardsmen there, but I held my own !

Dancing till 4 a.m. took it out of me a bit, but it revivified me and I renewed my strength like the Eagle ! . . . I hope the King talked politics with McKenna, who is very acute and would sacrifice himself for the King. Didn't you think McKenna excellent, the night he dined with me, as to the course the King should pursue? You see he knows so exactly how the Cabinet will be actuated. . . .

There are great risks. Both political sides unscrupulous. . . .

P.S.—Wasn't it the Emperor Diocletian who doffed the Imperial Purple to plant cabbages? and d—d fine cabbages, no doubt! So don't blackguard me for leaving the Admiralty of my own free will, to plant roses!

1910.
*Feb. 18th.*

. . . Things look ugly. . . . However, I'm a pure outsider! There will be desperate efforts to supplant Wilson, so I hear from trustworthy quarters. But McKenna will be the real loss to the Navy. The sacred fire of efficiency burns brightly in him! and he's a born fighter and a good hater, which I love (as Dr. Johnson did) with all my heart. You really *must* come here when the weather is nicer—it's lovely! I've never known till now what joy there is in Nature. Even beauteous woman fades in the comparison! I've just seen the wild swans flying over the Lake! " The world forgetting—By the world forgot!" is appropriate to me now! . . . I've just thought of a lovely Preamble for my approaching " Midshipman's Vade-Mecum " . . . I rather think it's Blackie, though perhaps not his words :

" Four Things for a Big Life
I. A great Inspiration
II. A great Cause
III. A great Battle
IV. A great Victory

Having got those 4 things then you can preach the Gospel of Rest and Build an Altar to Repose."

1910.
*March 14th.*

. . . I lunched with Asquith, he was *more than cordial !*
How funny it is that I did *infinitely more* for the Conservatives than for the *Radicals*, and yet the Radicals
have given me all I have got and the Conservatives have
only given me abuse and calumny !

The Radicals gave me my Pension and a Peerage,
and yet I increased the Radical estimates nearly ten
millions ! I decreased the estimates 9 millions and
reduced prospective charges by nineteen millions sterling
for the Conservatives, and they never lifted even a little
finger to help me, *but on the contrary* have heaped dunghill abuse on me ! *How do you explain this ?*

McKenna, whose life has been a burden on my account,
gives me a thing that would do for an Ascot Gold Cup
with the inscription I enclose—luckily it's in Latin or I
dare not let it be seen ! (The Craven Scholar writes
to me it's the best Latin he ever read in his life !) I
wouldn't write all this to anyone else, but *is it not all
of it phenomenally curious ?* Well, *longo intervallo* I took
your advice and seized an opportunity which called for
my communicating with Winston, and he sent me *by
return of post* a most affectionate letter and says I am
the one man in the world he really loves ! (Well ! I
really love him because he's a great Fighter.) What a
joke if you, I and George Clarke were put on to reform
the House of Lords !

1910.
*March 24th.*

I sent you a telegram from Ely on my way down (I
caught my train by ½ a minute !) as my cogitations impelled me to suggest to you that Asquith obviously does
not see the fallacy of ——'s reasoning, which as you very
acutely observed would kill the Defence Committee as
a whole in its *guiding*, but not its administrative or
executive power, which are non-existent and inimical

to its existence. But its "*guiding*" power is England's all-in-all, if only its sufficiency and efficiency could be digested.

I had an immense talk with McKenna. . . . He was " dead on " for your Committee. Of course the Ideal was your being President, but I suppose the " Shifting Man " as President, according to the subject and the Department concerned, has its merits and advantages.

1910.
*April 8th.*

Old Stead's letter in *Standard* on 2 keels to ⌐1 is unsurpassable ! *It ought to be circulated in millions as a leaflet !* . . . What d—d fools the Tories are not to swallow it whole—the 2 keels to 1 ! . . . I told " the Islanders " secretly I could do more as the " mole," so not to put my name down—(The Mole is my *métier !* only to be traced by upheavals !) Get Stead's letter sent all over the Nation as a leaflet.

I am to meet you on April 19th, Suez Canal.

I don't know Wilson's views. These are mine :—

General principle : The Admiralty should *never* engage itself to lock up a single vessel even—not even a torpedo-boat, or submarine—anywhere *on any consideration whatever. The whole principle of Sea fighting is to be free to go anywhere with every d—d thing the Navy possesses.* The Admiralty should engage to do their best but to reserve entire freedom of action. The responsibility of the Suez Canal therefore cannot be theirs. If this clashes with your views you had better cancel me on Committee, for I'll fight like Hell for the above vital War Principle !

1910.
*April 25th.*

I congratulate you on the latest by " Historicus " ; but do you sufficiently intensify the intolerable tyranny of the permanent Tory majority in the Lords that has meant a real single chamber government for so many years ? The Radicals are on the win and no one can stop it. We exaggerate the consequences. The silly thing is to have a General Election. Who gains ? Everybody loses ! Certainly the Tories won't win. Tariff Reform dead. Winston's last speeches have been very high class, especially where he shows how far greater issues are settled by the Government than anything appertaining to legislation without the House of Lords having a voice and we have always taken those risks in the past without a thought !

What is this about Kitchener hoisting out French as Inspector General ? Anything to get Kitchener out of England !

[King Edward VII. died on May 6th, 1910.]

1910.
*May.*
(*Saturday.*)

What an *inexpressible* sorrow ! ! How we both know the loss ! What a great National Calamity ! And *personally* what can I say ? *What a splendid and steadfast friend !* No use saying any more to each other—is it ? *I really feel heart broken !*

1910.
*May 24th.* KILVERSTONE HALL.

. . . I really can't get over the irreparable loss. *I think of nothing else !* Treves gave me a wonderful account of the King's last day. I rather think the King was coming to see me here, had he remained at Sandringham. The Queen [Queen Alexandra] has been very sweet to me. She stopped to notice me going up the steps of St. George's Chapel and so did her Sister [the Empress Marie]. I appreciated it very much —but most of all my interview with her. . . . She told me she would come here to see me and how the King

198

had told her about me being disappointed at her not having been to Kilverstone before. You'll think me morbid writing like this.

I dined with Asquith, McKenna and George Murray last week in London. If the Tories weren't such d—d stupid idiots I should rejoice at things being certain to go well. . . . My day is past. I have no illusions. You will enjoy the roses I've planted when you come here. How one's life does change!

1910.
*May 27th.*

. . . The Commonwealth Government [of Australia] have just sent a confidential telegram to Sir George Reid to ask me to go as their Guest to advise on the Navy. I've declined. I'd go as Dictator but not as Adviser. Also they have commenced all wrong and it would involve me in a campaign I intend to keep clear of with the soldiers. By the wording of the telegram I expect further pressure. Besides what a d—d fine thing to get me planted in the Antipodes! [Kitchener and the Australians, in drawing up their scheme of defence, forgot that Australia was an island. So do we here in England.]

1910.
*June 7th.*

. . . I can't shake off my sense of loss in the King's death. Though personally it practically makes no difference of course—yet I feel so curious a sense of isolation —which I can't get over—and no longer seem to care a d—n for anything! . . .

As you told me, it was miraculous I left the Admiralty when I did! It was the nick of time! A. K. Wilson is doing splendidly and is unassailable. I had much pressure to emerge the other day, but I won't, nor have I the heart now.

199

# MEMORIES

*August 5th.* KILVERSTONE HALL.

McKenna has just been here on his second visit (so he liked the first, I suppose! I mention this as an inducement to you to come!) He has shewn me various secret papers. *He is a real fighter*, and the Navy Haters will pass over his dead body! If our late Blessed Master was alive I should know what to do ; but I feel my hands tied now. Perhaps a kindly Providence put us both on the Beach at the right moment! Who knows ?

" *The lights begin to twinkle on the rocks* " ! I've told —— and others that the 2 keels to 1 policy is of inestimable value because it eliminates the United States Navy, *which never ought to be mentioned—criminal folly to do so*—Also it gives us such an ample margin as to allow for discount !

The insidious game is to have an enquiry into Ship Designs, which means delay and no money !

Two immense episodes are doing Damocles over the Navy just now. I had settled to shove my colleagues over the precipice about both of them, but as you know I left hurriedly to get in Wilson—so incomparably good ! We pushed them over the precipice about Water Tube Boilers, the Turbine, the Dreadnought, the Scrapping [of ships that could neither fight nor run away], the Nucleus Crews—the Redistribution of the Fleet, &c., &c. In each and all it was *Athanasius contra mundum*, but each and all a magnificent success ; so also these two waiting portents full of immense developments.

1. Oil Engines and internal combustion, about which I so dilated at our dinner and bored you. Since that night (July 11th) Bloom & Voss in Germany have received an order to build a Motor Liner for the Atlantic Trade. *No engineers, no stokers, and no funnels, no boilers ! Only a d—d chauffeur ! The economy prodigious !* as the Germans say " *Kolossal billig* " ! But what will it be for War ? *Why ! all the past pales before the prospect ! ! !*

I say to McKenna : " Shove 'em over the precipice ! *Shove !* " But he's all alone, poor devil !

The Second is that this Democratic Country won't stand 99 per cent. *at least* of her Naval Officers being drawn from the " Upper Ten." It's amazing to me that anyone should persuade himself that an aristocratic Service can be maintained in a Democratic State. The true democratic principle is Napoleon's : " *La carrière ouverte aux talents !* " The Democracy will shortly realise this, and there will be a dangerous and mischievous agitation. The secret of successful administration is the intelligent anticipation of agitation. Again I say to McKenna " *Shove ! ! !* " *Shove them over the preci- pice.*" I have the plan all cut and dried.

The pressure won't come from inside the Navy but from outside—an avalanche like A.D. 1788 (the French Revolution)—and will sweep away a lot more than desirable ! It is essentially a political question rather than a Naval question proper. *It is all so easy*, only the d—d Tory prejudices stand in the way ! But I gave you a paper about all this printed at Portsmouth, so won't bore you with more. I am greatly inclined to leave the Defence Committee and move out in the open on these two vital questions on the Navy. The one affects its fighting efficiency as much as the other. I am doing the mole, and certain upheavals will appear shortly, but it wants a Leader in the open !

1911.
*May 1st.*

. . . I want you to think over getting the Prime Minister to originate an enquiry for a great British Governmental Wireless Monopoly, or rather I would say " English Speaking " Monopoly ! No one at the Admiralty or elsewhere has as yet any *the least idea* of the *immense* revolution both for Peace and War purposes which will be brought about by the future development of wireless ! . . . The point is that this scheme wants to be

engineered by the Biggest Boss, i.e. the Prime Minister.
. . . *Believe me* the wireless in the future is the soul and
spirit of Peace and War, and therefore must be in the
hands of the Committee of Defence ! *You can't cut
the air !* You can cut a telegraph cable !

1911.
*June 25th.*                                          BAD NAUHEIM.

. . . You will see in the *Standard* of May 29th the
London Correspondent of the *Irish Times* lets out
about Lord Fisher and war arrangements, but as the
*Standard* in the very same issue makes this announcement in big type : " We (Great Britain) are in the satisfactory position of having *twice as many Dreadnoughts*
in commission as *Germany and a number greater by one
unit than the whole of the rest of the world put together !* "
I don't think there is the very faintest fear of war ! How
wonderfully Providence guides England ! Just when
there is a quite natural tendency to ease down our Naval
endeavours comes AGADIR !

> " Time and the Ocean and some Guiding Star
> In High Cabal have made us what we are ! "

" The Greatest Power on ' Airth,' " as Mr. Champ
Clarke would say ! (You ought to meet Champ Clarke.)
He is likely to succeed Taft as President, *but I put my
money on Woodrow Wilson.* He is Bismarck and Moltke
rolled into one ! . . . I need not say that I remain in
the closest bonds with the Admiralty. I never did a
wiser thing than coming abroad and remaining abroad
and working like a mole. *I shall not return till July*, 1912.
Most damnable efforts against me continue in full swing :
nevertheless like Gideon—" Faint yet pursuing " is my
motto. . . . And yet because in 1909 at the Guildhall
when our Naval supremacy had been arranged for in
the Navy Estimates of the year I said to my countrymen
" Sleep quiet in your beds ! " I was vehemently vilified
with malignant truculence, and only yesterday I got a

letter from an Aristocrat of the Aristocrats, saying he had heard it stated by a Man of Eminence the day before that I was in the pay of Germany ! It is curious that I can't get over the personal great blank I feel in the death of our late blessed Friend King Edward ! There was something in the charm of his heart that still chains one to his memory—some magnetic touch !

1911.
*Sept 20th.*                                         LUCERNE.

Through dancing with a sweet American (and indeed they are truly delightful, especially if you have the same partner all the evening!) I hear via a Bremen multi-million-aire that though the most optimistic official assurances of peace emanate from Berlin yet there is the most extreme nervousness amongst the German business men because of the revelation to them of the French power both financially and fightingly, so unexpected by them. I suppose if a Pitt or a Palmerston had now been guiding our destinies we should have war. They would say any Peace would be a bad Peace because of the latent damnable feeling in Germany against England. It won't be France any more, it will be England that will be the red rag for the German Bull ! And as we *never* were so strong as at present, then Pitt & Co. would say the present is the time to fight. Personally I am confident of Peace. I happen to know in a curious way (but quite certainly) that the Germans are in a blue funk of the British Navy and are quite assured that 942 German merchant steamers would be " gobbled up " in the first 48 hours of war, and also the d—d uncertainty of *when* and *where* a hundred thousand troops embarked in transports and kept " in the air " might land ! N.B.—There's a lovely spot only 90 miles from Berlin ! Anyhow they would demobilize about a million German soldiers ! But I am getting " off the line " now ! I really sat down to write and tell you of a two days' visit paid to me here by the new

American Ambassador to Berlin. *He is a faithful friend.*
He is *very*, *very* PRO-English (he has such a lovely daughter
whom I have been dancing with, A PERFECT GEM! if she
don't turn Wilhelm's head I'll eat my hat !).   My friend
was American Ambassador at Constantinople when I was
Commander-in-Chief of the Mediterranean Fleet—you
know it was a ticklish time then, at the worst of the Boer
War and the British Navy kept the Peace !   That old
Sultan [Abdul Hamid] told me so, and gave me a
500-guinea diamond star, bless him !  and he called Lord
Salisbury a d—d fool for having left him in the lurch
and for having said that " England had put her money
on the wrong horse " in backing Turkey.   The Turks
being the *one* people in the whole world to be England's
fast (and if put to it) *only* friend !   Well, my dear Friend !
Leishman saw this *then* in 1899, and sees it *now*, and hence
we were locked up for hours in a secret room here !   It
all bears immensely on the present Franco-German
Crisis !   That *" greater-than-Bismarck "* who is now
German Ambassador at Constantinople (Marschall von
Bieberstein), and who is the real director of German
policy (Waechter is only his factotum !  as I will prove
to you presently !) sees his rear and flanks quite safe by
having the Turks in the palm of his hand (as Leishman
describes it !) and so has been led to bluff at Agadir—
but those choice words of Lloyd George upset the German
apple-cart in a way it was never upset before !   (I
suppose they were " written out " words and Cabinet
words, and they were d—d fine words !)   Before I go on
with the next bit of my letter I must explain to you that
Leishman is a very great friend and admirer of Marschall
von Bieberstein and also of Kiderlen-Waechter, the
present German Foreign Minister.   When Marschall
went on his annual 4 months' leave from Constantinople
he always had Waechter to take his place while away,
who was then the German Minister at Bucharest !
Leishman is also an ardent admirer of the German

Emperor, and he is also the most intimate friend possessed by Mr. Philander Knox, the American Secretary of State, who has forced Leishman to Berlin when he was in Paradise at Rome (at all events his family were !) Well ! dear Friend, it's a good thing that Leishman loves England. I couldn't possibly write to Sir E. Grey what I am writing to you (I shouldn't write to you except that this letter goes through France only !) and it would be simply fatal to Leishman if it ever leaked out about his conversations with me, but his heart is with us. I knew this when I spent many weeks at Constantinople (and we had no friends then, 1899 and 1900 !). He says *our Turkish policy is the laughing stock of Diplomacy !* " Every schoolboy knows " that we have a Mahomedan Existence and the Turks love us, but all we do is to kick their —— ! As Leishman truly says, the Germans were in the dust by the deposition of Abdul Hamid and England was " all " to the New Turks, but slowly Marschall has worked his way up again, and the Germans again possess the Turks, instead of England. The Turkish Army, the very finest fighting army in the world, was ours for the asking, and " *Peace—perfect Peace* " in India, Egypt and Persia ; but we've chucked it all away because we have had d—d fools as our Ambassadors ! But how can it be otherwise unless you put in men from outside, like for instance Bryce at Washington ? Our strength is Mahomedan, but we are too d—d Christian to see it ! and fool about Armenian atrocities and Bulgarian horrors ! Tories and Radicals are both the same. Isn't it wonderful how we get along ! I repeat again to you my copyright lines :—

> " Time and the Ocean and some Guiding Star
> In High Cabal have made us what we are ! "

Look at Delagoa Bay, that might have been ours—indeed *was* ours only we " fooled " it away ! Look at Lord Granville and the Cameroons ! Well ! I haven't given Leishman away, I don't think ! The real German *bonne bouche* was the complete belt across Africa, but this only if the right of pre-emption as regards the Belgian Congo could have been acquired. I simply tremble at the consequences if the British Redcoats are to be planted on the Vosges Frontier [meaning the dread of Conscription and a huge Army for Continental Warfare].

1911.
*October 10th.*                                        LUCERNE.

 . . . I yesterday had a long letter from McKenna begging me to return and " put the gloves on again," and in view of his arguments I am going to do so when A. K. Wilson vanishes early next year ! It is, however, distasteful to me. I've had a lovely time here.

1911.
*October 29th.*                        REIGATE PRIORY, SURREY.

 . . . I am here 3 days with Winston and many of the Cabinet. I got a very urgent letter to come here, and I think my advice has been fully and completely digested, but don't say a word, please, to a soul ! I am returning direct to Lucerne on Wednesday, after Tuesday at Kilverstone.

1911.
*November 9th.*                                        LUCERNE.

These are very ticklish times indeed ! I have got to be extremely careful. I must not get between Winston and A. K. W. in any way—it would not only be very wrong but fatal to any smooth working. So I begged Winston not to write to me. With extreme reluctance I went to Reigate as I did, but McKenna urged me on the grounds of the good of the Navy, and from what Winston has since said to a friend of mine I think I did right in going.

1911.
*December.*                                              LUCERNE.

. . . I shouldn't have written again so soon except for just now seeing in a Paris paper that Sir John French, accompanied by four Officers, had landed at Calais *en route* to the French Head Quarters, and expatiating on the evident intention of joint military action! Do you remember the classic interview we had with the late King in his Cabin? If this is on the tapis again then we have another deep regret for the loss of that sagacious intuition! King Edward may not have been clever, but he never failed in his judgment on whose opinion to rely. . . . Of course there may be nothing in it! Nor do I think there is the least likelihood of war. ENGLAND IS FAR TOO STRONG! Yet I daily get letters anticipating my early return. . . .

I enclose you a letter from ——, received a little time ago. He is a very eminent Civil Engineer. There is a "dead set" being made to get the Midshipmen under the new scheme to rebel against "engineering"! ——, —— & Co. are persistently at it through their friends in the Fleet, and calling those Midshipmen who go in for engineering—"Greasers." The inevitable result of the present young officers of the Navy disparaging and slighting this chief necessary qualification of engineering in these engineering days will be to force the throwing open of entry as officers in the Navy *to all classes of the population* and adopting State paid Education and support till the pay is sufficient to support!

1911.
*December 24th.*

. . . I have had a hectic time with four hurricanes crossing the Channel and balancing on the tight-rope with one end held by Winston and the other by McKenna, but they both held tight and I am all right. Without doubt McKenna is a patriot to have encouraged ME to help Winston as he has done! I have not heard what

the War Staff is doing.  It does not trouble me.  My
sole object was to ensure Jellicoe being Commander-in-
Chief of the Home Fleet on December 19th, 1913, and that
is being done by his being appointed Second-in-Command
of the Home Fleet, and he will automatically be C.-in-C.
in two years from that date.  All the recent changes
revolved round Jellicoe, and No ONE sees it !

1912.
*Jan. 3rd.*                                          NAPLES.

 . . . I fully agree with you about the Navy want of
first-class Intellects.  Concentration and Discipline combine to cramp the Sea Officer. . . . Great views don't
get grasped.  Winston urges me to come back, but he
forgets the greatest of all the great Napoleonic sayings :
" *J'ordonne, ou je me tais.*"  Besides, you see, I was the
First Violin.  However, Winston is splendidly receptive.
I can't possibly write what has happened, *but he is a
brave man*.  And as 16 Admirals have been scrapped I
am more popular than ever ! ! !  A lovely woman two
days ago sent me this riddle : " Why are you like
Holland ? "  " Because you lie low and are dammed all
round."  But there it is.  Jellicoe will be Admiralissimo
when Armageddon comes along, and *everything that was
done revolved round that*, and *no one has seen it*.  He has
all the attributes of Nelson, and his age.

1912.
*March 7th.*                                          NAPLES.

You nearly saw me to-day, as a King's Messenger
roused me out the day before yesterday with papers I
really thought I could not cope with by letter ; but as
obviously the object was to avoid the gossip my appearance
in London would cause I did my best with my pen.  But
I see clearly I am in the middle of the whirlpool again
and must force what I feel a great disinclination for and
participate once more in the fight.  I have had strangely
intimate opportunities of learning the very inside of

### THE ANNIVERSARY OF TRAFALGAR.

NELSON (*in Trafalgar Square*) :—" I was on my way down to lend
them a hand myself, but if Jacky Fisher's taking on the job there's
no need for me to be nervous, I'll get back on my pedestal."

Nelson looking up Sir John Fisher on his first day as First Sea
Lord, Trafalgar Day, 1904.

German feeling towards England. *It is bitterly intense and widespread.* Without any doubt whatever the Germans thought they were going to squeeze France out of Morocco. You can take that as a fact, no matter what lies are told by the German Foreign Minister; and Clemenceau's unpublished speech would have proved it. but he said enough. And how treacherous to England was M. Caillaux.—What a dirty business! Anyhow, as a German Admiral of *high repute* wrote confidentially and privately a few days since : " German public opinion is roused in a way I had not before thought possible." And as far as I can make out, the very worst possible thing was Haldane's visit—a British Cabinet Minister crawling up the back stairs of the German Foreign Office in carpet slippers! and judging from all that is told me, it has made the Germans worse than ever, and for a variety of quite opposite reasons, all producing the same result. Any more Heligolands would mean certain war. It's very peculiar how we have left our impregnable position we occupied before Haldane's visit, to take up a most humiliating, weak and dangerous one.

1912.
*April 2nd.*

. . . As you say, Winston has done splendidly. He and I last November discussed every brick of his speech in Devonport Dockyard while visiting the 33-knot *Lion-* Dreadnought by night alone together, and don't accuse me of too much egotism, but he stopped dramatically on the Dockyard stones and said to me " You're a Great Man!" . . . We are lagging behind in out-Dread-noughting the Dreadnought! A plunge of course—a huge plunge—but so was the Dreadnought—so was the Turbine—so was the water-tube boiler, and last of all so was the $13\frac{1}{2}$-inch gun which now holds the field, and the whole Board of Admiralty (bar Jellicoe) and all the experts dead against it—but we plunged! So it is now

—we want more speed—less armour—a 15-inch gun—
more sub-division—oil only—and chauffeurs instead of
Engineers and Stokers, and a Dreadnought that will go
round the world without requiring to replenish fuel!
The *Non-Pareil*! Winston says he'll call her the
" Fisher ! " *I owe more than I can say to McKenna.*
I owe nearly as much to Winston for scrapping a dozen
Admirals on December 5th last so as to get Jellicoe 2nd in
Command of the Home Fleet. If war comes before 1914,
then Jellicoe will be Nelson at the Battle of St. Vincent :
if it comes in 1914 then he'll be Nelson at Trafalgar ! . . .
Again, I've had quite affectionate letters from three
important Admirals. Why should I come home and
filch their credit ? All this is to explain to you why I
keep abroad, as you ask me what are my future plans.
Your letter in *The Times* on the German Book quite
excellent. Bernstorff's book is even more popular in
Germany : " The War Between England and Germany "
—with the picture of the " Dreadnought " with all her
guns trained for action ! Every little petty German
newspaper is dead-on for war with England ! *that I can
assure you of!* So *anything* would kindle a war ! . . .
The banner unfurled on October 21st, 1904, by the d—d
scoundrel who on that day became First Sea Lord had
inscribed on it :

" *The fighting efficiency of the Fleet* "
and
" *Its instant readiness for War.*"

and, as Winston bravely said, that is now the case and
no credit to himself, but he ought to have gone further
back than McKenna for the credit. *It was Balfour !*
He saw me through—no one else would allow 160 ships
to be scrapped, &c., &c., &c. But you've had enough !

1912.
*April 25th.*
. . . When I was a Delegate at the Hague Conference

of 1899—the first Conference—I had very animated conversations, which, however, to my lasting regret it was deemed inexpedient to place on record (on account of their violence, I believe!), regarding " Trading with the Enemy." I stated the primordial fact that " *The Essence of War is Violence ; Moderation in War is Imbecility.*" And then in my remarks I went on to observe, as is stated by Mr. Norman Angell in the " Great Illusion," where he holds me up as a Terror! and as misguided—perhaps I went a little too far when I said I would boil the prisoners in oil and murder the innocent in cold blood, &c., &c., &c. . . . but it's quite silly not to make War damnable to the whole mass of your enemy's population, which of course is the secret of maintaining the right of Capture of Private Property at Sea. As you say, it must be proclaimed in the most public and most authoritative manner that direct and indirect trade between Great Britain, *including every part of the British Empire*, and Germany must cease in time of war. . . . When war does come " *Might is Right !* " *and the Admiralty will know what to do !* Nevertheless, it is a most serious drawback not making public to the world beforehand what we mean by War! It is astounding how even very great men don't understand War ! You must go to the Foreigner to appreciate our Surpassing Predominance as a Nation. I was closeted for two hours lately—in a locked room—with a great Foreign Ambassador, who quoted great names to me as being in agreement with him that never in the History of the World was the British Nation (as at the present moment) surpassed in power ! And therefore we could do what we liked ! . . . I fully agree with you that the schemes of the General Staff of the British Army are grotesque. Their projects last August, had we gone to war, were wild in the extreme. You will remember a famous interview we two had with King Edward in his Cabin on board the Royal Yacht—how he stamped on the idea (that then enthused the War Office mind) of England once more engaged in a great Continental War! "Marlboroughs Cheap To-day!" was the kettle of fish advertised by the Militarists!

I walked the sands of Scheveningen with General Gross von Schwartzhoff in June, 1899. The German Emperor said he (Schwartzhoff) was a greater than Moltke. He was the Military German Delegate at the Hague Conference; he was designated as Chief of the General Staff at Berlin, but he was burnt to death in China instead. I had done him a very good turn indeed, so he opened his heart to me. There was no German Navy then. We were doing Fashoda; and he expatiated on the *rôle* of the British Army—how the absolute supremacy of the British Navy gave it such inordinate power far beyond its numerical strength, because 200,000 men embarked in transports, and God only knowing where they might be put ashore, was a weapon of enormous influence, and capable of deadly blows—occupying perhaps Antwerp, Flushing, &c. (but, of course, he only was thinking of the Cotentin Peninsula), or landing 90 miles from Berlin on that 14 miles of sandy beach [in Pomerania], impossible of defence against a battle fleet sweeping with devastating shells the flat country for miles, like a mower's scythe—no fortifications able to withstand projectiles of 1,450 lb.

Yes! you are *so* right! the average man is incapable of a *wide* survey! he looks through a pinhole and only sees just a little bit much magnified! Napoleon and Cromwell! Where are they?

1912.
*April 29th.*                                         NAPLES.

. . . You say to me—" Come home! "—you remind me of "*personal influence.*" I KNOW IT! Three days ago I was invited to name one of three week-ends in June to meet two very great men at a country house— no one else. Day before yesterday Winston Churchill asks me. Hardly a week passes without such similar pressure from most influential quarters—" *Why don't I come home and smash and pulverize?* " Of course, they one and all exaggerate—that in ten minutes I could " *sweep the board* " and so on ! I know exactly what I can do. I've been fighting 50 years ! *But I don't want a personal victory !*

. . . I am going to take my body and what little money I have . . . to the United States in the near future. It would be no use my coming home. *The mischief is done !* . . . From patriotic motives I've given Winston of my very best in the replies going to him this day from Brindisi by King's Messenger, as regards designs and policy and fighting measures.

1912.
*May 15th.*

. . . Well ! as you say, every blessed thing at Weymouth [the Fleet Inspection] *absolutely* dates from 1909, except the aviation, and even that I pressed to its present condition dead against great opposition, but I wrote so strongly that —— took the bit between his teeth on that subject ! And you ask me the question " How goes it for the future ! "

Well ! Lloyd George is the real man, and so far judging from his most intimate conversation with me, *all is well !* . . . A propos of all this I've been specially invited to meet four people of importance at a week-end meeting—*no others.* I was asked twice before—and again now repeated ; but I think it best to abstain. I think you will approve of my not going. I have declined to go with W. C. in the Admiralty Yacht.

1912.
*May 19th.*                                      NAPLES.

I have a letter from W. C. this morning that he and the Prime Minister have decided to come direct here to

Naples to spend a few days, and a telegram has just
come saying they arrive on May 23rd . . . . I suppose the
coming Supplementary Estimates and also types of new
ships about which I am in deadly antagonism with every
living soul at the Admiralty, and one of the consequences
has been that a great Admiralty official has got the
boot ! ! ! So Winston is right when he writes to me
this morning that in all vital points I have had my way !
He adds : " The Future of the Navy rests in the hands of
men in whom your confidence is as strong as mine . . .
and no change of Government would carry with it any
change of policy in this respect."

1912.                KILVERSTONE HALL,
*June 30th.*              THETFORD.

My plot is working exactly as forecast. By and by
you'll say it's the best thing I ever did. The Prime
Minister and Winston would not listen at Naples to my
urgent cry " Increase your margin ! " They have got
to recruit without stint and build 8 " Mastodons "
instead of 4. Wait and see !
The recruiting HAS begun. The 8 will follow.

      We want 8
      We won't wait.

No other course but that now in progress would have
done it. I don't mind personal obloquy, but it's a bit
hard to undergo my friends' doubts of me ; but the
clouds will roll by. . . . I've got all my " working bees "
round me here of the Royal Commission [on Oil and the
Internal Combustion engine]. We shall stagger humanity !

1912.
*July 6th.*           KILVERSTONE HALL.

. . . Really all my thoughts are with my Royal Commission. I expect you will see that the course of action

will inevitably result in what I ventured to indicate *if only* the Admiralty will keep their backs to the wall of the irreducible margin required in Home Waters. The only pity was that dear old —— said we were sufficiently strong for two years or more, which of course is quite true, but his saying so may prevent Lloyd George being hustled (*as he otherwise would have been*). Luckily I prevented —— saying even more of our present great preponderance—but let us hope " All's well that ends well." Ian Hamilton came in most effectively with his witnessing the armoured Cruiser " Suffolk " laden with a Battalion of the Malta Garrison being twice torpedoed by a submarine.

1912.
*July 15th.*

. . . This instant the news has come to me that there are 750 eligible and selected candidates for 60 vacancies for Boy-Artificers in the Navy at the approaching examination ! When I introduced this scheme 8 years ago every man's hand was against me, and the whole weight of Trades Unionism inside the House of Commons and out of it was organised against me. . . . We were dominated by the Engineers ! We had to accept Engine Room artificers for the Navy who had been brought up on making bicycles ! *Now*, these boys are suckled on the marine engine ! and they have knocked out the old lot completely. Our very best Engine Room artificers now in the Navy are these boys ! Not one of my colleagues or anyone else supported me ! *Do you wonder that I don't care a d—n what anyone says?* The man you are going to see on Wednesday—how has he recognised that we are at this moment stronger than the Triple Alliance ? The leaders of both political parties—how have they recognised that 19 millions sterling of public money *actually allocated* was saved and the re-arrangement of British Sea Power so stealthily carried out that not a sign appeared of any remark by either our own or by any Foreign ·Diplomatists, until an obscure article in the *Scientific American* by Admiral Mahan stated that of a sudden he (Mahan) had discovered that 88 per cent. of the Sea Power of England was concentrated on Germany ? But the most ludicrous thing of all is that up to this very moment no one has really recognised that the Dreadnought caused such a deepening and dredging of German harbours and their approaches, and a new Kiel Canal, as to cripple Germany up to A.D. 1915, and make their coasts accessible, which were previously denied to our ships because of their heavy draught for service in all the world !

1912.
*August 2nd.*

At the Defence Committee yesterday . . . we had a regular set-to with Lloyd George (supported by Harcourt and Morley chiefly) against the provision of defence for Cromarty as a shelter anchorage for the Fleet, and the Prime Minister adjourned the discussion to the Cabinet as the temperature got hot ! As you know, I've always been " dead on " for Cromarty and hated Rosyth, which is an unsafe anchorage—the whole Fleet in jeopardy the other day—and there's that beastly bridge which, if blown up, makes the egress very risky without examination. . . . Also Cromarty is strategically better than Rosyth. . . . Also Lloyd George had a row about the airships—Seely's Sub-Committee. We *must* have airships.

1912.
*August 7th.*

I still hate Rosyth and fortifications and East Coast Docks and said so the other day ! but what we devise at

Cromarty is for another purpose—to fend off German Cruisers possibly by an accident of fog or stupidity getting loose on our small craft taking their ease or re-fuelling in Cromarty (Oil will change all this in time, but as yet we have for years coal-fed vessels to deal with). . . . I've got enthusiastic colleagues on the oil business! They're all bitten! Internal Combustion Engine Rabies!

1912.
*September.*

. . . What an ass I was to come home! but it was next door to impossible to resist the pressure put on me, and then can you think it was wise of me to plunge once more into so vast a business as future motor Battleships? Changing the face of the Navy, and, as Lloyd George said to me last Friday, getting the Coal of England as my mortal enemy!

1912.
*Sept. 14th.*

*This Royal Commission* [on oil] is a wonder! We have our first meeting on September 24th, and practically it is finished though it will go on for years and years and never submit a Report! You will love the *modus operandi* when some day I expound it to you! . . . In the second week of December we have an illustration on the scale of 12 inches to a foot of producing oil from coal. Twenty-five tons a day will be produced as an example. All that is required is to treble the retorting plant of all gas works in the United Kingdom where there is a Mayor and Corporation, and to treble their " through put " of coal! We get two million tons of oil that way! We only want one million.

I addressed the Directors of the S.E. & Chatham Railway last Tuesday, and hope I persuaded them to build a motor vessel of 24 knots between Calais and Dover, and proved to them they could save an hour between Paris and London—the whole side of the vessel falls down and makes a gangway on to a huge pontoon at Calais and Dover and all the passengers march straight out (" Every man straight before him," like the Israelites did at Jericho, and the walls fell down before them !)  No more climbing up Mont Blanc up a narrow precipitous gangway from the steamer to the jetty in the rain, and an old woman blocking you with her parcels and umbrella jammed by the stanchions, and they ask her for her ticket and she don't know which pocket it's in ! and the rain going down your neck all the time !  A glass roof goes over the motor vessel—she has no funnels, and her telescopic wireless masts wind down by a 2 h.p. motor so as not to go through the glass roof.  But all this is nothing to H.M.S. " Incomparable "—a 25 knot battleship that will go round the whole earth without refuelling ! . . . The plans of her will be finished next Monday, and I wrote last night to say I proposed in my capacity as a private British Citizen to go over in three weeks' time in the White Star " Adriatic " to get Borden [the Canadian Prime Minister] to build her at Quebec. The Building Yard put up there by Vickers is under a guarantee to build a Dreadnought in Canada in May and the great Dreadnought Dock left Barrow for Quebec on August 31st. No English Government would ever make this plunge, which is why I propose going to Canada—to that great man, Borden—and take the Vickers people to make their bargain for building.

1912.
*Sept. 20th.*

. . . My idea now is to raise a syndicate to build the " Non-Pareil " !  A few millionaires would suffice, and I know sufficient of them to do it.  All the drawings and designs quite ready.  The one *all pervading, all absorbing* thought is to get in first with motor ships before the Germans ! Owing to our apathy during the last two years they are ahead with internal combustion engines ! *They have killed 15 men in experiments with oil engines and we have not killed one !* And a d—d fool of an English politician told me the other day that he thinks this creditable to us !

Without any doubt (I have it from an eye-witness of part of the machinery for her at Nuremberg) a big German oil engine Cruiser is under weigh ! We must press forward. . . . These d—d politics are barring the way. . . . " *What !* " (say these trembling idiots) " ANOTHER *Dreadnought Revolution !* " and these boneless fools chatter with fear like apes when they see an elephant ! The imagination cannot picture that " *a greater than the Dreadnought is here !* " Imagine a silhouette presenting a target 33 per cent. less than any living or projected Battleship ! No funnels—no masts—no smoke—she carries over 5,000 tons of oil, enough to take her round the world without refuelling ! Imagine what that means ! Ten motor boats carried on board in an armoured pit in the middle of her, where the funnels and the boilers used to be. Two of these motor boats are over 60 feet long and go 45 knots ! and carry 21-inch Torpedoes that go five miles ! Imagine these let loose in a sea fight ![1] Imagine projectiles far over a ton weight ! going over a mile or more further than even the $13\frac{1}{2}$-inch gun can carry, and that gun has rightly staggered humanity !— Yes ! that $13\frac{1}{2}$-inch gun that all my colleagues (bar one ! and he is our future Nelson ! [Jellicoe]) thought me mad to force through against unanimous disapproval ! *and see where we are now in consequence !* We shall have 16 British Dreadnoughts with the $13\frac{1}{2}$-inch gun before the Germans *have one ! ! !* So it will be with the " Non-Pareil " ! WE HAVE GOT TO HAVE HER

---

[1] N.B.—These very motor boats here described sank two battleships of the Bolshevists only the other day. *See* Chapter IV.—F. 21/9/19.

# MEMORIES

*. . . I've worked harder over this job than in all my life before !*[2]

1912.
*Dec.* 29*th.*

   . . . I'm getting sick of England and want to get back to Naples and the sun ! and the " *dolce far niente !* " What fools we all are to work like we do ! Till we drop !


   [2] *Then after this came the* 15-*inch gun ; then the* 18-*inch gun, actually used at sea in the War ; and then the* 20-*inch gun, ready to be built and go into the " Incomparable," of* 40,000 *tons and* 40 *knots speed, on May* 22*nd,* 1915. —*F.* 21/9/19.

# CHAPTER XIII

## AMERICANS.

MY very best friends are Americans. I was the Admiral in North America, and saw "American Beauties" at Bermuda. (Those American roses and the American women are equal!) And without question they are the very best dancers in the world! (I suppose it's from so much skating!) My only son married an American lady (which rejoiced me), and an American gentleman on the steamer complimented me that she had come over and vanquished him instead of his going, as the usual way is, to America to capture her! I had such a time in America when I went over to the wedding! I never can forget the hospitality so boundless and sincere! I really might have spent three years in America (so I calculated) in paying visits earnestly desired. The Reporters (25 of them) asked me when I left what I thought of their country (I tried to dodge them, but found them all in my cabin when I went on board!) I summed it up in the one word I greatly admire— "HUSTLE!" and I got an adhesive label in America which I also loved! Great Black Block letters on a crimson ground—

```
RUSH
```

You stick it on a letter or the back of a slow fool. Mr. McCrea, the President of the Pennsylvania Railway, had his private car to take me to Philadelphia from New York. We went 90 miles in 90 minutes, and such a dinner! Two black gentlemen did it all. And I found my luggage in my room when I arrived labelled:

" MR. LORD FISHER "

(How it got there so quick I can't imagine.) I was bombed by a photographer as we arrived late at night, and an excellent photograph he took, but it gave me a shock! I had never been done like that! I had the great pleasure of dining with Mr. Woodrow Wilson. I predicted to the reporters he would be the next President for sure! I was told I was about the first to say so—anyhow, the 25 reporters put it down as my news!

I met several great Americans during my visit; but the loveliest meeting I ever had was when, long before, a charming company of American gentlemen came on July 4th to Admiralty House at Bermuda to celebrate " Independence Day ! " I got my speech

in before theirs! I said George Washington was
the greatest Englishman who ever lived! England
had never been so prosperous, thanks *solely* to him,
as since *his time and now!* because he taught us
how to associate with our fellow countrymen when they
went abroad and set up house for themselves! And
that George Washington was the precursor of that
magnificent conception of John Bright in his speech of
the ages when he foretold a great Commonwealth—yes
a great Federation—of all those speaking the same tongue
—that tongue which is the " *business* " tongue of the
world—as it expresses in fewer words than any other
language what one desires to convey! And I suppose
now we have got Palestine that this Federal House of
Commons of the future will meet at Jerusalem, the
capital of the lost Ten Tribes of Israel, whom we are
without doubt, for how otherwise could ever we have so
prospered when we have had such idiots to guide us and
rule us as those who gave up Heligoland, Tangier,
Curaçoa, Corfu, Delagoa Bay, Java, Sumatra, Minorca,
etc., etc. ? I have been at all the places named, so am
able to state from personal knowledge that only congenital idiots could have been guilty of such inconceivable
folly as the surrender of them, and again I say : " Let
us thank God that we are the lost ten tribes of Israel ! "
Mr. Lloyd George, in a famous speech long ago in the
War, showed how we had been 14 times " too late ! "
How many more " too lates " since he made that
memorable speech ? Especially what about our shipbuilding and the German submarine menace and Ration-

ing ? (The only favoured trades seem to be Brewing and Racing ! Both so flourishing !)

The American barber on board the " Baltic " told me a good story. He was a quaint man, clean shaved and wore black alpaca throughout. Halfway across the Atlantic I was waiting to have my hair cut, when a gentleman bounced in on him, kicking up a devil of a fuss about wanting something at once ! The barber, without moving a muscle, calmed him by saying : " Are you leaving to-day, Sir ? " But this was his story. He was barber in the train from Chicago to New York that never stops " even for a death " (so he told me) when the train suddenly stopped at a small village and a lady got out. Mr. Thompson, the President of the Railway, was in the train, and asked why ? The conductor showed an order signed by a great man of the Railway to stop there. When Mr. Thompson got to New York he asked this great man " What excuse ? " and added : " I wouldn't have done it for my wife'! " and the answer he got was : " No more would I ! "

But the sequel of the story is that I told this tale at an international cosmopolitan lunch party at Lucerne and said : " The curious thing is I knew the man ! " when Mr. Chauncey Depew wiped me out by saying that " he knew the woman ! "

This American Barber quaintly praised the Engine Driver of this Chicago train by telling me that " *he was always looking for what he didn't want!* " and so had avoided the train going into a River by noticing something wrong with the points !

224

AMERICA AND THE BLOCKADE.

"Why Mr. Wilson should expect this country to refrain from exercising
a right in return for Germany's refraining from committing wrongs is
not very clear to the ordinary intelligence."—*Daily Paper.*

DAME WILSON (*to P. C. Fisher*) :—"Oh, Constable! Don't hurt him.
I'm sure he won't murder anyone else!"

Admiral Sampson brought his Squadron of the United States Navy to visit me at Bermuda. I was then the Admiral in North America. At the banquet I gave in his honour I proposed his health, and that of the United States. He never said a word. Presently one of his Officers went up and whispered something in his ear. I sent the wine round, and the Admiral then got up, and made the best speech I ever heard. All he said was: " It was a d—d fine old hen that hatched the American Eagle ! " His chaplain, after dinner, complimented me on the Officers of my Flagship, the " Renown." He said : " He had not heard a single ' swear ' from ' Soup to Pea-nuts ' " !

### *Lord Fisher on John Bright*

(FROM " BRIGHT'S HOUSE JOURNAL ")

At a dinner held in London the other day to Mr. Josephus Daniels, Secretary to the United States Navy, Lord Fisher made the following speech in which he referred to a speech by Mr. John Bright :—

"Admiral of the Fleet Lord Fisher, who was called upon also to respond, was received with cheers, the whole company standing up and drinking his health. He said he had no doubt it would be pleasing to them if he spoke about America. He was there one week. Mr. Daniels had been here about one week. He was in America one week because his only son was married there to the only daughter of a great Philadelphian.

    •    •    •    •    •    •

" ' King Edward who was a kind friend to me—in fact he was my only friend at one time '—remarked Lord

Fisher, ' said to me, " You are the best hated man in the British Empire," and I replied, " Yes, perhaps I am." The King then said, " Do you know I am the only friend you have ? " I said, " Perhaps your Majesty is right, but you have backed the winner." Afterwards I came out on top when I said, " Do you remember you backed the winner and now everyone is saying what a sagacious King you are ? The betting was a thousand to one." '

\* \* \* \* \* \*

" But he was going to tell them about America, and some of them would hear things they had never before heard about their own country. When he was at Bermuda a deputation of American citizens waited upon him on July 4th. To tell the honest truth he had forgotten about it. He told the deputation he knew what they had come there for. ' You know,' he said to them, ' the greatest Englishman that ever lived was George Washington. He taught us how to rule our Colonies. He told us that freedom was the thing to give them. Why, if it had not been for George Washington America might have been Ireland.' ' I shook hands with them,' continued Lord Fisher, ' and they went away and said nothing they had come to say. . . .

" ' Now I will talk about the League of Nations. In A.D. 1910 an American citizen wished to see me ; and he said to me, taking a paper out of his pocket, " Have you read that ? " I looked at it and saw it was a speech by John Bright, mostly in words of one syllable—simplicity is, of course, the great thing. That speech is really very little known on this side of the Atlantic or on the other, but it so impressed me at the time that I have been thinking of it ever since. John Bright said he looked forward to the time when there would be a compulsory peace—when those who spoke with the same tongue would form a great federation of free nations joined together.' "

# AMERICANS

The following is an extract from the speech by Mr. John Bright. It was delivered at Edinburgh in 1868 :—

" I do not know whether it is a dream or a vision, or the foresight of a future reality that sometimes passes across my mind—I like to dwell upon it—but I frequently think the time may come when the maritime nations of Europe—this renowned country of which we are citizens, France, Prussia, resuscitated Spain, Italy, and the United States of America—may see that vast fleets are of no use ; that they are merely menaces offered from one country to another ; and that they may come to this wise conclusion—that they will combine at their joint expense, and under some joint management, to supply the sea with a sufficient sailing and armed police which may be necessary to keep the peace on all parts of the watery surface of the globe, and that those great instruments of war and oppression shall no longer be upheld. This, of course, by many will be thought to be a dream or a vision, not the foresight of what they call a statesman."

## Sir Hiram Maxim

When Sir Hiram Maxim—that great American—was very little known, he came to see me when I was Captain of the Gunnery ship at Portsmouth, bringing with him his ever-famous Maxim gun, to be tried by me. So we went to Whale Island to practise with the gun ; and when he was ready to fire I adopted the usual practice in trying all new guns and ordered the experimental party to get under cover ; and at that order they were supposed to go into a sort of dug-out. Evidently old Maxim considered this an insult to his gun, and he roared out at the top of his voice : " Britishers under cover, Yankees out in the open ! " The gun didn't burst and it was all right ; but it might have, all the same.

Admiral Hornby the bravest of the brave, was one of the Britishers ; and he came to lunch with me, being extremely fascinated with Hiram's quaintness. Hiram was a delightful man in my opinion, and I remember his telling me that if I wanted to live long and see good days the thing was to eat Pork and Beans. I never had the chance, till 1910, of eating them cooked *à l'Améri-caine ;* and I then agreed with Hiram Maxim—no more delicious dish in the world, but you can't get it in England ! After lunch there were some oranges on the table ; and to my dying day I shall never forget the extraordinary look on Sir Geoffrey Hornby's beautiful, refined face as Hiram reached out and grasped an orange from the centre of the table—tore it apart, and buried his face sucking out the contents, emerging all orange. He told us that was the way to enjoy an orange. We neither of us were up to it !

# CHAPTER XIV

## SOME SPECIAL MISSIONS

I was sent as a very young Lieutenant to a little fishing village called Heppens in Oldenburg. It is now Wilhelms-haven, chief Naval Port of Germany. Its river, the Jahde, was then a shallow stream. The occasion for my visit was the cession to King William of Prussia, as he was then, of this place, Heppens, by the Grand Duke of Oldenburg; and there I met King William, to whom I sat next but one at lunch, and Bismarck and von Moltke and von Roon were there. We had a very long-winded speech from the Burgomaster, and Bismarck, whom I was standing next to, said to me in the middle of it : " I didn't know this was going to happen, or I would have cut him short." The King asked me at lunch why I had been sent, and if there was no one else who knew about torpedoes. Well, I don't think there was. It was an imposing and never-to-be-forgotten sight, that lunch. They all wore their helmets and great-coats at lunch— so mediæval—and telegrams kept coming to Bismarck, who would get up and draw the King aside, and then they would sit down again. Von Roon I thought very

229

*débonnaire*, and Moltke was like an old image, taciturn and inscrutable, but he talked English as well as I did.

Years after this, Prince Adalbert's Naval Aide-de-camp, who was a great friend of mine, told me that on the day of mobilization in the war with France he was sent to von Moltke with a message from Prince Adalbert, who was King William's brother and Head of the Navy, to ask him whether he could see Prince Adalbert for a few moments. To his astonishment, my friend found Moltke lying on a sofa reading " Lady Audley's Secret," by Miss Braddon, and he told him he could see the Prince for as long as he liked and whenever he liked. The word " Mobilize " had finished all his work for the present.

On the occasion of my visit I imagined and reported what Heppens would become, and so it did. I never can make out why I didn't get a German decoration. I think perhaps they thought me too young. However, I had the honour of an empty sentry-box placed outside the little inn where I was staying ; and if I had been of higher rank there would have been a sentry in it. The little inn was very unpretentious, and when the landlord had carved for us he came and sat down at table with us. Some days after, at a very exclusive Military Club in Berlin, I met the King's two illegitimate brothers. They were exactly like him ; also I breakfasted with the Head of the German Mining School. I remember it, because we only had raw herring and black bread for breakfast. He was very poor, although he was exceeding clever, and had as his right-hand man a wonderful chemist.

# SOME SPECIAL MISSIONS

So far as I know, the present German mine is nearly what it was then, and the sea-gulls rested on the protuberances as they do now, for I went to Kiel Bay to see them. There was a lovely hotel at Kiel, where they treated me royally. I recommended the adoption of these German mines, and it's a pity we didn't. They hold the field to this very day. However, the First Sea Lord of that date didn't believe in mines or torpedoes or submarines, and I was packed off to China in the old two-decker " Donegal," as Commander of the China Flagship. Long afterwards Sir Hastings Yelverton, who became First Sea Lord, unburied my Memorandum headed " Ocean Warfare," and supported the views in it. It enunciated the principle of " Hit first, hit hard, and keep on hitting," and discoursed on Submarines and Mines.

## REVAL

You are remarking to me of a charming letter written to me by the late Emperor of Russia's youngest sister—the Grand Duchess Olga. She is a peculiarly sweet creature. Her nickname amongst the Russians was " Sunshine." Stolypin, the Prime Minister, told me that, and he also said to me that she was a kind of life-buoy because if you walked about with her you would not get bombed by an anarchist. All loved her.

I made her acquaintance first at Carlsbad. On my arrival at the hotel I found King Edward's Equerry waiting in the hall. I had written to tell the King, who was at Marienbad, in answer to his enquiry, as to the day

I should arrive and what time; and he came over to
Marienbad from Carlsbad. I went then and there and
found him just finishing lunch with a peculiarly charming
looking young lady, who turned out to be the Grand
Duchess Olga, and her husband, the Grand Duke of
Oldenburg, from whom happily she is now divorced (I
didn't like the look of him at all). The King, having
satisfied himself that I had had lunch, and he then
smoking a cigar as big as a capstan bar, after talking of
various things which interested him, told me that his
niece, the Grand Duchess Olga, did not know anyone
in Carlsbad, and he relied on me to make her time there
pleasant, so I promptly asked her if she could waltz.
She said she loved it, but she somehow never got the
step properly, whereupon I asked the King if he had
any objection to getting into the corner of the room while
I moved the table and took the rugs up to give her
Imperial Highness a lesson. He made some little
difficulty at first, but eventually went into the corner;
and when the lesson began he was quite pleased and
clapped his hands and called out " Bravo ! " The best
waltz tune in the world is one of Moody and Sankey's
hymns. I don't know whether Sankey originated the
saying that he didn't see why the Devil should have all
the good music. I don't by that implicate that the
waltz was the devil's ; but, without any doubt, there is
a good deal of temptation in it, and when you get a
good partner you cleave to her all the evening.

This dancing lesson was an unalloyed success, so I
asked her to a dance the next night at the Savoy Hotel ;

and after some more words with the King I left, and walking down the stairs to go to my hotel, I thought to myself : " How on earth are you going to get up a dance when you don't know a soul in the place ? " when who should I meet but a friend of mine—a Spanish Grandee, the Marquis de Villa Vieja, and he arranged what really turned out to be a ball, as he knew everybody, and I having some dear American friends at Marienbad I telegraphed them to come over and dine with the Grand Duchess and stay the night for the ball, and they did. When the dance had begun, and the Grand Duchess was proving quite equal to her lesson of the day before, suddenly an apparition of extraordinary grace and loveliness appeared at the door. Villa Vieja took on the Grand Duchess and I welcomed the beautiful Polish Countess and danced with her many waltzes running in spite of a hint I received that her husband was very jealous and a renowned duellist. Next day, by telegram from the King, I was told by His Majesty that Isvolsky, the Russian Minister of Foreign Affairs, was to be asked by me to lunch on his arrival that day from St. Petersburg. I invited him ; and just as we sat down to lunch the Polish angel of the night before came through the door and petrified Isvolsky, and the more so as she kissed her hand to me. He never took his eyes off her, and as she walked to her table I heard him breathe a sigh, and say *sotto voce*, " Alas, in heaven no woman ! " I said to him : "Monsieur Isvolsky, pray pardon me ; perhaps you did not intend it to be heard, but if it be true what you say, it takes away much of the charm which I had anticipated finding there."

He turned to me and said—quoting chapter and verse in the Revelations, " There was silence in heaven."

So when I met the Grand Duchess Olga again, when I accompanied King Edward on that memorable visit to Reval—when, as Prince Orloff, the Emperor's principal aide-de-camp, said to me, King Edward changed the atmosphere of Russian feelings towards England from suspicion to cordial trust—there was quite an affectionate meeting, and we danced the " Merry Widow " waltz— a then famous stage performance—with such effect as to make the Empress of Russia laugh. They told me she had not laughed for two years. At the banquet preceding the dance the Grand Duchess and I, I regret to say, made such a disturbance in our mutual jokes that King Edward called out to me that I must try to remember that it was not the Midshipmen's Mess ; and my dear Grand Duchess thought I should be sent to Siberia or somewhere. We sailed at daylight, and I got a letter from her when I arrived in England saying she had made a point of seeing Uncle Bertie and that it was all right, I was not going to be punished. Then she went on to describe that she had had a very happy day (being her birthday) picnicking in the woods ; the only drawback was, she told me, that the gnats would bite her ankles. Being, at that period, both a courtier and a sycophant, I telegraphed to her at some Palace she was at in Russia to say " I wished to God I had been one of the gnats." It was weeks before she got the telegram, as the Russian Secret Department believed it was from some anarchist, and was a cypher for bombing the Emperor or something of the sort, and there was a lot of bother to trace out who had sent it.

I find among my papers another charming letter which I received from the Grand Duchess Olga. It runs:

PETERHOF.
11/25 *July*, 1909.

DEAR ADMIRAL,

I have been going to write to you for ever so long and now is a chance to send you a few lines.

How are you getting on ?  We speak of you very often. I suppose you'll be going to Carlsbad this autumn—and I am very sorry that we are not going—so as to meet you there !

I have a great favour to ask you—but as I believe and think you *can* grant it—I shall ask : Lieutenant —— of your Royal Navy—whom we got to like very much two years ago at Sorrento—is willing to come this autumn and spend a month with us at our country place—*if* he gets leaves of course ; I write all this to you as I don't know who else can help and give him leave.

We should like to have him about the middle of your September (the very beginning of ours).  If you think he can get leave just then would you kindly telegraph to me—then I could write and ask him (I suppose he will be at Cowes ?).  Today is my nameday, and having received any amounts of presents—we are going to Church—as one always does—on such occasions and then there will be a rather big lunch and the band will play— All this glorious occasion is not only for me—but also for my niece Olga.

My sister Xenia—who does not know you—says she is sorry not to have that honour and pleasure !

My husband sends his best love (or whatever one says). Goodbye dear Admiral.  I wish I was going to see you soon it would be awfully amusing. Write to me later on when you will be free please !

Much love and good wishes.

OLGA.

P.S. Mrs. Francklin sends lots of kind messages and love. Mama sends her best love too.

That visit of King Edward to Russia was really quite remarkable for the really eloquent speech the King made, without a note of any sort. I said to him at breakfast the next morning, when they brought in a copy of what they thought he had said, that I wondered on such a momentous occasion he didn't have it written out. " Well ! " he said to me, " I did try that once, when the French President Loubet came to visit me, and I learnt the speech off by heart in the garden of Buckingham Palace. When I got up to say it, I could not remember it, and had to keep on beginning again at the beginning. So I said to myself, ' Never again ' ! " And I must say I share his conviction that there is no such eloquence as when out of the abundance of the heart the mouth speaketh. Emotion and earnestness will do much more than move mountains ; they will move multitudes—and that was what King Edward was able to do.

I have spoken elsewhere of what I deemed was a suitable epitaph for him—those great words of Pascal : " le cœur a ses raisons que la raison ne connaît point." The heart has reasons that the mind knows nothing about.

God bless him !

Stolypin, when we met him at Reval on King Edward's

visit to the Czar, was described to us as the greatest, the bravest and most single-minded Prime Minister that Russia had ever possessed. He spoke English fluently, and certainly was very pro-English. He was beyond deception. His only daughter, he told me, had been killed by a bomb while he was walking with her in the garden, and one of his hands was greatly mutilated by the same explosion. He was murdered at the theatre at Moscow not very long afterwards. We had many conversations together. He said it was criminal folly having the capital of Russia elsewhere than inland, as at Moscow, for that Petersburg was open to German attack by sea. He seemed to have a prophetic view of England's imbecility as regards using her enormous sea supremacy to prevent the Baltic becoming a German lake, as it became in the war, though we were five times stronger than the German Fleet. So it passed by as an idle dream, any idea of England's interference, and alas ! he remembered our betrayal of Denmark when the Germans took Kiel and Schleswig-Holstein.

Stolypin repeatedly said to me the German frontier was his one and only thought, and he was devoting all his life to make that frontier impregnable against Germany, both in men and munitions, and strategic arrangements. But he did not live long enough to carry out his scheme.

### CARTAGENA

I also went with King Edward to Cartagena, when he returned the King of Spain's visit. King Alfonso, whom

I had previously met in England, was very cordial to me because we had seven " Dreadnoughts " ready before the Germans had one. In fact, when I told him this piece of news, as we were walking up and down the deck, with King Edward and Queen Alexandra watching us from two deck-chairs, King Alfonso was so delighted that he threw his arms round my neck, cried " You darling ! " and kissed me. Then he put his hand in his waistcoat pocket, took out a chocolate and popped it into my mouth. He gave me the highest Spanish Order he could. But when the box came on board containing it, it turned out to be the Order of Isabella the Catholic, which is only given to Roman Catholics; but the interesting thing is that when I was a little Midshipman I had been reading "Ferdinand and Isabella," and I remember saying to my messmates that I intended some day to have the Order of Isabella the Catholic. And when, some years after, as a Lieutenant it was the fashion to wear medal ribbons in a rosette, upon some supercilious officer asking me what " that thing " was in my button-hole, I quite remember saying, by way of pulling his leg, that it was the Spanish Order of Isabella the Catholic. However, I got the proper Order in time to wear at the banquet.

The banquet was a very fine sight, as King Alfonso had brought down the tapestries, pictures and other ornaments from the Escurial. The Spanish Admirals were a grand sight. They wore the ancient uniform, and each had a great Malacca cane with a big gold top. They all came on board to call on King Edward in an old-fashioned pulling barge, and the sailors wore crimson and gold sashes. That rowing barge and the splendid uniforms lay at the root of one occasion when King Edward was really angry with me. I had been arranging for him the details of the great Naval Review and was summoned to Buckingham Palace to discuss them with him. I found no Equerries in attendance, no one about, and the King white with anger. " So ! " he cried out to me, " I'm to go by such and such a train, am I ? And I'm to embark at such and such a time, am I ? And I'm to use your barge because it's a better barge than mine, is it ? Look here, *am I the King or are you?* " The upshot of the interview was that he threw the papers on the floor, with " Have it your own way ! " But the secret cause of his anger was that he had made up his mind to go off in a rowing-boat like the Spanish Admirals, forgetting that there is no tide at Cartagena, whereas the tide at Cowes runs many knots, and it would have taken a rowing-boat hours to do what the barge could do in a few minutes.

### KIAMIL PASHA

One of the most pleasurable incidents of my holding the appointment of Commander-in-Chief of the Mediterranean Fleet was going to Smyrna to do honour to that splendid old Turk, Kiamil Pasha. He was then Vali, or Governor, of the Province of Smyrna. He was most hale and vigorous. He so delighted me with his conversations and experiences that it's a sincere joy to me now to recall, even in this humble way, what a magnificent old man he was, and how he had so often placed his life in jeopardy for the sake of right and for the good of his country, which last, he said (he spoke most fluent English), had been "imperishably bound up with England's righteous work in the East." He had been many times Grand Vizier, and he knew all the secret incidents following and preceding the Crimean War. And he said fervidly that England was the only nation that never asked and never schemed to get anything out of Turkey. And he said it was only the insensate folly of the English Authorities that could ever have dislodged England from her wonderful supremacy over the minds of the whole Turkish people. I told him, in return, that the English treatment of Turkey was only on a par with the English folly of giving up Heligoland, Corfu, Tangier, Minorca, Java, Sumatra, Curaçoa (the key of the Panama Canal), Delagoa Bay (the only harbour in Africa), and so on, and so on, and explained, to his delighted amusement, that we were a nation of Lions led by Asses. He pretty well foretold all that has happened since 1902.

With respect to Tangier, which was the dowry of Henrietta Maria, I diverge a moment to mention that a great Spaniard in high office once said to me that it was a curious fact that whenever Spain had left the side of England she had inevitably come to grief.

Following on Kiamil's wonderful prescience, I found on my visit to the Sultan, who had invited me to Constantinople, that all I had heard from him about Bulgaria was confirmed at Constantinople. One and all said that

Bulgaria was the fighting nation, and that Bulgaria was the Key of the East. I was so saturated with the importance of this fact that I spoke to Kitchener about it when the War commenced, but we did not give Bulgaria what she wanted, and when, a year afterwards, she was offered the same terms it was too late.

A great Bank always, I believe, has a travelling inspector who visits all the branches. We want such a personage to visit all our representatives in foreign lands, and see what they have done for England in the previous year.

# CHAPTER XV

AMONGST the 13 First Lords of the Admiralty I have had to deal with (and with nine of them I was very intimately associated) I should like to record that in my opinion Lord George Hamilton and Lord Spencer had the toughest jobs, because of the constitution of their respective Boards of Admiralty ; and yet neither of them received the credit each of them deserved for his most successful administration. With both of them their tact was unsurpassable. They had to deal with extremely able colleagues, and my experience is that it is not a good thing to have a lot of able men associated together. If you take a little of the best Port Wine, the best Champagne, the best Claret, and the best Hock and mix them together, the result is disastrous. So often is it with a Board of Admiralty. That's why I have suffered fools gladly ! But Lord George Hamilton and Lord Spencer had an awful time of it. To both of these (I consider) great men I am very specially beholden. Lord George Hamilton more particularly endured much on my behalf when I was Director of Naval Ordnance, fighting the War Office. It was his own decision that sent me to

Portsmouth as Admiral Superintendent of the Dockyard, and thus enabled me practically to prove the wisdom and the economy of concentrating workmen on one ship like a hive of bees and adopting piece-work to the utmost limit. Cannot anyone realise that if you have your men spread over many ships building, your capital is producing no dividend as compared with getting a ship rushed and sent to sea ready to fight ? I was held up as a dramatic *poseur* because the " Dreadnought " was built in a year and a day. Yes ! She was ready to fight in a year and a day. She did fire her guns. The " Inflexible," her famous prototype in former years, which I commanded, was four or five years building. I took up the battleship " Royal Sovereign " when I went as Superintendent of Portsmouth Dockyard and got her completed within two years, and thereby saw my way to doing it in a year. And so would I have done the famous " Hush Hush " ships, as I said I would ; only circumstances brought about my departure from the Admiralty, and apathy came back, and those " Hush Hush " ships consequently took more than a year to build. And some armchair quill-drivers still sling ink at 'em. And when I heard from an eye-witness how the whole lot of German cruisers did flee when they appeared and ought to have been gobbled up I rubbed my hands with malignant glee at the devastation of my pen-and-ink enemies. As usual in the war, on that occasion the business wasn't pushed home.

To revert to my theme—I owe also a great debt to Lord George Hamilton, when at a previous stage of my career he dissuaded me from accepting an offer from

Lord Rothschild, really beyond the dreams of avarice, of becoming the head of a great armament and shipbuilding combine, which accordingly fell through on my refusal. Had I gone, I'd have been a millionaire instead of a pauper as I am now ; but I wouldn't have been First Sea Lord from 1904 to 1910 and then " Sacking the Lot ! " Lord George also selected me to be Controller of the Navy.

Lord Spencer called a horse after me—almost as great an honour. Lord Spencer was really a very magnificent man, and he had the attributes of his great ancestor, who selected Nelson over a great many of his seniors to go and win the Battle of the Nile. There was no one else who would have done it ; and when Sir John Orde, one of the aggrieved Admirals, told the King that the selected Nelson was mad, he replied, " I wish to God he would bite you all ! " My Lord Spencer had the same gift of selection—it's the biggest gift that a man in such a position can have, and the life, the fate of his country may depend upon him. Only war finds out poltroons. Lord Spencer turned out his master, to whom he was faithfully devoted, when he saw the Navy was in danger and that Mr. Gladstone would not agree to strengthen it. His manners were superb. He satisfied that great description of what constitutes a gentleman : " He never hurt any man's feelings."

There's another First Lord I have too faintly alluded to—Lord Northbrook. He also was a great man, but he was not considered so by the populace. He was a victim to his political associates—they let him in. His finance at the Admiralty was bad through no fault of his, and he was persuaded to go to Egypt, which I think was a mistake. I stayed with him, and the microscope of home revealed him to me. His conceptions were magnificent and his decisions were like those of the Medes and Persians. Of all the awful people in the world nothing is so terrible as a vacillator. I am not sure the Devil isn't right when he says, " Tell a lie and stick to it." Lord Northbrook also in spite of intense opposition laid hold of my hand and led me forth in the paths I glory in, of Reform and Revolution. Stagnation, in my opinion, is the curse of life. I have no fellow-feeling with those placid souls who, like a duck-pond, torpid and quiescent, live the life of cabbages. I don't believe anybody can say, " Of such is the Kingdom of Heaven," because it is immortally shown that strife is the secret of a good life.

As with Lord Spencer, so was it with Lord Selborne. He again, as First Lord of the Admiralty, took the unusual course of kindly coming to Malta to see me when I commanded the Mediterranean fleet (the Boer War placed England in a very critical position at that time) ; and though there was a great strife with the Admiralty he chose me after my three years as Commander-in-Chief to be Second Sea Lord of the Admiralty and permitted me to unfold a scheme of education which came into being on the following Christmas Day without the alteration of a comma. More than that, he benevolently spared me from the Admiralty to become Commander-in-Chief at Portsmouth, to see that scheme carried out. Many letters have I that that step indicated the end of my naval career. I believe to that date it always has been so, but within a year I was First Sea Lord, and never did any First Lord hold more warmly the hand of his principal adviser than Lord Selborne held mine.

There are few people living to whom I am under a greater obligation than Admiral Sir Francis Bridgeman, G.C.B. This distinguished sailor aided me in the gradual building up of the Grand Fleet. As I have said before, it had to be done unostentatiously and by slow degrees, for fear of exciting the attention of the German Admiralty and too much embroiling myself with the Admirals whose fleets had to be denuded till they disappeared, so as to come under Admiral Sir Francis Bridgeman's command, with whom the Grand Fleet originated under the humble designation of the Home Fleet—a gathering and per-petuation of the old more or less stationary coast-guard ships scattered all round the United Kingdom and, as the old phrase was, " Grounding on their beef bones " as they swung with the tide at their anchors. In the Providence of God the animosities of the Admirals thus engendered caused the real success of the whole scheme — and what should have been as clear as crystal to the least observant onlooker was obscured by the fumes of anger exuding from these scandalized Admirals. I look back with astonishment at my Job-like conduct, but it had its compensations. I hope Sir Francis Bridgeman will forgive me for hauling him into this book—I have no other way of showing him my eternal gratitude ; and it was with intense delight that I congratulated Mr. Churchill on obtaining his services to succeed Sir Arthur

## SOME PERSONALITIES

Wilson, the First Sea Lord, who had so magnificently adhered to the scheme I left.

Sir Arthur refused a Peerage, and he was a faithful and self-effacing friend in his room at the Admiralty those seven fateful months I was First Sea Lord during the war. It was peculiarly fortunate and providential that the two immediately succeeding First Sea Lords after my departure on January 25th, 1910, should have been the two great sailors they were—otherwise there would have been no Grand Fleet—they altered nothing, and the glacier moved along, resistless and crushing all the obstacles in its path, and now, after the war, it has passed on ; the dead corpses of the foes of the scheme are disclosed, and we'll bury them without comment.

I began these talks by solemnly declaring that I would not mention a single living name—please let it stand— it shows what one's intention was ; but one is really forced to stand up to such outstanding personalities as Sir Arthur Wilson and Sir Francis Bridgeman, and I again repeat with all the emphasis at my command that it would have been impossible to have conducted those eight great years of ceaseless reform, culminating in the production of the most incomparable fleet that ever existed, had not the two Political Administrations, four First Lords, and every member of the several Boards of Admiralty been, as I described them in public, united, determined, and progressive. Never for one instant did a single Board of Admiralty during that time lay on its oars. For to rest on our oars would not have been standing still ; the malignant tide was fierce against us,

247

and the younger Officers of the fleet responded splendidly.

On January 3rd, 1903, I wrote as follows in reply to some criticism of me as First Sea Lord :—

" Our Fleets are 50 per cent. more at sea, and we hit the target 50 per cent. more than we did two years ago.
" In the first year there were 2,000 more misses than hits !
" In the second year there were 2,000 more hits than misses ! "

The very first thing I did when I returned to the Admiralty as First Sea Lord for those seven months in the first year of the war was instantly to get back Sir Percy Scott into the Fighting Arena. I had but one answer to all his detractors and to the opposition to his return :—

" *He hits the target !* "

He *also* was maliciously maligned. I don't mean to say that Sir Percy Scott indulges in soft soap towards his superiors. I don't think he ever poured hot water down anybody's back. Let us thank God he didn't !

I have repeatedly said (and I reiterate it whenever I get the chance) that Nelson was nothing if he was not insubordinate. Nelson's four immortal Big Fights are brilliant and everlasting testimonies to the virtues of Self-Assertion, Self-Reliance, and Contempt of Authority. But of Nelson and the Nelsonic attributes I treat in another place. (Ah ! Lord Rosebery, if only you had written " Nelson's Last Phase " ! I entreated you, but without avail !) (Again a repetition !) Nelson's *Life* not yet written ! Southey's *Life*, meant only for school-boys, still holds the field. W. T. Stead might have done it, for the sacred fire of Great Emotions was the calorific of Stead's Internal Combustion Engine. Suffice it to say of Sir Percy Scott that it was he and he alone who made the first start of the Fleet's hitting the enemy and not missing him. Why hasn't *he* been made a Viscount ? But that is reserved for those in another sphere !

" The Tides—and Sir Frederick Treves."—One of my greatest benefactors (he saved my life. Six doctors wanted to operate on me—he wouldn't have it ; the conse-quence—I'm better now than ever I was in my life) is Sir Frederick Treves, Surgeon, Orator, Writer, " De-veloper of the Powers of Observation." He, this morning, September 16th, 1919, gives me something to think about. It has relation to my dear and splendid friend Sir Charles Parsons, President of the British Association and inventor of the Turbine, who said the other day at Bournemouth that our coal bids fair to fail and we must seek other sources of power. Considering that Sir Charles invented the Turbine—derided by everyone as a box of tricks, and it now monopolises 80 per cent. of the horse-power of the world—we ought to listen to him. His idea is to dig a twelve-mile hole into the earth to get hold of power. Now Sir Frederick in his letter this morning uses these words :

" *England is an Island*. We are surrounded on all sides with the greatest source of power in the world—the *Tides*.

" There is enough force in the Tides to light and heat

the whole country, *and to run all its railways*. It is running to waste while we are bellowing for coal."

I know exactly what the Royal Society will say to Sir Frederick Treves. The Royal Society, not so many years ago, said through one of its most distinguished members that the aeroplane was a physical impossibility. When I said this to Sir Hiram Maxim he placed his thumb to his nose and extended his fingers ; and, as I have remarked elsewhere, aeroplanes are now as plentiful as sparrows. So do not let us put Sir Frederick Treves in the waste paper basket. He's a great man. When Lord Lister and my dear friend Sir Thomas Smith were beholding him operating on King Edward at the time when his illness stopped his Coronation—even those two wonderful surgeons held their breath at Treves's astounding skill and confidence. He kept on, and saved King Edward's life. There was no " Not running risks " with him. He snatched his King from death. The others both thought Death had won, and they both exclaimed !

Sir Frederick won't see this until he reads it in his presentation copy of this book, or he wouldn't have it.

And then he is so choice in his educational ideas. Here's a lovely morsel, which I commend to School-masters (Curse 'em ! they ruined Osborne). Sir Frederick. says :—

" Our present system of education is on a par with the Training of Performing Dogs, they're merely taught tricks ! and Trick antics do not help a boy much in the serious business of life. There is no attempt to get at the mind of a boy, and still less any attempt to find out his particular abilities. The only thing is, Is he good at Mental Acrobatics ? A very fine book on ' The New Education '[1] was published in the Autumn of last year, 1918. It shows up the wasteful absurdities of the present Educational System. Of course, no attention has been paid to it, because it is so simple, so evident, and so human. . . . Years are spent in teaching a boy Latin Verses, but never a moment to teach him ' *How to develop powers of Observation.*' "

I could tell my readers instances of Sir Frederick's powers in this last regard ; and the medical students during the many years he was their Lecturer could all of them do Sir Frederick greater justice than I can.

" *God bless Sir Frederick Treves !* "

Of all the famous men I have known, Lord Kelvin had the greatest brain. He went to sea with me in many new ships that I commanded. Once, in a bleak March east wind at Sheerness I found him on deck on a high pedestal exposed to the piercing blast watching his wonderful compass, and he had only a very thin coat on. I said : " For goodness sake, Sir William, come down and put on a great coat." He said : " No, thank you, I am quite warm. I've got several vests on." His theory was that it was much warmer wearing many thin vests than one thick one, as the interstices of one were filled up by the next one, and so on. I explained this afterwards, as I sat one day at lunch next to the Emperor of Russia, when he asked me to explain my youth and good health, and I hoped that he would follow Lord Kelvin's example, as

[1] "The New Teaching," edited by John Adams. Hodder and Stoughton

I did. Lord Kelvin got this idea of a number of thin vests instead of one thick one from the Chinese, who, in many ways, are our superiors.

For instance, a Chinaman, like an ancient Greek or Roman, maintains that the liver is the seat of the human affections. We believe that the heart is. So a Chinese always offers his hand and his liver to the young lady of his choice. Neither do they ever kiss each other in China. Confucius stopped it because the lips are the most susceptible portion of the human body to infection. When two Chinese meet, they rub their knees with their hands, and say " Ah " with a deep breath. A dear friend of mine went to the Viceroy of Nankin to enquire how his newly-raised Army was getting on with the huge consignment of magnificent rifles sent out from England for its use. The Chinese Viceroy told my friend he was immensely pleased with these rifles, and the reports made to him showed extraordinary accuracy, as the troops hit the target every time. The Viceroy sent my friend up in a Chinese gunboat to see the Army. When my friend landed he was received by the Inspector-General of Musketry, who was a peacock feather Mandarin, and taken to see the soldiers firing. To my friend's amazement the soldiers were firing at the targets placed only a few hundred yards off, and he explained to the Mandarin that these wonderful rifles fitted with telescopic sights were meant for long ranges, and their accuracy was wonderful. The Mandarin replied to him: " Look here ! my orders from the Viceroy are that every man in the army should hit the target, because these rifles are so wonderfully good, and so they do, and the Viceroy is very pleased at my reports." And he added : " You know, we go back 2,000 years before your people in our knowledge of the world."

Lord Kelvin had a wonderful gift of being able to pursue abstruse investigations in the hubbub of a drawing room full of visitors. He would produce a large green book out of a gamekeeper's pocket he had at the back of his coat, and suddenly go ahead with figures. I had an interesting episode once. Sir William Thomson, as he then was, had come with me for the first voyage of a new big cruiser that I commanded. I had arranged for various responsible persons to report to me at 8 a.m. how various parts of the ship were behaving. One of them reported that a rivet was loose, and there was a slight leak. I said casually : " I wonder how much water would come in if the rivet came out altogether." Sir William was sitting next me at breakfast, very much enjoying eggs and bacon, and he asked the Officer : " How big is the rivet ? " and whereabouts it was, etc. The Officer left, and Sir William went on with his eggs and bacon, and I talked to Sir Nathaniel Barnaby on the other side of me, who was the designer of the ship that we were in. Presently, Sir William, in a mild voice, never having ceased his eggs and bacon, said so much water would come in. Sir N. Barnaby thereupon worked it out on paper and said to Sir William : " You made a good guess." He replied : " I didn't guess. I worked it out."

The Midshipmen idolised Lord Kelvin, and they were

very intimate with him. I heard one of them, who was four-foot-nothing, explain to Sir William how to make a magnet. Sir William listened to the Midshipman's lecture on magnetism with the greatest deference, and gave the little boy no idea of what a little ass he was to be talking to the greatest man on earth on the subject of magnetism. The same little boy took the time for him in observing the lighthouse flashes, and Sir William wrote a splendid letter to *The Times* pointing out that the intervals of darkness should be the exception, and the flashes of light the rule, in a lighthouse, where-upon the Chief Engineer of the Lighthouse Department traversed Sir William's facts. The little boy came up to Sir William and asked him if he had read the letter, and he hadn't, so he told him of it and then asked Sir William if he would like him to write to *The Times* to corroborate him. Sir William thanked him sweetly, but said he would take no notice, as they would alter the flashes, and so they did.

This little boy was splendid. He played me a Machiavellian trick. We had an ass one night as Officer of the Watch, and in the middle watch I was nearly jerked out of my cot by a heavy squall striking the ship. I rushed up on deck (raining torrents) and we got in what was left of the sails, and I came down soaked through and bitterly cold, and on the main deck I met my young friend, the little Midshipman, with a smoking hot bowl of cocoa. I never enjoyed anything more in my life, and I blessed the little boy, but it suddenly occurred to me that he was as dry as a bone. I said : " How is it you

are dressed ? " He said : " I am Midshipman of the
watch." I said : " The devil you are ! How is it you
aren't wet ? " " Well, sir," he said, " I thought I
should be best doing my duty by going below and making
you a bowl of cocoa." I felt I had sold myself, like
Esau, for a mess of pottage. He was a splendid boy,
and he wrote me periodically till he died. He was left
a fortune. He was turned out of the Navy for knocking
his Captain down. I received a telegram to say that
he was ill and delirious and talking of me only, and
almost immediately afterwards a telegram came to say
he was dead.

Sir Nathaniel Barnaby, the eminent Director of Naval
Construction at the Admiralty, was also a great man,
but he never had recognition. He was not self-assertive.
He was as meek as Moses, and he was a saint. It was
he conceived the wonder of the time—the " Inflexible " ;
and I was her first Captain. He went out in her with
me to the Mediterranean. We had an awful gale in
the Bay of Biscay. Sir Nathaniel nearly died with sea-
sickness. I was cheering him up, and he whispered in
reply : " Fools build houses for wise men to live in.
Wise men build ships for fools to go in."

If ever there was a great Christian, he was. After he
retired he devoted his whole life to Sunday schools, not
only in this country, but in America. There was some
great scheme, of which he gave me particulars at the time,
of a vast association of all Sunday schools wherever the
English tongue is spoken. Perhaps it is in being now—
I don't know ; but it was a fine conception that on some

specified day throughout the world every child should join in some hymn and prayer for that great idea of John Bright's—the Commonwealth of Free Nations, all speaking the same grand old English tongue. I was too busy ever to follow that up, as I would have liked to have done, and been his missionary.

A letter which he wrote to me in 1910, and a much earlier note of mine to him, which he enclosed with it, are interesting, and I give them here:

*Letter from Sir Nathaniel Barnaby, K.C.B. (formerly Chief Constructor of the Navy) to Lord Fisher.*

MORAY HOUSE,
LEWISHAM, S.E.
*15th January,* 1910.

MY DEAR ADMIRAL,

I suppose the enclosed brief note must have been written by you to me over a quarter of a century ago. You were meditating " Dreadnoughts " even then and finding in me the opposition on the ground of " the degradation of our other Ironclads " through the introduction of the " 18-knot ' Nonsuch.' "

I have said to you before that I love a man who knows his own mind, and insists on getting his way. I have therefore no complaint to make.

In a note dated two days earlier I see you say, " Bother the money ! if we are all agreed that will be forthcoming."

And they accuse you of cheeseparing and starving the Navy !

It was I that stood for economy—see enclosed, on the principal events affecting and indicating Naval Policy, 1866–1884, drawn up by me for Mr. Campbell-Bannerman.

256

SIR JOHN FISHER AT THE HAGUE PEACE CONFERENCE,
MAY, 1899.

# SOME PERSONALITIES

See also the other side of me in a letter to the Peace Society People, and see a little hymn written for children to " Russian National Anthem " and now widely sung.

With sincere respect and good wishes,

Yours always,

(Signed)     NATHANIEL BARNABY.

Please return your note to me ; nothing else.

This was the old letter of mine which he enclosed :—

*From Lord Fisher to Sir N. Burnaby in* 1883.

*January 25th.*

I have delayed sending you this letter hoping to find copy of a brief article I wrote on H.M. Ironclad " Nonsuch " of 18 knots, after seeing your design A ; I can't find it, and have written for the original, which I will send for your amusement.    I don't think your argument is a sound one as to the " degradation of our other ironclads by the construction of an 18-knotter." Isn't the principle right to make each succeeding iron-clad an improvement and as perfect as you can ?

THERE IS NO PROGRESS IN UNIFORMITY ! !

We've had enough of the " Admiral " class of ship.    Now try your hand on a " Nonsuch " (of vast speed !).

In violent haste,

Ever yours,

(Sgd.)     J. A. F.

" Build few, and build fast,
Each one better than the last."

Two of Sir Nathaniel Barnaby's great successors in that arduous and always thankless post of Director of Naval Construction are Sir Philip Watts and Sir Eustace

Tennyson-D'Eyncourt. These two great men have each of them done such service as should have brought them far greater honour than as yet they have received. The " Dreadnought " could not have been born but for Sir Philip Watts. I commend to all who wish to have a succinct account of the ships of the British Navy that formed the line of battle on the outbreak of war on the 4th August, 1914, to read the paper delivered by Sir Philip Watts at the Spring Meeting of the Naval Architects on the 9th April, 1919, when a very excellent Sea Officer with more brains than most people I have met presided—being the Marquis of Bristol. And it was a great delight to me that he commanded the " Renown," my favourite ship, to bring to England King Alfonso—an equally admired hero of mine. If ever there was a brave man it is King Alfonso.

My other scientific hero besides Sir Philip Watts is Sir Eustace D'Eyncourt. He also was the practical means, besides his wonderful professional genius, of bringing forth what are known as the " Hush Hush " ships on account of the mystery surrounding their construction ; and notwithstanding the armchair " Know-alls " who have done their best to blast their reputation, they achieved—the five of them—a phenomenal success. Sir Eustace D'Eyncourt also gave us those incomparable Monitors, with their bulges under water, which were " given away " through the unmitigated folly of the Censors, who permitted a newspaper correspondent to describe how he had seen men, like St. Peter, walking on the water—they were walking on the protuberance which extended under the surface as the absolute protection against submarines; and when an old first-class cruiser called the " Grafton " had been so made submarine-proof, the captain of her, after receiving a torpedo fired at him at right angles and hitting him amidships, reported to the Admiralty that she went faster than before, simply because her hull proper had not been touched; the submarine had only blown away the submarine obstruction that Sir Eustace had fitted to her. Has he been made a lord ? Personally I should say the tanks could never have existed without him ; of that I am quite sure. Sir Philip Watts and Sir Eustace D'Eyncourt are enshrined in my heart.

Previously in this chapter I mentioned Mr. Gladstone. I sat next to him at dinner once. At the other side of him was a very beautiful woman, but she was struck dumb by awe of Mr. Gladstone, so he turned round to me and asked me if I had ever been in China. Yes, I had. And he asked me who were the best missionaries. I said the Roman Catholics were the most successful as they wore the Chinese dress, were untrammelled by families, so they got better amongst the people in the interior, but furthermore in their chapels they represented our Saviour and His Apostles with pigtails and dressed as Chinamen. Yes, he said, he remembered that, and he told me the name of the Head of the Roman Catholic Mission, whose name I had forgotten, and said to me that the Pope considered he had gone too far in that respect, and had recalled him. That had happened some twenty years previously, and I had forgotten all about it. Someone

said what a pity that all that is now being said is being
lost. Mr. Gladstone said : " Nothing is lost. Science
will one day take off the walls of this room what we have
been saying." This was years before the gramophone
and the dictaphone and the telephone. He told us a
great deal about Abraham and pigs, and why Abraham
was so dead against them, and how he, Gladstone, had
been driven by Daniel O'Connell in a four-in-hand, and
how the Bishops in his early days were so much handsomer
than now. One Bishop he specially named was called
" The Beauty of Holiness." When he left, he asked me
to walk home with him, which I did. Mrs. Gladstone
said, seated inside the brougham which was waiting at
the door : " Come in, William." He said : " No, I
am going to walk with this young man." It was midnight,
and Piccadilly was quite alive. He was living with Lady
Frederick Cavendish, I think, at Carlton Gardens. We
were nearly run over, as he was regardless of the traffic.
I remember his saying : " Do right, and you can never
suffer for it." I thought of that, when, in my own case
later on, it was " Athanasius contra Mundum." I was
urged only to attack one vested interest at a time, but I
said, " No, if you kick everyone's shins at the same time
they won't trouble about their neighbours," and it
succeeded ; but alas ! I gave up one thing, which was
the real democratic pith and marrow, the Free Education
of the Naval Officer, and a competence from the moment
of entry, and open to all. King Edward said to me about
this : " You're a Socialist." I said that a white shirt
doesn't imply the best brain. We have forty million to

select from, and we restrict our selection to about one-fortieth of the population.

I here relate an episode which made a deep impression on me and one never effaced. At the time of Gladstone's death I was looking at his picture in a shop window. Two working men were doing the same. The one said to the other : " That man died poor, but could have died rich, had he used his knowledge as Prime Minister to make investments quite lawfully ; but he didn't ! "

It really is a very fine thing in the public men of this nation.

I have always worshipped Abraham Lincoln. I have elsewhere related how he never argued with Judge or Jury or anyone else, but always told a story, thus following that great and inestimable example in Holy Writ : " And without a parable spake he not unto them." But one wishes it were more known how great were his simple views. His sole idea of a Christian Church was to preach the Saviour's condensed statement " to love God and your Neighbour ! " He said that summed up all religion. He gloried in having been himself a hired labourer and believed in a system which allowed labourers " to strike " when they wanted to, and did not oblige them to labour whether you pay them or not. He said : " I do not believe in a law to prevent a man getting rich (that would do more harm than good), so while we do not propose any war upon Capital we do wish to allow the humblest an equal chance to get rich with everybody else. I want every man to have a chance to better his condition." And what Lincoln says of diligence is very good :

" The leading rule for the man of every calling is
DILIGENCE ! Whatever piece of business you have
in hand, before stopping do all the labour pertaining to
it which can be done."

That most moving account of Lincoln's simple eloquence at the graves of Gettysburg is a most touching
episode. The thousands listening to him never uttered
a sound. There was a dead silence, when he stopped
speaking. He left thinking himself a failure. It was
the success of his life. A great orator just before him
had moved the multitude to cheer unboundedly ! but
after Lincoln their feelings made them dumb.

While on personalities, I should like to say a little
on one of the best friends I ever had and in my
opinion the greatest of all journalists. Lord Morley
once told me that he had never known the equal of
W. T. Stead in his astounding gift of catching the
popular feeling. He was absolute integrity and he
feared no man. I myself have heard him tackle a Prime
Minister like a terrier a rat. I have known him go to a
packed meeting and scathe the whole mob of them. He
never thought of money ; he only thought of truth. He
might have been a rich man if he hadn't told the truth.
I know it. When he was over sixty he performed a
journalistic feat that was wondrous. By King Edward's
positive orders a cordon was arranged round the battle-
cruiser " Indomitable," arriving late at night at Cowes with
the Prince of Wales on board, to prevent the Press being
a nuisance. Stead, in a small boat, dropped down with
the tide from ahead and swarmed up a rope ladder under

the bows, about 30 feet high and then along a sort of greasy pole, known to sailors as the lower boom, talked to one of the Officers, who naturally supposed he couldn't be there without permission ; and the *Daily Mail* the next morning had the most perfect digest I have ever read of perhaps one of the most wonderful passages ever made. This big battle cruiser encumbered with the heaviest guns known, and with hundreds and hundreds of tons of armour on her side, beat the " Mauretania," the greyhound of the seas, built of gingerbread, carrying no cargo, and shaped for no other purpose than for speed and luxury.

Of course no other paper had a word.

Stead always told me he would die in his boots. Strife was his portion, he said. I am not sure that my friend Arnold White would not have shot him at sight in the Boer War. Stead was a pro-Boer, and so was I. I simply loved Botha, and Botha gave me great words. He said: " English was the business language of the globe "— that's good ! Of course every genius has a strain of queerness. Does not the poet say : " Great wits to madness often are allied ? " I remember a book which had a great circulation, entitled " The Insanity of Genius." I very nearly wrote a letter to *The Times* only I was afraid they might think *me* mad, and I was afraid that Admiral Fitzgerald might not think me modest (see his letter in *The Times* of Sept. 8th, 1919). This was my letter to *The Times* :—

" Genius is not insanity, it only means the man is before his time. That's all."

# MEMORIES

That was the whole of the letter.

There was a very great scientist (he is a very great friend of mine and he discovered something I can't remember the name of) who said : " A man must be mad to think of flying machines ! " and he lived to see them as plentiful as sparrows.

Without saying a word to me or even letting me know, in a few hasty hours Stead wrote in the " Review of Reviews " in February, 1910, the most extraordinarily accurate *résumé* of every date and name connected with my career. It would have taken any other man a month. However, he made one great mistake in it. He only spoke in it, like all other things that have been said of me, of " The full corn in the ear ! " What really is a man's life is the endurance and the adversity and the non-recognition and the humiliating slights and the fighting morning, noon and night, of early life. That brings fortune. I like that word " fortune." Those inspired men who translated the Great Bible never said a thing " happened," they always said it " fortuned."

I here insert a letter kindly lent me by Lord Esher. As it was written on the spur of the moment and out of the abundance of the heart, I give it verbatim. Esher loved Stead as much as I did. I knew it, and that's why I wrote to him. We felt a common affliction :—

*April* 22, 1912.                HOTEL EXCELSIOR, NAPLES.

This loss of dear old Stead numbs me ! Cromwell and Martin Luther rolled into one. And such a big heart. Such great emotions. You must write something.

*All I've read quite inadequate.* The telegrams here say he was to the forefront with the women and children, putting them in the boats ! *I can see him !* and probably singing " Hallelujah," and encouraging the ship's band to play cheerfully. He told me he would die in his boots. So he has. *And a fine death.* As a boy he had threepence a week pocket money. One penny bought Shakespeare in weekly parts, the other two pennies to his God for Missions. And the result was he became editor of a big newspaper at 22 ! And he was a Missionary himself all his life. Fearless even when alone, believing in his God —the God of truth—and his enemies always rued it when they fought him. He was an exploder of " gas- bags " and the terror of liars. He was called a " wild man " because he said " Two keels to one." He was at Berlin—the High Personage said to him : " Don't be frightened ! " Stead replied to the All Highest : " Oh, no ! we won't ! *for every Dreadnought you build we will build two !* " *That* was the genesis of the cry " Two keels to one." I have a note of it made at the time for my " Reflections." But, my dear friend, put your concise pen to paper for our Cromwellian Saint. He deserves it.

Yours always,

FISHER.

" You cannot do anyone more good than by trying unsuccessfully to do him an injury," was one of the aphorisms of Lord Dalling (Sir Henry Bulwer) ; and it occurred to me forcibly on one occasion when I went to stay with my very great friend, Henry Labouchere (the proprietor of *Truth*. On the way I had been reading a peculiarly venomous attack on me in his paper ; and when he greeted me as affectionately as ever, I showed it to him, saying : " Don't put your arm on my shoulder ! Read that damned thing there ! " Labouchere glanced at it and replied, "Where would you have been if I hadn't persistently maligned you?"

When I was with him at his villa at Florence, he used to smoke the most beastly cigarettes at ten a penny, yet he left over a million sterling, and was generous to absurdity to those he loved.

He had none but Italian servants; he told me he was always extremely polite to them for the knife came so easy to them. He said he didn't realise this until, after he had had some words with an English friend, his Italian gardener, who had overheard the altercation, asked Labouchere if he would like him (the gardener) to deal with his friend, and he tapped the stiletto in his waistband.

His own wit was as ready as his gardener's stiletto. On one occasion he was at Cologne railway station, and the Custom House Officer was turning his portmanteau inside out. Labouchere had a telegraph form in his pocket; he wrote out a telegram with a stylographic pen and handed it to the official who was standing behind the Custom House Officer and told him it was a Government telegram. This was the telegram:

PRINCE BISMARCK,
                BERLIN.

Can't dine with you to-night. Missed train through a damned ass of a Custom House Officer. Will let you have his name.

                                LABOUCHERE, Cologne.

They offered him a special train. Labouchere had

never seen Bismarck in his life. This was the occasion
on which Labouchere was reprimanded by the Foreign
Office for his delay in taking up his appointment as attaché
at St. Petersburg. His excuse was that the money
allowed him only permitted his travelling by railway as
far as Cologne ; the rest of the way he walked.

This book would be incomplete if I did not draw
attention to the great debt the nation owes to three men
yet unmentioned in this volume.

Mr. George Lambert, M.P., twice refused office and
sacrificed his political prospects and with a glorious
victory sustained the whole Government effort to kick
him out of Parliament ; but he conquered with a magnificent majority of over two thousand ! Why ?

Because after serving for over seven years in the
Admiralty he could speak of his own knowledge that the
War administration and the fighting Sea Policy were
shamefully effete.

The Recording Angel will mark down opposite Mr.
Lambert's name : " Well done, thou good and faithful
servant ! " But may he also have his reward here and
now, as many years of good work here below may lie
between him and Heaven as yet.

Commodore Hugh Paget Sinclair is another "Stalwart "
of the War. His business was to provide the officers
and men to man the Fleet—imagine the stupendous task
that was his !

*We never wanted for Officer or Man !*

He is now Director of Naval Intelligence ; and may
his ascent in the Navy be what is his splendid due !

Sir Alfred Yarrow I select for mention, for without him Mesopotamia would have been a bigger crime than it was, and throughout all ages it will be branded for gross and culpable and criminal ineptitude. If I was asked to name the Capturer of Bagdad I would unhesitatingly reply it was Sir Alfred Yarrow.

The Navy has not had its due credit for the Capture of Bagdad. If Sir Alfred Yarrow with his usual astounding push, and without regard to red tape or thanks or recognition, had not sent those splendid light-draught gunboats of his to Mesopotamia, packed up in bits like portmanteaux, then Bagdad would not have been ours. The Viceroy of India sent us (acting on the advice he had received) the wrong draught of water. We ignored the Viceroy and all his crew. It took *eighteen* days to get this pressing vital business through the Government Departments concerned. It took us *one* day to accomplish the whole procedure, with Sir Alfred Yarrow, and we chucked all the Departments. So 24 light-draught gunboats grew up like Jonah's Gourd, which came up in a night (Jonah, iv, 10).

I append a memorandum compiled from the Official papers :—

### *History of Provision of 24 Light-draught Gunboats for Mesopotamia.*

*Note.*—These Vessels played a great part in the capture of Bagdad.

January 9th, 1915.—Telegram from Viceroy to India

Office that Admiralty be asked to provide 4 gunboats—draught 4½ feet for Tigris.[1]

January 11th, 1915.—India Office asked Admiralty to meet Viceroy's wishes.

January 29th, 1915.[2]—Admiralty Departments suggested various types. War Staff proposed 3 from Egypt be sent.

January 29th, 1915.—Lord Fisher ordered 24 light-draught gunboats. In order to save time, Captain [now Rear-Admiral Sir S. S.] Hall, R.N., (Lord Fisher's Secretary) was directed by Lord Fisher *to co-operate with Mr. Yarrow*[3] *and carry the operation through without reference to Admiralty Departments or any other Departments.*"

January 29th, 1915.—*Conference held. Design settled.*[4]

January 30th, 1915. ⎧Captain Hall toured the country
February 1st, 1915. ⎨ for likely firms to construct
⎩ the 24 gunboats.

February 2nd, 1915.[5]—Proposals made for placing orders approved by Lord Fisher and First Lord, and orders were placed as follows :—

12 Small by Yarrow.

4 Large by Barclay Curle.

2 Large by Lobnitz.

2 Large by Ailsa Shipbuilding Co.

2 Large by Wood Skinner.

2 Large by Sunderland Shipbuilding Co.

[1] This shows how badly advised the Navy was by the India Office, as *under 3 feet was vital*, and the order was given accordingly.
[2] Eighteen days going through Departments.
[3] Mr. Yarrow had technical charge of the whole business and was the sole designer—and there was no paper work whatever.
[4] All this action on the same day.
[5] All the rest of the required action taken in 4 days.

February 8th, 1915.—Captain Hall was appointed Commodore-in-Charge of the Submarine Service, but was directed by Lord Fisher to continue supervision of the provision of 24 gunboats.

Sir Alfred Yarrow ought (like Mr. Schwab) to have been made a Duke, and I wrote to Sir John Jellicoe, when he was First Sea Lord, and told him so.

The history of the Flotillas of light-draught gunboats built both for Mesopotamia and the Danube will ever be associated with the good service done by Sir Alfred Yarrow, and for which he was only made a Baronet. Those built for the Tigris led our Army to Bagdad and far beyond, and were at times unsupported far ahead of the military force; and without any question whatever without them the Mesopotamian muddle could never have emerged into a glorious victory. The speed with which these vessels were constructed and despatched in small parcels to Mesopotamia and there put together in an extemporary dockyard arranged by Sir Alfred Yarrow's staff was as much a feature as any other part of their production. It necessitated masses of natives of different religious persuasions being gathered together to assist the skilled artizans in bolting the pieces together and launching them on the Tigris. Their differing hours of prayer were a disturbing element in the rapidity of the construction; but my splendid friend the foreman from the Scotstoun Yard of Messrs. Yarrow contrived a prayer compromise. The Danube Flotilla arranged for with a number of other builders was equally remarkable; and Commodore (now Admiral) Bartolomé wrote me a commendatory letter of their good service there.

I must also mention Commodore (now Admiral) Sir S. S. Hall, but for whose continual journeys from shipyard to shipyard these vessels would never have been delivered on the scene of action in the time required.

Within six months all these Flotillas were thought of —designed—built—and in service, and nothing gave me intenser delight than the visit I paid to these craft as they were all built and then taken to pieces for transit to their destination in packages that any motor car could have transported.

The world at large can have little conception of the remarkability of those comparatively large hulls with good speed and practically drawing but a few inches of water—the propellers (which were too large in diameter for the depth of water) being made by an ingenious device to revolve in a well above the water-line, the water being drawn up by suction. I thought to myself as I viewed these miracles of ingenuity and rapidity: "England can never succumb."

# CHAPTER XVI

## THINGS THAT PLEASE ME

" I have culled a Garland of Flowers—
Mine is the string that binds them."

\*　　　\*　　　\*

Thou shalt not kill, but needst not strive
Officiously to keep alive !
(When catching Submarines).

\*　　　\*　　　\*

Seest thou a man diligent in business—he shall stand
before Kings—he shall not stand before mean men.

\*　　　\*　　　\*

God who cannot be unjust,
Heedeth all who on Him trust.
Them who call on Him for aid,
Anguish shall not make afraid.
Trust him then in life.　In death
He can give thee Living Breath !
After death the Life now thine
He can make the Life Divine.

\*　　　\*　　　\*

I never bother to bother about anyone who doesn't
bother to bother about me !

\*　　　\*　　　\*

COMMANDER-IN-CHIEF OF THE MEDITERRANEAN FLEET, 1899–1902.

## THINGS THAT PLEASE ME

"Put on the impenetrable armour of contempt and fortitude."

\* \* \*

When danger threatens and the foeman nigh,
" *God and our Navy !* " is the Nation's cry.
*But*, the danger over and the Country righted,
God is forgotten and the Sailor slighted.

\* \* \*

Never fight a Chimney Sweep; some of the soot comes off on you.

\* \* \*

Pas de Culte sans mystère.

\* \* \*

Ode to an Apple—

Newton saw an apple fall,
Eve an apple did enthral ;
It played the devil with us all,
The Devil making Eve to fall.

\* \* \*

" Liberty of Conscience " means doing wrong but not worrying about it afterwards.

\* \* \*

" Tact " is insulting a man without his knowing it.

\* \* \*

Even a man's faults may reflect his virtues.

\* \* \*

Sincerity is the road to Heaven.

\* \* \*

I thought it would be a good thing to be a missionary, but I thought it would be better to be First Sea Lord.

\* \* \*

# MEMORIES

Think in Oceans—shoot at sight.

\* \* \*

Big conceptions and Quick Decisions.

\* \* \*

Napoleonic in Audacity.
Cromwellian in Thoroughness.
Nelsonic in Execution.

\* \* \*

" Surprise " the pith and marrow of war !

\* \* \*

Audacity and Imagination beget surprise.

\* \* \*

Rashness in war is Prudence.

\* \* \*

Prudence in war is Imbecility.

\* \* \*

Hit first ! Hit hard ! Keep on hitting ! ! (The 3 H's).

\* \* \*

The 3 Requisites for Success—Ruthless, Relentless,
Remorseless (The 3 R's).

\* \* \*

BUSINESS—Call on a Business man in Business hours
only on Business. Transact your Business and go about
your Business, in order to give him time to finish his
Business, and you time to mind your own Business.
[I had this printed on cards, one of which was handed
to every caller on me at the Admiralty.]

\* \* \*

# THINGS THAT PLEASE ME

The Nelsonic Attributes—

- (*a*)  Self Reliance.
- (*b*)  Power of Initiative.
- (*c*)  Fearlessness of Responsibility.
- (*d*)  Fertility of Resource.

\* \* \*

Originality never yet led to Preferment.

\* \* \*

Mediocrity is the Road to Honour.

\* \* \*

Repetition is the Soul of Journalism.

\* \* \*

No difficulty baffles great zeal.

\* \* \*

The Pavement of Life is strewn with Orange Peel.

\* \* \*

Inconsistency is the bugbear of Silly Asses.

\* \* \*

Never Deny: Never Explain: Never Apologise.

\* \* \*

> " To defy Power that seems omnipotent . . .
> Never to change, nor falter, nor repent."
> 
> (SHELLEY.)

\* \* \*

Cardinal Rampolla got his Hat at a younger age than any preceding Cardinal. Asked to account for his phenomenal success, he replied :—It's due to 3 things :

I never { asked for / refused / resigned } anything.

\* \* \*

# MEMORIES

The best scale for an experiment is 12 inches to a foot.

\*     \*     \*

Dread Nought is over 80 times in the Bible (" Fear Not "). So I took as my motto " Fear God and Dread Nought."

\*     \*     \*

Moltke wrote as follows :

" A clever military leader will succeed in many cases in choosing defensive positions of such an offensive nature from a strategic point of view that the opponent is compelled to attack us in them."

\*     \*     \*

In looking through a packet of ancient papers I find some youthful thoughts of my own and some others which evidently I thought very choice.

" Anything said before a lecture muddles it."
" Anything after weakens it ! "

\*     \*     \*

" There is nothing you can't have if you want it enough."

\*     \*     \*

The following extract is from Blake :

> " He who bends to himself a joy,
> Does the winged life destroy ;
> But he who kisses the joy as it flies
> Lives in Eternity's Sunrise."

\*     \*     \*

Dean Swift satirized the vulgar exclusiveness of those

276

who desired the infinite meadows of Heaven only to be frequented by the religious sect they adorned on earth :

> " We are God's chosen few !
> All others will be damned !
> There is no place in Heaven for you,
> We can't have Heaven crammed ! "

* * *

Lord Dalling (Sir Henry Bulwer) codified his life in axioms and phrases. His intimate friend, Sir Drummond Wolff, says so. (By the way, Wolff's father was a marvellous Bible scholar. I heard him preach the sermon of my life : it was extempore, on " The Resurrection." A great friend of his told me that Wolff did really know the Bible by heart.) These are Lord Dalling's sayings ; he quotes Talleyrand for one of his rules of life :

" Acknowledge the receipt of a book from the author at once : this relieves you of the necessity of saying whether you have read it."

Again this is excellent :

" You cannot do anyone more good than by trying unsuccessfully to do him an injury." (Mr. Labouchere gave me the same reason for attacking me in his paper *Truth*.)

" Nothing is so foolish as to be wise out of season."

" The best trait in a man's character is an anxiety to serve those who have obliged him once and can do so no more."

* * *

Nelson's Ipsissima Verba.

" Do not imagine I am one of those hot-brained people who fight at an immense disadvantage without an adequate object . . . in a week's time I shall get

277

reinforcements and the enemy will get none, and then I must annihilate him."

It was not "Victory" that Nelson ever desired. It was "Annihilation!"

＊　　　＊　　　＊

Moses, Gideon and Cromwell.

Moses and Gideon were each of them summoned straight from their simple daily task to go and help their fellow countrymen, and both were able to perform the task allotted to them in spite of their first great doubts of their fitness for the work. The figure of Moses looms through the Ages as gigantic as the Pyramids, and nearer home and in a lesser sphere stands our English Cromwell, the Great Protector!

"I would have been glad," said Cromwell, "to have lived on my woodside or kept a flock of sheep rather than have undertaken a government like this." And yet in the end he had undertaken it because he said he "had hoped he might prevent some imminent evil."

＊　　　＊　　　＊

Suffragettes.

The nine Muses were all women.

The three Graces were all women.

＊　　　＊　　　＊

A great philosopher has stated that a woman can be classed under two categories:

1. A mother, a mistress and a friend; or,

2. A comrade and queen and child.

A woman is really rooted in physical reality, and all

278

the above six attributes of the philosopher always live in her.

Thus the Song of Solomon produced a passionate commodity, but it required the Mary Magdalene of the Gospel to express the *summum bonum* of a woman of " Greatly Loving."

In the first prayer book of A.D. 1549 there was a Collect for her ! No other woman had a Collect except the Virgin Mary.

Emotion, self-surrender, selflessness, immortal courage, wondrous physical beauty ! Mary Magdalene was a great human reality. It is quite obvious she was no debauchee or her Beauty would have failed, nor could she have been a " hardened " sinner or she would have scoffed !

What was her history ? What caused her lapse ? Who was her Betrayer ?

" Her sins, which are many, are forgiven ; for she loved much. Verily I say unto you, Wheresoever this Gospel shall be preached in the whole world, there shall also this, that this woman hath done, be told for a memorial of her."

And is it not very striking that St. Peter, who dictated St. Mark's Gospel, records in the 16th chapter, verse 9, of St. Mark, that the first person in the world to whom the Saviour showed Himself after His Resurrection was Mary Magdalene ?

" Now when Jesus was risen early the first day of the week, He appeared *first* to Mary Magdalene, out of whom he had cast seven devils. And she went and told

279

MEMORIES

them that had been with Him as they mourned and
wept. And they, when they heard that He was alive
and had been seen of her, believed not."

* * *

A Sun-Dial that I Love.
    Que Dieu éclaire les heures que je perds.
    (May God light up the hours that I fail to light.)

* * *

      Though hidden yet from all our eyes,
      He sees the Gideon who shall rise
      To save us and His sword.

# `EPILOGUE

## MOUNT PISGAH

IT is stated that the historian, Lecky, O.M. (I assisted at the operation of his receiving the Order of Merit) gave more thought and time to the book of his last years, " The Map of Life," than to any other of all his works, and it is said that for three years he kept on revising the last of its chapters.

The book was derided to me by a literary friend of great eminence as being " The Pap of Life ! "  I read its last chapters with great avidity.  If for nothing else, the book is worthy of immortality for the reason that it so emphasises those great words of Dryden as being appropriate to the close of a busied life—

> " Not Heaven itself upon the past has Power,
>     What has been has been, and I have had my hour."

Whenever (as I often do) I pass Dryden's bust in Westminster Abbey I invariably thank him for those lines.

Mr. Lecky urges his readers to leave the active scenes of life in good time and not to " Lag superfluous on the

MEMORIES

Stage " (I believe Mr. Gladstone recommended this also, but didn't do it !).

To illustrate Mr. Lecky we have that great and splendid Trio of Translation to Heaven at the very zenith of their powers. Elijah was hurrying along (that great, hairy, weird old man) so that Elisha could hardly keep pace with him, and he is suddenly caught up in a Chariot of Fire to Heaven ! I ask, " Was not Nelson's leaving this earth quite a similar glorious departure ? "

> " Partial firing continued until 4.30 p.m. when a victory having been reported to Admiral Lord Viscount Nelson, K.B., and Commander-in-Chief, he THEN died of his Wound."

Moses (with whom I am now more particularly concerned) also left this life in a similar glorious way, for God was his companion when his Spirit left this Earth, and it markedly is recorded of Moses that—

> " His eye was not dim,
> Nor his natural force abated ! "

Mr. Lecky doesn't quote my three men above. I consider them superior to Noah, Daniel and Job, who are the three named in Scripture as being so dear to the pious man. Ezekiel, chapter xiv., verse 14.

I reiterate that the advice of the derided Lecky seems to me excellent, to leave active life at one's zenith, and thus anticipate senility.

The Archbishop of Seville is a lovely story by Cervantes. All Spain came to hear him preach. Indeed he had to preach every day, the crowds were so great, and he said to his faithful Secretary: "Tell me when you notice me waning, for a man never knows it himself." The Secretary did so, and the Archbishop gave him the sack! Yes! The Archbishop had passed the Rubicon, and this dismissal was the proof. Having this fear, I left Office on my birthday in 1910, though for a few short months in 1914 I enjoyed the " dusky hues of glorious war," and exceedingly delighted myself in those seven months in arranging a new Armada against Germany of 612 vessels, and in sending Admiral von Spee and all his ships to the bottom of the sea.

The following much-prized lines were sent me on the Annihilation of Admiral von Spee's Squadron off the Falkland Islands on December 8th, 1914. He had sunk Admiral Cradock's Squadron five weeks before. The " Dreadnought " Battle Cruisers, " Inflexible " and " Invincible," sent to sink von Spee, made a passage of 14,000 miles without a hitch and arrived just a few hours before von Spee. It was a timely arrangement :—

From the President of Magdalen College, Oxford, Sir Herbert Warren (Professor of Poetry).

Merserat Ex-spe Spem, rediit spes, mergitur Ex-spes.

" Von Spee sent the 'Good Hope' to the bottom : hope revived ; he is sunk himself, without hope."

From Mr. Godley, the Public Orator at Oxford University.

Hoc tibi Piscator Patria debet opus.

" Your country owes this exploit to you, O Fisher ! "

# MEMORIES

But that Great Providence, that shapes our course, rough hew it how we will, ordained my departure from the conduct of the War. Amongst the masses of regretful letters at my departure I choose one from an Admiral then 88 years old, who satisfies the great Dr. Weir Mitchell's dictum of the clear brain becoming clearer with age. This Admiral annexed a Continent for England, abounding in riches in New Guinea; but he got no thanks; and England gave away his gift. But his name lives there. I conclude with his letter :—

DEAR OLD FISHER,

It is marvellous how all variations of our lives are unravelled by Divine Inspiration that cannot err.
" No one can ' hustle ' Providence."
(That's one of your sayings !)
Think of Moses !

" He was the truest warrior that ever buckled sword.
He the most gifted Poet that ever breathed a word :
And never Earth's Philosopher traced with his golden pen,
On the Deathless Page, truths half so sage as he wrote down for
    men ;
Yet no man knows his sepulchre, and no man saw it e'er,
For the Angels of God up-turned the sod and laid the Dead Man
    there."

Moses saved his people. He prepared them for the conquest in which he was to take no part. He was the meekest man on earth, yet he could be the most ruthless !
· Doubtless you saved England at the Falkland Islands.
Doubtless you prepared our Fleet for this war !
(Nothing to boast of ! You the clay in the hands of the Potter !) And it seems likely that some Joshua will

284

# EPILOGUE

reap what you have sown! Yet history will put it right.

"O lonely grave in Moab's land!   O dark Beth-Peor's hill!
Speak to these curious hearts of ours and teach them to be still!

Ever faithfully yours,

(Signed) J. MORESBY.

# INDEX

.

# INDEX

## A

Abdul Hamid, 55 ; the Pope and, 91 *et seq.*, 204, 205

Aboukir Bay, French Fleet in, 161

Adalbert, Prince, 230

Adams, John, editor of " The New Teaching," 251 *n.*

Admiralty clerks and the Naval War Staff, 102 *et seq.*

Aircraft, 124 *et seq.*

Alcester, Lord, 140

Alexandra, Queen, 12, 20, 198, 238

Alfonso, King, 237–238, 258

Americans, 221 *et seq.*

Anderson, Mr. J. W. S., 111

Angell, Mr. Norman, 126, 211

Arbuthnot, Sir R., 60

Arnold-Forster, Rt. Hon. H. O., 169–171, 179

Asquith, Rt. Hon. H. H., 42, 50, 58, 59, 70, 74, 196, 199

## B

Bacon, Admiral Sir Reginald, 104, 128

Baddeley, Mr. V W., 111

Balfour, Rt. Hon. A. J., 36, 64, 82, 182, 210

Barnaby, Sir Nathaniel, 253, 255 ; letter to Lord Fisher, 256–257

Barnardo, Dr., 160

Bartolomé, Admiral Sir Charles de, 104, 270

Battenberg, Prince Louis of, 168

Beatty, Lord, 37, 40, 121

Beilby, Sir George, 116

Beit, Mr., 4, 33, 34, 182

Benbow, Admiral, 163

Bernstorff, Count von, 210

Bieberstein, Marschall von, 204, 205

Birdwood, General Sir William R., 82

Bismarck, Prince, 229

" Blücher," sinking of the, 149–150

Booth, General, 160

Borden, Rt. Hon. Sir R. L., 218

Botha, General, 136, 263

Boys, Admiral, 168

Bridgeman, Admiral Sir Francis, 246, 247

Bridgman, Mr., 92

Bright, John, 23, 100, 223, 225–227, 256

# INDEX

# INDEX

# INDEX

# INDEX

# INDEX

# INDEX

PRINTED IN GREAT BRITAIN BY
RICHARD CLAY AND SONS, LIMITED,
BRUNSWICK STREET, STAMFORD STREET, S.E. I,
AND BUNGAY, SUFFOLK.

*Photo J. Russell and Sons.*

1882.   CAPTAIN OF H.M.S. "INFLEXIBLE."

# RECORDS

BY
ADMIRAL OF THE FLEET
## LORD FISHER,

HODDER AND STOUGHTON
LONDON     NEW YORK     TORONTO
MCMXIX

JOHN

# *Preamble*

THE main purpose of this second book is obvious from its title. It's mostly a collection of "Records" confirming what has already been written, and relates almost exclusively to years after 1902. As Lord Rosebery has said so well, "The war period in a man's life has its definite limits"; and that period is what interests the general reader, and for that reason all attempt at a biography has been discarded.

In our present distress we

certainly want badly just now Nelson's "Light from Heaven"! Nelson had what the Mystics describe as his "seasons of darkness and desertion." His enfeebled body and his mind depressed used at times to cast a shade on his soul, such as we now feel as a Nation, but (if I remember right) it is Southey who says that the Sunshine which succeeded led Nelson to believe that it bore with it a prophetic glory, and that the light that led him on was "Light from Heaven." We don't see that "Light" as yet. But England never succumbs.

# PREFACE

NAPOLEON at St. Helena told us what all Englishmen have ever instinctively felt—that we should remain a purely Maritime Power; instead, we became in this War a Conscript Nation, sending Armies of Millions to the Continent. If we stuck to the Sea, said Napoleon, we could dictate to the World; so we could. Napoleon again said to the Captain of the British Battleship " Bellerophon " : " Had it not been for you English, I should have been Emperor of the East, but wherever there was water to float a ship, we were sure to find you in the way." (Yes ! we had ships only drawing two feet of water with six-inch guns, that went up the Tigris and won Bagdad. Others, similar, went so many thousand miles up the Yangtsze River in China that they sighted the Mountains of Thibet. Another British Ship of War so many thousand miles up the Amazon River that she sighted the Mountains of Peru, and there not being room to turn she came back stern first. In none of these cases had any War Vessel ever before been seen till these British Vessels investigated those waters and astounded the inhabitants.)

# PREFACE

Again, Napoleon praised our Blockades (Les Anglais bloquent très bien) ; but very justly of our Diplomacy he thought but ill. Yes, alas ! What a Diplomacy it has been ! ! ! If our Blockade had been permitted by the Diplomats to have been effective, it would have finished the War at once. Our Diplomats had Bulgaria in their hands and lost her. It was " Too Late " a year after to offer her the same terms as she had asked the year before. We " kow-towed " to the French when they rebuffed our request for the English Army to be on the Sea Flank and to advance along the Belgian Coast, supported by the British Fleet ; and then there would have been no German Submarine War. At the very beginning of the War we deceived the German Ambassador in London and the German Nation by our vacillating Diplomacy. We wrecked the Russian Revolution and turned it into Bolshevism.

I mention these matters to prove the effete, apathetic, indecisive, vacillating Conduct of the War—the War eventually being won by an effective Blockade.

# CONTENTS

## CHAPTER I

## CHAPTER II

## CHAPTER III

## CHAPTER IV

## CHAPTER V

## CHAPTER VI

ix

# CONTENTS

# CONTENTS

## CHAPTER XV

# LIST OF ILLUSTRATIONS

# LIST OF ILLUSTRATIONS

# RECORDS

# RECORDS

## CHAPTER I

### EARLY YEARS

OF all the curious fables I've ever come across I quite think the idea that my mother was a Cingalese Princess of exalted rank is the oddest !   One can't see the foundation of it !

" The baseless fabric of a vision ! "

My godfather, Major Thurlow (of the 90th Foot), was the " best man " at my mother's wedding, and very full of her beauty then—she was very young—possibly it was the " Beauté du diable ! "   She had just emerged from the City of London, where she was born and had spent her life !   One grandfather had been an officer under Nelson at Trafalgar, and the other a Lord Mayor ! He was Boydell, the very celebrated engraver.  He left his fortune to my grandmother, but an alien speculator (a scoundrel) robbed her of it.  My mother's father had, I believe, some vineyards in Portugal, of which the wine pleased William the Fourth, who, I was told, came to his counting house at 149, New Bond Street, to taste it !   Next door Emma, Lady Hamilton, used to clean the door steps !   She was housemaid there.

I                    B

I don't think the Fishers at all enjoyed my father (who was a Captain in the 78th Highlanders) marrying into the Lambes! The " City " was abhorred in those days, and the Fishers thought of the tombs of the Fishers in Packington Church, Warwickshire, going back to the dark ages! I, myself, possess the portrait of Sir Clement Fisher, who married Jane Lane, who assisted Charles the Second to escape by disguising his Majesty as her groom and riding behind him on a pillion to Bristol.

The Fishers' Baronetcy lapsed, as my ancestor after Sir Clement Fisher's death wouldn't pay £500 in the nature of fees, I believe. I don't think he had the money—so my uncle told me. This uncle, by name John Fisher, was over 60 years a fellow of Magdalen College, Oxford, and told me the story of an ancestor who built a wing of Balliol at Oxford, and they—the College Authorities—asked him whether they might place some inscription in his honour on the building! He replied :

" Fisher—non amplius,"

(but someone else told me it was :—

" Verbum non amplius Fisher ! ")

My uncle explained that his ancestor only meant just to put his name, and that's all.

But the College Authorities put it all on :

" *Fisher !* Not another blessed word is wanted."

One of my ancestors changed his motto and took these words (I have them on a watch !) :—

" Ubi voluntas—ibi piscatur."
(We fish where we like).

2

A Poacher, I suppose! or was there a " double entendre " ?

I'm told in the old days you could change your motto and your crest as often as you liked, but not your coat of arms !

A succession of ancestors went and dwelt at Bodmin, in Cornwall—all clergymen down to my grandfather, who was Rector of Wavendon, in Bucks, where is a tablet to his brother, who was killed close to the Duke of Wellington at Waterloo, and who ordered his watch to be sent to my uncle's relatives with the dent of the bullet that killed him, and that watch I now have.

My uncle was telling this story at a *table d'hôte* at Brussels a great many years afterwards, and said he had been unable to identify the spot, when an old white-haired gentleman at the table said he had helped to bury him, and next day he took him to the place.

I remember a Dean glancing at me in a Sermon on the Apostles, when he said the first four were all Fishers !

On the death of Sir Robert Fisher of Packington in 1739, a number of family portraits were transferred apparently to the Rev. John Fisher of Bodmin, born January 27th, 1708. The three principal portraits are a previous Sir Robert Fisher, his son Sir Clement Fisher, who died 1683, and Jane Lane, his wife. Another portrait is a second Sir Clement Fisher, son of the above and of Jane Lane. This Sir Clement Fisher died 1709, and was succeeded by his only brother, Sir Robert Fisher, who died A.D. 1739, one year before his niece, Mary Fisher, wife of Lord Aylesford. All these portraits were

B 2

transmitted in direct inheritance to Sir John Fisher. The four generations of Reverend John Fishers of Bodmin, commencing with John Fisher born 1708, were none of them in a position to incur the heavy expenses involved for their assumption of the Baronetcy. They were descended from a brother of the Sir Robert Fisher who lived before the year A.D. 1600.

I was born in 1841, the same year as King Edward VII. There was never such a healthy couple as my father and mother. They never married for money—they married for love. They married very young, and I was their first child. All the physical advantages were in my favour, so I consider I was absolutely right, when I was nine months old, in refusing to be weaned.

> " She walks in beauty like the night
> Of cloudless climes and starry skies ;
> And all that's best of dark and bright
> Meets in her aspect and her eyes :
> Thus mellow'd to that tender light
> Which heaven to gaudy day denies."

These lines were written by Lord Byron of my god-mother, Lady Wilmot Horton, of Catton Hall, Burton-on-Trent. She was still a very beautiful old lady at 73 years of age when she died.

One of her great friends was Admiral Sir William Parker (the last of Nelson's Captains), and he, at her request, gave me his nomination for entering the Navy. He had two to give away on becoming Port Admiral at Plymouth. He gave the other to Lord Nelson's own niece, and she also filled in my name, so I was doubly nominated by the last of Nelson's Captains, and my first

ship was the " Victory " and it was my last ! In the
" Victory " log-book it is entered, " July 12th, 1854,
joined Mr. John Arbuthnot Fisher," and it is also entered that Sir John Fisher hauled down his flag on October
21st, 1904, on becoming First Sea Lord.

A friend of mine (a yellow Admiral) was taken
prisoner in the old French War when he was a Midshipman ten years old, and was locked up in the fortress of
Verdun. He so amused me in my young days by telling
me that he gave his parole not to escape ! as if it mattered
what he did when he was only four foot nothing ! And he
did this, he told me, in order to learn French ; and when
he had learned French, to talk it fluently, he then cancelled his parole and was locked up again and then he
escaped ; alone he did it by filing through the iron bars of
his prison window (the old historic method), and wended
his way to England. I consider this instance a striking
testimony to the inestimable benefit of sending little boys
to sea when they are young ! What splendid Nelsonic
qualities were developed !

But it was quite common in those days of my old yellow
Admiral for boys to go to sea even as young as seven
years old. My present host's grandfather went to sea as
a Midshipman at seven years old ! Afterwards he was
Lord Nelson's Signal Midshipman, his name was Hamilton, and his grandson was Midshipman with me in two
ships. He is now the 13th Duke of Hamilton ! It is
interesting as a Nelsonic legend that the wife of the 6th
Duke of Hamilton (she was one of the beautiful Miss
Gunnings ; she was the wife of two Dukes and the

5

# RECORDS

mother of four) peculiarly befriended Emma, Lady Hamilton, and recognised her, as so few did then (and, alas! still fewer now, as one of the noblest women who ever lived—one mass of sympathy she was!

The stories of what boys went through then at sea were appalling. I have a corroboration in lovely letters from a little Midshipman who was in the great blockade of Brest by Admiral Cornwallis in 1802. This little boy was afterwards killed just after Trafalgar. He describes seeing the body of Nelson on board ship on its way to Portsmouth. This little Midshipman was only eleven years old when he was killed! This is how he describes the Midshipman's food: "We live on beef which has been ten or eleven years in a cask, and on biscuit which makes your throat cold in eating it owing to the maggots, which are very cold when you eat them! like calves-foot jelly or blomonge—being very fat indeed!" (It makes one shudder!) He goes on again: "We drink water the colour of the bark of a pear tree with plenty of little maggots and weevils in it, and wine, which is exactly like bullock's blood and sawdust mixed together"; and he adds in his letter to his mother: "I hope I shall not learn to swear, and by God's assistance I hope I shall not!" He tried to save the Captain of his Top (who had been at the "Weather earing") from falling from aloft. This is his description: "The hands were hurried up to reef topsails, and my station is in the foretop. When the men began to lay in from the yards (after reefing the topsails) one of them laid hold of a slack rope, which gave way, and he fell out of the top on deck and was dashed to pieces

6

and very near carried me out of the top along with him as I was attempting to lay hold of him to save him ! ! ! " Our little friend the Midshipman was eight years old at this time ! What a picture ! this little boy trying to save the sailor huge and hairy ! His description to his mother of Cornwallis's Fleet is interesting : " We have on board Admiral Graves, who came in his ten-oared barge, and as soon as he put his foot on shipboard the drums and fifes began to play, and the Marines and all presented their arms. We are all prepared for action, all our guns being loaded with double shot. We have a fine sight, which is the Grand Channel Fleet, which consists of 95 sail of the line, each from 120 down to 64 guns."

That is the Midshipman of the olden day, and one often has misgivings that the modern system of sending boys to sea much older is a bad one, when such magnificent results were produced by the old method, more especially as in the former days the Captain had a more paternal charge of those little boys coming on board one by one, as compared with the present crowd sent in batches of big hulking giants, some of them. However, there is more to learn now than formerly, and possibly it's impossible (all the entrance examination I had to pass was to write out the Lord's Prayer, do a rule of three sum and drink a glass of sherry !) ; but one would like to give it a trial of sending boys to sea at nine years old. Our little hero tried to save the life of the Captain of his Top when he was only eight years old ! Still, the Osborne system of Naval education has its great merits ; but it has been a grievous blow to it, departing from the original conception of entry at eleven years of age.

However, the lines of the modern Midshipman are laid in pleasant places ; they get good food and a good night's rest.   Late as I came to sea in 1854, I had to keep either the First or Middle Watch every night and was always hungry !   Devilled Pork rind was a luxury, and a Spanish Onion with a Sardine in the Middle Watch was Paradise !

In the first ship I was in we not only carried our fresh water in casks, but we had some rare old Ship's Biscuit supplied in what were known as " bread-bags." These bread-bags were not preservative ; they were creative. A favourite amusement was to put a bit of this biscuit on the table and see how soon all of it would walk away. In fact one midshipman could gamble away his " tot " of rum with another midshipman by pitting one bit of biscuit against another. Anyhow, whenever you took a bit of biscuit to eat it you always tapped it edgeways on the table to let the " grown-ups " get away.

The Water was nearly as bad as the Biscuit.   It was turgid—it was smelly—it was animally.   I remember so well, in the Russian War (1854-5), being sent with the Watering Party to the Island of Nargen to get fresh water, as we were running short of it in this old Sailing Line of Battleship I was in (there was no Distilling Apparatus in those days).   My youthful astonishment was how on earth the Lieutenant in charge of the Watering Party discovered the Water.   There wasn't a lake and there wasn't a stream, but he went and dug a hole and there was the water !   However, it may be that he carried out

8

the same delightful plan as my delicious old Admiral in China. This Admiral's survey of the China Seas is one of the most celebrated on record. He told me himself that this is how he did it. He used to anchor in some convenient place every few miles right up the Coast of China. He had a Chinese Interpreter on board. He sent this man to every Fishing Village and offered a dollar for every rock and shoal. No rock or shoal has ever been discovered since my beloved Admiral finished his survey. Perhaps the Lieutenant of the Watering Party gave Roubles !

I must mention here an instance of the Simple Genius of the Chinese. A sunken ship, that had defied all European efforts to raise her, was bought by a Chinaman for a mere song. He went and hired all the Chinamen from an adjacent Sponge Fishery and bought up several Bamboo Plantations where the bamboos were growing like grass. The way they catch sponges is this—The Chinaman has no diving dress—he holds his nose—a leaden weight attached to his feet takes him down to where the sponges are— he picks the sponges—evades the weight—and rises. They pull up the weight with a bit of string afterwards. The Chinese genius I speak of sent the men down with bamboos, and they stuck them into the sunk ship, and soon "up she came "; and the Chinaman said :

> " Ship hab Bamboo—
> No hab Water ! "

It's a pity there's no bamboo dodge for Sunk Reputations !

An uncle of mine had a snuff box made out of the Salt Beef, and it was french-polished! That was his beef —and ours was nearly as hard.

There were many brutalities when I first entered the Navy—now mercifully no more. For instance, the day I joined as a little boy I saw eight men flogged—and I fainted at the sight.

Not long ago I was sitting at luncheon next to a distinguished author, who told me I was " a very interesting person ! " and wanted to know what my idea of life was, I replied that what made a life was not its mature years but the early portions when the seed was sown and the blossom so often blasted by the frost of unrecognition. It was then that the fruit of after years was pruned to something near the mark of success. " Your great career was when you were young," said a dear friend to me the other day. I entered the Navy penniless, friendless and forlorn. While my mess-mates were having jam, I had to go without. While their stomachs were full, mine was often empty. I have always had to fight like hell, and fighting like hell has made me what I am. Hunger and thirst are the way to Heaven !

When I joined the Navy, in 1854, the last of Nelson's Captains was the Admiral at Plymouth. The chief object in those days seemed to be, not to keep your vessel efficient for fighting, but to keep the deck as white as snow and all the ropes taut. We Midshipmen were allowed only a basin of water to wash in, and the basin was inside one's sea-chest ; and if anyone spilt a drop of water on the deck he was made to holy-stone it himself.

And that reminds me, as I once told Lord Esher, when I was a young First Lieutenant, the First Sea Lord told me that *he* never washed when he went to sea, and he didn't see " why the Devil the Midshipmen should want to wash now ! " I remember one Captain named Lethbridge who had a passion for spotless decks ; and it used to put him in a good temper for the whole day if he could discover a " swab-tail," or fragment of the swabs with which the deck was cleaned, left about. One day he happened to catch sight of a Midshipman carefully arranging a few swab-tails on deck in order to gratify " old Leather-breeches' " lust for discovering them ! And as for taut ropes, many of my readers will remember the old story of the lady (on the North American station) who congratulated the Captain of a " family " ship (officered by a set of fools) because " the ropes hung in such beautiful festoons ! "

There was a fiddler to every ship, and when the anchor was being weighed, he used to sit on the capstan and play, so as to keep the men in step and in good heart. And on Sundays, everyone being in full dress, epaulettes and all, the fiddler walked round the decks playing in front of the Captain. I must add this happened in a Brig commanded by Captain Miller.

After the " Victory," my next ship was the " Calcutta," and I joined it under circumstances which Mr. A. G. Gardiner has narrated thus :—

" One day far back in the fifties of last century a sailing ship came round from Portsmouth into Plymouth Sound, where the fleet lay. Among the passengers was a little

midshipman fresh from his apprenticeship in the
'Victory.' He scrambled aboard the Admiral's ship,
and with the assurance of thirteen marched up to a
splendid figure in blue and gold, and said, handing him a
letter : ' Here, my man, give this to the Admiral.' The
man in blue and gold smiled, took the letter, and opened
it. ' Are you the Admiral ? ' said the boy. ' Yes, I'm
the Admiral.' He read the letter, and patting the boy on
the head, said : ' You must stay and have dinner with
me.' ' I think,' said the boy, ' I should like to be getting
on to my ship.' He spoke as though the British Navy had
fallen to his charge. The Admiral laughed, and took
him down to dinner. That night the boy slept aboard the
' Calcutta,' a vessel of 84 guns, given to the British Navy
by an Indian merchant at a cost of £84,000. It was the
day of small things and of sailing-ships. The era
of the ironclad and the ' Dreadnought ' had not
dawned."

I think I must give the first place to one of the first of
my Captains who was the seventh son of the last Vice-
Chancellor of England, Sir Lancelot Shadwell. The
Vice-Chancellor used to bathe in the Thames with his
seven sons every morning. My Shadwell was about the
greatest Saint on earth. The sailors called him, somewhat
profanely. " Our Heavenly Father." He was once heard
to say, " Damn," and the whole ship was upset. When,
as Midshipmen, we punished one of our mess-mates for
abstracting his cheese, he was extremely angry with us, and
asked us all what right we had to interfere with his cheese.
He always had the Midshipmen to breakfast with him, and
when we were seasick he gave us champagne and gingerbread nuts. As he went in mortal fear of his own steward,
who bossed him utterly, he would say : " I think the

aroma has rather gone out of this champagne. Give it to the young gentlemen." The steward would reply: " Now you know very well, Sir, the aroma *ain't* gone out of this 'ere champagne "; but all the same we got it. He always slept in a hammock, and I remember he kept his socks in the head clews ready to put on in case of a squall calling him suddenly on deck. I learned from him nearly all that I know. He taught me how to predict eclipses and occultations, and I suppose I took more lunar observations than any Midshipman ever did before.

Shadwell's appearance on going into a fight I must describe. We went up a Chinese river to capture a pirate stronghold. Presently the pirates opened fire from a banana plantation on the river bank. We nipped ashore from the boats to the banana plantation. I remember I was armed to the teeth, like a Greek brigand, all swords and pistols, and was weighed down with my weapons. We took shelter in the banana plantation, but our Captain stood on the river bank. I shall never forget it. He was dressed in a pair of white trousers, yellow waistcoat and a blue tail coat with brass buttons and a tall white hat with a gold stripe up the side of it, and he was waving a white umbrella to encourage us to come out of the bananas and go for the enemy. He had no weapon of any sort. So (I think rather against our inclinations, as the gingall bullets were flying about pretty thick) we all had to come out and go for the Chinese.

Once the Chinese guns were firing at us, and as the shell whizzed over the boat we all ducked. " Lay on your oars, my men," said Shadwell ; and proceeded to explain very deliberately how ducking delayed the progress of the boat—apparently unaware that his lecture had stopped its progress altogether !

His sole desire for fame was to do good, and he requested for himself when he died that he should be buried under an apple tree, so that people might say : " God bless old Shadwell ! " He never flogged a man in his life. When my Captain was severely wounded, I being with him as his Aide-de-Camp (we landed 1,100 strong, and 463 were killed or wounded), he asked me when being sent home what he could do for me. I asked him to give me a set of studs with his motto on them : " Loyal au mort," and I have worn them daily for over sixty years. When this conversation took place, the Admiral (afterwards Sir James Hope, K.C.B.) came to say good-bye to him, and he asked my Captain what he could do for him. He turned his suffering body towards me and said to the Admiral : " Take care of that boy." And so he did.

Admiral Hope was a great man, very stern and stately, the sort of man everybody was afraid of. His nickname was composed of the three ships he had commanded : " Terrible. . . Firebrand. . . Majestic." He turned to me and said : " Go down in my boat " ; and everyone in the Fleet saw this Midshipman going into the Admiral's boat. He took me with him to the Flagship ; and I got on very well with him because I wrote a very big hand which he could read without spectacles.

He promoted me to Lieutenant at the earliest possible

date, and sent me on various services, which greatly helped me.

My first chance came when Admiral Hope sent me to command a vessel in Chinese waters on special service. His motto was " Favouritism is the secret of efficiency," and though I was only nineteen he put me over the heads of many older men because he believed that I should do what I was told to do, and carry out the orders of the Admiral regardless of consequences. And so I did, although I made all sorts of mistakes and nearly lost the ship. When I came back everyone seemed to expect that I should be tried by Court-Martial; but the Admiral only cared that I had done what he wanted done ; and then he gave me command of another vessel.

The Captain of the ship I came home in was another sea wonder, by name Oliver Jones. He was Satanic ; yet I equally liked him, for, like Satan, he could disguise himself as an angel ; and I believe I was the only officer he did not put under arrest. For some reason I got on with him, and he made me the Navigating Officer of the ship. He told me when I first came on board that he thought he had committed every crime under the sun except murder. I think he committed that crime while I was with him. He was a most fascinating man. He had such a charm, he was most accomplished, he was a splendid rider, a wonderful linguist, an expert navigator and a thorough seaman. He had the best cook, and the best wines ever afloat in the Navy, and was hospitable to an extreme. Almost daily he had a lot of us to dinner, but after dinner came hell ! We dined with him in tail coat and epaulettes. After dinner he had sail drill, or preparing the ship for battle, and persecution then did its utmost.

Once, while I was serving with him, we were frozen in out of sight of land in the Gulf of Pechili in the North of China. And there were only Ship's provisions, salt beef, salt pork, pea soup, flour, and raisins. Oliver Jones was our Captain, or we wouldn't have been frozen in. The Authorities told him to get out of that Gulf and that's why he stayed in. I never knew a man who so hated Authority. I forget how many degrees below zero the thermometer was, and it was only by an unprecedented thaw that we ever got out. And with this intense cold he would often begin at four o'clock in the morning to prepare for battle, and hand up every shot in the ship on to the Upper Deck, then he'd strike Lower Yards and Topmasts (which was rather a heavy business), and finish up with holystoning the Decks, which operation he requested all the Officers to honour with their presence. And when we went to Sea we weren't quite sure where we would go to (I remember hearing a Marine Officer say that we'd got off the Chart altogether). Till that date I had never known what a delicacy a sea-gull was. We used to get inside an empty barrel on the ice to shoot them, and nothing was lost of them. The Doctor skinned them to make waistcoats of the skins— the insides were put on the ice to bait other seagulls, and a rare type of onion we had (that made your eyes water when you got within half a mile of them) made into stuffing got rid of the fishy taste.

KING EDWARD VII. AND THE CZAR, 1909.

On the way home he landed me on a desert island
to make a survey. He was sparse in his praises;
but he wrote of me : " As a sailor, an officer, a Navigator
and a gentleman, I cannot praise him too highly." Confronted with this uncommon expression of praise from
Oliver Jones, the examiners never asked me a question.
They gave me on the spot a first-class certificate.

This Captain Oliver Jones raised a regiment of cavalry
for the Indian Mutiny and was its Colonel, and Sir Hope
Grant, the great Cavalry General in the Indian Mutiny,
said he had never met the equal of Oliver Jones as a cavalry
leader. He broke his neck out hunting.

When I was sent to the Hythe School of Musketry as a
young Lieutenant, I found myself in a small Squad of
Officers, my right hand man was a General and my left
hand man a full Colonel. The Colonel spent his time
drawing pictures of the General. (The Colonel was really
a wonderful Artist.) The General was splendid. He
was a magnificent-looking man with a voice like a bull
and his sole object was Mutiny! He hated General
Hay, who was in Command of the Hythe School of
Musketry. He hated him with a contemptuous disdain,
In those days we commenced firing at the target only a
few hundred yards off. The General never hit the
target once! The Colonel made a beautiful picture of
him addressing the Parade and General Hay : " Gentlemen! my unalterable conviction is that the bayonet is
the true weapon of the British Soldier!" The beauty
of the situation was that the General had been sent to
Hythe to qualify as Inspector-General of Musketry.

After some weeks of careful drill (without firing a shot) we had to snap caps (that was to get our nerves all right, I suppose !) ; the Sergeant Instructor walked along the front of the Squad and counted ten copper caps into each outstretched hand. At that critical moment General Hay appeared on the Parade. This gave the General his chance ! With his bull-like voice he asked General Hay if it was believable after these weeks of incessant application that we were going (each of us) to be entrusted with ten copper caps ! When we were examined *vivâ voce* we each had to stand up to answer a question (like the little boys at a Sunday School). The General was asked to explain the lock of the latest type of British Rifle. He got up and stated that as he was neither Maskelyne and Cooke nor the Davenport Brothers (who were the great conjurers of that time) he couldn't do it. Certainly we had some appalling questions. One that I had was, " What do you pour the water into the barrel of the rifle with when you are cleaning it ? " Both my answers were wrong. I said, " With a tin pannikin or the palm of the hand." The right answer was " *with care* " ! Another question in the written examination was, " What occurred about *this* time ? " Only one paragraph in the text-book had those words in it " About *this* time there occurred, etc." ! All the same I had a lovely time there ; the British Army was very kind to me and I loved it. The best shot in the British Army at that date was a confirmed drunkard who trembled like a leaf, but when he got his eye on the target he was a bit of marble and " bull's eyes "

every time ! So, as the Scripture says, never judge by
appearance. Keble, who wrote the " Christian Year,"
was exceedingly ugly, but when he spoke Heaven shone
through ; so I was told by one who knew him.

It's going rather backwards now to speak of the time
when I was a Midshipman of the " Jolly Boat " in 1854,
in an old Sailing Line of Battleship of eighty-four guns.
I think I must have told of sailing into Harbour every
morning to get the Ship's Company's beef (gale or no
gale) from Spithead or Plymouth Sound or the Nore.
We never went into harbour in those days, and it was
very unpleasant work. I always felt there was a chance
of being drowned. Once at the Nore in mid-winter all
our cables parted in a gale and we ran into the Harbour
and anchored with our hemp cable (our sole remaining
joy) ; it seemed as big round as my small body was then,
and it lay coiled like a huge gigantic serpent just before
the Cockpit. Nelson must have looked at a similar
hemp cable as he died in that corner of the Cockpit
which was close to it. All Battleships were exactly
alike. You could go ashore then for forty years and
come on board again quite up to date. On our Quarter
Deck were brass Cannonades that had fired at the French
Fleet at Trafalgar. No one but the Master knew about
Navigation. I remember when the Master was sick and
the second Master was away and the Master's Assistant
had only just entered the Navy, we didn't go to Sea
till the Master got out of bed again. There was a
wonderfully smart Commander in one of the other
Battleships who had the utmost contempt for Science ;

he used to say that he didn't believe in the new-fangled sighting of the guns, " Your Tangent Sights and Disparts ! " What he found to be practically the best procedure was a cold veal pie and a bottle of rum to the first man that hit the target. We have these same " dears " with us now, but they are disguised in a clean white shirt and white kid gloves, but as for believing in Engineers—" Sack the Lot " !

It is very curious that we have no men now of great conceptions who stand out above their fellows in any profession, not even the Bishops, which reminds me of a super-excellent story I've been told in a letter. My correspondent met by appointment three Bishops for an expected attack. Before they got to the business of the meeting, he said, " Could their Lordships kindly tell him in the case of consecrated ground how deep the consecration went, as he specially wanted to know this for important business purposes." They wrangled and he got off his " mauvais quart d'heure." My correspondent explained to me that his old Aunt (a relation of Mr. Disraeli) said to him when he was young " Alfred, if you are going to have a row with anyone—*always you begin !* "

I come to another episode of comparatively early years.

Yesterday I heard from a gentleman whom I had not seen for thirty-eight years, and he reminded me of a visit to me when I was Captain of the " Inflexible." I was regarded by the Admiral Superintendent of the Dockyard as the Incarnation of Revolution. (What upset him most was I had asked for more water-closets and got them.) This particular episode I'm going to relate was that I wanted the incandescent light. Lord Kelvin had taken me to dine with the President of the Royal Society, where for the first time his dining table was lighted with six incandescent lamps, provided by his friend Mr. Swan of Newcastle, the Inventor in this Country of the Incandescent light, as Mr. Edison was in America (it was precisely like the discovery of the Planet Neptune when Adams and Leverrier ran neck and neck in England and France). After this dinner I wrote to Mr. Swan to get these lamps for the " Inflexible," and he sent down the friend who wrote me the letter I received yesterday (Mr. Henry Edmunds) and we had an exhibition to convert this old fossil of an Admiral Superintendent.

Here I'll put in Mr. Henry Edmunds's own words :—

At last we got our lamps to glow satisfactorily ; and at that moment the Admiral was announced. Captain Fisher had warned me that I must be careful how I answered any questions, for the Admiral was of the stern old school, and prejudiced against all new-fangled notions. The Admiral appeared resplendent in gold lace, and accompanied by such a bevy of ladies that I was strongly reminded of the character in " H.M.S. Pinafore " " with his sisters, and his cousins, and his aunts." The Admiral immediately asked if I had seen the " Inflexible." I replied that I had. " Have you seen the powder magazine ? " " Yes ! I have been in it." " What would happen to one of these little glass bubbles in the event of a broadside ? " I did not think it would affect them. " How do you know ? You've never been in a ship during a broadside ! " I saw Captain Fisher's eye fixed upon me ; and a sailor was dispatched for some

gun-cotton. Evidently everything had been ready prepared, for he quickly returned with a small tea tray about
two feet long, upon which was a layer of gun-cotton,
powdered over with black gun-powder. The Admiral
asked if I was prepared to break one of the lamps over
the tray. I replied that I could do so quite safely, for
the glowing lamp would be cooled down by the time
it fell amongst the gun-cotton. I took a cold chisel,
smashed a lamp, and let it fall. The Company saw the
light extinguished, and a few pieces of glass fall on the
tray. There was no flash, and the gun-powder and
gun-cotton remained as before. There was a short
pause, while the Admiral gazed on the tray. Then he
turned, and said to Lord Fisher, " We'll have this light
on the ' Inflexible.' "

And that was the introduction of the incandescent
light into the British Navy.

Talking about water-closets, I remember so well long
ago that one of the joys on board a Man-of-War on
Christmas Day was having what was called a " Free
Tank," that is to say, you could go and get as much
fresh water as ever you liked, all other days you were
restricted, so much for drinking and so much for washing.
The other Christmas Joy was " Both sides of the ' Head '
open " ! What that meant was that right in the Bows
or Head of the Ship were situated all the Bluejackets'
closets, and on Christmas Day all could be used ! " all
were free." Usually only half were allowed to be open
at a time. It was a quaint custom, and I always thought
outrageous. " Nous avons changé tout cela."

When I was out in the West Indies a French Frigate
came into the Harbour with Yellow Fever on board.
My Admiral asked the Captain of the English Man-of-

War that happened to be there what kindness he had shown the French Frigate on arrival ? He said he had sent them the keys of the Cemetery. This Captain always took his own champagne with him and put it under his chair. I took a passage with him once in his Ship, he had a Chart hanging up in his cabin like one of those recording barometers, which showed exactly how his wine was getting on. When he came to call on the Admiral at his house on shore, he always brought a small bundle with him, and after his Official visit he'd go behind a bush in the garden and change into plain clothes ! All the same, this is the stuff that heroes are made of. Heroes are always quaint.

## CHAPTER II.

KING EDWARD paid a visit to Admiralty House, Portsmouth, 19th February to 22nd February, 1904, while I was Commander-in-Chief there; and after he had left I received the following letter from Lord Knollys :—

> BUCKINGHAM PALACE,
> *22nd February*, 1904.

MY DEAR ADMIRAL,

I am desired by the King to write and thank you again for your hospitality.

His Majesty also desires me to express his great appreciation of all of the arrangements, which were excellent, and they reflect the greatest credit both on you and on those who worked under your orders.

I am very glad the visit was such a great success and went off so well. The King was evidently extremely pleased with and interested in everything.

> Yours sincerely,
> KNOLLYS.

I can say that I never more enjoyed such a visit. The only thing was that I wasn't Master in my own house, the King arranged who should come to dinner and himself arranged how everyone should sit at table; I never had a look in. Not only this, but he also had the Cook up in the morning. She was absolutely the best cook I've ever known. She was cheap at £100 a year. She was a remarkably lovely young woman. She died suddenly walking across a hay field. The King gave her some decoration, I can't remember what it was. Some little time after the King had left—one night I said to the butler at dinner, " This soup was never made by Mrs. Baker; is she ill?" The butler replied, " No, Sir John, Mrs. Baker isn't ill, she has been invited by His Majesty the King to stay at Buckingham Palace." And that was the first I had heard of it. Mrs. Baker had two magnificent kitchenmaids of her own choosing and she thought she wouldn't be missed. I had an interview with Mrs. Baker on her return from her Royal Visit, and she told me that the King had said to her one morning before he left Admiralty House, Portsmouth, that he thought she would enjoy seeing how a Great State Dinner was managed, and told her he would ask her to stay at Buckingham Palace or Windsor Castle to see one! Which is only one more exemplification of what I said of King Edward in my first book, that he had an astounding aptitude of appealing to the hearts of both High and Low.

My friends tell me I have done wrong in omitting countless other little episodes of his delightful nature.

" One touch of nature makes the whole world kin ! "

This is a sweet little episode that occurred at Sandringham. The King was there alone and Lord

Redesdale and myself were his only guests. The King was very fond of Redesdale, and rightly so. He was a most delightful man. He and I were sitting in the garden near dinner time, the King came up and said it was time to dress and he went up in the lift, leaving Redesdale in the garden. Redesdale had a letter to write and rushed up to his bedroom to write the letter behind a screen there was between him and the door; the door opened and in came the King, thinking he had left Redesdale in the garden, and went to the wash-hand-stand and felt the hot water-can to see if the water was hot and went out again. Perhaps his water had been cold, but anyhow he came to see if his guest's was all right.

On another occasion I went down to Sandringham with a great party, I think it was for one of Blessed Queen Alexandra's birthdays (I hope Her Majesty will forgive me for telling a lovely story presently about herself). As I was zero in this grand party, I slunk off to my room to write an important letter; then I took my coat off, got out my keys, unlocked my portmanteau and began unpacking. I had a boot in each hand; I heard somebody fumbling with the door handle and thinking it was the Footman whom Hawkins had allocated to me, I said " Come in, don't go humbugging with that door handle ! " and in walked King Edward, with a cigar about a yard long in his mouth. He said (I with a boot in each hand !) " What on earth are you doing ? " " Unpacking, Sir." " Where's your servant ? " " Haven't got one, Sir." " Where is he ? " " Never had one, Sir ; couldn't afford

it." "Put those boots down; sit in that arm chair."
And he went and sat in the other on the other side of
the fire. I thought to myself, " This is a rum state of
affairs ! Here's the King of England sitting in my
bedroom on one side of the fire and I'm in my shirt
sleeves sitting in an armchair on the other side ! "

" Well," His Majesty said, " why didn't you come and
say, ' How do you do ' when you arrived ? " I said, " I
had a letter to write, and with so many great people
you were receiving I thought I had better come to my
room." Then he went on with a long conversation,
until it was only about a quarter of an hour from dinner
time, and I hadn't unpacked ! So I said to the King,
" Sir, you'll be angry if I'm late for dinner, and no doubt
your Majesty has two or three gentlemen to dress you,
but I have no one." And he gave me a sweet smile
and went off.

All the same, he could be extremely unpleasant ; and
one night I had to send a telegram for a special messenger
to bring down some confounded Ribbon and Stars,
which His Majesty expected me to wear. I'd forgotten
the beastly things (I'm exactly like a Christmas Tree
when I'm dressed up). One night when I got the
King's Nurse to dress me up, she put the Ribbon of
something over the wrong shoulder, and the King
harangued me as if I'd robbed a church. I didn't like
to say it was his Nurse's fault. Some of these Ribbons
you put over one shoulder and some of them you have
to put over the other ; it's awfully puzzling. But the
King was an Angel all the same, only he wasn't always

27

one. Personally I don't like perfect angels, one doesn't feel quite comfortable with them. One of Cecil Rhodes's secretaries wrote his Life, and left out all his defects; it was a most unreal picture. The Good stands out all the more strikingly if there is a deep shadow. I think it's called the Rembrandt Effect. Besides, it's unnatural for a man not to have a Shadow, and the thought just occurs to me how beautiful it is—" The Shadow of Death "! There couldn't be the Shadow unless there was a bright light! The Bright Light is Immortality! Which reminds me that yesterday I read Dean Inge's address at the Church Congress the day before on Immortality. If I had anything to do with it, I'd make him Archbishop of Canterbury. I don't know him, but I go to hear him preach whenever I can.

The Story about Queen Alexandra is this. My beloved friend Soveral, one of King Edward's treasured friends, asked me to lunch on Queen Alexandra's sixtieth birthday. After lunch all the people said something nice to Queen Alexandra, and it came to my turn, I said to Her Majesty, " Have you seen that halfpenny newspaper about your Majesty's birthday ? " She said she hadn't, what was it ? I said these were the words :—

> " The Queen is sixty to-day !
> May she live till she looks it ! "

Her Majesty said " Get me a copy of it ! " (Such a thing didn't exist !) About three weeks afterwards (Her Majesty has probably forgotten all about it now, but she hadn't then) she said, " Where's that halfpenny newspaper ? " I was staggered for a moment, but recovered myself and said " Sold out, Ma'am ; couldn't get a copy ! " (I think my second lie was better than my first !) But the lovely part of the story yet remains. A year afterwards she sent me a lovely postcard which I much treasure now. It was a picture of a little girl bowling a hoop, and Her Majesty's own head stuck on, and underneath she had written :—

" May she live till she looks it ! "

I treasure the remembrances of all her kindnesses to me as well as that of her dear Sister, the Dowager Empress of Russia. The trees they both planted at Kilverstone are both flourishing ; but strange to say the tree King Edward planted began to fade away and died in May, 1910, when he died—though it had flourished luxuriantly up till then. Its roots remain untouched— and a large mass of " Forget-me-nots " flourishes gloriously over them.

For very many consecutive years after 1886 I went to Marienbad in Bohemia (eight hundred miles from London and two thousand feet above the sea and one mass of delicious pine woods) to take the waters there. It's an ideal spot. The whole place is owned by a Colony of Monks, settled in a Monastery (close by) called Tepl, who very wisely have resisted all efforts to cut down the pine woods so as to put up more buildings.

I had a most serious illness after the Bombardment of

Alexandria due to bad living, bad water, and great anxiety. The Admiral (Lord Alcester) had entrusted me (although I was one of the junior Captains in the Fleet) with the Command on shore after the Bombardment. Arabi Pasha, in command of the Rebel Egyptian Army, was entrenched only a few miles off, and I had but a few hundreds to garrison Alexandria. For the first time in modern history we organised an Armoured Train. Nowadays they are as common as Aeroplanes. Then it excited as much emotion as the Tanks did. There was a very learned essay in the *Pall Mall Gazette*.

I was invalided home and, as I relate in my " Memories," received unprecedented kindness from Queen Victoria (who had me to stay at Osborne) and from Lord Northbrook (First Lord of the Admiralty), who gave me the best appointment in the Navy. I always have felt great gratitude also to his Private Secretary at that time (Admiral Sir Lewis Beaumont). For three years I had recurrence of Malarial Fever, and tried many watering places and many remedies all in vain. I went to Marienbad and was absolutely cured in three weeks, and never relapsed till two years ago, when I was ill again and no one has ever discovered what was the matter with me ! Thanks be to God—I believe I am now as well as I ever was in all my whole life, and I can still waltz with joy and enjoy champagne when I can get it (friends, kindly note !).

At Marienbad I met some very celebrated men, and the place being so small I became great friends with them. If you are restricted to a Promenade only a few hundred yards long for two hours morning and evening, while you are drinking your water, you can't help knowing each other quite well. How I wish I could remember all the splendid stories those men told me !

Campbell-Bannerman, Russell (afterwards Chief Justice), Hawkins (afterwards Lord Brampton), the first Lord Burnham, Labouchere (of *Truth*), Yates (of the *World*), Lord Shand (a Scottish Judge), General Gallifet (famous in the Franco-German War), Rumbold (Ambassador at Vienna), those were some of the original members. Also there were two Bevans (both delightful) —to distinguish them apart, they called the " Barclay Perkins " Bevan " poor " Bevan, as he was supposed to have only two millions sterling, while the other one was supposed to have half a dozen ! (That was the story.) I almost think I knew Campbell-Bannerman the best. He was very delightful to talk to. I have no Politics. But in after years I did so admire his giving Freedom to the Boers. Had he lived, he would have done the same to Ireland without any doubt whatever. Fancy now 60,000 British soldiers quelling veiled Insurrection and a Military Dictator as Lord Lieutenant and Ireland never so prosperous ! I have never been more moved than in listening to John Redmond's brother, just back from the War in his Soldier's uniform, making the most eloquent and touching appeal for the Freedom of Ireland ! *It came to nothing.* I expect Lord Loreburn (who was Campbell-Bannerman's bosom friend) will agree with me that had Campbell-Bannerman only known what a literally overwhelming majority he was going to obtain

31

at the forthcoming Election, he would have formed a
very different Government from what he did, and I
don't believe we should have had the War. King
Edward liked him very much. They had a bond in
their love of all things French. I don't believe any
Prime Minister was ever so loved by his followers as
was Campbell-Bannerman.

Sir Charles Russell, afterwards Chief Justice, was
equally delightful. We were so amused one day (when
he first came to Marienbad) by the Head Waiter whis-
pering to us that he was a cardsharper! The Head Waiter
told us he had seen him take a pack of cards out of his
pocket, look at them carefully, and then put them back!
Which reminds me of a lovely incident in my own
career. I had asked the Roman Catholic Archbishop to
dinner; he was a great Saint—we played cards after
dinner. We sat down to play—(one of my guests was a
wonderful conjurer). "Hullo!" I said, "Where are
the cards gone to?" The conjurer said, "It doesn't
matter: the Archbishop will let us have the pack of
cards he always carries about in his pocket"! The
Holy Man furtively put his hand in his pocket (thinking
my friend was only joking!) and dash it! there they
were! I never saw such a look in a man's face! (He
thought Satan was crawling about somewhere.)

Lord Burnham was ever my great Friend, he was also
a splendid man. I should like to publish his letters.
I have spoken of Labouchere elsewhere. As Yates,
of the *World*, Labouchere, and Lord Burnham (those
three) walked up and down the Promenade together

Two photographs of King Edward VII. and Sir John Fisher on board H.M.S. "Dreadnought" on her first cruise.

(Lord Burnham being stout), Russell called them " The World, the Flesh, and the Devil." I don't know if it was original wit, but it was to me.

Old Gallifet also was splendid company ; he had a silver plate over part of his stomach and wounds all over him. I heard weird stories of how he shot down the Communists.

Sir Henry Hawkins I dined with at some Legal Assemblage, and as we walked up the Hall arm in arm all the Law Students struck up a lovely song I'd never heard before : " Mrs. 'enry 'awkins," which he greatly enjoyed. On one occasion he told me that when he was still a Barrister, he came late into Court and asked what was the name of the Barrister associated with him in the Case ? The Usher or someone told him it was Mr. Swan and he had just gone out of the Court. (I suppose he ought to have waited for Sir Henry.) Anyhow Sir Henry observed that he didn't like him " taking liberties with his Leda." I expect the Usher, not being up in Lemprière's Dictionary, didn't see the joke !

Dear Shand, who was very small of stature, was known as the " Epitome of all that was good in Man." He reeked with good stories and never told them twice. Queen Victoria fell in love with him at first sight (notwithstanding that she preferred big men) and had him made a Lord. She asked after his wife as " Lady Shand " ; and, being a Scottish Law Lord, he replied that " Mrs. Shand was quite well." There are all sorts of ways of becoming a Lord.

Rumbold knocked the man down who asked him

for his ticket ! He wasn't going to have an Ambassador treated like that (as if he had travelled without a ticket !)

As the Czechs hate the Germans, I look forward to going back to my beloved Marienbad once more every year. The celebrated Queen of Bohemia was the daughter of an English King ; her name was Elizabeth. The English Ambassador to the Doge of Venice, Sir Henry Wootton, wrote some imperishable lines in her praise and accordingly I worshipped at Wootton's grave in Venice. The lines in his Poem that I love are :—

> " You Common People of the Skies,
> What are You, when the Moon shall rise ? "

In dictating the Chapter on " Some Personalities," that appears in my " Memories," I certainly should not have overlooked my very good friend Masterton-Smith (Sir J. E. Masterton-Smith, K.C.B.). I can only say here (as he knows quite well) that never was he more appreciated by anyone in his life than by me. Numberless times he was simply invaluable, and had his advice been always taken, events would have been so different in May 1915 !

I have related in " Memories " how malignancy went to the extent not only of declaring that I had sold my country to the Germans (so beautifully denied by Sir Julian Corbett), but also that I had formed " Syndicates " and " Rings " for my own financial advantage, using my official knowledge and power to further my nefarious schemes for making myself quickly rich ! I have denied this by the Income Tax Returns—and I have also explained

I am still poor—very poor—because one-third of my pension goes in income tax and the remaining two-thirds is really only one-third because of depreciation of the pound sterling and appreciation of food prices !

But let that pass. However, I've been told I ought to mention I had another very brilliant opportunity of becoming a millionaire in A.D. 1910, but declined. And also it has been requested of me to state the fact that never in all my life have I belonged to any company of any sort beyond possessing shares, or had any place of profit outside the Navy. That is sufficiently definite, I think, to d——n my enemies and satisfy my friends.

My finances have always been at a low ebb (even when a Commander-in-Chief), as I went on the principle of " whatever you do, do it with all your might," and there is nothing less conducive to " the fighting efficiency of a Fleet and its instant readiness for war " than a Stingy Admiral ! The applications for subscriptions which were rained upon me I countered with this inestimable memorandum in reply, invented by my sympathetic Secretary :—" The Admiral deeply regrets being unable to comply with your request, and he deplores the reason—but his Expenditure is in excess of his Receipts." I always got sympathy in return, more especially as the Local Applicants were largely responsible for the excess of expenditure.

At an early period of my career I certainly did manage on very little, and it is wonderful what a lot you can get for your money if you think it over. I got breakfast for tenpence, lunch for a shilling and dinner for eighteen

# RECORDS

pence and barley water for nothing and a bed for three
and sixpence (but my bedroom had not a Southern aspect).
The man I hired a bedroom from was like a Father
to me, and I have never had such a polish on my shoes.
(I remember saying to a German Boots, pointing to my
badly-cleaned shoes, " Spiegel ! "—looking-glass ;  he
took away the shoes and brought them back shining
like a dollar.  Hardly anyone will see the joke !)  But
what I am most proud of is that, financial necessity once
forcing me to go to Marienbad quite alone, I did a three
weeks' cure there, including the railway fare and every
expense, for twenty-five pounds.  I don't believe any
Economist has ever beaten this.  I preserve to this day
the details of every day's expenditure, which I kept in
a little pocket-book, and read it all over only a couple of
days ago, without any wish for past days.

I recall with delight first meeting my beloved old
friend, Sir Henry Lucy ; he had with him Sir F. C. Gould,
who never did a better service to his country than when
he portrayed me as an able seaman asking the Con-
scriptionists (in the person of Lord Roberts) whether
there was no British Navy.  The cartoon was reproduced in my " Memories " (p. 48).  In my speech at
the Lord Mayor's Banquet in 1907 (see Chapter VI
of this volume) I had spoken of Sir Henry Lucy as
"gulled by some Midshipman Easy of the Channel
Fleet " (Sir Henry had been for a cruise in the Fleet),
who stuffed him up that the German Army embarking
in the German Fleet was going to invade England !
And in the flippant manner that seems so to annoy people,

36

I observed that Sir Henry might as well talk of embarking St. Paul's Cathedral on board a penny steamer as of embarking the German Army in the German Fleet! He and Gould came up to me at a *séance* on board the " Dreadnought," and had a cup of tea as if I had been a lamb !

On the occasion of that same speech, a Bishop looked very sternly at me, because in my speech, to show how if you keep on talking about war and always looking at it and thinking of it you bring it on, I instanced Eve, who kept on looking at the apple and at last she plucked it ; and in the innocence of my heart I observed that had she not done so we should not have been now bothered with clothes. When I said this in my speech I was following the advice of one of the Sheriffs of the City of London, sitting next me at dinner, who told me to fix my eyes, while I was speaking, on the corner of the Ladies' Gallery, as then everyone in the Guildhall could hear what I said. And such a lovely girl was in that corner, I never took my eyes off her, all the time, and that brought Eve into my mind !

# CHAPTER III

I HAVE just been listening to another very eloquent sermon from Dr. Hugh Black, whom I mention elsewhere in this book (see Chapter V). Nearly all these Presbyterians are eloquent, because they don't write their sermons.

The one slip our eloquent friend made in his sermon was in saying that the A.D. 1611 edition of the Bible (the Authorised Version) was a better version of the Bible than the Great Bible of A.D. 1539, which according to the front page is stated to be as follows :—

" The byble in English that is to say the content of all the Holy Scripture both of the old and new testament truly translated after the verity of the Hebrew and Greek texts by the diligent study of diverse excellent learned men expert in the aforesaid tongues.

" Printed by Richard Grafton and Edward Whitchurch. Cum privilegio ad imprimendum solum.

### 1539."

It is true, as the preacher said, that the 1611 edition, the Authorised Version, is more the literal translation of the two, but those " diverse excellent learned men " translated according to the spirit and not the letter of the original ; and our dear brother (the preacher) this morning in his address had to acknowledge that in the text he had chosen from the 27th Psalm and the last verse thereof, the pith and marrow which he rightly seized on—being the words " Wait on the Lord "—were more beautifully rendered in the great Bible from which (the Lord be thanked !) the English Prayer Book takes its Psalms, and which renders the original Hebrew not in the literal words, " Wait on the Lord," but " *Tarry thou the Lord's leisure*," and goes on also in far better words than the Authorised Version with the rest of the verse : " Be strong and He shall comfort thine heart."

When we remonstrated with the Rev. Hugh Black after his sermon, he again gainsaid, and increased his heinousness by telling us that the word " Comfort," which doesn't appear in the 1611 version, was in its ancient signification a synonym for " Fortitude " ; and the delightful outcome of it is that that is really the one and only proper prayer— to ask for Fortitude or *Endurance*. You have no right to pray for rain for your turnips, when it will ruin somebody else's wheat. You have no right to ask the Almighty— in fact, He can't do it—to make two and two into five. The only prayer to pray is for Endurance, or Fortitude. The most saintly man I know, daily ended his prayers with the words of that wonderful hymn :

> " Renew my will from day to day,
> Blend it with thine, and take away
> All that now makes it hard to say,
> Thy will be done."

39

# RECORDS

It must not be assumed that I am a Saint in any way in making these remarks, but only a finger-post pointing the way. The finger-post doesn't go to Heaven itself, yet it shows the way. All I want to do is to stick up for those holy men who were not hide-bound with a dictionary, and gave us the spirit of the Holy Word and not the Dictionary meaning.

Here I feel constrained to mention a far more beautiful illustration of the value of those pious men of old.

In Brother Black's 1611 version, the most famous of the Saviour's words : " Come unto me all ye that labour and are heavy laden and I will give you rest," is, in the 1539 version, " I will *refresh* you ! " There is no *rest* this side of Heaven. Job (iii, 17) explains Heaven as " Where the wicked cease from troubling and where the weary be at rest." The fact is—the central point is reached by the Saviour when He exemplifies the Day of Perfection by saying : " In that day ye shall ask me nothing."

I have been told by a great scientist that for the tide to move a pebble on the beach a millionth of an inch further would necessitate an alteration in the whole Creation. And then we go and pray for rain, or to beat our enemies !

Again, I say—The only thing to pray for is *Endurance*.

Some people in sore straits try to strike bargains with God, if only He will keep them safe or relieve them in the present necessity. It's a good story of the soldier who, with all the shells exploding round him was heard to pray : " O Lord, if You'll only get me out of this d—d mess I will be good, I will be good ! "

# THE BIBLE, AND OTHER REFLECTIONS

I am reminded of what I call the " Pith and Marrow " which the pious men put at the head of every chapter of the Bible, and which, alas! has been expunged in the literary exactitudes of the Revised Version. Regard Chapter xxvi, for instance, of Proverbs—how it is all summed up by those " diverse excellent learned men." They wrote at the top of the chapter " Observations about Fools." Matthew xxii : the Saviour " *Poseth* the Pharisees." Isaiah xxi : " The *set* time." Isaiah xxvii (so true and pithy of the Chapter!): " Chastisements differ from Judgments " ; and in Mark xv : " The Clamour of the Common People "— descriptive of what's in the chapter. All these headings, in my opinion, as regards those ancient translators, are for them a " Crown of Glory and a Diadem of Beauty " ; and I have a feeling that, when they finished their wondrous studies, it was with them as Solomon said, " The desire accomplished is sweet to the Soul."

## DR. GINSBURG

*March 27th, 1918.*

DEAR FRIEND,

When I was at Bath I read in the local paper a beautiful letter aptly alluding to the Mount Fiesole of Bath and quoting what has been termed that mysterious verse of David's :

" I will lift up mine eyes unto the hills ——."

Well! the other day a great friend of that wonderful Hebrew scholar, Dr. Ginsburg—he died long since at Capri—told me that Ginsburg had said to him that all the Revisers and Translators had missed a peculiar

41

Hebraism which quite alters the signification of this opening verse of the 121st Psalm : It should read :

"*Shall* I lift up mine eyes to those hills ?  DOTH my help come from thence ? "

And this is the explanation :

Those hills alluded to were the hills in which were the Groves planted in honour of the idols towards which Israel had strayed.  So in the second verse the inspired tongue says :

" No ! My help cometh from the Lord ! He who hath made Heaven and Earth ! (not these idols)."

I have had an admiration for Ginsburg ever since he shut up the two Atheists in the Athenæum Club, Huxley and Herbert Spencer, who were reviling Holy Writ in Ginsburg's presence and flouting him.  So he asked the two of them to produce anything anywhere in literature comparable to the 23rd Psalm as translated by Wyclif, Tyndale, and Coverdale.  He gave them a week to examine, and at the end of it they confessed that they could not.

One of them (I could not find out which it was) wrote :

" I won't argue about nor admit the Inspiration claimed, but I say this—that those saintly men whom Cromwell formed as the company to produce the Great Bible of 1539 *were inspired*, for never has the spirit of the original Hebrew been more beautifully transformed from the original harshness into such spiritual wealth."

Those are not the exact words, I have not got them by me, but that was the sense.

The English language in A.D. 1539 was at its very maximum.  Hence the beauty of the Psalms which come from the Great Bible as produced by that holy company of pious men, who one writer says : " Did not wish their names to be ever known."  I send you the title page.

Yours, etc.,

(Signed) FISHER.

27/3/18.

# THE BIBLE, AND OTHER REFLECTIONS

I enclosed with this letter the front page of the first edition of the Great Bible, A.D. 1539, often known as Cranmer's Bible, but Archbishop Cranmer had nothing whatever to do with it except writing a preface to it ; it was solely due to Cromwell, Secretary of State to Henry VIII., who cut off Cromwell's head in July, 1540. Cranmer wrote a preface for the edition after April, 1540. Cranmer was burnt at the stake in Mary's reign. Tyndale was strangled and burnt, Coverdale, Bishop of Exeter, died of hunger. Coverdale headed the company that produced the Great Bible, and Tyndale's translation was taken as the basis. (So those who had to do with the Bible had a rough time of it !)

John Wyclif, in A.D. 1380, began the translation of the Bible into English. This was before the age of printing, so it was in manuscript. Before he died, in A.D. 1384, he had the joy of seeing the Bible in the hands of his countrymen in their own tongue.

Wyclif's translation was quaint and homely, and so idiomatic as to have become out of date when, more than one hundred years afterwards, John Tyndale, walking over the fields in Wiltshire, determined so to translate the Bible into English " that a boy that driveth the plough should know more of the Scriptures than the Pope," and Tyndale gloriously succeeded ! But for doing so, the Papists, under orders from the Pope of Rome, half strangled him and then burnt him at the stake. Like St. Paul, he was shipwrecked ! (Just as he had finished the Book of Jonah, which is curious, but

43

there was no whale handy, and so he was cast ashore in Holland, nearly dead !)

Our present Bible, of A.D. 1611, is almost word for word the Bible of Tyndale, of round A.D. 1530, but in A.D. 1534, Miles Coverdale, Bishop of Exeter, was authorised by Archbishop Cranmer and Thomas Cromwell (who was Secretary of State to Henry VIII.) to publish his fresh translation, and he certainly beautified in many places Tyndale's original !

In 1539, " Diverse excellent learned men expert in the ' foresaid tongues ' " (Hebrew and Greek), under Cromwell's orders made a true translation of the whole Bible, which was issued in 1539–40 in four editions, and remained supreme till A.D. 1568, when the Bishops tried to improve it, and made a heavenly mess of it ! And then the present Authorised Version, issued in A.D. 1611, became the Bible of the Land, and still holds its own against the recent pedantic Revised Version of A.D. 1884. No one likes it. It is literal, but it is not spiritual !

In the opinion of Great and Holy men, Cranmer's Bible (as it is called), or " the Great Bible "—the Bible of 1539 to 1568—holds the field for beauty of its English and its emotional rendering of the Holy Spirit !

Alas ! we don't know their names ; we only know of them as " Diverse excellent learned men ! " It is said they did not wish to go down to Fame !

" It is the greatest achievement in letters ! The Beauty of the translation of these unknown men excels (far excels) the real and the so-called originals ! All nations and tongues of Christendom have come to admit reluctantly that no other version of the Book in the English or any other tongue offers so noble a setting for the Divine Message. Read the Prayer Book Psalms! They are from this noble Version—English at its zenith! The English of the Great Bible is even more stately, sublime, and pure than the English of Shakespeare and Elizabeth."

## ACTION

" Ye men of Galilee ! Why stand ye gazing up into Heaven ? " (Acts, Chapter i., verse 11.)

The moral of this one great central episode of the whole Christian faith (which, if a man don't believe with his utmost heart he is as a beast that perisheth, so Saint Paul teaches in I. Corinthians, Chapter xv.), the moral of it is that however intense at any moment of our lives may be the immediate tension that is straining our mental fibre to the limit, yet we are to " get on ! " and not stand stock still " gazing up into Heaven ! " Inaction must be no part of our life, and we must " get on " with our journey as the Apostles did— " to our own City of Jerusalem ! "

It is curious that Thursday (Ascension Day) was not made the Christian Sabbath. No scientific agnostic could possibly explain the Ascension by any such theories as those that try to get over the fact of the Resurrection by cataleptic happenings or an inconceivable trance ! The agnostic can't explain away that He was seen by the Apostles to be carried up into Heaven when in the

45

act of lifting up His hands upon them to bless them " and a cloud received Him out of their sight ! "

*Vide* the Collect for the Sunday after Ascension Day !

## RESENTMENT

The prophet Zechariah says in Chapter xiv., verse 7 :

" At evening time
It shall be light ! "

And I conclude that in the last stage of life, as pointed out so very decisively by Dr. Weir Mitchell (that great American), " the brain becomes its best," and so we rearrange our hearts and minds to the great advantage of our own Heaven and the avoidance of Hell to others ! " Resentment " I find to fade away, and it merges into the feeling of Commiseration ! (" Poor idiots ! " one says instead of " D—n 'em ! ") But I can't arrive as yet at St. Paul, who deliberately writes that he's quite ready to go to Hell so as to let his enemy go to Heaven ! You've got really to be a real Christian to say that ! I've not the least doubt, however, that John Wesley, Bishop Jeremy Taylor and Robertson of Brighton felt it surely ! Isn't it odd that those three great saints (fit to be numbered " with these three men, Noah, Daniel and Job," Ezekiel, Chapter xiv., verse 14) each of them should have a " nagging " wife !

Their Home was Hell !

And I've searched in vain for any one of the three saying a word to the detriment of the other sex ! They might all have been Suffragettes ! (St. Paul does indeed

46

say that he preferred being single! But Peter was married!)

But this "Resentment" section hinges entirely on "Charity" as defined and exemplified by Mr. Robertson, of Brighton, in one of the best of his wonderful Trinity Chapel Sermons.


## DEAN INGE

I heard the Dean of St. Paul's (Dr. Inge) preach in Westminster Abbey on the 17th Chapter of St. Matthew, verse 19 : " Then came the disciples to Jesus apart, and said, ' Why could not we cast him out ? ' "

The sermon was really splendiferous!

The Saviour had just cast out a devil that had been too much for the disciples, and He told them their inability to do so was due to their want of Faith, and added : " Howbeit this kind goeth not out but by prayer." The Dean explained to us that some ascetic annotator 400 years afterwards had shoved in at the end of these two additional words—" and fasting." That, of course, was meant by the Dean as " one in the eye " for those who fast like the Pharisees and for a pretence make long prayers! Then the Dean was just too lovely as to " Prayer ! " He said he was so sick of people praying for victory in the great War ! And speaking generally he was utterly sick of people praying for what they wanted ! (as if *that* was Prayer !) No ! the Dean divinely said, " Prayer was the exaltation of the Spirit of a Man to dwell with God and say in the Saviour's

47

words, ' Not my will but Thine be done.' " " Get right thus with God," said the Dean, " and then go and make Guns and Munitions with the utmost fury. That (said the Dean) was the way to get Victory, and not by silly vain petitions as if you were asking your Mamma for a bit of barley sugar." (I don't mean to say the Dean used these exact words !) Then he said an interesting thing that " this event of the disciples ignominiously failing to cast out the devil " happened to these chief of His apostles just after their coming down from the Mount of Transfiguration, where they had been immensely uplifted by the Heavenly Vision of the Saviour talking with Moses and Elijah. The Dean said " that it was really a curious fact of large experience that when you were thus lifted up in a Heavenly Spirit it was a sure precursor of a fierce temptation by the Devil ! " These highly-favoured disciples, after such a communion with God, thought that they themselves, by themselves, could do anything ! Pride had a fall ! They could not cast out that devil ! They trusted in themselves and did not give God the praise ! And so it was that Moses didn't go over Jordan, for he struck the rock and said, " How now, ye rebels ! " (I'll show you who I am !)

The Dean also observed that it was the Drains that had to be put right when there was an Epidemic of Typhoid Fever ! " Prayer " wasn't the Antidote !

The holy man Saint Francis summed up all religion and the Christian life in his famous line :

" How we are in the sight of God !—That is the only thing that matters ! "

PHOTOGRAPH, TAKEN AND SENT TO SIR JOHN FISHER BY THE EMPRESS MARIE OF RUSSIA, OF A GROUP ON BOARD
H.M.S. "STANDARD," 1909.

1. Lord Hamilton of Dalzell.
2. The Chevalier de Martino.
3. Sir Arthur Nicholson.
4. M. Stolypin, Russian Prime Minister.
5. The Czarina.
6. M. Isvolsky, Russian Minister of Foreign Affairs.
7. Sir John Fisher.
8. Sir Charles Hardinge.
9. Baron Fredericks.
10. The Grand Duchess Olga.
11. The Czar.
12. The Princess Victoria.
13. The Grand Duke Michael.
14. Count Benckendorff, Russian Ambassador.

# THE BIBLE, AND OTHER REFLECTIONS

It fortuned this morning that I read Joseph's interview with his Brethren just after the death of their Father Jacob. They, having done their best to murder Joseph quite naturally thought that he would now be even with them, so they told a lie. They said that Jacob their Father had very kindly left word with them that he hoped Joseph would be very nice with his brethren after he died. Jacob said no such thing. Jacob knew his Joseph. But it gave Joseph a magnificent opportunity for reading one of Mr. Robertson's, of Brighton, Sermons—he said to them, " Am I in the place of God ? " Meaning thereby that no bread and water that he might put them on, and no torturing thumbscrews, would in any way approach the unquenchable fire and the undying worm that the Almighty so righteously reserves for the black-guards of this life. Which reminds me of the best Sermon I ever heard by the present Dean of Salisbury, Dr. Page-Roberts. He said : " There is no Bankruptcy Act in Heaven. No 10s. in the £1 there. Every moral, debt has got to be paid in full," and consequently Page-Roberts, though an extremely broad-minded man, was the same as the extreme Calvinist of the unspeakable Hell and the Roman Catholic's Purgatory. How curious it is how extremes do meet !

# CHAPTER IV

## I.—MR. GLADSTONE'S FINAL RESIGNATION.

I WAS Controller of the Navy when Lord Spencer was First Lord of the Admiralty and Sir Frederck Richards was First Sea Lord. Mr. Gladstone, then Prime Minister, was at the end of his career. I have never read Morley's " Life of Gladstone," but I understand that the incident I am about to relate is stated to have been the cause of Mr. Gladstone resigning—and for the last time. I was the particular Superintending Lord at the Board of Admiralty, who, as Controller of the Navy, was specially responsible for the state and condition of the Navy; and it was my province, when new vessels were required, to replace those getting obsolete or worn out. Sir Frederick Richards and myself were on the very greatest terms of intimacy. He had a stubborn will, an unerring judgment, and an astounding disregard of all arguments. When anyone, seeking a compromise with him, offered him an alternative, he always took the alternative as well as the original proposal, and asked for both. Once bit, twice shy; no one ever offered him an alternative a second time.

50

However, he had one great incapacity. No one could write a more admirable and concise minute ; but he was as dumb as Moses. So I became his Aaron. The moment arrived when that magnificent old patriot, Lord Spencer, had to choose between fidelity to his life-long friend and leader, Mr. Gladstone, and his faithfulness to his country. Sir Frederick Richards, the First Sea Lord, had convinced him that a certain programme of ship-building was vitally and urgently necessary. Mr. Gladstone would not have it. Sir Frederick Richards and myself, in quite a nice way, not quite point-blank, intimated that the Sea Lords would resign. (My bread and cheese was at stake, but I did it !) Lord Spencer threw in his lot with us, and conveyed the gentle likelihood to Mr. Gladstone ; whereupon Sir William Harcourt and Sir Henry Campbell-Bannerman were alternately turned on to the three of us (Lord Spencer, Sir F. Richards and myself) sitting round a table in Lord Spencer's private room. I loved Sir William Harcourt ; he was what might be called " a genial ruffian," as opposed to Sir Michael Hicks-Beach, who, when he was Chancellor of the Exchequer, was a perfect beast, without a single redeeming feature that I ever found out. Sir William Harcourt always started the conversazione by insulting Lord Spencer (quite in a friendly way) ; then he would say to Sir Frederick Richards, " I always thought that one Englishman was equal to three Frenchmen, and according to this table of ships required, which has been presented to the Prime Minister, it takes three Englishmen to manage one Frenchman." Old Richards would grow livid with anger ; he wanted to say, " It's a damned lie ! " but he couldn't get the proper words out !

He had an ungovernable temper. I heard him once say to one of the principal Officers in his ship : " Here ; don't you look sulky at me, I won't have it ! " There was a famous one-legged cabman at Portsmouth whom Sir Frederick Richards hired at Portsmouth railway station by chance to drive him to the Dockyard. He didn't recognise the man, but he was an old ship-mate who had been with him when Sir Frederick Richards commanded a brig on the coast of Africa, suppressing the Slave Trade—he led them all a dog's life. The fare was a shilling, and ample at that ; and as old Richards got out at the Admiral's door he gave the cabman five shillings, but the cabby refused it and said to old Richards : " You *drove* me for nothing on the Coast of Africa, I will drive you for nothing now," and he rattled óff, leaving old Richards speechless with anger. He used to look at Sir William Harcourt in exactly the same way. I thought he would have apoplexy sometimes.

Dear Lord Spencer was pretty nearly as bad in his want of lucid exposition ; so I usually did Aaron all through with Sir William Harcourt, and one of the consequences was that we formed a lasting friendship.

When I was made a Lord, Stead came to my house that very morning and said he had just had a message from Sir William Harcourt (who had then been dead for some years), saying how glad Sir William was ; and the curious thing was that five minutes afterwards I got a

letter from his son, now Lord Harcourt, congratulating
me on my Peerage, which had only been made known an
hour before. I think Stead said Sir William was in
Heaven. I don't think he ever quite knew where the
departed were !

Campbell-Bannerman was a more awkward customer.

But it was all no use. We got the ships and Mr.
Gladstone went.


II.—THE GREAT LORD SALISBURY'S BROTHER-IN-LAW.

It really is very sad that those three almost bulky
volumes of my letters to Lord Esher—which he has so
wonderfully kept—could not all have been published
just as they are. This is one of the reasons for
my extreme reluctance, which still exists, for these
" Memories" and " Records " of mine being
published in my lifetime. When I was dead there
could be no libel action ! The only alternative is to
have a new sort of " Pilgrim's Progress " published—
the whole three volumes—and substitute Bunyan names.
But that would be almost as bad as putting their real
names in—no one could mistake them !

I think I have mentioned elsewhere that Lord Ripon,
when First Lord, whom I had never met, had a design
to make me a Lord of the Admiralty, but his colleagues
would not have it and called me " Gambetta." Lord
Ripon said he had sent for me because someone had
maligned me to him as " a Radical enthusiast." Well,
the upshot was that in 1886 I became Director of Ordnance

of the Navy ; and after a time I came to the definite conclusion that the Ordnance of the Fleet was in a very bad way, and the only remedy was to take the whole business from the War Office, who controlled the Sea Ordnance and the munitions of sea war. A very funny state of affairs !

Lord George Hamilton was then First Lord and the Great Lord Salisbury was Prime Minister. Lord Salisbury's brother-in-law was the gentleman at the War Office who was solely responsible for the Navy deficiencies, bar the politicians. When they cut down the total of the Army Estimates, he took it off the Sea Ordnance. He had to, if he wanted to be on speaking terms with his own cloth. I don't blame him ; I expect I should have done the same, more particularly as I believe in a Citizen Army—or, as I have called it elsewhere, a Lord-Lieutenant's Army. (The clothes were a bit different ; but Lord Kitchener's Army was uncommonly like it.) Lord George Hamilton, having patiently heard me, as he always did, went to Lord Salisbury. Lord George backed me through thick and thin. The result was a Committee— the Prime Minister, Lord Salisbury, Chairman ; W. H. Smith, Secretary for War ; Lord George Hamilton, First Lord of the Admiralty ; the Director of Ordnance at the War Office, and myself. It was really a very remarkably unpleasant time. I had an awful bad cold—much worse than General Alderson, the Prime Minister's brother-in-law—and Lord Salisbury never asked after it, while he slobbered over Alderson. I just mention that as a straw indicating which way the wind blew. The result, after immense flagellations administered to the Director of the Sea Ordnance, was that the whole business of the munitions of war for the Navy was turned over to the Admiralty, " lock, stock and gun barrel, bob and sinker," and by Herculean efforts and the cordial co-operation of Engelbach, C.B., who had fought against me like a tiger, and afterwards helped like an Angel, and of Sir Ralph Knox, the Accountant-General of the Army, a big deficit, in fact a criminal deficit, of munitions for the Fleet was turned over rapidly into a million sterling of surplus.

They are nearly all dead and gone now, who worked this enormous transfer, and I hope they are all in Heaven.

This story has a lovely sequel ; and I forgave Lord Salisbury afterwards for not asking after my cold when, in 1899, many years after, the Hague Peace Conference came along and he submitted my name to Queen Victoria as the Naval Delegate, with the remark that, as I had fought so well against his brother-in-law, there was no doubt I should fight at the Peace Conference. So I did, though it was not for Peace ; and M. de Staal, who was a great friend of mine, and who was the President of the Conference, told me that my remarks about boiling the crews of hostile submarines in oil when caught, and so forth, were really unfit for publication. But W. T. Stead tells that story infinitely better than I can. It is in the " Review of Reviews " for February, 1910.

But there is another providential sequel to the events with which I began this statement. I made great friends at the Peace Conference with General Gross von Schwarzhoff and Admiral von Siegel, the Military and

Naval German Delegates, and I then (in 1899) imbibed those ideas as to the North Sea being our battle ground, which led to the great things between 1902 and 1910.

### III.—Ship-building and Dockyard Workers.

I have been asked to explain how I got rid of 6,000 redundant Dockyard workmen, when Mr. Childers nearly wrecked his Government by turning out but a few hundred. Well, this was how it was done. We brought home some 160 ships from abroad that could neither fight nor run away; enough men were thus provided for the fighting portion of the crews for all the new ships then lying in the Dockyards, which were not only deteriorating in their hulls and equipment for want of care, but were inefficient for war because officers and men must have practice in the ship they fight as much as the Bisley shot with his rifle, the jockey with his race-horse and the chef with his sauces. It is practice that makes perfect. The original plan for mobilising the Navy for war was that on the outbreak of war you disorganised the ships already fully manned and efficient by taking a portion of the trained crew, thus impairing the efficiency of that ship, and putting them into the un-manned ships and filling up both the old and the new—the former efficient ships and those in the dockyards—with men from the Reserve. So the whole Navy got disorganised. And that was what they called " Preparing for War ! " By what Mr. Balfour called a courageous stroke of the pen, in his speech at Manchester, when he was Prime Minister, every vessel in the Fleet by the new system had its fighting crew complete.

Those who were to fill up the hiatus were the hewers of wood and the drawers of water. The brains were there ; only the beef had to come, and the beef might have been taken from the Army.

When are we going to have the great Army and Navy Co-operative Society, which I set forth to King Edward in 1903—that the Army should be a Reserve for the Navy ? When shall we be an amphibious nation ? This last war has made us into a conscript Nation.

Well, to revert to the subject of how we got rid of the 6,000 redundant dockyard workmen. When that mass of Officers and men set free by the scrapping of the 160 ships that couldn't fight nor run away came back to Chatham, Portsmouth, Devonport, Pembroke, and Queenstown, then in those dockyard towns the tradesmen had the time of their lives, for the money that had flowed into the pockets of the Chinese, the Chileans, the Peruvians, the Boers, the Brazilians, made the shopkeepers of the dockyard towns into a mass of Liptons, so that when the 6,000 Dockyard workers tried, as they had done in the time of yore (in the time of Childers), to get the dockyard tradespeople to agitate and turn out their Members of Parliament, the tradespeople simply replied, " You be damned ! " and I arranged to find congenial occupation for these redundant dockyard workmen in private yards where they were much needed.

When I became Admiral Superintendent of Portsmouth Dockyard, I took another drastic step in concentrating all the workmen then leisurely building several different ships, and put them all like a hive of bees on to one ship and extended piece-work to the utmost limit that was conceivable. The result was that a battle-ship which would have taken three years to build was built in one year ; for the work of building a ship is so inter-laced, when they are working by piece-work especially, that if one man does not work his fellow workmen cannot earn so much, so this piece-work helps the overseers because the men oversee each other.

But there is another great principle which this hides. The one great secret of the fighting value of a battleship is to get her to sea quickly :—

> " Build few, and build fast,
> Each one better than the last."

You will come across some idiots whose minds are so deliciously symmetrical that they would prefer ten tor-toises to one greyhound to catch a hare, and it was one of the principal articles of the ancient creed that you built ships in batches. They strained at the gnat of uniformity and so swallowed the camel of inferiority. No progress—they were a batch.

### IV.—" JOLLY AND HUSTLE."

I have just been asked by an alluring, though somewhat elusive friend, to describe to you quite an excellent illustration of those famous words in " Ecclesiastes " " Cast thy bread upon the waters for thou shalt find it after many days." That's the text this alluring friend suggested to me to exemplify. For myself, I prefer the more heavenly text where the Scripture says : " Be not forgetful to entertain strangers : for thereby some have entertained angels unawares." It was quite an angel that I had to do with, and he ate my bread as follows :—

One day, when I was Admiral in North America, I received a telegram : " The President of the Grand Trunk Railway with forty distinguished American friends was arriving in about an hour's time on some business connected with railway affairs, and could they be permitted to see the battleship ' Renown.' " The "Renown " was my flagship. I sent a reply to the next station their special train was stopping at, asking them to lunch on board on their arrival at 1 p.m. I sent for Monsieur Augé, my wonderful chef, who on the produce of his service with me afterwards set up a restaurant in Paris (he really was excellent—but so extravagant !) and told him : " Lunch for forty, in an hour's time." All he said was " Oui, Monsieur," and he did it well ! I myself being really amazed.

The Company greatly enjoyed themselves. I had some wonderful champagne obtained from Admiral McCrea— of immortal memory as regards that requisite—which effectively seconded M. Augé's magnificent lunch.

Years after—it was in March, 1902—I was in a serious dilemma as to the completion of the necessary buildings at Osborne for the new scheme of entry of Officers to be inaugurated by the King in person, who was to open the new establishment on the fourth day of August following. Every effort had failed to get a satisfactory

# RECORDS

contract, when after a prolonged but fruitless discussion, I was sitting thinking what the devil I should do, when an Officer came in to see me on some business and mentioned casually that he had just come from lunching at the Carlton and had happened to overhear a man at an adjacent table say that he would give anything to see Sir John Fisher, as he had given him—with many others—the very best lunch he had ever had in his life. I sent the Officer back to the Carlton to bring him. On his arrival in my room I didn't remember him, but he at once thanked me—not for seeing the " Renown " and all the other things—but only for the lunch. He said he belonged to St. Louis and was over in England on business. He had completed a big hotel in three months, which no one else would contract to build under three years.

Then I thought of that angel whom I had entertained unawares ; certainly the bread that was cast came back all right. I explained my difficulty to him—I had all the particulars. He said he had his American staff over here, who had been working at the Hotel, and he would attend with the contract and the drawings in forty-eight hours. And he did. The contract was signed, and King Edward opened the buildings on August 4th.

An expert of our own who participated in the final proceedings asked the American gentleman's foreman how he did it, and especially how he had managed that hotel in the three months. I overheard the American's answer : " Well," he said, " this is how our boss does it ; when he is a-laying of the foundations he is a-thinking of the roof." " What is his name ? " said the English expert. " Well,"

60

replied the American, " his name is Stewart, but we always
call him ' JOLLY & HUSTLE.' " " Oh ! " said the
English expert, " Why that name ? " " Well, " he says,
" I will tell you. There's not one of his workmen, not
even the lower grades, gets less than fifteen shillings a day,
and as much as he likes to eat and drink—free of cost.
Well, that's *jolly*. But we has to work sixteen hours a
a day—that's *hustle*."

So when the defences of the Humber came into my
mind and no contractor could be got for so gigantic a
business, I telegraphed for " Jolly & Hustle," and when he
came over and said he would do it and that he was going
to bring everything, from a pin up to a pile-driver, from
America, it made the contractors at home reconsider the
position—and they did the work.

### V.—" Buying up Opportunities."

The words I take to head this section are as applicable
to the affairs of common life as they are to religion, with
reference to which they were originally spoken.

What these words signify is that Faith governs all
things. Victories on Earth have as their foundation the
same saving virtue of Faith.

One great exercise of Faith is " Redeeming the Time,"
as Paul says. (I'm told the literal meaning of the
original Greek is " buying up opportunities.") Most
people from want of Faith won't try again. Lord
Kelvin often used to tell me of his continuous desire of
" redeeming the time." Even in dressing himself he

61

sought every opportunity of saving time (so he told me)
in th'nking of the next operation. However his busy
brain sometimes got away from the business in hand,
as he once put his necktie in his pocket and his handker-
chief round his neck. (Another wonderfully clever
friend of mine, who used to think in the Differential
Calculus, I once met immaculately dressed, but he had
his trousers over his arm and not on.) And yet I am told
he was an extraordinarily acute business man. Every sailor
owes him undying gratitude for his " buying up opportunities " in the way he utilised a broken thigh, which
compelled him to go in a yacht, to invent his marvellous
compass and sounding machine. At the Bombardment
of Alexandria the firing of the eighty ton guns of the
" Inflexible " with maximum charges, which blew my
cap off my head and nearly deafened me, had no effect
on his compasses, and enabled us with supreme advantage to keep the ship steaming about rapidly and so get
less often hit whilst at the same time steering the ship
with accuracy amongst the shoals. So it was with the
ancient sounding machine : one had to stop the ship to
sound, and it was a laborious operation and inaccurate.
Lord Kelvin devised a glass tube which by the height
of the discoloration gave you the exact depth, no matter
how fast the ship was going ; and the beauty of it was
you kept the tubes as a register.

It was an immense difficulty getting the Admiralty to
adopt Lord Kelvin's compass. I was reprimanded for
having them on board. I always asked at a Court-
Martial, no matter what the prisoner was being tried for,

# EPISODES

whether they had Lord Kelvin's compass on board. It was only ridicule that got rid of the old Admiralty compass. At the inquiry the Judge asked me whether the Admiralty compass was sensitive (I was a witness for Lord Kelvin). I replied, " No, you had to kick it to get a move on." But what most scandalised the dear old Fossil who then presided over the Admiralty compass department was that I wanted to do away with the points of the compass and mark it into the three hundred and sixty degrees of the circle (you might as well have asked them to do away with salt beef and rum !). There could then never be any mistake as to the course the ship should steer. However, a landsman won't understand the beauty of this simplicity, and the " Old Salts " said at that time " There he is again—the d—d Revolutionary ! "

But to revert to " buying up opportunities " : I know no more signal instance of the goodness of Paul's advice both to the Ephesians and Colossians in things temporal as in things spiritual than as exemplified by the Gunnery Lieutenant of the " Inflexible " in discovering a fracture in one of her eighty-ton guns. He was always thinking ahead in everything—" Buying up Opportunities."

After the Bombardment of Alexandria we two were walking along the shore ; he stopped and said, " Hullo ! that's a bit of one of our shell, and it burst in the bore of the gun." As there were no end of pieces of burst shell about, which had exploded in striking the fort, I said, " How do you know it is ? " He pointed to the marks of the rifling on the shell, which showed that it had burst

63

in the bore and had been pressed into the grooves of the rifling, instead of being rotated by the copper band on its passage through the bore. Then he put his hand in his pocket, took out his clinometer, laid it on the marks of the rifling on the bit of burst shell ; and the rifling of our eighty-ton guns having an increasing spiral, he calculated the exact spot in the gun where the shell had burst. And when he got on board he had himself shoved up the bore of the gun holding a piece of hot gutta percha, like that with which the dentist takes the impression of your mouth for a set of false teeth, and brought me out the impression of where the gun had been cracked by the explosion of the shell. Younghusband was his name—perhaps the most gifted man I ever met, but, as unusual with genius, he was not indolent and was always practising himself in seizing opportunities. When the constituted authorities came to inspect the gun, though Younghusband put the broken bit of shell before them, they took a long time to find that crack. One night at Portsmouth someone told Younghusband, who was having his third glass of port after dinner, that he was too fat to walk. For a considerable bet he got up there and then and walked seventy-two miles to London. Younghusband never went to any school in his life ; he never left home ; he never had a governess or a tutor. He was taught by his mother.

### VI.—How the Great War was Carried on.

Six weeks after I left the Admiralty on May 22nd, 1915—that deplorable day, the particulars of which I

A GROUP ON BOARD H.M.S. "STANDARD," 1909.
The Czar, The Grand Duchess Olga, and
Sir John Fisher.

am not at present at liberty to mention—I received most cordial letters from both Mr. Asquith and Mr. Balfour welcoming me to fill a Post of great magnitude.

I am impelled to digress here for a few moments to tell a very excellent story of Dean Hole (famous for the cultivation of roses). He said to his Curate one day, " I am sick of hearing the name of that poor man whom we pray for every Sunday ; just say ' the prayers of the Congregation are requested for a member of the Congregation who is grievously ill.' " Next Sunday the Curate said at the usual place in Divine Service, " The prayers of the Congregation are requested for a gentleman whose name I'm not at liberty to mention ! " That's my case in regard to what happened between Saturday, May 15th, and Saturday, May 22nd, during which time I received communications which I hold in my hand at this moment, and which some day when made public will be just astonishing ! I am advised that the Law does not permit even an outline of them to be given.

I was invited by Mr. Balfour to preside over an Assemblage of the most Eminent Men of Science for War purposes ; the chief point was the German Submarine Menace. Also we had to consider Inventions, as well as Scientific Research.

My three Super-Eminent Colleagues of the Central Committee of this great Scientific Organisation were very famous men :—

(1) Sir J. J. Thomson, O.M., President of the Royal Society and now Master of Trinity. I am told (and I believe it) a man unparalleled in Science.

(2) The Hon. Sir Charles Parsons, K.C.B., the Inventor of the Turbine, which has changed the whole art of Marine Engineering, and enabled us to sink Admiral von Spee. We couldn't have sunk von Spee without Parsons's Turbine, as those two great Fast Battle-Cruisers " Invincible " and " Inflexible " could not have steamed otherwise 14,000 miles without a hitch (there and back). They only arrived at the Falkland Islands a few hours before Admiral von Spee.

(3) Sir George Beilby, F.R.S., one of the greatest of Chemists, who, if we don't take care, will give us a smokeless England, by getting rid of coal in its present beastly form, and turning it into oil and fertilisers, dyes, etc., etc. The Refuse he sells to the Poor fifty per cent. cheaper than coal and without smoke or ashes.

The Advisory Panel of other Distinguished Men was as famous as these Magi. There were also many Eminent Associates.

I felt extreme diffidence in occupying the Chair ; however, I put it to them all in the famous couplet of the French author who, in annexing the thoughts of other people, took this couplet as the text of his book :—

" I have cull'd a garland of flowers,
Mine only is the string that binds them."

I said to them all at our first Assemblage : " Gentlemen, You are the Flowers, I am the String ! "

You would have thought that such a Galaxy of Talent would have been revered, welcomed, and obeyed—on the contrary, it was derided, spurned, and ignored.

# EPISODES

The permanent " Expert Limpets " did for us ! All the three First Lords at the Admiralty whom we dealt with in succession were most cordial and most appreciative, but all three were equally powerless. Just a couple or so of instances will suffice to illustrate the reason why we at last said to Sir Eric Geddes :—

" Ave Geddes Imperator !
" Morituri te Salutant."

(1) The chief object of this magnificent Scientific Organisation being to counter the German Submarine Menace, we naturally asked for a Submarine to experiment with. The answer was " one could not be spared."

(2) We asked to be furnished with all the details of the destruction of German Submarines that had already taken place, which of course lay at the root of further investigation. This was denied us !

(3) A " Submarine Detector " was developed under the auspices of the Central Committee by May, 1916. A year was allowed to elapse before it was taken up ; and even then its progress was cancelled because nothing more than a laboratory experiment with a competing invention came to the notice of the " Limpets."

(4) The Scientific Members of our Association had conceived and practically demonstrated a most astoundingly simple method of discovering the passage of German Submarines. It was termed " The Loop Detection " scheme. It was turned

down—And then two years afterwards was violently
taken up, with astoundingly successful results.

I think I have said enough.   And really, after all, what
is the good of raking up the past ?

I have had two pieces of advice given me referring
to the trials I had experienced.   One was :—

" When sinners entice thee, consent thou not !—
But take the name and address for future reference."

And the other was :—" Fear less—hope more ; eat
less—chew more ;  whine less—breathe more (deep
breathing) ; talk less—say more ; hate less—love more,
and all good things are yours."

# CHAPTER V

*" Government of the people—by the people—for the people."*
*(President Abraham Lincoln at Gettysburg, 1863.)*

SOME time ago the Vice-Chancellor of Cambridge University presided at a lecture on Democracy given at Cambridge by the Professor of History at Chicago (A. C. McLaughlin). I gather that he implied that Democracy is helpless in the game of secret diplomacy and secret treaties. Democracy now all depends upon the purpose and desire of the English-speaking people.

It's an opportune moment to repeat John Bright's very famous speech on a great federation of the nations that speak the Anglo-Saxon tongue.

The speech was given me when crossing the Atlantic by a splendid citizen of the United States, where I had just been receiving boundless hospitality and a wonderful welcome, and had realised the truth about a prophet when not in his own country, and had been asked to " stump the Middle West " to advocate the cause of friendship amongst all those who speak our incomparable tongue, and to establish a Great Commonwealth of Free Nations. There can be no secret treaties and no secret

69

diplomacy when the Government is of the People, by the People, for the People.

This is John Bright's speech :

" Now what can one say of the future of our race and of our kinsmen ?  Is that merely a dream ?  By no means. . . .  Look where we are now ? . . .

" In this country, in Canada, and in the United States there are, or soon will be, one hundred and fifty millions of population, nearly all of whom owe their birth and origin to the comparatively small country in which we live.  It is a fact that is not paralleled in any past history, and what may come in the future to compare with it or excel it, it is not for us to speak of, or even with any show of reason to imagine ; but we have in all these millions the same language, the same  literature, mainly the same laws and the institutions of freedom.  May we not hope for the highest and noblest  federation to be established among us ?  That is a question to which I would ask your special and sympathetic attention.  The noblest kind of federation among us, under different Governments it may be, but united by race, by sympathy, by freedom of industry, by communion of interests and by a perpetual peace, we may help to lead the world to that better time which we long for and which we believe in, though it may not be permitted to our mortal eyes to behold it."

That was said by John Bright.

The time has now come for this great federation which he desired—for this great Commonwealth of Free Nations.

There is only one type of treaty which is effective—" Community of Interests."

All other treaties are " Scraps of Paper."

# DEMOCRACY

It is maintained by eminent men that the late appalling and disastrous war, in which so many millions of human beings have been massacred or maimed, would never have occurred *had there been a real Democracy in power in England.* They say, as a small instance, that the great Mutiny at the Nore and other mutinies were brought about by trampling on Democracy.

This is what pure and unadulterated Democracy is, and we have not got it in England :—

## "EQUAL OPPORTUNITY FOR ALL."

For instance, no parent with less than nearly a £1000 a year can now send his boy into the Navy as an Officer!

Nature is no respecter of birth or money power when she lavishes her mental and physical gifts.

*We fight God when our Social System dooms the brilliant clever child of the poor man to the same level as his father.*

Therefore, we must have such State provision and such State education as will enable the very poorest in the land to let their eligible children rise to Admirals, Generals, Ambassadors, and Statesmen.

Can it be conceived that a real Democracy would have permitted secret treaties such as have been divulged to us, or have scouted the terms of Peace which were allowed only to be seen by Kings and Prime Ministers ; or would a real Democracy have flouted the Russian Revolution in its first agonizing throes when gasping for help and recognition ?

71

In a real Democracy, would true Labour leaders have waited on the doormat ?

Would a real Democracy wave the red rag of " Empire " in front of these noble self-governing peoples all speaking our tongue in their own free Parliaments, and all of them praying for the hastening of the time when " England, the Mother of Free Parliaments, shall herself be free " ?

But the Glorious Epoch is now fast approaching !   ·

A Prime Minister once complimented me on a casual saying of mine at his luncheon table.   I was accounting for part of my success against

> " Many giants great and tall,"

and I ventured to state that :—

" The secret of successful administration was the intelligent anticipation of agitation."

*Anticipate the Revolution.*   Do the thing yourself in your way before the agitators get in before you and do it in their way.   Get rid of the present obsolete Forms and Antique Ceremonies which grate on the masses, and of Figureheads who are laughing-stocks, and of sinecures which are exasperating—and so anticipate another Cromwell, who is certainly now coming fast along to " Remove another Bauble ! "

I forget what they did to the man who tried to import poisonous snakes into New Zealand (finding that happy island unblessed with this commodity).   It was something quite drastic they did to *him !*   They killed the snakes.

The Canadian House of Commons adopted by a majority of 33 a motion by Sir Robert Borden, on behalf

of the Canadian Government, asking that no more
hereditary titles should be bestowed in Canada, and
declaring that the Canadian Government should make
all recommendations for honours of any kind. This
motion was a compromise designed to damp down the
popular outcry against titles which has arisen in Canada.
In one debate Sir Wilfrid Laurier offered to throw his
own title on a common bonfire. He urged that all titles
in Canada should be abolished.

Why should Great Britain lag behind Canada and the
United States? Hereditary titles are ludicrously out of
date in any modern democracy, and the sooner we sweep
away all the gimcracks and gewgaws of snobbery the
better. The fount of so-called honour has become a
deluge, and the newspapers are hard put to it to find
room for even the spray of the deluge.

The war has not begotten simplicity and austerity in
this respect. On the contrary, it has made what used to
be a comedy a screaming farce. There was a time when
the Birthday Honours List could be printed on one day,
but it is now a serial novel. The first chapter of the
latest Birthday list was long, but the *Times* warned us
that it was only " the first of a series which already
threatens to outlast the week—quite apart from the
gigantic Order of the British Empire."

Chicago's great Professor of History, Mr. McLaughlin,
made the statement at the Kingsway Hall, in his address
to British teachers, that now the United States have over
100 millions of people, and fifty years from now they
may well have 200 millions—a great Atlantic and Pacific

Power. The Professor added that this great War was " *to protect Democracy against the greatest menace it has ever had* " (in the present rule of Kings and Secret Treaties, etc., etc.). Another points out as a striking example of present old-time conditions (so pernicious to freedom and efficiency) the positive fact now existing that our Military Leaders, by a class distinction, were only selected from one twenty-fifth of the ore which we have at our disposal though we had brought five million men under arms, as all our generals commanding armies, army corps, divisions, and in most cases brigades, were drawn from among the Regular Forces who handled our small pre-War Army of two hundred thousand men. And the writer adds :

" If considered purely from the standpoint of the law of averages, one would expect to find more good brains if one searched the entire Army than in merely looking for material in one twenty-fifth of it."

General Currie, who so ably commands all the Canadian Forces, was a Land Agent before the War. Neither Napoleon nor Wellington ever commanded a regiment. Marlborough never handled an army till he was fifty-two years of age. Clive was a Bank Clerk. Napoleon's maxim was " *La carrière ouverte aux talents.*" Are we ever going to adopt it ?

### PEACE

This truth is (*and ever will be*) the fact that the only pact that ever holds, and the only treaty that ever lasts is :

" *COMMUNITY OF INTEREST !* "

and we can only have Community of Interest in the masses of a People always being on the side of Peace, because it's the masses who are massacred, not the Kings and Generals and Politicians (they are plentifully fed and comfortably housed, and have the best white bread—*vide* the American Dentist, Davies, when he stayed with the German Emperor).

Well! the only way the masses of the People can act effectively is by means of Republics. Because then no secret diplomacy ever answers, and no one man can make war, or no coterie of men. In a Republic we get " Government of the People, by the People, for the People."

It's a cheap sneer to ask how long the same Government ever exists in Republican France! Nevertheless, sooner millions of changes of Government and Peace than a stable Government with War! *A Republic is always Peace-loving!* except when righteous fury in a gust of popular rage sweeps it into war, as lately in America; but it took four years to move them! The People pushed the President. We are going to have Bolshevism unless we foster these German Republics, and it will spread righteously to England.

These Leagues of Nations and Freedoms of the Seas and all the other items are all d—d nonsense! When War does come, then " Might is Right." " La raison du plus fort est toujours la meilleure! " and every treaty is a Scrap of Paper!

> The Essence of War is Violence.
> Moderation in War is Imbecility.

75

# RECORDS

You hit first, you hit hard, and keep on hitting.
You have to be Ruthless, Relentless and Remorseless.
It's perfect rot to talk about " Civilised Warfare ! "
You might as well talk about a " Heavenly Hell ! "


### FROM LORD FISHER TO A FRIEND.

MY DEAR ——,

I wrote to a distinguished friend to note (but not to congratulate him) that he had been made " a Companion of Honour " (what that is I don't know !), and told him one of the disadvantages of even a " Limited Monarchy " was the making of us all into Christmas Trees to hang Decorations upon ! He replied he had declined it, as he did not wish " to be regarded as a dab of paint to camouflage this new Order instituted for Labour Leaders ! " Haven't I always told you we are a Nation of Snobs, and that even the Labour Leaders don't resent being kept hanging about on the door mat ?

My dear friend adds : " I feel sure your conception of Democracy will be realised." (I had sent him my Paper on Democracy that you didn't like !) " *Liberty means a Country where every man or woman has an equal chance."*

" The race of Life in a civilised Country is a race carried out under a system of handicaps, and the people who do the handicapping are the people of the least brains.

" The prophecy you send me is wonderful."

I think the words of this my friend will interest you, *though perhaps not convince you !*

Yours till death,

F.

9/6/18.

# DEMOCRACY

## The Battle Hymn of the Republic.

I have been sitting this morning under a Presbyterian
Minister, Dr. Hugh Black, whose eloquence so moved
the Prime Minister, Mr. Lloyd George (who kindly
gave me a seat in his pew, on the other side of
me being President Wilson, at the Presbyterian Church
in Paris on May 25th, 1919), that the moment the
service was ended the Prime Minister went straight
to him in the pulpit and told him it was one of the
best sermons he had ever heard.  And it probably
was.  One word Dr. Black used was very descriptive.
He described us all, except those homeless ones for whom
the Saviour pleaded in Dr. Black's text, as the " sheltered "
classes.  I think also our feelings in the congregation
(not that I wish to derogate from the sermon) had been
intensely moved by the magnificent singing on the part
of the great congregation (mostly American Citizens) of
the Battle Hymn of the American Republic, composed
by Julia Ward Howe.  The tune (" John Brown's Body "),
as Mr. Sankey said, no doubt has much to do with the
glorious emphasis of the chorus ;  but certainly the words
are magnificent :—

### BATTLE HYMN OF THE REPUBLIC.

Mine eyes have seen the Glory of the Coming of the Lord ;
He is trampling out the vintage where the grapes of wrath are
   stored ;
He hath loosed the fatal lightning of His terrible swift sword,
His truth is marching on.

    Glory ! Glory ! Hallelujah ! Glory ! Glory ! Hallelujah !
    Glory ! Glory ! Hallelujah ! His truth is marching on.

77

# RECORDS

I have seen Him in the watch-fires of a hundred circling camps ;
They have builded Him an altar in the evening dews and damps ;
I can read His righteous sentence by the dim and flaring lamps,
His day is marching on.

>  Glory, etc.

I have read a fiery gospel writ in burnished rows of steel ;
" As ye deal with my contemners, so with you my grace shall deal "
Let the Hero born of woman crush the serpent with His heel,
Since God is marching on.

>  Glory, etc.

He has sounded forth the trumpet that shall never call retreat ;
He is sifting out the hearts of men before His Judgment seat ;
Oh, be swift, my soul, to answer Him ! be jubilant, my feet !
Our God is marching on.

>  Glory, etc.

In the beauty of the lilies Christ was born across the sea ;
With the glory in His bosom that transfigures you and me ;
As He died to make men holy, let us die to make men free,
While God is marching on.

>  Glory, etc.

It reminded me of the 76th Psalm, sung by those old Covenanters when they vanquished Claverhouse at Drumclog. We see the Battle Field of Drumclog from the room where we are now talking.

>  " In Judah's land God is well known,
>  His name's in Isr'l great."

I began a letter (but diffidence made me stop it) to Sir William Watson the poet, to ask him if he couldn't give us some such great Hymn for the Nation.

" God Save the King " is worn out. We don't individualise now. It is as worn out as knee breeches for Court Functions or Gold Lace Coats for Sea Officers.

# CHAPTER VI

I HAVE made four accurately reported public speeches, the fifth one (at Mr. Josephus Daniels's reception by the American Luncheon Club) is too inadequate to include here. For none of these four speeches had I any notes, except for the one of a hundred words and one of fifty words, both delivered in the House of Lords. The other two were simply and solely my exuberant verbosity, and they must be read with that remark in mind. I was saturated with the subject ; and when the *Times* reporter came and asked me for my speech before I'd made it, I told him with truth that I really didn't know what I was going to say. I might have been like Thackeray (What a classic case his was !). He was the Guest of Honour. He got up, was vociferously cheered, and was dumb. After a death-like silence he said these words, and sat down :—" If I could only remember what I thought of to say to you when I was coming here in the cab, you really would have had a delightful speech ! "

## I.—THE ROYAL ACADEMY BANQUET, 1903.

The Navy always readily appreciates the kind words in which this toast is proposed, and also the kind manner in which it is always received. I beg to thank you especially, Mr. President, for your kind reference to Captain Percy Scott, which was so well deserved. He was indeed a handy man. (Cheers.) Personally I have not the same pleasurable feelings on this occasion as I enjoyed last year, when I had no speech to make. I remember quite well remarking to my neighbour : " How good the whitebait is, how excellent the champagne, and how jolly not to have to make a speech." He glared at me and said : " I have got to make a speech, and the whitebait to me is *bête noire*, and the champagne is real pain." (Laughter.) He was so ready with his answer that I thought to myself : " You'll get through it all right," and sure enough he did, for he spoke thirty minutes by the clock without a check. (Laughter.) I am only going to give you three minutes (cries of " No.") Yes. I always think on these occasions of the first time I went to sea on board my first ship, an old sailing two-decker, and I saw inscribed in great big gold letters the one word " Silence." (Laughter.) Underneath was another good motto : " Deeds, not words." (Cheers.) I have put that into every ship I have commanded since. (Cheers.) This leads me to another motto which is better still, and brings me to the point of what I have to say in reply to the toast that has been proposed. When I was Commander-in-Chief in the Mediterranean I went to inspect a small Destroyer, only 260 tons, but with such pride and swagger that she might have been 16,000 tons. (Laughter.) The young Lieutenant in command took me round. She was in beautiful order, and I came aft to the wheel and saw

1.      2.      3.  4.    5.

A GROUP ON BOARD H.M.S. "STANDARD," 1909.

1. The Empress Marie of Russia.   3. Sir John Fisher.
2. The Czarina.                   4. The Grand Duchess Olga.
5. The Czar.

there the inscription : " Ut Veniant Omnes." " Hallo,"
I said, " what the deuce is that ? " (Laughter.) Saluting
me, he said : " Let 'em all come, Sir." (Great laughter
and cheers.) Well, that was not boasting ; that was the
sense of conscious efficiency—(cheers)—the sense that
permeates the whole Fleet—(cheers)—and I used to
think, as the Admiral, it will be irresistible provided the
Admiral is up to the mark. The Lord Chief Justice,
sitting near me now, has kindly promised to pull me down
if I say too much ! (Laughter.) But what I wish to
remark to you is this—and it is a good thing for everybody
to know it—there has been a tremendous change in Navy
matters since the old time. In regard to Naval warfare
history is a record of exploded ideas. (Laughter and
cheers.) In the old days they were sailors' battles ;
now they are Admirals' battles. I should like to recall
to you the greatest battle at sea ever fought. What was
the central episode of that ? Nelson receiving his death-
wound ! What was he doing ? Walking up and down
on the quarter-deck arm-in-arm with his Captain. It is
dramatically described to us by an onlooker. His
Secretary is shot down ; Nelson turns round and says :
" Poor Scott ! Take him down to the cockpit," and then
he goes on again walking up and down, having a yarn with
his Captain. What does that mean ? It means that in
the old days the Admiral took his fleet into action ; each
ship got alongside the enemy ; and, as Nelson finely said,
" they got into their proper place." (Cheers.) And
then the Admiral had not much more to do. The ships
were touching one another nearly, the Bos'un went with

some rope and lashed them together so as to make them quite comfortable—(laughter)—and the sailors loaded and fired away till it was time to board. But what is the case now ? It is conceivable that within twenty minutes of sighting the enemy on the horizon the action will have begun, and on the disposition of his Fleet by the Admiral —on his tactics—the battle will depend, for all the gunnery in the world is no good if the guns are masked by our own ships or cannot bear on the enemy ! In that way I wish to tell you how much depends on the Admirals now and on their education. Therefore, joined with this spirit, of which the remark of the young Lieutenant I mentioned to you is an indication, permeating the whole Service, we require a fearless, vigorous, and progressive administration, open to any reform—(loud cheers)— never resting on its oars—for to stop is to go back—and forecasting every eventuality. I will just take two instances at hazard.

*Look at the Submarine Boat and Wireless Telegraphy. When they are perfected we do not know what a Revolution will come about.*

In their inception they were the weapons of the weak. Now they loom large as the weapons of the strong.

*Will any Fleet be able to be in narrow waters ?*

Is there the slightest fear of invasion with them, even for the most extreme pessimist ? I might mention other subjects ; but the great fact which I come to is that we are realising—the Navy and the Admiralty are realising —*that on the British Navy rests the British Empire.* (Loud cheers.) Nothing else is of any use without it, not even the Army. (Here the gallant Admiral, amid laughter, turned to Mr. Brodrick, the Secretary for War, who sat near him.) We are different from Continental nations. No soldier of ours can go anywhere unless a sailor carries him there on his back. (Laughter.) I am not disparaging the Army. I am looking forward to their coming to sea with us again as they did in the old days. Why, Nelson had three regiments of infantry with him at the battle of Cape St. Vincent, and a Sergeant of the 69th Regiment led the boarders, and, Nelson having only one arm, it was the Sergeant who helped him up. (Cheers.) The Secretary for War particularly asked me to allude to the Army or else I would not have done it. (Loud laughter.) In conclusion, I assure you that the Navy and the Admiralty recognise their responsibility. I think I may say that we now have a Board of Admiralty that is united, progressive, and determined—(cheers)—and you may sleep quietly in your beds—(loud cheers).

## II.—The Lord Mayor's Banquet, 1907.

As to the strength, the efficiency, and the sufficiency of the Navy, I am able to give you indisputable proofs. Recently, in the equinoctial season in the North Sea we have had twenty-six of the finest battleships in the world and twenty-five of the finest cruisers, some of them equal to foreign battleships, and over fifty other vessels, under eleven Admirals, and all working under a distinguished Commander-in-Chief, under very trying circumstances and in a very stormy time, and I look in vain to see any equal to that large Fleet anywhere. (Cheers.) That is only a fraction of our power. (Cheers.) And that large Fleet is *nulli secundus*, as they say, whether it is ships or officers or men. (Cheers.) Now, I turn to the other point, the gunnery of the Fleet. The gunnery efficiency of the Fleet has surpassed all records—it is unparalleled—and I am lost in wonder and admiration at the splendid unity of spirit and determination that must have been shown by everybody from top to bottom to obtain these results. (Cheers.) I am sure that your praise and your appreciation will go forth to them, because, remember, the best ships, the biggest Navy— my friend over there talked about the two-Power standard —a million-Power standard (laughter) is no use unless you can hit. (Cheers.) You must hit first, you must hit hard, and you must keep on hitting. (Cheers.) If these are the fruits, I don't think there is much wrong with the government of the Navy. (Cheers.) Figs don't grow on thistles. (Laughter and cheers.) But a gentleman of fine feeling has lately said that the recent Admiralty administration has been attended with the devil's own luck. (Laughter.) That interesting personality (laughter)—his luck is due to one thing, and one thing only—hesitates at nothing to gain his object. That is what the Board of Admiralty have done, and our object has been the fighting efficiency of the Fleet and its instant readiness for war ; and we have got it. (Cheers.) And I say it because no one can have a fuller knowledge than myself about it, and I speak with the fullest sense of re-sponsibility. (Cheers.) So I turn to all of you, and I turn to my countrymen and I say—Sleep quiet in your beds (laughter and cheers), and do not be disturbed by these bogeys—invasion and otherwise—which are being periodically resuscitated by all sorts of leagues. (Laughter.) I do not know what league is working this one. It is quite curious what reputable people lend themselves to these scares. This afternoon I read the effusions of a red-hot and most charmingly interesting magazine editor. He had evidently been victimised by a *Punch* correspondent, and that *Punch* correspondent had been gulled by some Midshipman Easy of the Channel Fleet. He had been there. And this is what the magazine editor prints in italics in this month's magazine—that an army of 100,000 German soldiers had been practising embarking in the German Fleet. The absolute truth is that one solitary regiment was embarked for manœuvres. That is the truth. To embark 100,000 soldiers you want hundreds and thousands of tons of transport. You might just as well talk of practising embarking St. Paul's Cathedral in a penny steamer. (Laughter.) I have no doubt that equally silly stories are current in Germany. I have no doubt that there is terror there that the English Fleet will swoop down all of a sudden and gobble up the German Fleet. (Laughter.) These stories are not only silly—they are mischievous, very mischievous. (Hear, hear.) If Eve had not kept on looking at that apple (laughter)—and it was pleasant to the eyes—she would not have picked it, and we should not have been now bothered with clothes. (Loud laughter.) I was very nearly forgetting something else

85

that the *Punch* correspondent said. I put it in my pocket as I came away to read it out to you. He had been a week in the Channel Fleet and he had discussed everything, from the admiral down to the bluejacket. He does not say anything about that Midshipman Easy. " In one matter I found unanimity of admission. It was that in respect to the number of fighting ships, their armament, and general capacity the British Navy was never in so satisfactory a condition as it floats to-day." (Cheers.) So we let him off that yarn about the 100,000 German troops. (Laughter.)

### III.—THE HOUSE OF LORDS, NOVEMBER 16, 1915.

LORD FISHER, rising from the cross-benches immediately before public business was called, said :— " I ask leave of your lordships to make a statement. Certain references were made to me in a speech delivered yesterday by Mr. Churchill. I have been 61 years in the service of my country, and I leave my record in the hands of my countrymen. The Prime Minister said yesterday that Mr. Churchill had said one or two things which he had better not have said, and that he necessarily and naturally left unsaid some things which will have to be said. I am content to wait. It is unfitting to make personal explanations affecting national interests when my country is in the midst of a great war."

Lord Fisher, having delivered his brief statement, immediately left the House.

# PUBLIC SPEECHES

## IV.—The House of Lords, March 21, 1917.

Lord Fisher addressed the House of Lords.

Immediately prayers were over he rose from a seat on one of the cross-benches. He said :—

" With your Lordships' permission, I desire to make a personal statement. When our country is in great jeopardy, as she now is, it is not the time to tarnish great reputations, to asperse the dead, and to discover our supposed weaknesses to the enemy ; so I shall not discuss the Dardanelles Reports—I shall await the end of the war, when all the truth can be made known."

# CHAPTER VII

SIR WILLIAM ALLAN, M.P., with the torso of a Hercules and the voice of a bull and the affectionate heart of Mary Magdalene, did not know Latin, and he asked me what my motto meant:

" Fiat justitia—ruat cœlum."

I had sent it to him when he was malignantly attacking me because, as Controller of the Navy, I had introduced the water-tube boiler. Sir William Allan was himself a boiler-maker, and he had to scrap most of his plant because of this new type of boiler.

I said the translation was : " Do right, and damn the odds."

This motto has stood me in good stead, for by attending to it I fought a great battle in a righteous cause with Lord Salisbury, when he was Prime Minister, and conquered. I have related this elsewhere. Years after, Lord Salisbury, in remembrance of this, recalled me from being Commander-in-Chief in America to be British delegate at the First Peace Conference at The Hague in 1899, and from thence I went as Commander-in-Chief of the Mediterranean Fleet.

## THE ESSENTIALS OF SEA FIGHTING

While I was in command of the Mediterranean Fleet, from 1899 to 1902, when I became Second Sea Lord of the Admiralty, I arranged to have lectures for the officers of the Fleet. I extract now from the notes of my lectures some points which may be of general interest, as illustrating the new strategy and tactics necessitated by the change from wind to steam.

After setting forth a few of the problems which would have to be solved in sea-fighting under the new conditions, the lecturer went on to elaborate the themes from such rough notes as I give here of the principal ideas.

All Officers without exception should be unceasingly occupied in considering the various solutions of these problems, as who can tell who will be in command after the first five minutes of a close engagement, whether in an individual ship or in command of the whole Fleet! Otherwise we may have a stampede like that of riderless horses! The Captain or Admiral is *hors de combat*, and the next Officer, and, perhaps, the next, and the next don't know what to do when moments mean victory or defeat!

" The man who hesitates is lost ! " and so it will be with the Fleet if decision is wanting !

" Time, Twiss, time is everything ! " said Nelson (speaking to General Twiss when he was chasing the French Fleet under Villeneuve to the West Indies); " a quarter of an hour may mean the difference between Victory and Defeat ! "

This was in sailing days. Now it will be quarters of a minute, not quarters of an hour !

It is said to have been stated by one of the most eminent of living men, that sudden war becomes daily more probable because public opinion is becoming greater in power, and that popular emotion, once fairly aroused, sweeps away the barriers of calm deliberation, and is deaf to the voice of reason.

Besides cultivating the faculty of Quick Decision and consequent rapid action, we must cultivate Rashness.

Napoleon was asked the secret of victory. He replied, " *L'audace, l'audace, l'audace, toujours l'audace !* "

There is a rashness which in Peace is Folly, but which in War is Prudence, and there are risks that must be undertaken in War which are Obligatory, but which in peace would be Criminal !

As in War, so in the preparation for War, Rashness must have its place. We must also reflect how apt we are to suppose that the enemy will fit himself into our plans !

The first successful blow on either side will probably determine the final issue in sea-fighting. Sustained physical energy will be the required great attribute at that time for those in command as well as those who administer. Collingwood wrote two years before Trafalgar, when blockading Rochefort—and Nelson then off Toulon, Pellew off Ferrol, and Cornwallis off Brest— that " *Admirals needed to be made of iron !* " The pressure then will test the endurance of the strongest, and the rank of Admiral confers no immunity from the operation of the natural law of *Anno Domini !* Nelson was 39 years old at the Battle of the Nile, and died at 47. What is our average age of those actively responsible for the control, mobilisation, and command of our Fleets ? As age increases, audacity leaks out and caution comes in.

An instant offensive is obligatory. Mahan truly says:—

" The assumption of a simple defensive in war is ruin. War, once declared, must be waged offensively, aggressively. The enemy must not be fended off, but smitten down. You may then spare him every exaction, relinquish every gain. But till down he must be struck incessantly and remorselessly."[1]

---

[1] *Was that our Sea Policy during the War ?* Did we not keep our Fleet in cotton wool ?

## THE ESSENTIALS OF SEA FIGHTING

All will depend on the instant start, the sudden blow !
Napoleon again, " *Frappez vite et frappez fort !* " That
was the whole of his orders.

The question of armament is all-important !

If we have the advantage of speed, *which is the first
desideratum in every class of fighting vessel (Battleships
included), then, and then only*, we can choose our distance
for fighting. If we can choose our distance for fighting,
then we can choose our armament for fighting ! But how
in the past has the armament been chosen ? Do we
arrange the armament to meet the proposed mode of
fighting ? Doesn't it sometimes look like so many of each
sort, as if you were peopling the Ark, and wanted representatives of all calibres ?

*Whoever hits soonest and oftenest will win !*

" The effectiveness of a fighting weapon," wrote
Mahan, " consists more in the method of its use and in
the practised skill of the human element that wields it
than in the material perfection of the weapon itself. The
sequel of a long period of peace is a demoralisation of
ideals. Those who rise in peace are men of formality
and routine, cautious, inoffensive, safe up to the limits
of their capacity, supremely conscientious, punctilious
about everything but what is essential, yet void altogether
of initiative, impulse and originality.

" This was the difference between Hawke and Matthews. Hawke represented the spirit of war, the ardour,
the swift initiative, the readiness of resource, the im-
patience of prescription and routine, without which no
great things are done ! Matthews, the spirit of peace, the
very reverse of all this ! "

Peace brings with it the reign of old men.

The sacred fire never burnt in Collingwood. Nelson,
with the instinct of genius, intended the Fleet to anchor,
turning the very dangers of the shoals of Trafalgar into
a security. Collingwood, simply a naval machine, and
never having been his own master all his life, and not

being a genius, thought a shoal was a thing to be avoided, and, consequently, wrecked the ships unfitted to cope with a gale, and so to weather these shoals ! Collingwood ought to have had the moon given him for his crest, for all his glory was reflected from Nelson, the sun of glory ! Collingwood was an old woman !

History is a record of exploded ideas. In what sense ? Fighting conditions are all altered. The wind formerly determined the course of action ; now it is only the mind of man. One man and the best man is wanted—not a fossil ; not a careful man. Fleets were formerly days coming into action, now only minutes.

Two Fleets can now be fighting each other in twenty minutes from first seeing each other's smoke.

Formerly sea battles were Sailors' battles, now they are Officers'.

At Trafalgar, Nelson was walking up and down the Quarter-Deck and having a yarn with his Flag Captain, Hardy, at the very zenith of the Action ! It was the common sailors only who were then at work. How different now ! *The Admiral everything !*

Now, the different phases of a Naval War are as capable of as exact a demonstration as a proposition in Euclid, because steam has annihilated wind and sea. We are now trained to a higher standard, and the arts of strategy and tactics have accordingly been immensely magnified. Make an initial mistake in strategy or tactics, and then it may be said of them as of women by Congreve :

" Hell has no fury like a woman scorn'd."

The last place to defend England will be the Shores of England.

The Frontiers of England are the Coasts of the Enemy. We ought to be there five minutes before war breaks out.

Naval Supremacy once destroyed is destroyed for ever. Carthage, Spain, Holland, the great commercial nations of the past, had the sea wrested from them, and then they fell.

A successful Mercantile Marine leads to a successful War Navy.

It is solely owing to our command of the sea that we have been able to build up our magnificent Empire.

Admiral Mahan's most famous passage is :—

" The world has never seen a more impressive demonstration of the influence of Sea Power upon its history. Those far-distant, storm-beaten ships of Nelson, upon which the Grand Army never looked, stood between it and the dominion of the World."

" SECRECY AND SECRETIVENESS."

There are three types of Secrecy :—

I. The Ostrich.
II. The Red Box.
III. The Real Thing.

I. The ostrich buries his head in the sand of the desert when pursued by his enemy, and because he can't see the enemy concludes the enemy can't see him ! Such is the secrecy of the secretive and detestable habit which hides from our own officers what is known to the world in other Navies.

II. The secrecy of the Red Box is that of a distinguished Admiral who, with great pomp, used to have his red despatch box carried before him (like the umbrella of an African King), as containing the most secret plans ; but one day, the box being unfortunately capsized and burst open, the only contents that fell out were copies of " La Vie Parisienne " !

Such, it is feared, was the secrecy of those wonderful detailed plans for war we hear of in the past as having been secreted in secret drawers, to be brought out " when the time comes," and when no one has any time to study

93

them, supposing, that is, they ever existed; and, remember, it is detailed attention to minutiæ and the consideration of trifles which spells success.

III. There is the legitimate secrecy and secretiveness of hiding from your dearest friend the moment and the nature of your rush at the enemy, and which of all the variety of *operations you have previously practised with the Fleet* you will bring into play ! But all your Captains will instantly know your mind and intentions, for you will hoist the signal or spark the wireless message, Plan A, or Plan B . . . , or Plan Z !

" After I have made known my intentions," began Nelson's last order ; and it expressed the experience of a hundred battles—that the Second in Command (and in these days it may well be amplified into the individual officers in command) are to fulfil the spirit of the peace manœuvre teaching, and assist by the teaching in carrying out the meaning of brief signals to the destruction of the enemy's Fleet. The secret of success lies in the first part of the sentence : " *After I have made known my intentions.*"

Confidence is a plant of slow growth. Long and constant association of ships of a Fleet is essential to success. A new-comer is often more dangerous than the enemy.

An Army may be improvised in case of war, but not a Navy.

Immense importance of constant readiness at all times. A Fleet always ready to go to sea at an hour's notice is a splendid national life preserver ! Here comes in the water-tube boiler ! Without previous notice or even an inkling, we have been ready to start in one hour with water-tube boiler ships. You can't exaggerate this ! One bucket of water ready on the spot in the shape of an instantly ready Fleet will stop the conflagration of war which all the Fire Brigades of the world won't stop a little later on ! Never forget that from the very nature of sea fighting an initial Naval disaster is irretrievable, irreparable, eternal. Naval Colensos have no Paardebergs !

*Suddenness* is the secret of success at sea, because suddenness is practicable, and remember that rashness may be the height of prudence. How very rash Nelson was at the Nile to go in after dark to fight the French Fleet with no chart of the shoals of Aboukir !

But you must be sure of your Fleet and they must be sure of you ! Every detail previously thought out. Trust no one ! (My friend, Maurice Bourke, used to tell a story of the Yankee barber, who put up in his shop : " To trust is to bust, and to bust is hell ! " which means " no credit given "). Make the very best of things as they are. Criminal to wait for something better. " We strain at the gnat of perfection and swallow the camel of unreadiness."

## " THE GREAT SILENT NAVY."

The usual motto is " Silence " or " Deeds, not words," which you will see ornamenting some conspicuous place in a ship.[1] It has been said by landsmen that the most striking feature to them in a British man-of-war when at sea is the noiseless, ceaseless, sleepless, yet unobtrusive, energy that characterises everyone and everything on board ! If so, we sailors don't notice it, and it is the result of nature ! Gales of wind, sudden fogs, immense speeds, the much multiplied dangers of collision and wreck from these terrific speeds, as in Destroyers and even in large ships, all these circumstances automatically react on all on board and are nature's education by environment. There is no place for the unthinking or the lethargic. He is a positive danger ! Every individual in a man-of-war has his work cut out ! " Think and act for yourself "

[1] These mottoes were painted up in my first ship, and I have had them in every ship I have commanded since.

95

is to be the motto of the future, not " Let us wait for orders ! "

Such may be said of sea fights ! No mountains delay us, and, as Scripture says, the way of a ship is trackless ! The enemy will suddenly confront us as an Apparition ! At every moment we must be ready ! Can this be acquired by grown men ? No ! it is the force of habit. You must commence early. Our Nelsons and Benbows began the sea life when they first put their breeches on ! The brother of the Black Prince (John of Gaunt) joined the Navy and was in a sea fight when he was 10 years of age ! Far exceeding anything known in history does our future Trafalgar depend on promptitude and rapid decision, and on every eventuality having been foreseen by those in command. But these attributes cannot be acquired late in life, nor by those who have lived the life of cabbages ! So begin early and work continuously. Then if there is war your opportunity must come ! Like Kitchener, you will then walk over the cabbages !

A Group at Langham House. Photograph taken and sent to Sir John Fisher by the Empress Marie of Russia.

1. Mrs. Neeld.   2. Miss Diana Neeld.   3. The Princess Victoria.   4. Lady Fisher.
5. Queen Alexandra.   6. Miss Kitty Fullerton.   7. Sir John Fisher.

# CHAPTER VIII

JONAH'S GOURD

"Came up in a night
And perished in a night."

JONAH, chap. iv, verse 10.

THE above words came into my mind late last night
when tired out with destroying masses of papers and
letters (mostly malignant abuse or the emanations of
senile dotage), I sat back in my chair and soliloquised
over what had happened to all these pestilent attackers
of mine; and I said to myself in those immortal
words in Jonah, "*Doest thou well to be angry?*"
and for a few brief moments I really quite felt like
Stephen praying for his enemies when they stoned
him! What has become of all these stone-throwers
and backbiters, I asked myself! Like Jonah's Gourd
—"A worm has smote them all"—and they have
withered into obscurity. But yet it's interesting, as
this is a Book of Records, to tear out one sheet or so and
reproduce here some replies to the nefarious nonsense
one had to deal with at that time of democratising the
Navy. I reprint verbatim a few pages I wrote in October,
1906. These particular words that follow here were

97                              H

directed against those who assailed my principles of (1) The fighting efficiency of the Fleet, (2) Its instant readiness for war.

### ADMIRALTY POLICY : REPLIES TO CRITICISMS.

[In the autumn of 1906 there was considerable criticism of the Government's naval policy, particularly in the daily and weekly Press. Just before the dissolution of Mr. Balfour's administration, Lord Cawdor, then First Lord, had issued a memorandum on " Admiralty Work and Progress," dated November 30th, 1905, in which it was stated that " At the present time strategic requirements necessitate an output of four large armoured ships annually." In July, 1906, however, it was announced in Parliament that only three battleships would be included in the current programme, the reason for the abandonment of the fourth ship being that there was a temporary cessation of warship building on the Continent caused by the advent of the " Dreadnought " and the " Invincibles." Coming in the first year of office of the new Liberal administration, however, the reduction in the British programme aroused genuine disquiet among certain people, and by others was utilised for a political attack on the Government, who were alleged to be jeopardising the security of the country. In addition, there was another body of opinion strongly adverse to certain features in the design of the new " Dreadnoughts." The following notes were prepared by Lord Fisher at the time for use by Lord Tweedmouth and Mr. Edmund Robertson (afterwards Lord Lochee), who were then First Lord and Parliamentary Secretary respectively.]

The most brilliant preacher of our generation has said what a stimulus it is to have always some friends to save us from that " Woe unto you when all men shall speak well of you " ! When criticism goes, life is done ! You must squeeze the fragrant leaf to get the delicious scent ! Hence, it may be truly said that the Board of Admiralty should just now heartily shake hands with themselves, because Korah, Dathan, and Abiram (in the shape of three Retrograde Don Quixotes) are trying to raise a rebellion, but the earth will now open and swallow them all up quick as in the days of Moses. They and all their company, with their small battleships and their slow speeds, and their invasion fright and foreign shipbuilding houses of cards are each and all capable of absolute pulverisation ! Why people don't laugh at it all is the wonder ! Here, for instance, is a military correspondent lecturing the Board of Admiralty on types of ships ; and Admirals, whose names were bywords of inefficiency and ineptitude when they were afloat, and who never—one single one of them—left anything better than they found it, are being seriously quoted by serious magazines and serious newspapers as " a most distinguished Admiral," etc., etc. " These prophets prophesy falsely and the people love to have it so," as Jeremiah says ! This is because of the inherent pessimistic British instinct !

Perhaps the most laughable and silly emanation of these Rip Van Winkles is the outcry against large ships and high speeds, and an Admiral has gone so far as to resort to mathematics and trigonometrical absurdities to prove that slow speed and 6-inch guns are of primary import- ance in a sea fight ! ! ! Archbishop Whately dealt

with a similar critic by a celebrated *jeu d'esprit* entitled
" Historic Doubts relative to Napoleon Buonaparte." The
Archbishop by a process of fallacious reasoning demonstrated with all the exactitude of a mathematical problem
the impossibility of the existence of such a person as
Buonaparte ! But as someone has well said, if these strange
oddities can convert our enemies (the Germans) to the
priceless advantage of slow ships and small guns they are
patriots in disguise, and Providence is employing them
(as it employs worms and other such things) in assisting
to work out the unfailing and invincible supremacy
of the British Navy.

But to say no more—the plain man sees that it is of
vital importance that we should obtain the highest
possible speed in order that, in face of emergencies on
the south or east or west of the British Isles, we may
be able to concentrate adequate Naval Force with as
little delay as possible, and that had the British Admiralty held the opinions expressed by " the Blackwood
Balaam " our battleships would still be steaming at
about 10 knots an hour, because he must remember
that the progress which has been made from 10 knots
to 22 knots (as attained in " Dreadnought " at deep, or
war load draught) has been gradual, and at any period
during this progression it was quite open to other
Balaams to retard the action of the Admiralty by pointing
out that the slight gain in speed which has been chron-
icled year by year in battleships was really not worth
the price which was being paid for it ! But, Blessed
be God ! In this and all other criticisms of Admiralty

Policy the public pulse is totally unaffected, and the reputation of the Admiralty unlowered.

For 12 months past not a single battleship has been laid down in Europe, and this simply and solely owing to the dramatic appearance of the " Dreadnought," which upset all the calculations in Foreign Admiralties and deserved the calculated letter written by Lord Selborne to the Committee on Designs. The Admiralty has done more than all the Peace party with all their dinners to arrest the contest for Sea Power !

In the criticisms we are dealing with, " Party " as usual has come before " Patriotism," but the Sea Lords can, each one of them, confidently say, with the poet's version of a patriot's motto,

> " Sworn to no party, of no sect am I,
> I can't be silent and I will not lie,"

and so the Sea Lords have no desire to avoid any odium the Tory papers [1] may be pleased to bring upon them. There is undoubted authority for stating that a skilfully organised " Fleet Street " conspiracy aided by Naval Malcontents is endeavouring to excite the British public against the Board of Admiralty, but it has fallen flat.

There is, however, a very serious danger in the

---

[1] ONE SAMPLE OUT OF MANY.—" Lord Tweedmouth and Mr. Robertson, having tasted blood in their reduction of this year's Estimates, are about to strike a blow at the vital efficiency of the Navy. But what are we to think of the naval officers on the Admiralty Board, men who cannot plead the blindness and ignorance of their civilian colleagues ?   No one knows better than Sir John Fisher the real nature and the inevitable consequences of those acts to which he is a consenting party. And we are not speaking at random when we assert that more than any one man, the responsibility and the guilt for those reductions lies at his door." (The *Globe*, 21 Sept. 1906.)

propagation of the view so ably combated by Sir C. Dilke in his speech at Coleford, Forest of Dean, on September 27th last, that this country requires a military force of 640,000 men !

His comparison of Navy and Army expenditure is illuminating but has been totally ignored by the Press and the country. The " Fiery Cross " has been sent round to resuscitate the " Invasion Bogey."

There has been for many years past a general feeling in this country that questions of international relationship and of national defence should be withdrawn as far as possible from the arena of party politics. Such divergences of opinion as must exist on these topics have no obvious connection with the divisions of our internal politics ; and it is surely legitimate to go further than this, and say that the main problems in these departments can be dealt with in such a way as to win the assent of every reasonable man, whatever his opinions may be on Trade Unionism or Elementary Education.

At any rate successive Boards of Admiralty have for something like 20 years acted on the assumption— which has hitherto been justified—that their policy would be accepted by the public as based on a fully considered estimate of the requirements of national defence, and, if criticised (as it was bound to be from time to time), criticised on other than partisan grounds. Between the date of the Naval Defence Act and 1904 the Navy Estimates were approximately trebled. The increase was continuous under four successive First Lords, and under both Liberal and Conservative Governments. In 1904 the maximum of the curve of expenditure was reached, and the Navy Estimates began to decline, at first rapidly, under a Conservative Government, then more slowly, and in part subject to certain provisos, under the present Liberal Government. And this, it appears, is the moment chosen for the first considerable outbreak of political rancour in naval affairs since the modern Navy came into existence !

It is, however, of such supreme importance to the Navy that the Admiralty Board should not be suspected of being governed in its decisions on matters of national defence by partisan considerations that it may be well to set out again, and very explicitly, what are the reasons which have led the Board to adopt the policy now impugned.

Here we have to go back to first principles. It has become too much the fashion to employ the phrase " a two-Power standard " as a mere shibboleth. The principle this phrase embodies has been of the utmost value in the past, and is likely to be so in the future ; but if used unintelligently at the present moment it merely gives the enemy cause to blaspheme. Great Britain must, it is agreed, maintain at all costs the command of the sea. Therefore we must be decisively stronger than any possible enemy. Who then is the possible enemy ? Ten years ago, or even less, we should probably have answered, France and Russia in alliance. As they were then respectively the second and third naval Powers, the two-Power standard had an actuality which it has since lost. The United States and Germany are competing for the second place which France has already almost yielded. Russia's fleet has practically disappeared. Japan's has sprung to the front rank. Of the four Powers which are primarily in question, Japan is our ally, France is our close friend, America is a kindred State with whom we may indeed have evanescent quarrels, but with whom, it is scarcely too much to say, we shall never have a parricidal war. The other considerable naval Powers are Italy and Austria, of whom we are the secular friends, and whose treaty obligations are in the highest degree unlikely to force them into a rupture with us which could in no possible way serve their own interests.

There remains Germany. Undoubtedly she is a possible enemy.[1] While there is no specific cause of dispute there is a general commercial and—on the German side—political rivalry which has unfortunately but indisputably caused bad blood between the two countries. For the moment, it would be safe to build against Germany only. But we cannot build for the moment : the Board of Admiralty are the trustees of future generations of their countrymen, who may not enjoy the same comparatively serene sky as ourselves. The ships we lay down this year may have their influence on the international situation twenty years hence, when Germany—or whoever our most likely antagonist may then be—may have the opportunity of the co-operation (even if only temporary) of another great naval Power. Hence a two-Power standard, rationally interpreted, is

---

[1] This was written in October, 1906.

by no means out of date. But it is not a rational interpretation to say that we must instantly lay down as many
ships as any other two Powers are at this moment laying
down. We must take long views ; we must be sure
what other Powers are doing ; we must take the average
of their efforts, and average our own efforts in response.

Now this matter of averaging the shipbuilding, of
equalising the programme over a number of years,
deserves further consideration. Some Powers, notably
Germany, attempt to achieve this end by creating long
statutory programmes. The British Admiralty has abandoned the idea since the Naval Defence Act. For us,
in fact, it would be a thoroughly vicious system. For
a Power which is trying to " set the pace," and which is
glad to avoid annual discussion of the financial aspect
of the question, it, no doubt, has its advantages. But
Great Britain does not build to a naval strength that
can be determined *a priori ;* she builds simply and solely
to maintain the command of the sea against other
Powers. For this end the Admiralty must have its
hands free to determine from year to year what the
shipbuilding requirements are. But, again, this does
not mean that our efforts must be spasmodic, that because foreign Powers lay down six ships one year and
none the next, therefore we must do the same. For
administrative reasons, which should be obvious, and
which in any case this is not the place to dilate upon,
it is very necessary that shipbuilding should approximate
year by year, so far as practicable, to some normal
figure, and that increases or decreases, when they become

necessary, should be made gradually. This double principle, of determining the programme from year to year, and yet averaging the number of ships built over a number of years, has to be firmly grasped by anyone who desires to understand the Admiralty shipbuilding policy.

With this preamble we are in a position to discuss the actual situation. And first we have to consider what is the existing relative strength of Great Britain and the other naval Powers. About this there is really no difference of opinion—British naval supremacy was never better assured than at the present moment. Even admitting the combination of two of the three next naval Powers (France, Germany, and the United States) to be conceivable, it is certain that any two of them would hesitate to attack us, and it is more than probable that if they did they would be defeated, even without the assistance of our Japanese allies. The alleged alarm as to our naval strength is therefore admittedly in regard to the future, not in regard to the present. And here (to digress for a moment) we may remark that agitations have occurred in earlier years when it was supposed that some foreign Power or combination of Powers was actually in a position to sweep us off the Channel, but never before have we been invited to panic by prophecy. Is there not something slightly absurd in alarm—not calculation, for that is justifiable enough, but alarm—about our position in 1920 ? At any rate, it is clear that it is the future which we are called on to consider.

In this connection two facts have to be remembered : first, that we start in a position of security, and need therefore be in no undue haste to build more ships ; *secondly, that we are on the threshold of a new era in naval construction,* and can therefore not rest content with the advantage which we secured in an era which is passing away. The problem need not be complicated by a somewhat futile attempt to bring the existing and the new ships of our own and foreign navies to a common denominator ; we must build new ships to meet new ships, always, however, remembering that until the new ships are in commission we have got plenty of the old ones to fight with.

But here it is really impossible to avoid commenting on the gross insincerity of some recent attacks on the Admiralty. It was no doubt only to be expected that the four ships of the Cawdor memorandum, which were explicitly stated to be a maximum, should always be quoted as a minimum by anyone who wishes to belabour the present Board. But there is a further point which the convenient shortness of the journalistic memory has suffered to be overlooked. When the Cawdor memorandum was issued, it was generally (though wrongly) assumed that only two of the four ships would be battleships, and two " armoured cruisers." *And at that time the public had certainly no idea what the " Invincible "* Fast Battle Cruiser type was like, with its 6 knots superiority of speed to everything afloat, and the biggest guns alive. The " Invincibles " are, as a matter of fact, perfectly fit to be in line of battle with the battle fleet, and *could more correctly be described as battleships which, thanks to their speed, can drive any-*

*thing afloat off the seas.* But this was not known, and
the calculations generally made in the Press added only
two units per annum to our battle fleet. Yet there
was no outcry ; that was reserved to a later date, when
it was beginning to be understood that the " Invincibles "
could be reckoned side by side with the " Dreadnought,"
and it had been announced that three new " Dreadnoughts," instead of two, were to be laid down this
winter. Surely the ways of the party journalist are
past finding out.

In this connection it may be well also to make some
observations on the diminution by the authority of the
Board of programmes of shipbuilding already approved
by Parliament. The allegation that there is anything
unconstitutional in the procedure may be left to the
constitutional lawyer to pulverise. Probably all that is
usually meant by the statement is that it is desirable
to let Parliament know of the change in the programme
as soon as convenient after it has been decided, and to
this there would usually be no possible objection. But
the idea that, because Parliament has voted a certain
sum of money for the current year's programme, and
certain commitments for future years (a much more
important matter), therefore the Board is bound to build
ships it really does not want, is not only pernicious,
but also ridiculous in the extreme. The only legitimate
ground for complaint, if any, would be that the Board
had misled Parliament in the first instance by over-
estimating the requirements. The Board are faced
each summer with the necessity of saying what they

expect to have to lay down 18 months later. This, of course, is prophecy. Generally it is found to be pretty accurate, but the advent of the new era in ship-building (which is principally due to the lessons of the only big naval war of modern times) has made prophecy more than usually difficult. Moreover, if the matter is at all in doubt, the prophet has special inducements to select the higher rather than the lower figure. Increase of a programme during a given year will involve a supplementary estimate with all its accompanying inconveniences. If on the other hand it is found that the original programme was unnecessarily extensive, it is a comparatively simple matter to cut it down. It is best of course to have the right number of new ships in the Navy Estimates; but it is next best to have a number in excess of that ultimately required, which can be pruned as requisite.

Let us repeat : sufficient unto the year is the ship-building thereof. Panic at the present time is stupid. The Board of Admiralty is not to be frightened by paper programmes. They will cautiously do all that they judge necessary to secure the existing naval supremacy of this country : the moment that is threatened they will throw caution to the winds and outbuild our rivals at all costs.

H.M. Ships " Dreadnought " and " Invincible."

The accompanying papers [1] contain arguments in support of the " Dreadnought " and " Invincible."

[1] Not reprinted.

The features of these novel designs, which have been most adversely criticised, are :—

    1. The uniform Big Gun armament.
    2. The great increase in speed.

It is admitted that strategically speed is of very great importance. It enables the fleet or fleets possessing it to concentrate at any desired spot as quickly as possible, and it must therefore exercise an important influence on the course of a naval war, rapid concentration being one of the chief factors of success.

Many adverse critics of high speed maintain that it is the weapon of the weaker Fleet, the only advantage conferred being the ability to refuse an action by running away : two cases may be cited from the actions of the late war in the East showing the fallacy of this argument and that the Japanese successes were solely due to a command of speed.

In the battle of the 10th August, 1904, after the preliminary manœuvres, the Russian Admiral turned to the eastward at 2.30 p.m. to escape to Vladivostok. The Japanese Fleet was then on the starboard quarter of the Russian and practically out of range. Captain Pakenham, the British Naval Attaché, who was on board Admiral Togo's flagship, in his report, states that the " ' Tzæsarevitch ' (leading the Russian line) was almost out of sight." A slightly superior speed in the Russian line would have ensured their escape, but the excess of speed lay with the Japanese and they slowly drew up into range and reopened the action ;

but it was late in the evening before they drew far enough ahead to concentrate a heavy fire on the leader of the Russian line and so break up their formation. When this was accomplished it was nearly dark and the Russians, though thrown into confusion and beaten, were not destroyed, for the approaching darkness and the destroyer threat necessitated the Japanese Battle Fleet hauling off, yet the retreat to Vladivostok was prevented.

A higher speed in the Japanese line would have wrought confusion to the Russians earlier in the day, and probably have allowed a sufficient period of daylight for their total destruction.

Again. At the opening of the Battle of the Sea of Japan in May, the Japanese Fleet, due to skilful handling, held a commanding position, giving a concentration of fire on the heads of the Russian lines. Had they not possessed superior speed, the Japanese would rapidly have lost this advantage, as the Russians turned away to starboard and compelled the Japanese to move along a circle of larger radius ; their greater speed enabled the Japanese to maintain their advantage and so continue the concentration of fire on the Russian van until so much damage had been inflicted that the Russians lost all order and were crushed.

These, therefore, are two of the most convincing instances that could now be given, where speed was of overwhelming tactical value to the victorious side, and such evidence is unanswerable and is a justification of the speeds adopted in the designs of the new ships.

### DEFECTS AND REPAIRS

[Lord Fisher found fruitful scope for his reforming
energy in the Royal dockyards, and was very keen on
making them efficient in working as well as economical
in administration. The former tendency had been for
ships to accumulate defects until they went into dock,
when their stay was accordingly prolonged, and the
longer they were in dockyard hands the more work was
provided for the officials and workmen, so that there
was a double incentive to spend money. In the following
memorandum, Lord Fisher insists that this drain upon
the limited funds available for the Navy must stop, and
explains how the Admiralty meant to discriminate
between vessels which it was essential to keep thoroughly
efficient and others which were not worth any, or so
much, money for repairs. Elsewhere in this volume
Lord Fisher has shown how he got rid of 6,000 redundant
dockyard workmen.]

The head has got to wag the tail. The tail sometimes
now wags the head. It is for the Admiralty, and the
Admiralty alone, to decide *whether*, *how*, or *when* the
defects and repairs of the Fleet are to be taken in hand.

*The sole governing condition is what the Admiralty
require for fighting purposes!* It is desirable to put an
extreme case to accentuate this :—

In the secrets of Admiralty Fighting Policy undesir-
able to make known to our enemies there are certain
vessels never going to be used for actual fighting, but
they serve an extremely useful purpose for subsidiary
purposes. In such vessels there are defects and repairs
of a particular character that might stand over till
Doomsday! whilst there are other vessels where only

SIR JOHN FISHER GOING ON BOARD THE ROYAL YACHT.

defects affecting purely seagoing and actually direct fighting efficiency should be attended to. All this entirely depends on our probable enemy and may vary from time to time, and the sole judge can only be the Admiralty. But what it is feared now obtains is a blind rushing at all defects and repairs of all kinds and classes in all vessels. It is perfectly natural that the Commander-in-Chief and Admirals Superintendent may wish for the millennium of having all their vessels perfect—but this cannot be. What does it lead to ? Extreme local pressure accentuated by Parliamentary action to enter more Dockyard workmen. What does this mean ? It means in some recent cases that practically the upkeep of three cruisers is swallowed up in pay to Dockyard workmen ! No—the Admiralty Policy is sound, consistent and irrefutable, which is *never* to exceed the normal number of Dockyard workmen as now fixed by the recent Committee, and have such a great margin of Naval strength—such as we now possess—as admits of a leisurely and economical refit of ships without extravagant overtime or inefficient hustling of work. Therefore, what it comes to is this :—The Admiralty decide what vessels they require first and what defects and repairs in those vessels are most material, and they give orders accordingly. It is *not* the responsibility of the local authorities at all to say that this vessel or that vessel must be completed at once,for,as before-mentioned, it may be that in the Admiralty scheme of fighting those vessels are not required at all.

The Controller has great difficulties to contend with

because he has not the free hand of a private employer who can discharge or enter men just as he requires. To get rid of a Dockyard workman involves agitation in every direction—in Parliament, at the Treasury and locally, and even Bishops throw themselves into the fray, like the Bishop of Winchester at Portsmouth, instead of looking after his own disorganised and mutinous Established Church. There is now a plethora of shipwrights at Chatham, because the Treasury will not allow their transfer to other yards, and a paucity of boilermakers because unwanted men occupy their places, and the scandal exists of men being entered at Devonport with men having no work at Chatham. But, of course, this is one of the blessings of Parliamentary Government, Treasury Control, and a Free Press !

Where the special influence of the Commander-in-Chief is desired by the Admiralty is to bring before them cases where defects have not been dealt with in the initial stages by the ship's artificers and so allowed to increase as to necessitate Dockyard intervention. Such cases would be drastically dealt with by the Admiralty if only they could be informed of them, but there is an amiable desire to avoid severe punishments, and the dire result is that the zealous and efficient are on the same footing as the incompetent and the careless who get more leave and time with their friends because their vessels are longer in Dockyard hands.

It is desired to give prominence to the following facts :—It is a matter of everyday occurrence that vessels come home from Foreign stations, often immense distances, as from China or Australia, and are inspected by the Commander-in-Chief on arrival home and reported thoroughly efficient, and praise is given by the Admiralty accordingly, and the full-power steam trial is conducted with great care, and the mere fact of the vessel having steamed home those thousands of miles is itself a manifest evidence of her propelling machinery being efficient, and yet instantly after paying off we are asked to believe that such a vessel instantly drops down to a totally incapable condition of either seagoing or fighting efficiency, by our being presented with a bill of thousands upon thousands of pounds.

The attention of the Commanders-in-Chief of the Home Ports and of the Admirals Superintendent will be specially drawn to a new series of instructions which will specifically detail their responsibility in carrying out the orders of the Admiralty in regard to defects and repairs. It is admitted that no comprehensive statement has as yet been issued as to the order and urgency in which both Fleet and Dockyard labour should be applied.

This statement is now about to be issued—it is based, and can only be based, on the knowledge of what vessels are most required for war at that particular time, and so must emanate direct from the Admiralty, who alone can decide on this matter. For instance, at this present moment there are vessels, even in the first line as some might suppose, which would not be employed until the last resort, whilst there are others almost believed to be out of the fighting category which under certain present conditions might be required for the first blow. This fact came so notably into prominence some months since that it has led to the adoption of what may be termed the " sliding scale " of nucleus crews, with the Torpedo craft and Submarines at almost full complement down to the vessels in " Special Reserve " with only a " skeleton " crew capable of raising steam periodically and working only the heavy armament. So no local knowledge could determine from day to day which are the first vessels required. This is changing from day to day and it is the duty of the necessarily *very few* to determine the daily fighting requirements. The ideal is for only *one* to know, and the nearer this is adhered to the more likely are we to surprise our enemies.

### The Use of the Gunboat.

[The notes and letters which follow were prepared by Lord Fisher in the course of his advocacy that the Navy Estimates and the Service itself should not be saddled with establishments not directly contributing to the fighting efficiency of the Fleet and its instant readiness for war. Such services, he maintained, not only reduced the sum of money available for the real work of the Navy, but constituted elements of weakness in the event of hostilities. The first document concerns the maintenance of small craft on foreign stations, on which a number of " gunboats " were kept to fulfil duties for departments other than the Admiralty. Lord Fisher differentiates between vessels which the Board should rightly supply, and others which had no naval value but were retained for duties connected with the Foreign or Colonial Offices—for which, if necessary, a proper fighting ship could be lent temporarily and then returned to her squadron. The second document deals with the Coastguard, which no longer served the purpose of a reserve for the Navy, and which had come to be mainly employed on duties connected with revenue, life-saving, etc., although paid for out of Navy Votes and employing Navy personnel. Thirdly, the Admiralty letter on Observatories shows that heavy expense was borne upon naval funds for duties no longer necessary to the Royal Navy.]

In the Cawdor memorandum of last year (1905) will be found an exposition of the Admiralty policy in this matter, and attention may particularly be drawn to the following passage :—

" Gunboats, and all vessels of like class, have been gradually losing value except for definite purposes under special conditions. As far as this country is concerned, the very places consecrated as the sphere of gunboat activity are those remote from the covering aid of large ships. Strained relations may occur at the shortest notice ; the false security of the period of drifting imperceptibly into actual hostilities is proverbial, and the nervous dread of taking any action that might even be construed into mere precautionary measures of defence, which experience has shown to be one of the peculiar symptoms of such a period, is apt to deprive these small vessels of their last remaining chance of security by not allowing them to fall back towards material support. The broadcast use of gunboats in peace time is a marked strategic weakness, and larger vessels can generally do the work equally well, in fact far better, for they really possess the strength necessary

117

to uphold the prestige of the flag they fly, whereas the gunboat is merely an abstract symbol of the power of the nation, not a concrete embodiment of it.

"It might be thought that the withdrawal of the small non-effective vessels and the grouping of fleets and squadrons at the strategic positions for war involved the loss of British prestige, and of the 'Showing the Flag' (as it was termed). But the actual fact is that never before in naval history has there been a more universal display of sea power than during this year by this country. The Channel Fleet in the North Sea and Baltic receiving the courtesies of Holland, Denmark, and Germany ; the Atlantic Fleet at Brest ; the Mediterranean Fleet at Algiers ; the Fourth Cruiser Squadron, consisting of five powerful fighting vessels, now in the West Atlantic ; a powerful squadron of six of the finest armoured cruisers in the world visiting Lisbon, Canada, Newfoundland, and United States ; a squadron of cruisers, under a Commodore, proceeding from Labrador to Cape Horn and back by the coast of Africa, and two cruisers visiting the Pacific Coast and the adjacent islands ; the movements of the Cape Squadron and of the Eastern Fleet in China, Australia, and the Indian Ocean : so imposing and ubiquitous a display of the flag and of naval power has never before been attained by our own Navy."

The statement goes on to explain the special circumstances—use in shallow inland waters, etc., etc., which alone are held by the Admiralty to justify the use of gunboats.

This policy is from time to time impugned by people who have no need to count the cost of the alternative policy. Doubtless it would be convenient, as a temporary emergency arises here or there over the surface of the globe, if at that very spot some British cruiser or gunboat promptly appeared ready to protect British interests, or to sink in the attempt. Indeed, for some time this was the ideal at which the Admiralty aimed. But since the redistribution of the Fleet the Empire has had to do without the ubiquitous gunboat, and, if the truth be told, scarcely seems to have missed it. There are one or two valuable cases in point. For a long time the Foreign Office, or rather the Ambassador at Constantinople, pressed for the restoration of the second stationnaire. The Admiralty sternly refused. The only noticeable result of this dangerous policy so far has been that the French have followed our example and withdrawn their second vessel.

An even more remarkable case occurred in Uruguay. A poaching Canadian sealer had been captured by the Uruguayan authorities, and language was used as if the disruption of the Empire would follow a refusal on the part of the Admiralty to liberate her crew by force. For a time the Admiralty was practically in revolt against H.M. Government, and then—everything blew over. The dispute was settled by diplomatic action and the local courts of law.

The question of the small vessel for police duties will long be with us. Vice-Consuls and Resident Commissioners will, no doubt, continue to act on the great principle : When in doubt wire for a gunboat. The Foreign and Colonial Offices, to whom the dispatch of a gunboat means no more than persuading a gentleman in Whitehall to send a telegram saying she is to go, will probably never quite realise why the gentleman should be so perverse as to refuse. But the matter is really now a " chose jugée " ; the Admiralty battle has been fought and won, and it only remains for the Admiralty to adhere to its principles and decline to give way simply for the sake of a quiet life.

## COAST GUARD

*June, 1906.*

The Coast Guard Service was transferred from the control of the Commissioners of Customs to that of the Admiralty by the Coast Guard Service Act, 1856, in order to make better provision for—

(i) The defence of the coasts of the realm ;
(ii) The more ready manning of His Majesty's Navy in case of war or sudden emergency ;
(iii) The protection of the Revenue ;

and there is little doubt that at that time the Coast Guard force was required for these three purposes.

Since that date, however, these requirements have been greatly modified by the great developments that have taken place in steam, in electricity, and generally in the conduct of Naval warfare, and also as regards the inducements and facilities for smuggling.

It is now considered that about 170 War Signal and

Wireless Telegraphy Stations in the United Kingdom are sufficient to give warning of the approach of an enemy's ships, and that, as far as the use of the Coast Guard for Coast Defence is concerned, the remaining 530 Stations and their personnel are quite unnecessary.

*As an Active Service force the Coast Guard is far from fulfilling modern fighting requirements, which are so exacting that a man's efficiency depends upon his being* continuously *associated with highly technical duties on board ship, and employment in the Coast Guard (even with the arranged periodical training in the Fleet) is found to be inconsistent with these requirements.*

Again, as a Reserve, though it fulfils the requirements of such a force, yet its cost (largely due to the heavy expense of housing the men and their families) is out of all proportion to that at which the efficient Royal Fleet Reserve can now be maintained.

The Coast Guard being treated as an Active Service force in the Estimates, the numbers are included in the number of men voted for the Fleet, and help to make up the total of 129,000 ; but as the 4,000 Coast Guard men are appropriated for duties away from the chief Naval ports, they are not available for the ordinary work of the Fleet, and the peace resources are correspondingly reduced, while the extra charges for the Coast Guard tend largely to increase the expense of maintaining the Active Service force.

If, on the other hand, the Coast Guard be treated as a Reserve only, the expense is still more disproportionate, as, in comparison with the small retainers, charges for a week's annual drill and small prospective pension, which make up the whole expense entailed in the maintenance of the Royal Fleet Reserve, there are the Full Pay, Victualling, Housing, and numerous miscellaneous allowances and charges of a permanent force maintained in small units under the most expensive conditions.

Therefore, the maintenance of the Coast Guard by the Admiralty not only entails a reduction of the number of highly-trained active service ratings in the Fleet at sea, but also an unnecessarily large expenditure on a Reserve.

As regards the use of the Coast Guard for the protection of the Revenue, the arrangements made when the Coast Guard was transferred to the control of the Admiralty might now be considerably modified. A large proportion of the coast of the United Kingdom is still patrolled nightly by the Coast Guard as a precaution against smuggling, but looking to the increase in population and the number of towns and villages round the coasts, the development of telegraphic communication, and the great reduction in the inducements to smuggling, this service seems to be no longer required ; and some other adequate arrangement for the protection of the Revenue might be made by a small addition to the present Customs Force, assisted by the local Police, in addition to the watch still kept at those Coast Guard Stations which would be maintained as Naval Signal Stations.

Even in the cases in which the existing Coast Guard may be considered to afford valuable protection to the

Revenue, it must be remembered that in case of War or for Great Manœuvres, the men would be withdrawn to the Fleet from all stations except the Naval War Signal Stations.

In any case the employment of highly-trained seamen to perform simple police duties on shore cannot be justified, and the expense is much greater than it would be were a civilian force to be employed.

Certain other duties, principally in connection with life-saving and wrecks, under the Board of Trade, have also been undertaken by the Coast Guard ; but these, however valuable, do not constitute a *raison d'être* for the Coast Guard, and it is quite feasible to make adequate local arrangements for carrying out these services, should the Coast Guard be removed. No more striking illustration of the feasibility of this can be given than the National Lifeboat Organisation, and to that body, aided perhaps by a Government grant, these services could, no doubt, be easily, economically, and efficiently transferred.

Owing to the growing naval armaments of other Nations, and the consequent necessary increase in the Navy, the Admiralty has found it necessary carefully to consider the whole question of the expenditure under the Naval Votes in order to eliminate therefrom any services which are unnecessary from the point of view of immediate readiness and efficiency for war. About £1,000,000 of the Naval Votes is diverted to services which only indirectly concern the Navy, and are not material to the fighting efficiency of the Service. Of this about half (£500,000) is annually absorbed by the Coast Guard.

From a Naval point of view the greater part of this heavy annual expenditure is wholly unnecessary, and it is also very doubtful, from what has been before pointed out, whether for Revenue purposes a force such as the Coast Guard is now required ; while if it be still required in certain localities, it would be more economical to replace the present expensive Naval detachments by a Civilian service. By such a transfer the whole of the present expense of training men as a fighting force would be saved and there would be no deterioration in an important part of the Naval active personnel such as is now inevitable.

There can be no comparison between the cost of a Revenue force and that of a Naval force, the cost of Naval training, which is very considerable, being dispensed with in the former case. Therefore, there is no doubt that, from the point of efficiency and economy, the substitution of civilians for Naval ratings would be a great saving to the State.

## OBSERVATORIES.

*21st August,* 1906.

In the past Greenwich Observatory has been of great importance to the Navy, inasmuch as all the data necessary for the navigation of ships by astronomical observation have been compiled there. The testing of chronometers has been carried out at Greenwich since their invention in 1762, while the Cape Observatory was instituted in 1820 in order to supply data concerning Southern stars not visible from Greenwich.

In recent years, however, the familiarity with Ocean routes that has been attained ; the greatly extended area of coast surveys, and the admirable system of lights and beacons established throughout the navigational zones of the world, have in the course of years caused the work of the Observatories to become of less importance to practical navigation, and more a matter of scientific research. The photographic mapping of the heavens, by which stars invisible to the naked eye are discovered, is not a necessity to navigation, nor to the Naval Service.

At the present time, therefore, it may be said that the only work done by the Observatories which is directly useful to the Navy, is the testing and storing of chronometers ; observing the astronomical changes connected with the heavenly bodies for the purpose of obtaining data for the correction of the Nautical Almanack ; supplying accurate time for time signals and meridian distance work, and taking magnetic observations.

This sphere of usefulness is not of advantage to the Navy alone. The Mercantile Marine derives equal benefit from the work of the Observatories. Greenwich time is indispensable to Railway Companies to enable them to work their complicated systems with accuracy, and it is equally indispensable to the Postal Authorities for the proper working of every post and telegraph office in the Kingdom. Although the staff of the Observatories is very largely occupied upon services of this public character, neither the Board of Trade, nor Lloyd's, nor the various Mercantile Shipping Associations, nor the Railway Companies, nor the General Post Office, have made any contribution towards their cost, while, on the other hand, in one case, that of the Post Office, the Admiralty is charged with a heavy annual payment for postal and telegraphic communications. The London Water Companies are greatly assisted by the Greenwich rainfall observations, but they pay nothing for them, neither do they supply the Admiralty with water gratuitously.

It is fitting that the British Empire should possess a National Observatory, but it is not equitable that Naval funds should bear the whole expense.

When criticism is directed against the magnitude of the Navy Estimates, it rarely happens that the critic takes the trouble to ascertain of what Items the Votes are made up ; on the other hand, money voted for the Royal Observatories is passed by the House without much question, because it happens to form part of Estimates which are of such great magnitude.

The present procedure tends therefore to obscure the actual sum total of the Navy Estimates, and at the same time it prevents the application to the Royal Observatories of the same Parliamentary criticism which is applied to the Civil Service Estimates.

# CHAPTER IX

## NAVAL PROBLEMS

[THE three privately printed volumes entitled "Naval Necessities," 1904, 1905, and 1906, contain papers written or collected by Sir John Fisher, as Commander-in-Chief at Portsmouth and as First Sea Lord of the Admiralty, bearing upon the Naval Reforms which he then introduced or contemplated. The following selections from these papers tell their own story.]

### *Sir John Fisher to Lord Selborne, First Lord of the Admiralty.*

DEAR LORD SELBORNE, . . .

You remember you glanced through some manuscript in my office at Portsmouth the day you embarked in "Enchantress," and I gathered that you saw much in them that commended itself to you. Well! having thus more or less got a favourable opinion from you, I elaborated that manuscript which you had read, and printed it with my confidential printer ; . . . then I gave it secretly to the five best brains in the Navy below the rank of Admiral to thresh out ; and associated two other brains for the consideration of the types of future fighting vessels ; then I selected out of those seven brains the one with the most facile pen and . . . said to him : " Write a calm and dispassionate précis for me to give the First Lord." You may be confident (as confident as I know you are) that the First Sea Lord won't ever sell you ! that these seven brains may be absolutely relied upon for secrecy. I have tested each of them for many years !

These are the seven brains : Jackson, F.R.S., Jellicoe, C.B., Bacon, D.S.O., Madden, M.V.O., Wilfred Henderson (who has all the signs of the Zodiac after his name !), associated with Gard, M.V.O., Chief Constructor of Portsmouth Dockyard, and who splendidly kept the Mediterranean Fleet efficient for three years, and Gracie, the best Marine Engineer in the world !

This is the " modus operandi " I suggest to you. If these proposals in their rough outline commend themselves to you and our colleagues on the Board, then let me have these seven, assisted by Mr. Boar (who is a mole in the Accountant-General's Department—you know of him only by upheavals of facts and figures !), and secretly these eight will get out a detailed statement supported by facts and figures for consideration before we take a step further ! . . .

Please now just a few words of explanation at the possibly apparent (but in no ways real) slight put on those at the Admiralty who might be thought the right persons to conduct these detailed inquiries instead of the eight brains I've mentioned !

In the first place, any such heavy extraneous work (such as is here involved) means an utter dislocation of the current work of the Admiralty if carried out by the regular Admiralty staff ! and as any such *extraneous* work must of necessity give place to any very pressing *current* work, then the extraneous work doesn't get done properly—so both suffer !—But further ! these seven other spirits (not more wicked than any of those at the Admiralty !) will be absolutely untrammelled by any remarks of their own in the official records in the Admiralty, and will not be cognisant (and so not influenced !) by the past written official minutes of the High and Mighty Ones, and so we shall get the directness and unfettered candour that we desire ! (Parenthesis :—

SIR JOHN FISHER AND SIR COLIN KEPPEL (CAPTAIN OF THE ROYAL YACHT).

A most distinguished man at the War Office used to think he had gained his point and blasted the Admiralty by collecting extracts 20 years old with opposing decisions ! absolutely regardless that what is right to-day may be wrong to-morrow ! but he traded on what we all dislike —*the charge of inconsistency !*—Why ! the two most inconsistent men who ever lived, the two greatest men who ever lived and the two most successful men who ever lived, were Nelson and Napoleon !)

Nelson most rightly said that no sailor could ever be such a born ass as to attack forts with ships (*he was absolutely right*), and then he went straight at them at Copenhagen. Napoleon said, " *L'audace, l'audace, toujours l'audace !* " and then he went and temporised at Warsaw for three solid weeks (was it a Polish Countess ?), and so got ruined at Moscow in consequence of this delay.

*Circumstances alter cases !* That's the answer to the charge of inconsistency. So please let us have this excellent and unparalleled small working Committee to thresh out all these details (when the general outlines have been considered), but this very special point will no doubt be borne in mind :—" Until you have these details how can you say you approve of the outline ? " So what has to be said finally is that if the facts and figures corroborate what is sketched out, then the proposals can be considered for adoption, so the ultimate result is this :— " Let the Committee get on at once."

J. A. FISHER.<br>19/10/04.

MAIN PRINCIPLES OF SCHEME.

*Future Types of Fighting Vessels.*

Four classes only of fighting vessels.

Uniform armament (except torpedo attack guns) in all classes of fighting vessels.

Inviolate watertight bulkheads.

Subdivision of magazines.

Protection of magazines.

Abolish Ram.

No guns on main deck (so splendid light and airy accommodation for officers, and crew, with huge square ports and magnificent deck space).

Reduction of all weights and scantlings.

### "Out of Date" Fighting Ships.

Removal as soon as possible of all "out of date" ships (that is, ships unfit for fighting).

To abolish gradually the employment of all *slow* vessels below 1st Class Armoured Cruisers.

To substitute efficient fighting vessels with nucleus crews for all the stationary obsolete vessels now in commission, and also for all the training vessels and all the Coastguard Cruisers.

### Revision of Stations.

South Atlantic, West Indies, and Cape to form a squadron under chief command of the Admiral of the Cape Station, who will be a Vice-Admiral in the future with three Rear-Admirals under him.[1]

The Commander-in-Chief in China to have the chief command and strategic handling of the squadrons in China, Australia, East Indies, and Pacific. He can be a full Admiral with two Vice-Admirals and two Rear-

[1] There are two alternative schemes which may possibly be preferred to this.

Admirals under him. *The object is to employ Flag Officers as much as possible at sea.*

Effective Cruisers to be substituted for the present varying types of vessels forming all these squadrons.

### Personnel.

Reduction in entry of Boys, and increase of entry of Non-continuous Service Men and of " Northampton " lads.

Introduction of new system of Reserve (long service tempered by short service !)

### Nucleus Crews.

Two-yearly commissions to be instituted, and with no material change of officers and men during the two years.

All the fighting vessels in Reserve to have an efficient nucleus crew of approximately two-fifths of the full crew, together with all important Gunnery ratings as well as the Captain of the ship and the principal Officers.

The periodical exercise and inspection of the ships by the responsible Flag Officer who will take them to the war.

This Flag Officer will suffer for any want of efficiency and preparation for war of these vessels. These vessels to be collected in squadrons at Portsmouth, Plymouth, and Chatham, according to the Station to which they are going as the reinforcements.

### *Signals.*

Revision of our methods of Signalling to be based on the class of Signals that will be used in war.

To abolish all systems and all Signals that are only of use in peace time.

The Signal and Exercise Books of the Fleet to be ruthlessly revised and cut down with this in view.

The present establishment of Signalmen on board all vessels to be reduced to the numbers that *are necessary* in war (present system of superabundance of Signalmen embarked in Flagships criminally wrong).

### *Defence of Naval Ports.*

Modern conditions necessitate certain floating defences requiring seamen to manipulate them. Soldiers apparently can't do it !

Divided control of defence of Naval Ports impossible between Navy and Army.

Admiralty must have sole responsibility that all our Naval Arsenals are kept open for egress and ingress of our Fleet in war.

Local defences should, therefore, apparently be under the Naval Commander-in-Chief.

But all these arrangements for any such transfer of responsibility from War Office to Admiralty must be so planned as to obviate all possibility of Fleet men being used for shore work in war, *and there must be no risk of lessening the sea experience of the officers and men of the Fleet ;* hence it will be imperative that there should be an entire transference of the whole of the Garrison Artillery from Army to Navy, as well as the responsibility for all ordnance.

All this involves so immense an addition to the responsibilities of the Admiralty, apart from the one chief function of the Navy of seeking out and fighting the enemy's fleets, that we have to hesitate ; but we can't let matters go on as at present.

### Notes by Sir John Fisher on New Proposals.

#### Organisation for War.

> " If the Trumpet give an uncertain sound, who shall prepare himself to the battle ? "
> (St. Paul, 1 Corinthians, xiv. 8.)

The object of the following remarks is to make clear what has now to be done to organise and prepare for war. What are the two great essentials ?

I. *The Sufficiency of Strength and the Fighting Efficiency of the Fleet.*

II. *Absolute Instant Readiness for War.*

To get these two essentials an immense deal is involved ! It is believed they can both be got with a great reduction in the Navy Estimates !

This reduction, combined with an undeniable increase in the fighting efficiency of the Navy, involves great changes and depends absolutely on one condition :—

*The Scheme herein shadowed forth must be adopted as a whole !*

Simply because all portions of it are absolutely essential

133

—and it is all so interlaced that any tampering will be fatal !

The country will acclaim it ! the income-tax payer will worship it ! the Navy will growl at it ! (they always do growl at first !)

*But we shall be Thirty per cent. more fit to fight and we shall be ready for instant war !*

and in time when we get rid of our redundancies in useless ships and unnecessary men it will probably be 30 per cent. cheaper !

The outline of the various proposals will first be given. *No one single point must be taken as more important than another. Each is part of a whole ;* As St. Paul well observes in the xii. Chapter of the I Corinthians :—

" *The eye cannot say unto the hand, I have no need of thee : nor again the head to the feet, I have no need of you. Nay, much more those members of the body, which seem to be more feeble, are necessary.*"

So is it of this scheme ! All its parts are essential for the perfection we must have if England is to remain the " Mistress of the Seas " !

The British Nation floats on the British Navy ! So we must have no doubt whatever about its fighting supremacy and its instant readiness for war ! To ensure this and at the same time *to effect the economy which the finances of the country render imperative* there must be drastic changes ! To carry these out we must have the three R's ! We must be Ruthless, Relentless, Remorseless ! We must tell interested people whose interests are going to be ignored that what the Articles of War have said since the time of Queen Elizabeth is truer than ever !

"*It is the Navy whereon under the good providence of God, the wealth, peace, and safety of this country doth chiefly depend !*"

If the Navy is not supreme, no Army however large is of the slightest use. It's not *invasion* we have to fear if our Navy is beaten,

*It's Starvation !*

What's the good of an army if it has got an empty belly ? In Mr. John Morley's famous and splendid words at Manchester on November 8th, 1893: "*Everybody knows, Liberals as well as Tories, that it is indispensable that we should have not only a powerful Navy, but I may say, an all-powerful Navy.*" And when we have that—then History may repeat itself, and Mahan's glorious .words *will be applicable in some other great national crisis !* the finest words and the truest words in the English language !

"*Nelson's far-distant, storm-beaten ships, upon which the Grand Army never looked, stood between it and the dominion of the world.*"—(Mahan, Vol. II., page 118.)

And the Navy must always so stand ! Supreme—unbeaten ! So we must have no tinkering ! No pandering to sentiment ! No regard for susceptibilities ! No pity for anyone ! We must be Ruthless, Relentless, and Remorseless ! And we must therefore have The Scheme ! The Whole Scheme !! And Nothing But The Scheme !!!

Just let us take one instance as an illustration of a mighty reform (lots more will follow later, but the sledge

hammer comes in handy here !). During the 12 months
ending June 30th, 1904 (this last month !) the ships of
the Home Fleet, the Channel Fleet, and the Cruiser
Squadron were in Portsmouth Dockyard for over 30 per
cent. of the year ! Disorganised and unfit for sea !
See what this means ! A battleship costs over £100,000
a year for its up-keep, irrespective of repairs, but it's
not the money waste ! *it's the efficiency waste !*

*Every day those Fleets and Squadrons are not together,
they are deteriorating !*

It is only human nature that when in Portsmouth
Dockyard, from the Admiral downwards, all are hankering
after their homes ! and somehow or other they get
there ! the fictions are endless and ingenious, and extend
from " the cradle to the grave ! " From an unexpected
confinement to the serious illness of an aged relative !
(nearly always a grandmother ! and the baby is always
the first one !)

What is the remedy ?

It's Nelsonic—and so simple !

Nelson could not leave Toulon with all his Fleet for
nearly four months out of the year ! No ! he stayed
there for two years without putting his foot on shore !
What he did was to send one or two ships away at a time
to get provisions and water, and to effect any needed
repairs. Let us do the same ! We want a fixed base
for each Fleet (and so fixed for war reasons). Thus, for
example, the Channel Fleet at Gibraltar, the Home
Fleet at Bantry, or the Forth, and so on. But this is
going into unnecessary detail, and anticipating other

parts of the scheme which must be adopted to make this work! Thus it will be seen later on, that to enable this great economy in money to be effected (*putting aside increase of fighting efficiency !*), we must have two years' commissions! But we can't have two years' commissions unless we have fewer ships in commission! But we can't have fewer ships in commission unless we have a redistribution of our Fleet! But we can't have a redistribution of our Fleet until we rearrange our strategy! and this strategy, strange to say, depends on our reserves, and our reserves depend on a fresh allocation of our personnel, and on a fresh system of service. *We must have the new scheme of Long Service tempered by Short Service!* And this again largely hangs on the types of fighting ships we are going to have! *But what is the type of ship?* Not one that goes to the bottom in two minutes from the effect of one torpedo, and drowns nearly a thousand men, and takes three years to replace, and costs over a million sterling! *How many types do we want!* This is quite easy to answer if we make up our minds *how we are going to fight!* Who has made up his mind? *How many of our Admirals have got minds?*

It will be obvious then that the whole of this business is a regular case of " the house that Jack built," for one thing follows on another, *they are all interlaced and inter-dependent!* That's why it was said to begin with :—

*The Scheme! The Whole Scheme!! And Nothing but the Scheme!!!*

One essential feature which has been overlooked must be mentioned before going further *because impera-*

*tively necessary to ensure instant readiness for war*, but it hangs on all the other points previously mentioned and which are going to be examined in detail.

The reduction in the number of ships in commission *which is as necessary for fighting efficiency (when the whole Navy is mobilised for war) as it is conducive to an immense economy must be accompanied by and associated with two vital requisites :*

I. Every fighting ship in reserve must have a nucleus crew.

II. The reinforcements for the fighting fleets and squadrons must be collected together while in the reserve at the most convenient ports and be placed under the Flag Officer who will take them to their war stations, and this Flag Officer to understand he will be shot like a dog in case of any inefficiency in these ships in war.

Unless this is carried out the great strategic scheme in contemplation could not be entertained nor could the number of ships in commission be reduced as is absolutely essential for the efficiency of those in reserve, *not on the score of economy at all, but the reduction of ships in commission is imperative for the fighting efficiency of the whole fleet when mobilised.*

So we thus get one more illustration of the inter-dependence of all portions of the scheme and beg again to refer to St. Paul as previously quoted.

It is convenient here to mention that the paucity of efficient Admirals is a most serious matter, and will probably compel the manufacture of Commodores or of Acting Admirals under a resuscitated Order-in-Council.

## NAVAL PROBLEMS

The least capable in the respective ranks of the Navy are the Admirals. It's not their own fault solely, they have had no education, and this blot will continue till we have a Naval War College established at Portsmouth, and Flag Officers and Captains, hoping for employment, can practically prove their capacity by manœuvring two fleets of destroyers against each other. This will be much cheaper and less risky to the Empire than their manœuvring with the big ships. *Experiments on the scale of 12 inches to a foot are not economical!*

Mr. Childers was our Attila! He was the "scourge" of the Navy in many ways, but most of all by his disastrous and frightfully costly retirement schemes. *The secret of efficiency lies in large lists of Officers!* You have then a large field of selection, and a great flow of promotion, and also no Officer considers it a stigma to be passed over in company with forty others, and so not to pose as a solitary monument of ineptitude as he appears at present to himself and his friends when passed over with the present small lists of Flag Officers.

Also "*Selection by non-employment*" goes so easily with large lists (and with large lists is accepted as a necessity, and not resented as a personal affront !).

### PURGING THE NAVY OF OBSOLETE VESSELS.

Out of 193 ships at present in commission (not counting destroyers) organised in fleets, 63 *only* are of such calibre as not to cause an Admiral grave concern if allowed to wander from the protection of larger ships. There are

.among these several ships which should be paid off as soon as possible, being absolutely of no fighting value. And there are, further, several ships having trained naval crews doing the work usually performed by small merchant tramps. Further still, there are in our Home Ports many ships taking up valuable berthing space, requiring maintenance and repair, which never under any circumstances whatever would be used in war time.

The above useless vessels being in commission means awful waste of money.

Every ship that has defects taken in hand, and which would not be of use in war, is a waste of money to the country.

Of course objections will be raised, and it will be shown that the Navy cannot be run without them, but wipe them out, and in a year no one will remember that they ever existed.

It is well to review generally our distant stations and the composition of their squadrons.

The Navy and the country have grown so accustomed to the territorial nomenclature of our distant squadrons that their connection with the sea is considerably obscured, and their association with certain lands has led to a tacit belief that those particular squadrons are for the protection of the lands they frequent, and not generally for the destruction of the enemy's fleet wherever it may happen to be. Of course no such idea is accepted by the Admiralty, but, in spite of the broad principles of strategy involved, certain fleets are composed largely with a view to work in restricted waters, which vessels would be a source of danger and weakness on the sudden outbreak of war with a combination of Powers.

Take the combination of ships on each of the following stations : North America, Cape of Good Hope, East Indies, and Australia. Remember the " Variag." What happened in the small area of the theatre of operations in the present war will be repeated in the larger theatre of operations of a conflict of European Powers when the whole world will be involved. What will happen to our " Odins," " Redbreasts," " Fantomes," " Dwarfs," etc. ? aye ! and what will happen to our " Scyllas," " Katoombas," and " Hyacinths," if caught sight of by first class cruisers of modern armament on foreign stations ?[1] Lucky if they can reach a neutral port, disarm, and have their crews interned for the remainder of the war. Lucky, indeed, if a far worse fate does not befall them. At all events, such wholesale scattering of the British foreign fleets would lead to irreparable loss of prestige among the smaller States where these little vessels were usually located.

Now is there any necessity for such numbers of useless fighting ships ? Cannot more efficient classes be substituted for them, or, at all events, some of them ?

What we have to face is the probability of a serious combination of strong Powers against us, for then we will be unable to spare two first class cruisers to go in search of individual enemy's first class cruisers, who, if

[1] The "Pegasus" was massacred at Zanzibar by the Germans !— F. 1919.

not caught, may sweep round and lick up or force into neutral ports all our inefficient small fry.

Surely the three Atlantic squadrons should be of such strength as to be able to rendezvous and form a fleet more or less absolutely self-protective, to say nothing of being offensive. Such a squadron, under one admiral in war time, would be an effective Atlantic squadron, and would protect our interests by holding the ocean against enemy's cruisers.

Such squadrons can be formed without increasing the personnel of the Navy, and, moreover, the crews would be in ships that would be used in war instead of being in " floating anxieties."

Now for the present, sufficient cruisers, first class, do not exist to meet the requirements of supplying ships to take the place of smaller obsolete ones, and also for reserve purposes.

For the present a large proportion of cruisers, second class, must be retained, but it is hoped that these will in time be replaced by cruisers, first class, in the proportion of one cruiser, first class, to three cruisers, second or third class. No one can argue that one first class cruiser is not a superior fighting unit to three cruisers second or third class. Also one defect list instead of three !

If it should be insisted on that certain ports require certain small vessels, then they should be earmarked for that purpose, and only such places be recognised which larger vessels cannot frequent, such as the rivers on the West Coast of Africa (our territory), shallow rivers in

China where no question of neutrality can arise, or special places of this nature. It should be overwhelmingly proved to the satisfaction of the Admiralty that essential conditions necessitate the presence of useless fighting ships before they relax their efforts to have such useless ships removed.

It should be accepted as a principle that the great aim and object of the Admiralty is to have nothing floating on the waters except the four fundamental types of fighting vessels, and that (for the present) lack of ships of the necessary classes prevents this being realised, but that as the delivery of ships takes place, the substitution will automatically follow.

The Foreign Office will in time be bound to recognise the real efficiency of the scheme, even if a consul *is* robbed of the shadow of support of a gunboat under his window, but has the substantial strength of a first class cruiser substituted at the end of a telegraph wire.

*The danger that is eternally present to the Navy is over confidence in our preparedness for war.*

The chief cause of unpreparedness for war is want of appreciation of the cumulative effect of daily small changes in our ships and armament on the whole question of strategy and shipbuilding.

Changes have slipped so gradually from wooden sailing ships through slow steam iron vessels to our present splendid ships of war that the tendency has always been to subordinate our strategy to our ship construction, rather than to mould our war ship design to suit our strategy.

*Strategy should govern the types of ships to be designed.*

*Ship design, as dictated by strategy, should govern tactics.*

*Tactics should govern details of armaments.*

In approaching the important question of ship design the first essential is to divest our minds totally of the idea that a single type of ship as now built is necessary, or even advisable, then to consider the strategic use of each different class, especially weighing the antagonistic attributes of nominally similar classes in the old wars.

To commence with the battleship.

The sole reason for the existence of the old line of battleship was that that ship was the only vessel that could not be destroyed except by a vessel of equal class. This meant that a country possessing the largest number of best equipped battleships could lay them alongside the enemy, or off the ports where the enemy were. Transports with the escort of a few battleships could then proceed to make oversea conquests. Squadrons of battleships or cruisers escorting the convoy of merchant ships and keeping the line of communications open. In each case the battleship, being able to protect everything it had under its wing from any smaller vessel, was the ultimate naval strength of the country. *Then* it was that, by means of the battleship only, was the command of the sea gained and held. *Let us be quite clear on the matter, it was solely from the fact that the battleship was unassailable by any vessel except a battleship that made the command of the sea by battleships a possibility !*

144

Hence battleships came to symbolise naval sea strength and supremacy. For this reason battleships have been built through every change of construction and material, although by degrees other vessels not battleships have arisen which can attack and destroy them.

Here therefore there is good ground for inquiry whether the naval supremacy of a country can any longer be assessed by its battleships. To build battleships merely to fight enemy's battleships, so long as cheaper craft can destroy them, and prevent them of themselves protecting sea operations, is merely to breed Kilkenny cats unable to catch rats or mice. For fighting purposes they would be excellent, but for gaining practical results they would be useless.

This at once forces a consideration as to how a battleship differs from an armoured cruiser. Fundamentally the battleship sacrifices speed for a superior armament and protective armour. It is this superiority of speed that enables an enemy's ships to be overhauled or evaded that constitutes the real difference between the two. At the present moment *naval experience is not sufficiently ripe to abolish totally the building of battleships* so long as other countries do not do so.

*But it is evidently an absolute necessity in future construction to make the speed of the battleship approach as nearly as possible that of the armoured cruiser.*

Next consider the case of the armoured cruiser.

In the old days the frigate was the cruiser, she was unarmoured, that is, her sides were so much thinner than those of the battleship that she was not able to fight in the line of battle, but the weak gun fire of those days permitted close scouting by such unprotected vessels, she could approach a battleship squadron very closely without fear of damage, she could sail round a fleet and count their numbers without danger to herself, unless chased off by other frigates, she was a scout and a commerce destroyer. Similarly with present day armoured cruisers, they can force their way up to within sight of a fleet, and observe them, unless chased off by other armoured cruisers, but to do this they have to be given a certain amount of protective armour.

The range of eyesight has remained constant, that of gunfire has increased. Speed is a necessity to ensure safety, armour protection to ensure vision.

It is evident, from the above considerations, that the functions of the frigate have devolved on the armoured cruiser to a greater extent than have the functions of the line of battleship devolved on the modern battleship.

But how about the unarmoured cruisers and those of low speed ?

With loss of protection a cruiser loses her power of reasonable approach for observation purposes, and if to this be added a loss of reasonable speed her safety is gone. Cruisers without high speed and protection are entirely and absolutely useless.

Every vessel that has not high scouting speed, or the highest defensive and offensive powers, *is useless for fighting purposes*.

This is true of every class of vessel between the first class armoured cruiser and the fast torpedo vessel.

146

### NUCLEUS CREWS.

It is impossible to exaggerate the vital importance to the nation of having all the reserve ships absolutely ready for instant war.

Our reserve ships, as they are now, are not, and cannot be made really efficient fighting units under several months of commission. There is no doubt that great strides towards rapid mobilisation have been made of late years, but merely to hustle a complement of the required ratings into a ship, is not to make her a really efficient fighting machine.

*The keystone of our preparedness for war has now to be inserted, namely, the provision of efficient nucleus crews.*

*This can be done to-morrow.*

A nucleus crew should consist of approximately two-fifths of her engine-room complement, the whole of her turret crews, gun layers and sight-setters for all guns, all important special ratings, and two-fifths of her normal crew, her captain, and all important officers.

The ship can proceed half-yearly, or quarterly, as may be required, to sea with her fighting ship's company to carry out firing exercises, or to work under the Admiral or Commodore who will command her and her consorts in war, and be as nearly perfectly efficient as any ship, not always at sea, can be.

No more men above our present requirements need be entered, training in gunnery and torpedo schools need not be interfered with, and a saving of money to the taxpayer effected.

# RECORDS

## SUBSIDIARY SERVICES OF WAR.

We are now busily engaged in perfecting each and all of these subsidiary services ; but they are not yet perfect. In some important respects we are as yet far from it (Rome was not built in a day !), but we now emphasise the fact in order that matters may be pushed on by all concerned, from the Prime Minister downwards, with the utmost energy and vigour !

The items are not taken in the order of their relative importance, but for convenience of argument.

There is the service of all the auxiliary vessels of the Fleet for supplying coal, ammunition, stores, provisions, water, materials for repairs, &c., and also the multitudes of fast mercantile vessels we require as Scouts ; and there is also the nature of the employment of the armed mercantile cruisers to be settled. All these points have been carefully considered in the past, but in all and every one of them there is that most deadly of all deadly drawbacks to fighting readiness, the leaving certain things to be dealt with " *when the time comes.*" The time will come like the Day of Judgment ! There won't be time for doing anything, not even for repentance ! We must go to the very utmost limit of preparedness, not one little item must be left to be dealt with " when the time comes." We want all these vessels, without any exception whatever, to be as ready for a sudden emergency as is now the main Fighting Fleet ! So therefore, day by day, we must know by name each vessel for every service, and the orders for every captain of

148

every single one of this multitude of mercantile auxiliaries must be prepared, and he (each several captain) must thoroughly understand these orders beforehand ; they must be explained to him by " one who knows," and when that captain leaves England for his next trade voyage (and his ship is therefore no longer available), then the operation must be repeated with the captain of the substituted vessel ! It must be laid down where every ship is to load, what route she is to follow, what eventualities she has to guard against ! *All, and together, must be detailed and day by day kept perfect !*

Again, who are the officers at every port superintending the imparting of this information every day of the year, to the daily fresh captains of daily fresh ships, replacing others daily, going on their usual trade voyages ? Who is the Flag Officer in supreme charge of all these superintending Port Officers ? What are the names of the retired Commissioned or Warrant Officers who may be allocated to take passage in all the more important auxiliary vessels ? such, for instance, and above all, as the Ammunition and Repair ships, so as to ensure the proper control and distribution of the cargo, as well as the efficient and prompt action of the ship herself, to be at the right place at the right time. Every Commander-in-Chief must know in minute detail every particular about every one of these vessels that are coming to him. He must know it *now*. He must know it *day by day !* He must have his own agent at home to look after his interests and to be responsible to him (the Commander-in-Chief) for the completeness of all the arrangements,

149

—if not complete, then this agent must report the Superintending Port Officers for their incompetency.

All this scheme above sketched out may involve immense labour and great expense, *but it has got to be done!* Not a bit of use having the Fleet at all, if you don't feed it, and also feed it well!

Quite as a separate service, apart from all that has been mentioned above, is the dissemination of intelligence and its suppression.

We must not (as has been hitherto accepted) permit the splendid costly fighting vessels of the Fleet to be criminally wasted by being sent here and there as messengers! Fast unarmoured mercantile steamers must constitute the squadrons of the Sea Intelligence Department, and instead of our Admirals running after information with costly armoured cruisers, we must run after the Admirals with the information, with easily obtainable cheap (because non-fighting), fast mercantile vessels.

All this is but a brief review of what is in progress, and what has to be done, but *there remains above all* that daily consideration at the Admiralty, and by every Admiral in command, of what would have to be done *that very day* in case of war, with the most unexpected, as well as the most expected opponent!

A RETROSPECT (JULY, 1906).

The most striking fact to an outsider is the astonishing confidence and loyalty of the Navy in its rulers which has been exhibited during he last two years of relentless reorganisation.

Naval Officers, as a class, are conservative and dislike change, and as a rule are prepared to resist it. The manner in which the recent changes have been received, root and branch and sweeping as they were, shows, as nothing else can, the necessity for reforms. Compare the insignificant agitation (which has, however, now entirely collapsed), in the Navy over the vast and drastic reforms of the last two years with the agitation in the Army over the trifling matter of getting rid of two battalions of Guards !

So let us be grateful—adequately grateful—to the officers and men of the Navy for their splendid loyalty during the introduction of reforms, some of which have hit them very hard, notably the sudden bringing home and paying off of the large number of vessels that were wiped out of the Navy as not being up to the required standard of fighting efficiency. And there was also the redistribution of the Fleet, which deprived many officers of advantageous appointments and seriously disturbed domestic arrangements.

But the fact is that the Navy sees the fighting advantages we have gained, and so has loyally responded to the demands on its sense of duty.

As an excellent writer in the " North American Review " for June so aptly expresses it, the Navy saw that it was steam-manship that was wanted, and so, as a body, they welcomed the new scheme of training both of officers and men. They saw also that to have every vessel of the Navy, large and small, mobilised and efficient to fight within three hours in the dead of night, as practically exemplified in the recent Grand Manœuvres, is a result which justifies all the drastic measures of the Board of Admiralty.

The Navy also recognises the incomparable fighting advantages of the new era in giving us an unparalleled gunnery efficiency, as exemplified in the fact that before that new era there were 2,000 more misses than hits in the annual gunlayers' competition, while in the year after there were 2,000 more hits than misses! In the new order the best ship is the one that can catch the enemy soonest, and hit him hardest and oftenest ; under the old system these considerations were certainly not the primary ones.

The Navy sees also that, while the fighting efficiency of the British Fleet and its instant readiness for war has become a household word amongst the Admiralties of the world, at the same time vast economies—to be reckoned in many millions—have been effected ; for instance, our harbours, docks, and basins are ridded of obsolete vessels and thus made adequate for the accommodation of our fighting fleet, for which there was no room previously, and no less a sum than 13 millions sterling was at one time contemplated as necessary to give the required accommodation. The whole of that 13 millions in proposed works has been cancelled.

Nor have the officers and men been forgotten. The men have had a quarter of a million sterling practically added to their pay ; one item alone is £75,000 a year for increase of pensions to petty officers, and another £47,000 a year in giving them their food allowance when on leave, and other similar and just concessions make up the balance. Further improvements in the position of the lower deck are now under consideration and will shortly be ready for announcement, *i.e.*, Ratings Committee.

The officers, again, no longer pay for the bands out of their own pockets, and the system of Nucleus Crews gives them an amount of Home Service combined with sea-time, with all its domestic advantages, beyond anything ever before obtaining in the Navy.

Again, it is recognised by all but a few misguided misanthropes that the new shipbuilding policy is a magnificent departure in fighting policy. *We ask the officers who are going to fight, what they want, and we build thereto.* Formerly vessels were simply belated improvements on their predecessors. Admirals had to make the best use they could of the heterogeneous assemblage of vessels which the idiosyncrasies of talented designers and Controllers of the Navy had saddled us with, to the embarrassment of those whose business it was to use them in battle, and to the bitter bewilderment of types in the brain of the Board of Admiralty ! Theory was entirely divorced from practice, with the lamentable result that when the two were recently brought together, and the " Dreadnought " was evolved, it was found that the whole Navy had practically become obsolete !

" First catch your hare " is the recipe in Mrs. Glasse's Cookery Book for " jugged hare," and so speed has been put in the forefront in every class of vessel from battleship to submarine, and as it's no use having the speed without the wherewithal to demolish the enemy, the armament of our new ships, as so fully exemplified in the " Dreadnought," has received such a development that that vessel is equal to any two and a half battleships at present existing.

The efficacy of the Nucleus Crew system has also been obvious to the whole Fleet in the unprecedented exemptions from machinery defects, and the unexampled gunnery efficiency, coupled with a saving of about 50 per cent. in repairs of ships, which incidentally has led in a large measure to the reduction of 6,000 Dockyard workmen. *And it must never be forgotten that every penny not spent in a fighting ship or on a fighting man is a penny taken away from the day of battle !*

The management of the Royal Dockyards has now been placed on a much sounder footing, more akin to the organisation in similar commercial establishments, where any undue extravagance or unnecessary executive machinery means loss of money to the shareholders, and is visited by pains and penalties on the officials directly responsible. At the same time the desirable possibilities of ready expansion in war time to suit the varying requirements of a purely naval repairing and building establishment have been maintained.

The Navy also sees the great strategic advantages of our Fleets exercising where they are likely to fight. As Nelson said, " *The battle ground should be the drill ground.*"

The placid waters and lovely weather of the Mediterranean do not fit our seamen for the fogs and gales of the North Sea, or accustom them to the rigours of a northern winter, when the icicles hang down over the bed or the hammock of the Torpedo Boat Commander and his men, as in the North Sea last winter when we sent 147 Torpedo Craft suddenly to exercise at sea ; and though sent on a full power trial of many hours, on first being mobilised, not a single defect or breakdown was experienced. Since that date the arrangements for the Torpedo Craft have been still further perfected, and now the Destroyers are all organised according to the strategic requirements of the situation of the moment, and are definitely detailed in flotillas and divisions, with their store and repair ships and reserves, according to the approved modern methods of torpedo warfare as exemplified in the Russo-Japanese War.

The Navy also sees and welcomes the untold advantage given by the Nucleus Crew system of instant war readiness, as exemplified when last July all our vessels, large and small, in reserve went to sea unnoticed by the Press and engaged in fighting Manœuvres in the Channel with 200 pendants under the chief command of the Admiral of the Channel Fleet.

No calling out of Reserves or such disorganisation as was incidental to the old system, when the crews of ships in commission had to be broken up to leaven the ships of the Reserve that then had no crews at all.

# CHAPTER X

## I.—COMMON ENTRY.

### (*Written in* 1905).

ON the 25th of December, 1902, the new system of entry and training of officers for the Navy was inaugurated.

The fundamental principles of this great reform are :—

(*a*) The common entry and training of officers of the three principal branches of the Service, viz., Combatant or Executive, Engineer, and Marine.

(*b*) The practical amalgamation of these three branches of officers.

(*c*) The recognition of the fact that the existence of the Navy depends on machinery, and that, therefore, all combatant officers must be Engineers.

(*d*) The adoption of the principle that the general education and training of all these officers must be completed before they go to sea, instead of, as heretofore, dragging on in a perfunctory manner during their service as midshipmen, to be finally completed by a short " cram " at Greenwich and Portsmouth.

156

When the details of the new scheme were published, it was stated that at about the age of 20 these officers, who up till then had all received an identical training, would be appropriated by selection to the three branches, viz., Executive, Marine, or Engineer ; however, this is unlikely to be carried out in its entirety, and when the time comes, the march of progress will have prepared us to recognise that differentiation to this extent is unnecessary, and that the Fleet will be officered by the combatant officer, who will be equally an Executive, Marine, or Engineer Officer.

Let us assume this to be true. In spite of the great revolution that has been brought about since Christmas, 1902, in the Navy, and the consequent awakening and development of the minds of all officers, there is not one in one hundred who realises fully what the effects of this great reform will be.

The Cadets who are at present at Osborne College are being educated primarily as Mechanical Engineers concurrently with the special training necessary to make them good seamen, good navigators, and good commanders. The most important training they have to receive is undoubtedly that of the Mechanical Engineer, which will ultimately make them capable of dealing with and handling ANYTHING of a mechanical nature. In process of learning this they acquire a mathematical training of a very high order, and, as pure mathematics are the same all the world over, the various other subjects which the Naval Officer of the future will be required to be proficient in only necessitate a little training in the

157

special application of the mathematics of which they possess a firm grasp. Navigation and nautical astronomy are simplicity exemplified once the student has learned trigonometry and algebra. Gunnery, torpedo, and electricity are simply special cases of mechanical problems. Modern seamanship is practically nothing else but a practical application of simple mechanical " chestnuts."

What, therefore, is the meaning of it all ?

It means that the Naval Officer of the future will regard machinery, mechanical work, and mechanical problems as his " bread and butter." He will think no more of handling machinery of any sort than the ordinary mortal does of riding a bicycle ; guns, gun-mountings, torpedoes, and electrical instruments and machines he will regard as special types, but differing no whit in principle from the primitive stock. Mystery will disappear. At present it is an unfortunate thing that departmental jealousy leads the members of each and every department of the Service to make a mystery of their particular speciality. The Gunnery Lieutenant, Torpedo Lieutenant, Engineer, and Marine Officer each resent discussion by " outsiders " of any point in connection with their speciality, as a piece of unwarrantable presumption, with the result that each knows all about his own job, and pursues it diligently, taking care not to poach on anybody else's preserves, but without any regard as to whether the Service might not gain in efficiency by a little more co-operation and collaboration.

From one point of view they are right in being exclusive, because they know that no one else knows anything about their work, and therefore discussion with " outsiders " is mere waste of breath, but in future all this will be changed. Specialities will disappear ; the Naval Officer of the future will see no greater difference between a gun-mounting and a torpedo, than an Engineer sees between the main engines and the feed pump.

However, although specialities will disappear, it will always be necessary to have " experts " in each department. We shall still require our Lieutenants G., T., and E. ; but as at the present time when a Lieutenant G. is promoted to Commander he drops the G., so also it seems logical to conclude that the future Lieutenant E. on promotion to Commander should drop the E.

It is absolutely safe to predict that the Naval Officer of 50 years hence will smile when he reads that his forefathers had to have an officer of Commander's rank appointed to a ship solely for charge of the main engines. Foreigners gasp when they hear that Lieutenants of two or three years standing command our destroyers ; in other navies destroyers are usually commanded by Captains de Corvette ; and then we smile when we remember youngsters like Lieutenant Rombulow-Pearse of the " Sturgeon," who rescued the crew of the sinking " Decoy " in a gale of wind, with only his small whaler to help him, and with the loss of only one man, who disappeared nobody knows how.

The ideal complement of officers of the future therefore will be : 1 Captain, 1 Commander, 1 Lieutenant G., 1 Lieutenant E., 1 Lieutenant T., 1 Lieutenant M.,

1 Lieutenant N., 1 Lieutenant P., and as many other watchkeepers as necessary.

Enough has been said in the meantime to show how completely the new system of entry and training of officers has remodelled the British Navy, and it is with the object of using the case of the officers as an argument in considering the case of the men, that it has been dilated on at such length.

### STATE EDUCATION IN THE NAVY.

*(This Paper was prepared in 1902 under great obligations to Mr. J. R. Thursfield.)*

Everyone must now feel that the new system of Entry and Education of Naval Officers must have a fair trial, and all reasonable people will hold that it deserves one.

There still remains to be faced an argument which is certain to appeal to democratic sentiment. Broadly stated, it is this—that the new system, as at present organised, must of necessity take all officers of the Navy from among the sons of parents who can afford to spend about £120 a year on their sons from the age of 12½ until they become Lieutenants at the age of about 20, or even over. In other words, the officers of the Navy will be drawn exclusively from the well-to-do classes.

Democratic sentiment will wreck the present system in the long run, if it is not given an outlet. But let us take the far higher ground of efficiency : is it wise or expedient to take our Nelsons from so narrow a class ?

Surely some small percentage of promising and intelligent boys from the other classes could be secured and

" The Dauntless Three," Portsmouth, 1903.

Sir John Fisher, Commander-in-Chief at Portsmouth.
Viscount Esher, President of the Committee of War Office
    Reconstruction.
Sir George Sydenham Clarke, late Governor of Victoria.

(if caught early enough, as is now the case) trained to be *officers and gentlemen* by the time they are grown up.

Nor is it the money barrier alone which excludes them. An exclusive system of nomination is distasteful, if not alien, to the democratic sentiment. Combined with the cost of the subsequent training, our present system absolutely excludes all but a very small fraction of the population from serving the King as naval officers. It admits the duke's son if he is fit, but it excludes the cook's son whether he is fit or not. It ought to admit both, *but only if both are fit.* The cook's son may not often be fit, but when he is, why exclude him? Brains, character, and manners are not the exclusive endowment of those whose parents can afford to spend £1,000 on their education.

There seems to be only one way of solving this problem. Initial fitness must be secured, as at present, by careful selection at the outset, and if the promise is not fulfilled as time goes on, ruthless exclusion, whether of duke's son or of cook's son, must be the inflexible rule. But do not exclude for poverty alone, either at the outset or afterwards. Let every fit boy have his chance, irrespective of the depth of his parents' purse. This might, of course, be done by a liberal system of reduced fees for cadets, midshipmen, and sub-lieutenants whose parents were in poor circumstances. But in the first place there would be a certain element of invidiousness in the selection of the recipients of the national bounty, and, in the second, mischievous class distinctions would inevitably arise among the cadets themselves—between those who were supported wholly or partially by the State and those who were not. It is most essential that there should be no such distinctions—that the cadets should be taught to look up only to those who are eminent in brains, character, and manners, and to look down only on those who are idle, vicious, vulgar, or incorrigibly stupid. Now, a common maintenance by the State would put them all on a common level of equality. Though the additional cost to the State would doubtless be great, the result would be well worth the extra expenditure.

The quarter of a million sterling required would be lost and unnoticeable in the millions of the Education Vote, yet it would be worth all the millions of the Education Vote if it makes the Navy more efficient, because

*The British Nation Floats on the British Navy.*

It would put the Navy once for all on a basis as broad as the nation ; it would immeasurably widen the area of selection, and place at the disposal of the Admiralty all the intellect and all the character of all classes of the people.

### The New Naval Education.

Masts and sails disappeared irretrievably with the demand for high speed.

Now, what went with them ? Why ! The education that the sole use of sail power gave to the eye, brain, and body, in battling with the elements !

It was a marvellous education which we had in the pure sailing days !

One was alert by instinct ! You never knew what might happen ! A topsail-sheet carrying away, or a weather brace going, or a sudden shift of wind, or squall !

One thus got habituated to being quick and resourceful, and it was more or less a slur and a stigma not to be so ! *Also (as Officer of the Watch) men's lives were in your hands !* For instance with men on the yards, and any lubberly stupidity with braces or helm !

Both for Officers and Men then we no longer have this magnificent education by *the Elements !*

Steam has practically annihilated the wind and the sea !

What are we to do to get the same ready and resourceful qualities by other methods ?

The answer is : The Gymnasium, Boat Sailing, the Destroyer, the Submarine, and the Engine Room.

Apparently, we are in this country in the infancy of Gymnastics for the training of the body when one reads of the Swedish system and its results. (" *Mens sana in corpore sano.*")

The one solitary element in which we are behind, and must be behind all nations, is " Men." We have no Conscription with the unlimited resources it gives ! How should we counterbalance this want ? " By introducing every possible form of labour-saving appliance," regardless of cost, weight, and space ; for instance, is it really impossible to devise mechanical arrangements for feeding the fires with coal instead of using the mass of men we now are obliged to employ for the purpose ?

The coal is got out of the bunkers in the same way now as in the first steamship ever built. It is not only we thereby save men—we ensure success (for the next Naval War will be largely a question of physical endurance and nerves).

" A machine has no nerves and doesn't tire ! "

The other point necessary to consider is " not to waste educated labour, and to utilise and cultivate specialities ! "

The present system of education both of Men and Officers is that we all go in at one end like the pigs of every type at Chicago, and come out a uniform pattern of sausages at the other !

Thus, what we want is, above all things, a " Corps d'Elite " of gun-firers ! I should call them the " Bull's Eye Party " (and give them all 10s. a day extra pay !)

They must do nothing else but practise hitting the target and lose their pay when they don't !

Where would your violin player be if he didn't daily practise ? And if you made him pick oakum, where would his touch be ?

This is what Paganini said : " The first day I omit to practise the violin I notice it myself !

" The second day my friends notice it ! !

" The third day the public notice it ! ! ! "

But if the " Bull's Eye Party " are to hit the enemy as desired (and as they can be made competent to do !) then the Admirals and Captains, and all others, must equally play their parts to allow the " Bull's Eye Party " to get within range and sight of the enemy. *Their* education is therefore equally important. Scripture comes in here appropriately, " The eye cannot say to the hand, nor the hand to the foot," etc., etc.

To put the matter very briefly :

" The education of all our Officers, without distinction, must be remodelled to cope with machinery, instead of sails ! "

The Gymnasium, the Engine-room, the Destroyer, the Submarine, and Boat Sailing must be our great educational instruments.

Not for a single moment is it put forward that a year in a workshop and a year in an engine-room will make an efficient Engineer Officer ! It is long experience in such work that does that !—as in every other thing ! But in a small way, the argument of the abolition of the old Navigating Class applies here very forcibly. It was said their abolition would be absolutely fatal to the efficient navigation of the Fleet.

But what has been the result ? There have been fewer cases of bad navigation since the old Navigating Class was done away with than in the whole history of the Navy ! And with this immense gain—that the knowledge of navigation is now widely diffused through the Fleet.

One can suppose cases where it would be of the utmost value to us were engineering knowledge and the handling of mechanical appliances more widely diffused amongst our Officers !

But that is not *the vital point ! The vital point* is that were a Midshipman to be continuously serving in the engine-room of Destroyers and larger vessels (continuously under weigh) at high speeds, he would get a training assimilating in its nature to that marvellous training of the old sailing days, which kept the wits of Officer of the Watch in the utmost state of tension, and produced the splendid specimens of readiness and resource which we read of in the sea Officers of Nelson's time and later !

TRAINING OF BOYS : No masts and sails—Gymnasium —Rifle and gun practice—Boat sailing—Little or no school. (No Binomial Theorem)—Destroyer work for sea-sickness—Sent straight from training-ships to hot foreign stations on the hot-house principle before bedding-out—Select from the very beginning the good shots and the smart signalmen and train them specially.

TRAINING OF THE MEN : Re-model instruction in Gunnery and Torpedo Schools—"Corps d'Elite" of three classes of (1) gun firers or "Marksmen" ; (2) gun loaders ; (3) gun manipulators—From the time the boy enters the Navy in the training-ship till he gets his pension, the sole object to be to select, train, and improve and retain "the good shot," and all training subordinated to this !

TRAINING OF OFFICERS : Return to early entry at 12 years of age—A much lower standard of entrance, educational examination, and a high standard of physical entrance examination—Colloquial French obligatory, no grammar, and no other language, dead or alive !—A combined course of "Britannia" and "Keyham"

Colleges with at least two years of engine-room and shop work and Destroyer practice.

These great changes are not fanciful ideas !

The stubborn fact that we cannot provide what is required on the present system forces the change both as regards Officers as well as Men and Boys.

NAVAL OFFICERS' TRAINING.

*Some Opinions on the Admiralty Scheme* (1902).

1. ADMIRAL LORD CHARLES BERESFORD.

In 1902 Lord Charles Beresford, in an interview on the then recent Admiralty memorandum on the subject of the entry, training, and employment of officers and men of the Royal Navy, said :—

" The strongest opponent of the scheme will acknowledge that it is a brilliant and statesmanlike effort to grapple with *a problem upon the sound settlement of which depends the future efficiency of the British Navy.* To-day the commander of fleets must possess a greater combination of characteristics than has ever before been required of him. He must not only be a born leader of men, but he must have the practical scientific training which the development of mechanical invention renders an absolute and indispensable essential. The executive officer of to-day should possess an intimate knowledge of all that relates to his profession. Up to now he has been fairly educated in the different branches. The most important, however—in that we depend entirely upon it—that relating to steam and machinery, has been sadly neglected. The duties of this branch have been delegated to, and well and loyally performed by, a body of officers existing for this special purpose, and there have been two results. *The executive officer has remained ignorant of one of the most important parts of his profession ; the engineer officer has never received that recognition to which the importance of his duties and responsibilities so justly entitled him.* The Board of Admiralty have now unanimously approved a plan which provides that naval officers shall have an opportunity of adding to their professional attainments the essential knowledge of marine engineering. Further than this, the Board have recognised that the present status of naval engineer officers could not continue, in fairness either to themselves or to the Service. *The abolition of distinction regarding entry has settled this point once and for ever, and it is satisfactory to find that constituted authority has taken the matter in hand before it became a political or party question.*

" There seems to be a doubt as to whether it will be possible under the new scheme for an executive officer to have the knowledge he should possess of marine engineering. There is no cast-iron secret or mystery with regard to marine engineering, as some seem to imagine. This being so, there is no reason why lieutenants (E.) should not be just as good and useful experts in their speciality as the gunnery, torpedo, or navigating lieutenant of the present day, without in the slightest degree detracting from their ability to become excellent executive officers. It is imperative that all officers of the present day should be well acquainted with all the general duties connected with the management of ships and fleets. The wider and fuller the education the naval officer receives in matters relating to science within his own profession, the more likely the Service is to produce men who will be capable of seeing that the fleet in its entirety is perfect for its work, and that there is no weak link in the chain that may jeopardise the whole.

" The memo. referring to the marines will be, I believe, received with the greatest satisfaction by that splendid corps as a whole as by the Service as a whole. *It is a marvel that the zeal and ability of the officers of the Royal Marines has not been effectively utilised long ago.* Many important positions will now be open to them, and *they will feel that they are taking a real part in the executive working of the ship and fleet which is so proud to own them as a component part.* It is to be hoped the way will now be open to give them appointments as general officers commanding at many of the naval bases. No part of the scheme will give the Service in its entirety more sincere pleasure than the improvements promised with regard to the position of the warrant officers. Promotion of warrant officers to lieutenant's rank has long been urged by those who argued that the lower deck were fully entitled to a right that had from time immemorial been engaged by the non-commissioned ranks of the sister Service. Placing the signal ratings on an equality with gunnery and torpedo ratings is of far more importance than is generally realised. The vital necessity of a good line of communication and good signalmen has never been thoroughly appreciated.

" *I consider the return to the early age of entry of infinite value.* It has not yet been decided whether on first going to sea midshipmen will be appointed to ships ordinarily in commission or to ships specially in commission for training purposes. I am strongly of opinion that it would be by far the best plan to send them to learn their duties in the ordinary ships of the regularly commissioned fleet. With regard to the proposed arrangement of nomination to branches, I consider it a fair contract, and it keeps the power of appointment to the various branches in the hands of the constituted authorities. In my opinion this gives the best young officer the fairest chance of holding the best positions.

" In conclusion, I am of the opinion that the plan is one that has been thoroughly matured and well thought out, and I believe that when its details have been definitely

settled it will make more complete the well-being, contentment, and efficiency of that Service on which the safety
of the empire absolutely depends."

## 2. SIR JOHN HOPKINS.

I succeeded Admiral Sir John Hopkins, one of the
most distinguished Officers in the Navy, in seven
different appointments—as Head of the Gunnery School
at Portsmouth, as Director of Naval Ordnance at the
Admiralty, as Admiral Superintendent of Portsmouth
Dockyard, as Controller of the Navy, as 3rd Sea Lord,
as Commander-in-Chief in North America, and as
Commander-in-Chief in the Mediterranean. In each
of these appointments force of circumstances compelled
me to have a revolution. So the following spontaneous
letter, which he wrote me long after, is the more gratifying
and shows his magnanimity :

GREATBRIDGE, ROMSEY,<br>16th April, 1906.

MY DEAR FISHER,

There is a small band of writing critics " making
mouths and ceasing not " at the Education Scheme ; but
let them not trouble you. The wonder will be in twenty
years' time how such a bold forecast could have been
made, that produced such excellent results ; and, in my
opinion, the " Common Entry " man will be as great a
success as the best friends of the Service could wish.

Believe me,<br>Sincerely yours,<br>(Signed) J. O. HOPKINS.

# NAVAL EDUCATION

3. CHIEF INSPECTOR OF MACHINERY, SIR HENRY BENBOW, K.C.B., D.S.O., R.N.

HABESHI, DORMAN'S PARK,
SURREY,
*20th April*, 1908.

DEAR SIR,

Permit me to congratulate you on the success of the new system of Entry and Education of Naval Cadets, which has always elicited my warmest sympathy as the only means of doing away with class prejudice. A relative and namesake of mine, a Lieutenant in the Service, only the other day spoke to me most highly of the mental and physical development of the present-day Cadets, and remarked how very favourably they compared with the Cadets entered under the old *régime*.

I remain, dear Sir,
Yours faithfully,
HENRY BENBOW.

Admiral of the Fleet
Sir JOHN FISHER, G.C.B., O.M.


## A NAVAL CANDIDATE'S ESSAY.

I give here an essay written on 20th February, 1908, by a candidate for entry at Osborne as a Naval Cadet. His age was $12\frac{1}{2}$; his height four foot nothing. The subjects were suddenly set to the candidates by the Interview Committee, and they were allowed only ten minutes to write the essay in. The original of this essay I sent to King Edward.

*What Nation ought we to protect ourselves most against —and why?*

"In my opinion we should protect ourselves most against Germany.

"The most important reason is that they have the second largest Navy in the world ; to which (their Navy) they are rapidly adding. They are also building three ships equal to our 'Dreadnought.' Their Army also is very formidable ; though they are suffering from flat-feet. It is also rumoured that the present German Emperor has a feud against King Edward ; namely, when they were young King Edward punched the German Emperor's head ; how far that is true, I don't know.

"I always think that Englishmen and Germans are, more or less, natural enemies. One of the reasons for this is, I think, that Englishmen and Germans are so different ; for most of the Germans I've met in Switzerland were not quarter so energetic as our English friends. They (the Germans) would never go much above the snow line. Also I think we rather despise the Germans, because of their habit of eating a lot. The Germans also would like a few of our possessions."

# CHAPTER XI

I BEGIN this chapter with a letter written to me on April 18th, 1918, by Colonel Sir Maurice Hankey, Secretary to the War Cabinet :—

MY DEAR LORD FISHER,

Last night I dined with Lord Esher. He showed me letters of yours dated 1904 describing in detail the German Submarine Campaign of 1917. It is the most amazing thing I have ever read ; not one letter only, but several.

Also some astonishing remarks of yours about the Generals who ought to man the War Office in case of war. All men who have come to the top were your nominees. Finally, General Plumer (whom few people knew about) you picked out for Quartermaster-General, with this remark : " Every vote against Plumer is a vote for paper boots and insufficient shells ! "[1]

Priceless, the whole thing ! Neck-busy though I am, I have come to the Office early to pay this tribute of my undying admiration, and to beg you to get hold of these astounding documents for your Memoirs. But anyhow, they will appear in Lord Esher's Memoirs, I suppose.

Yours ever,
(Signed)  M. P. A. HANKEY.

[1] For these predictions, see Letter to Lord Esher of (?) Jan., 1904 " Memories," p. 173.

# RECORDS

Now follows a letter which I wrote to a High Official in 1904, and which I had forgotten, until I came across it recently. It's somewhat violent, but so true that I insert it. I went as First Sea Lord of the Admiralty shortly after—very unexpectedly—and so was able to give effect (though surreptitiously) to my convictions. Not only Admirals afloat, but even Politicians ashore, dubbed submarines as " playthings," so the money had to be got by subterfuge (as I have explained in Chapter V. of my " Memories ").

ADMIRALTY HOUSE,<br>
PORTSMOUTH.<br>
April 20th, 1904.

MY DEAR FRIEND,

I will begin with the last thing in your letter, which is far the most important, and that is our paucity of submarines. I consider it the most serious thing at present affecting the British Empire !—That sounds *big*, but it's true. Had either the Russians or the Japanese had submarines the whole face of their war would have been changed for both sides. It really makes me laugh to read of " Admiral Togo's *eighth* attack on Port Arthur ! " Why ! had he possessed submarines it would have been *one* attack and *one* attack only ! It would have been all over with the whole Russian Fleet, caught like rats in a trap ! Similarly, the Japanese Admiral Togo outside would never have dared to let his transports full of troops pursue the even tenor of their way to Chemulpo and elsewhere !

It's astounding to me, *perfectly astounding*, how the very best amongst us absolutely fail to realise the vast impending revolution in naval warfare and naval strategy that the submarine will accomplish! (I have written a paper on this, but it's so violent I am keeping it!) Here, just to take a simple instance, is the battleship " Empress of India," engaged in manœuvres and knowing of the proximity of Submarines, the Flagship of the Second Admiral of the Home Fleet nine miles beyond the Nab Light (out in the open sea), so self-confident of safety and so oblivious of the possibilities of modern warfare that the Admiral is smoking his cigarette, the Captain is calmly seeing defaulters down on the half-deck, no one caring an iota for what is going on, and suddenly they see a Whitehead torpedo miss their stern by a few feet! And how fired? From a submarine of the " pre-Adamite " period, small, slow, badly fitted, *with no periscope at all*—it had been carried away by a destroyer lying over her, fishing for her!—and yet this submarine followed that battleship for a solid two hours under water, coming up gingerly about a mile off, every now and then (like a beaver!), just to take a fresh compass bearing of her prey, and then down again ᵢ

Remember, that this is done (and I want specially to emphasise the point), with the Lieutenant in command of the boat out in her for the first time in his life on his own account, and half the crew never out before either! why, it's wonderful! And so what results may we expect with bigger and faster boats and periscopes more powerful than the naked eye (such as the latest pattern one I saw the other day), and with experienced officers and crews, and with nests of these submarines acting together?

I have not disguised my opinion in season and out of season as to the essential, imperative, immediate, vital, pressing, urgent (I can't think of any more adjectives!) necessity for more submarines at once, at the very least 25 in addition to those now ordered and building, and a hundred more as soon as practicable, or we shall be caught with our breeches down just as the Russians have been !

And then, my dear Friend, you have the astounding audacity to say to me, " I presume you only think they (the submarines) can act on the *defensive* ! " . . . . Why, my dear fellow ! not take the offensive ? Good Lord ! if our Admiral is worth his salt, he will tow his submarines at 18 knots speed and put them into the hostile Port (like ferrets after the rabbits !) before war is officially declared, just as the Japanese acted before the Russian Naval Officers knew that war was declared !

In all seriousness I don't think it is even *faintly* realised—

*The immense impending revolution which the submarines will effect as offensive weapons of war.*

When you calmly sit down and work out what will happen in the narrow waters of the Channel and the Mediterranean—how totally the submarines will alter the effect of Gibraltar, Port Said, Lemnos, and Malta, it makes one's hair stand on end !

I hope you don't think this letter too personal !

Ever yours,<br>J. A. FISHER.

Note made on January 5th, 1904 :

Satan disguised as an Angel of Light wouldn't succeed in persuading the Admiralty or the Navy that in the course of some few years Submarines will prevent any Fleet remaining at sea continuously either in the Mediterranean or the English Channel.

Now follows a paper on " The Effect of Submarine Boats," which I wrote while I was Commander-in-Chief at Portsmouth, October, 1903.

*These remarks can only be fully appreciated by those who witnessed the Flotilla of Submarine Boats now at Portsmouth practising out in the open sea.*

SOME SHELLS FOR 18-INCH GUNS.

The shells for the 20-inch guns to be carried by H.M.S. "Incomparable" would have been far bigger, and would have weighed two tons.

# SUBMARINES

It is an historical fact that the British Navy stubbornly resists change.

A First Sea Lord told me on one occasion that there were no torpedoes when he came to sea, and he didn't see why the devil there should be any of the beastly things now!

This was *à propos* of my attracting the attention of his serene and contented mind to the fact that we hadn't got any torpedoes at that time in the British Navy, and that a certain Mr. Whitehead (with whom I was acquainted) had devised an automobile torpedo, costing only £500, that would make a hole as big as his Lordship's carriage (then standing at the door) in the bottom of the strongest and biggest ship in the world, and she would go to the bottom in about five minutes.

Thirty-five years after this last interview, on September 4th, 1903, at 11 a.m., the ironclad " Belleisle," having had several extra bottoms put on her and strengthened in every conceivable manner that science could suggest or money accomplish, was sent to the bottom of Portsmouth Harbour by this very Whitehead automobile torpedo in seven minutes.

This Whitehead torpedo can be carried with facility in Submarine Boats, and it has now attained such a range and such accuracy (due to the marvellous adaptation of the gyroscope), that even at two miles' range it possesses a greater ratio of power of vitally injuring a ship in the line of battle than does the most accurate gun. This is capable of easy demonstration (if anyone doubts it).

There is this immense fundamental difference between the automobile torpedo and the gun—the torpedo has no trajectory : it travels horizontally and hits below water, so all its hits are vital hits ; but not so the gun — only in a few places are gun hits vital, and those places are armoured. It is not feasible to armour the bottoms of ships even if it were effectual—which it is not.

But the pith and marrow of the whole matter lies in

the fact that the Submarine Boat which carries this automobile torpedo is up to the present date absolutely unattackable. When you see Battleships or Cruisers, or Destroyers, or Torpedo Boats on the horizon, you can send others after them to attack them or drive them away! You see them—you can fire at them—you can avoid them—you can chase them—but with the Submarine Boat you can do nothing! You can't fight them with other Submarine Boats—they can't see each other!

Now for the practical bearing of all this, and the special manner it affects the Submarine Boat and the Army and the Navy—for they are all inextricably mixed up together in this matter :—

As regards the Navy, it must revolutionise Naval Tactics for this simple reason—that the present battle formation of ships in a single line presents a target of such a length that the chances are altogether in favour of the Whitehead torpedo hitting some ship in the line even when projected from a distance of several miles. This applies specially to its use by the Submarine Boat ; but in addition, these boats can, in operating defensively, come with absolute invisibility within a few hundred yards to discharge the projectile, not at random amongst the crowd of vessels but with certainty at the Admiral's ship for instance, or at any other specific vessel desired to be sent to the bottom.

It affects the Army, because, imagine even one Submarine Boat with a flock of transports in sight loaded each with some two or three thousand troops! Imagine the effect of one such transport going to the bottom in a few seconds with its living freight!

Even the bare thought makes invasion impossible! Fancy 100,000 helpless, huddled up troops afloat in frightened transports with these invisible demons known to be near.

Death near — momentarily — sudden — awful —

invisible — unavoidable! Nothing conceivable more demoralising!

It affects the existence of the Empire, because just as we were in peril by the non-adoption of the breech-loading gun until after every Foreign nation had it, and just as we were in peril when Napoleon the Third built " La Gloire " and other French ironclads, while we were still stubbornly building wooden three-deckers, and just as we were in peril when, before the Boer War, we were waiting to perfect our ammunition and in consequence had practically no ammunition at all, so are we in peril now by only having 20 per cent. of our very minimum requirements in Submarine Boats, because we are waiting for perfection! We forget that " half a loaf is better than no bread "—we strain at the gnat of perfection and swallow the camel of unreadiness! We shall be found unready once too often!

In 1918 I wrote the following letter to a friend on " Submarines and Oil Fuel."

You ask for information in regard to a prophecy I made before the War in relation to Submarines, because, you say, that my statement made in 1912 that Submarines would utterly change Naval Warfare is now making a stir. However, I made that same statement in 1904, fourteen years ago.

I will endeavour to give you a brief, but succinct, synopsis of the whole matter. I have to go some way back, but as you quite correctly surmise the culmination of my beliefs since 1902 was the paper on Submarine Warfare which I prepared six months before the War.[1] . . . .

In May, 1912 (I am working backwards), Mr. Asquith, the Prime Minister, and Mr. Churchill, First Lord of the Admiralty, came to Naples, where I then was, and I was

[1] See below, p. 181.

N 2

invited to be Chairman of a Royal Commission on Oil Fuel for the Navy, and on Oil Engines. What most moved me to acceptance was to push the Submarine, because oil and the oil engine had a special bearing on its development.

Continuing my march backwards in regard to the Submarine, there was a cessation in the development of the Submarine after I left the Admiralty as First Sea Lord on January 25th, 1910. When I returned as First Sea Lord to the Admiralty in October, 1914, there were fewer Submarines than when I left the Admiralty in January, 1910, and the one man incomparably fitted to develop the Submarine had been cast away in a third-class Cruiser stationed in Crete. No wonder! An Admiral, holding a very high appointment afloat, derided Submarines as playthings!

In one set of manœuvres the young officer commanding a Submarine, having for the third time successfully torpedoed the hostile Admiral's Flagship, humbly said so to the Admiral by signal, and suggested the Flagship going out of action. The answer he got back by signal from the Admiral was : " You be damned ! "

I am still going on tracing back the Submarine. In 1907, King Edward went on board the " Dreadnought " for a cruise and witnessed the manœuvres of a Submarine Flotilla. I then said to His Majesty : " The Submarine will be the Battleship of the future ! "

In February, 1904, Admiral Count Montecuccoli, the Austrian Minister of Marine, invited himself to stay with me at Portsmouth, where I was then Commander-in-Chief. He had been Commander-in-Chief of the Austrian Navy at Pola when I was Commander-in-Chief in the Mediterranean. We became very great friends out there. The Austrian Fleet gave us a most cordial reception. He also was an ardent believer in the Submarine. That's why he invited himself to stay, but I refused to let him see our Submarines at Portsmouth, which were then

advancing by leaps and bounds. Admiral Bacon was
then the admirable Captain in charge of Submarines,
and he did more to develop the Submarine than anyone
living. The Submarine is not the weapon of the weak.
Had it only been properly used and developed, it's the
weapon of the strong, if you use your Naval Supremacy
properly, and

*seize the exits of the enemy, and make a blockade effectual
by Submarines and Mines, which our predominant and
overwhelming naval superiority renders feasible.*

All that was required to meet a German Submarine
Menace was the possession of Antwerp, the Belgian
Coast, and the Baltic. We could quite easily have
accomplished these three objects.

Nearly three months before the War, before the
meeting of the Committee of Imperial Defence held on
May 14th, 1914, I sent the Prime Minister the following
Memorandum which I had written in the previous
January ; and added :—

THE SUBMARINE IS THE COMING TYPE OF WAR VESSEL
FOR SEA FIGHTING.

But for that consummation to be reached we must
perfect the oil engine and we must store oil.

There is a strong animus against the submarine—of
course there is !

An ancient Admiralty Board minute described the
introduction of the steam engine as fatal to England's
Navy.

Another Admiralty Board minute vetoed iron ships,
because iron sinks and wood floats !

The whole Navy objected to breech-loading guns, and
in consequence sure disaster was close to us for years
and years.

There was virulent opposition to the water-tube boiler (fancy putting the fire where the water ought to be, and the water where the fire should be !)

The turbine was said by eminent marine engineers to have an " insuperable and vital defect which renders it inadmissible as a practical marine engine—its vast number of blades—it is only a toy." 80 per cent. of the steam-power of the world is now driving turbines.

Wireless was voted damnable by all the armchair sailors when we put it on the roof of the Admiralty, and yet we heard what one ship (the " Argyll ") at Bombay was saying to another (the " Black Prince ") at Gibraltar.

" Flying machines are a physical impossibility," said a very great scientist four years ago. To-day they are as plentiful as sparrows.

" Submarines are only playthings ! " was the official remark of our Chief Admiral afloat only a little while ago, and yet now submarines are talked of as presently ousting Dreadnoughts.

The above texts, extracted from comparatively modern naval history (history is a record of exploded ideas !), should make anyone chary of ridiculing the writer when he repeats :

THE SUBMARINE IS THE COMING TYPE OF WAR VESSEL FOR SEA FIGHTING.

And what is it that the coming of the submarine really means ? It means that the whole foundation of our traditional naval strategy, which served us so well in the past, has been broken down ! The foundation of that strategy was blockade. The Fleet did not exist merely to win battles—that was the means, not the end. The ultimate purpose of the Fleet was to make blockade possible for us and impossible for our enemy. Where that situation was set up we could do what we liked with him on the sea, and, despite a state of war, England grew steadily richer. But with the advent of the long-range ocean-going submarine that has all gone ! Surface ships can no longer either maintain or prevent blockade, and with the conception of blockade are broken up all the consequences, direct and indirect, that used to flow from it. All our old ideas of strategy are simmering in the melting pot ! Can we get anything out of it which will let us know where we are and restore to us something of our former grip ? It is a question that must be faced.

\* \* \* \* \* \*

Sea-fighting of to-day, or at any time, entails the removal of the enemy's sea forces. If, as is maintained, the submarine proves itself at once the most efficient factor for this purpose and also the most difficult sea force to remove, let us clear our minds of all previous obsessions and acknowledge the facts once and for all.

### HOSTILE SUBMARINES.

*It has to be freely acknowledged that at the present time no means exist of preventing hostile submarines emerging from their own ports and cruising more or less at will.*

It is, moreover, only barely possible that, in the future, mining and other blocking operations on a very extensive scale may so develop as to render their exit very hazardous ; but it is plain that such operations would require a large personnel, unceasing energy and vigilance, and an immense quantity of constantly replaceable materials.

\* \* \* \* \* \*

### THE SUBMARINE AND COMMERCE.

Again, the question arises as to what a submarine can do against a merchant ship when she has found her. She cannot capture the merchant ship ; she has no spare hands to put a prize crew on board ; little or nothing would be gained by disabling her engines or propeller ;

she cannot convoy her into harbour ; and, in fact, it is impossible for the submarine to deal with commerce in the light and provisions of accepted international law. Under these circumstances, is it presumed that the hostile submarine will disregard such law and sink any vessel heading for a British commercial port and certainly those that are armed or carrying contraband ?

There is nothing else the submarine can do except sink her capture, and it must therefore be admitted that (provided it is done, and however inhuman and barbarous it may appear) this submarine menace is a truly terrible one for British commerce and Great Britain alike, for no means can be suggested at present of meeting it except by reprisals. All that would be known would be that a certain ship and her crew had disappeared, or some of her boats would be picked up with a few survivors to tell the tale. Such a tale would fill the world with horror, and it is freely acknowledged to be an altogether barbarous method of warfare ; but, again, if it is done by the Germans the only thing would be to make reprisals. The essence of war is violence, and moderation in war is imbecility.

It has been suggested that it should be obligatory for a submarine to fire a warning gun, but is such a proceeding practical ? We must bear in mind that modern submarines are faster on the surface than the majority of merchantmen, and will not necessarily need to dive at all. Therefore, as the submarine would in most cases be sighted, and as she has no prize crew to put on board, the warning gun is useless, as the only thing the submarine could do would be to sink the enemy ; also, the apparently harmless merchant vessel may be armed, in which case the submarine may but have given herself away if she did not sink her.

The subject is, indeed, one that bristles with great difficulties, and it is highly desirable that the conduct of

# SUBMARINES

submarines in molesting commerce should be thoroughly considered. Above all, it is one of overwhelming interest to neutrals. One flag is very much like another seen against the light through a periscope, should he have thought it necessary to dive ; and the fear is natural that the only thing the officer of the hostile submarine would make sure of would be that the flag seen was not that of his own country.

Moreover, under numerous circumstances can a submarine allow a merchant ship to pass unmolested ? Harmless trader in appearance, in reality she may be one of the numerous fleet auxiliaries, a mine-layer, or carrying troops, and so on. Can the submarine come to the surface to inquire and lose all chance of attack if the vessel should prove to be faster than she is ? The apparent merchant ship may also be armed. In this light, indeed, the recent arming of our British merchant-men is unfortunate, for it gives the hostile submarine an excellent excuse (if she needs one) for sinking them ; namely, that of self-defence against the guns of the merchant ship.

What can be the answer to all the foregoing but that (barbarous and inhuman as, we again repeat, it may appear), if the submarine is used at all against commerce, she must sink her captures ?

For the prevention of submarines preying on our commerce, it is above all necessary that merchant shipping should take every advantage of our favourable geographical position, and that we should make the Straits of Dover as difficult as we possibly can.

It is not proposed here to enter into the technical details of such arrangements ; but even after every conceivable means has been taken, it must be conceded that there is at least a chance of submarines passing safely through ; while at night, or in thick weather, it is probable that they would not fail to pass in safety.

I conclude with some details of British Submarines before and during the War :—

I. When I left the Admiralty in January, 1910 :
Submarines ready for fighting    61
Building and on order    13

II. When I returned to the Admiralty, in October, 1914, as First Sea Lord :
Submarines fit for fighting    53
Building and on order    21
But of these 21, only 5 were any good !
2 were paid off as useless.
3 sold to the Italians, not of use to us.
4 sold to the French, not of use to us.
7 of unsatisfactory design.
———
16 leaving only 5 of oversea modern (" E ") Type.
———

Nominally, there were 77 Submarines when I returned in October, 1914, but out of these 24 were useless, or had gone to the Antipodes, as follows :

2 to Australia.
3 to Hong Kong.
1 sold to Italy useless.
8 " A " Class scrapped, 10 years old.
10 " B " Class scrapped, 9 years old.
———
24

77 − 24 = 53 total Submarines fit for Service when I returned in October, 1914.

There were 61 Submarines efficient when I left the Admiralty in January, 1910.

Of those that were on order when I returned, 14 were

of " G " Class, but were of an experimental type, and so were not ready till *June*, 1916, or one year after the Submarines were ready which I ordered on my return to the Admiralty in October, 1914.

Here may be stated the great service rendered by Mr. Schwab, of the Bethlehem Steel Works. I specially sent for him. I told him the ¡very shortest time hitherto that a Submarine had been built in was 14 months. Would he use his best endeavours to deliver in six months ? *He delivered the first batch in five months !* And not only that, but they were of so efficient a type (" H " Class) that they came from America to the Dardanelles without escort, and were of inestimable service out there, and passed into the Sea of Marmora, and were most effective in sinking Turkish Transports bringing munitions to Gallipoli.

The type of Submarine (" H " Class) he built hold the field for their special attributes. I saw one in dock at Harwich that had been rammed by a Destroyer—I think a German Destroyer—and had the forepart of her taken clean away, and she got back to Harwich by herself all right. The Commander of her, an aged man, was in the Merchant Service. (What a lot we do indeed owe to the Merchant Service, and especially to those wonderful men in the Trawlers !)

But Mr. Schwab did far more than what I have narrated above. He undertook the delivery of a very important portion of the armament of the Monitors.

The idea was followed up in making old Cruisers immune from German Submarines—the " Grafton," an old type Cruiser (and so also the " Edgar "), thus fitted, was hit fair amidships by a torpedo from a German submarine off Gibraltar, and the Captain of the " Grafton " reported himself unhurt and going all the faster for it (as it had blown off a good bit of the hull !), and those vessels were ever so much the better sea boats for it !

It is lamentable that no heed was given to the great sagacity of Mr. Churchill in his special endeavour to give further application to this invention.

In the Submarine Monitor M1, which carries a 12-inch gun, and which is illustrated in this volume, we have the type of vessel I put before the Admiralty in August, 1915. She is the forerunner of the Battleship of the future; but her successors should be built in a much shorter time than she was.

# CHAPTER XII

*How War and Peaceful Commerce will be Revolutionised by the Oil Engine.*

ON September 17th, 1912, at 3 a.m., I invited two very eminent experts, Sir Trevor Dawson and his coadjutor McKechnie, to leave their beds and come into my room to see an outline of the Fast Ship of the Future, both for War and Commerce, carrying sufficient fuel to go round the Earth with and with an increased capacity of 30 per cent. as compared with similar vessels of the same displacement using steam. At length a special Government Research Department has been set up to develop the Oil Engine, and a sum prohibitive in peace time has been cheerfully accorded by War reasoning to set up this establishment on a big basis. I reiterate what is said elsewhere, that the Oil Engine will revolutionise both War and Commerce when once it is perfected—through the enormous gain it affords in space and smaller crews through riddance of stokeholds and firemen, and facility of re-fuelling and cleanliness and absence of funnels, etc., etc.

189

# RECORDS

Here is a descriptive outline of H.M.S. " Incomparable," as set forth in the early morning of September 17th, 1912 :

Really a Gem ! She can be riddled and gutted outside the Central Diamond-shaped Armoured Citadel because nothing vital outside that Citadel ! So lightly built she'll weigh so little as to go Fast, with a hundred and fifty thousand horse power ! She'll shake to pieces in about 10 years ! What's the good of a warship lasting longer ? The d—d things get obsolete in about a year !

Ten 16-inch guns to begin with (afterwards 20-inch guns) for main armament.

Eight broadside Torpedo Tubes (21-inch Torpedo).

32 knots speed at least.

16-inch armour on citadel and belt amidships, thinning towards the end.

850 feet long—to be afterwards 1,000 feet ; 86 feet wide.

Four Torpedo Tubes each side to be well before the Citadel (submerged Tubes) so as not to interfere with machinery space.

Quadruple screws.

Anti-Submarine guns in small single turrets.

A Turtle-backed armoured hull, with light steel uninflammable structure before and abaft the armoured Diamond-shaped Citadel.

Two Conning Towers.

Hydraulic crane each side (very low in height) for lifting boats.

The light central steel hollow mast only for wireless

and for ventilation, made of steel ribbon to wind up and down at will.

Jam up the Citadel all that is possible right in centre of Hull, and squeeze the last inch in space so as to lessen amount of 16-inch armour.

Curved thick armour deck.

Ammunition service by Hydraulic power.

Oil right fore and aft the whole ship. Enough to go round the earth !

Very high double bottom—honeycombed.

Coffer dams everywhere stuffed with cork.

This, then, is the Fast Battle Cruiser " Incomparable " of 32 knots speed and 20-inch guns and no funnels, and phenomenal light draught of water, because so very long and built so flimsy that she won't last 10 years, but that's long enough for the War !

I have just found copy of a letter I sent Mr. Winston Churchill dated two months later, when those two very eminent men, having cogitated over the matter, very kindly informed me that the Visionary was justified. I omit the details they kindly gave me, as I don't wish to deprive them of any trade advantage in the furtherance of their great commercial intentions with regard to the oil engine, for it is just now the commercial aspect of the internal combustion engine which enthrals us. A ship now exists that has a dead weight capacity of 9,500 tons with a speed of eleven knots (which is quite fast enough for all cargo-carrying purposes) and she burns only a little over ten tons of oil an hour. Having worked out the matter, I conclude she would save roughly a thousand pounds in fuel alone over a similar sized steamship in a voyage of about 3,000 miles (say crossing the Atlantic); and, of course, as compared with coal, she could carry much additional cargo, probably about 600 tons more. Then the getting rid of boilers and coal bunkers gives another immense additional space to the oil engine ship for cargo, as the oil fuel would be carried in the double-bottom. A Swiss firm has put on board an ocean-going motor-driven ship a Diesel engine which develops 2,500 indicated Horse Power in one cylinder, so that a quadruple-screw motor ship could have 80,000 Horse Power with sixteen of these cylinders cranked on each shaft. I don't see why one shouldn't have a sextuple - screw motor ship with a hundred thousand Horse Power. So it is ludicrous to say that the internal combustion engine is not suited to big ships. For some reason I cannot discover, " Tramp " owners are hostile to the internal combustion engine. I hope they will not discover their error too late. I sent two marvellous pictures of a Motor Battleship to Mr. Winston Churchill on November 17th, 1912, saying to him :—

" These pictures will make your mouth water ! "

However, this type of ship is obsolete for war before she has been begun, as we have got to turn her into a submersible—not that there is any difficulty in that—it has already been described that in August, 1916, a submersible vessel with a 12-inch gun was proposed and after extreme hesitation and long delays in construction was built, but she was completed too late to take part in the war. She might have sunk a goodly number of the German Fleet at the Battle of Jutland. But our motto in the war was " Too Late." [1]

The whole pith and marrow of the Internal Combustion Engine lies in the science of metallurgy. We are lamentably behind every foreign nation, without exception, in our application of the Internal Combustion Engine to commercial purposes, because its reliability depends on Metallurgy, in which science we are wanting, and we are also wanting in scientific research on the scale of 12 inches to a foot. We have no scale at all !

*We are going to be left behind !*

The Board of Invention and Research, of which I was President, after much persistence obtained the loan of a small Laboratory at South Kensington, greatly aided by Professor Dalby, F.R.S., for research purposes as regards the Internal Combustion Engine ; but its capabilities were quite inadequate. Then the President of the Council (Earl Curzon) was to undertake the whole question of Research on a great and worthy scale, and I got a most kind letter from him. It ended with the letter !

In this connection I have had wonderful support from Sir Marcus Samuel, who staked his all on Oil and the Oil Engine. Where should we have been in this War but for this Prime Mover ? I've no doubt he is an oil millionaire now, but that's not the point. Oil is one of the things that won us the War. And when he was Lord Mayor of London he was about the only

[1] Only this morning (November 5th, 1919), I have arranged to deal with the drawings of a proposed Submersible Battleship carrying many Big Guns, and clearly a practicable production.

RECORDS

man who publicly supported me when it was extremely unfashionable to do so.

Oil is the very soul of future Sea Fighting. Hence my interest in it, and though not intending to work again, yet my consuming passion for oil and the oil engine made me accept the Chairmanship of a Royal Commission on Oil and the Oil Engine when Mr. Churchill and Mr. Asquith found me at Naples in May, 1912.

I have come to the conclusion that about the best thing I ever did was the following exuberant outburst over Oil and the Oil Engine. I observe it was printed in November 1912, written " currente calamo," and now on reading it over I would not alter a word. I am only aghast at the astounding stupidity of the British Shipbuilder and the British Engineer in being behind every country in the development of motor ships.

OIL AND THE OIL ENGINE (1912).

I.—With two similar Dreadnoughts oil gives 3 knots more speed—that is if ships are designed to burn oil only instead of oil and coal—*and speed is everything*.

II.—The use of oil fuel increases the strength of the British Navy 33 per cent., because it can re-fuel at sea off the enemy's Harbours. Coal necessitates about one-third of the Fleet being absent re-fuelling at a base (in case of war with Germany) some three or four hundred miles off !—*i.e.*, some six or eight hundred

194

miles unnecessary expenditure of fuel and
wear and tear of machinery and men.

III.—Oil for steam-raising reduces the present engine
and boiler room personnel some 25 per cent.,
and for Internal Combustion Engines would
perhaps reduce the personnel over 60 per cent.
This powerfully affects both economy and
discipline.

IV.—Oil tankers are in profusion on every sea and as
England commands the Ocean (*she must command the Ocean to live ! !*) she has peripatetic
re-fuelling stations on every sea and every
oil tanker's position known every day to a
yard ! Before very long there will be a million
tons of oil on the various oceans in hundreds
of oil tankers. The bulk of these would be
at our disposal in time of war. Few or none
could reach Germany.

V.—The Internal Combustion Engine with *one* ton
of oil does what it takes *four* tons of coal to
do ![1] And having no funnels or smoke is an
*indescribable fighting asset !* (Always a chance
of smoke in an oil steam-raising vessel where
of course the funnels which disclose a ship
such an immense distance off are obligatory.
Each enemy's ship spells her name to you by
her funnels as they appear on the horizon,
while you are unseen !)

VI.—The armament of the Internal Combustion Ship
is not hampered by funnels, so can give all-
round fire, an inestimable advantage because
the armament can all be placed in the central
portion of the Hull with all-round fire, and
giving the ship better seaworthy qualities by
not having great weights in the extremities,

[1] NOTE.—For steam raising 3 tons of oil are only equivalent to
4 tons of coal.

as obligatory where you have funnels and boilers.

VII.—But please imagine the blow to British prestige if a German warship with Internal Combustion Propulsion is at sea before us and capable of going round the World without re-fuelling! What an *Alabama ! ! !* What an upset to the tremblers on the brink who are hesitating to make the plunge for Motor Battleships !

According to a reliable foreign correspondent, the keel of a big Oil-Engine Warship for the German Navy is to be laid shortly. Krupp has a design for a single cylinder of 4,000 H.P.! He has had a six-cylinder engine of 2,000 H.P., each cylinder successfully running for over a year.

VIII.—Anyhow, it must be admitted that the burning of oil to raise steam is a roundabout way of getting power! The motor car and the aeroplane take little drops of oil and explode them in cylinders and get all the power required without being bothered with furnaces or boilers or steam engines, so we say to the marine engineer, " Go and do thou likewise ! "

The sailor's life on the 70,000 H.P. coal using *Lion* is worse than in any ship in the service owing to the constant coalings.

It's an economic waste of good material to keep men grilling in a baking fire hole at unnecessary labour and use 300 men when a dozen or so would suffice !

Certainly oil at present is not a cheap fuel ! but it *is* cheap when the advantages are taken into consideration. In an Internal Combustion Engine, according to figures given by Lord Cowdray, his Mexican oil would work out in England, when freights are normal, as equiva-

lent to coal at twelve to fifteen shillings a
ton !

Oil does not deteriorate by keeping. Coal does.
You can store millions of tons of oil without
fear of waste or loss of power, and England has
got to store those millions of tons, though this
reserve may be gradually built up. The
initial cost would be substantial but the in-
vestment is gilt-edged ! We must and can
face it. *Si vis pacem para bellum !*

You can re-fuel a ship with oil in minutes as
compared with hours with coal !

At any moment during re-fuelling the oil-engine
ship can fight—the coal-driven ship can't—
she is disorganised—the whole crew are black
as niggers and worn out with intense physical
exertion ! In the oil-driven ship one man
turns a tap !

*It's criminal folly to allow another pound of coal
on board a fighting ship !*—or even in a cargo-
ship either !—Krupp has a design for a cargo-
ship with Internal Combustion Engines to go
40,000 (forty thousand) miles without re-
fuelling ! It's vital for the British Fleet and
vital for no other Fleet, to have the oil engine.
That's the strange thing ! And if only the
Germans knew, they'd shoot their Dr. Diesel
like a dog !

Sir Charles Parsons and others prefer small units.
It is realised in regard to the multiplication of
small units (as the Lilliputians tied up Gulliver)
that though there is no important reason why
cylinders shall not be multiplied on the same
shaft yet the space required will be very large
—the engines thus spreading themselves in the
fore and aft direction—but here comes in the
ingenuity of the Naval Constructor and the

197

Marine Engineer in arranging a complete
fresh adaptation of the hull space and forthwith
immense fighting advantages will accrue ! Far
from being an insuperable objection it's a
blessing in disguise, for with a multiplicity of
internal combustion engines there undoubtedly
follows increased safety from serious or total
breakdown, provided that suitable means are
provided for disconnecting any damaged unit
and also for preventing in case of such failure
any damage to the rest of the system. The
storage of oil fuel lends itself to a remarkable
new disposition of the whole hull space.
Thus a battleship could carry some five or six
thousand tons of oil in her double bottoms—
sufficient to go round the earth without re-
fuelling. The " Non-Pareil " (being the French
for the " Incomparable ") will carry over 6,000
tons of oil in her double bottoms, with an
extra double bottom below those carrying the
oil. This is equal to 24,000 tons of coal !

This new arrangement of the hull space permits
some dozen motor boats being carried in a
central armoured pit (where the funnels used
to be). These 60-feet motor boats would
carry 21-inch Torpedoes and have a speed of
40 knots. Imagine these hornets being let
loose in a sea fight ! The 21-inch Torpedo
which they carry goes 5 miles ! And the
silhouette of an Internal Combustion Battleship is over 30 per cent. less than any living or
projected Battleship in the target offered to
the enemy's fire.

IX.—Finally :

*To be first in the race is everything !*

Just consider our immense gains in having been
first with the water-tube boiler ! First with

the turbine! First with the 13½-inch gun! Just take this last as an illustration! We shall have 16 ships armed with the 13½-inch gun before the Germans have a single ship with anything bigger than the 12-inch, and the 13½-inch is as superior to the 12-inch as the 12-inch is to a peashooter.

And yet we hesitate to plunge with a Motor Battleship! Why boggle at this plunge when we have plunged before, every time with success?

People say Internal Combustion Propulsion in a hundred thousand horse-power *Dreadnought* is similarly impossible! "Wait and see!"— The "Non-Pareil" is coming along!

The rapid development of the oil engine is best illustrated by the fact that a highly influential and rich German syndicate have arranged for six passenger steamers for the Atlantic and Pacific Trade, of 22 knots speed and 36,000 H.P. with nine of Krupp's cylinders of 4,000 H.P. each on three shafts.[1]

There need be no fear of an oil famine because of the immense sure oil areas recently brought to notice in Canada, Persia, Mesopotamia and elsewhere. The British oil area in Trinidad alone will be able to more than supply all the requirements of the British Navy. Assuming the present coal requirements of the Navy at 1¼ million tons annually, then less than half a million tons of oil would suffice when the whole British Navy is oil engined, and, as recently remarked by the greatest oil magnate, this amount would be a bagatelle compared with the total output of oil, which he expects before many years to reach an output of a

[1] The War stopped this.—F. 1919.

hundred million tons a year in consequence of
the great demand for developing its output
and the discovery of new oil areas and the
working of shale deposits.

We turned coal-burning Battleships that were building
in November, 1914, into oilers, with great increase of
efficiency and speed.

I have chanced upon a Memorandum on " Oil and
its Fighting Attributes," which I drew up on March 3rd,
1913, for the First Lord of the Admiralty.  It shows
what a Great Personality can effect.  I was told by an
enemy of Mr. Deterding (of whom I am speaking) that
when he came in as Manager of the Great Shell Oil
Combine, the Concern could have been bought for
£40,000.  When I wrote my Memorandum, it was
valued by a hostile Oil Magnate (who told me this himself) at forty millions sterling.  Whether it is Oil, or
Peace, or War, it's the Man, and not the System that
Wins.  And Mr. Deterding is the man who shifted the
centre of gravity of oil (together with an immense assemblage of clerks and chemists and all the paraphernalia of
a huge financial web) from abroad to this country.

" The ideal accumulator which everybody has been
after for the last 50 years, is oil.  There will never
be found another accumulator or source of power of
such small volume as oil.
" Just fancy !  Get a gallon of oil and a man can go
to Brighton and back again, carrying the weight of his
bicycle and himself by means of it. . . .
" It's a shame that anybody is allowed to put oil

under a boiler—for this reason, that when oil is used in an oil engine it realises about five times greater effect. . . .

" The moment the price of oil is £5 a ton it will not be used anywhere under a boiler for steam raising, and the whole world's supply will be available for the Navy and the Diesel Engine. . . .

" I am going to raise every penny I can get and build storage, and even when I have built five million tons of storage I am still going on building it and filling it, even if it is only for the pleasure of looking at it. It is always so much condensed labour stored for the future. . . .

" Oil fuel when stored, does not deteriorate as coal does. The stocks would therefore constitute a national asset, the intrinsic value of which would not diminish." . . . (Mr. Deterding before the Royal Commission on Oil and Oil Engines.)

My Memorandum was as follows :—

Mr. Deterding in his evidence before the Royal Commission, confesses that he possesses in Roumania, in Russia, in California, in the Dutch Indies, in Trinidad, and shortly in Mexico, the controlling interest in oil. The Anglo-Persian Company also say he is getting Mesopotamia and squeezing Persia which are practically untouched areas of immense size reeking with oil. Without doubt Mr. Deterding is Napoleonic in his audacity and Cromwellian in his thoroughness. Sir Thomas Browning in his evidence says that the Royal Dutch-Shell Combination is more powerful and aggressive than ever was the great Standard Oil Trust of America.

Let us therefore listen with deep attention to the words of a man who has the sole executive control of the most powerful organisation on earth for the production of a source of power which almost doubles the power of our Navy whilst our potential enemies remain normal in the strength of their fleets. *What does he advise?*

He says : " Oil is the most extraordinary article in the commercial world and the only thing that hampers its sale is its production. There is no other article in the world where you can get the consumption as long as you make the production. In the case of oil make the production first as the consumption will come. There is no need to look after the consumption, and as a seller you need not make forward contracts as the oil sells itself." Only what you want is an enormously long purse to be able to snap your fingers at everybody and if people do not want to buy it to-day to be able to say to them : " All right ; I will spend a million sterling in making reservoirs and then in the future you will have to pay so much more." " The great point for the Navy is to get oil from someone who can draw supplies from many spots, because no one spot can be absolutely relied on." There is not anybody who can be certain of his supply ; oil fields in my own experience which at the time yielded 18,000 barrels a day within five days went down to 3,000 barrels without the slightest warning.

*The British Empire " has the long purse " ; build reservoirs and store oil. Keep on building reservoirs and buy oil at favourable rates when they offer.*

*November 21st, 1917.*

The report below of the Secretary of the United States Navy is interesting. I have just been looking up the record in 1886, when high officials said I was an " Oil Maniac." I was at that time at the Admiralty as Director of Naval Ordnance, and was sent from that appointment to be Admiral Superintendent of Portsmouth Dockyard,

202

prior to being appointed Controller of the Navy, where I remained six years.   At Portsmouth Dockyard, while I was Admiral Superintendent, we paved the way for rapid shipbuilding in the completion of the Battleship " Royal Sovereign " in two years.   Afterwards, with the same superintendence but additional vigour, we completed the " Dreadnought " in one year and one day ready for Battle !

## OIL BURNING BATTLESHIPS.

WASHINGTON.

Mr. Daniels, Secretary of the Navy, issues a report urging that Congress should authorise the construction of three Battleships, one Battle Cruiser, and nine Fleet Submarines.   He favours oil-burning units, and says that the splendid work which has been accomplished by these vessels would not have been done by coal-burning ships.   *The use of any other power but oil is not now in sight.*

# CHAPTER XIII

## THE BIG GUN

PERHAPS the most convincing speech I ever read was made impromptu by Admiral Sir Reginald Bacon at a meeting of the Institution of Naval Architects on March 12th, 1913.

First of all Admiral Bacon disposed of the fallacy brought forward by one of the speakers, as to which is more effective in disabling the enemy, to destroy the structure of the ship or destroy the guns—the fact being that both are bound up together—if you utterly destroy the hull of the ship you thereby practically destroy the gun-fire. (This is one of those things so obvious that one greatly wonders how these clever experts lose themselves.)

Then Admiral Bacon in a most lovely parable disposed of the " Bow and Arrow Party," who want a lot of small guns instead of, as in the Dreadnought, but one type of gun and that the heaviest gun that can be made. This is Admiral Bacon :—

" I should like to draw your attention to some advice that was given many years ago by an old Post Captain to a Midshipman. He said, ' Boy, if ever you are dining and after dinner, over the wine, some subject like politics is discussed when men's passions are aroused, if a man throws a glass of wine in your face, do not throw a glass of wine in his : *Throw the decanter stopper !* ' And that is what we advocates of the Heavy Gun as mounted in the Dreadnought propose to do—not to slop the six-inch shot over the shirt-front of a battleship, but to go for her with the heaviest guns we can get ; and the heavier the explosive charge you can get in your shell and the bigger explosion you can wreak on the structure near the turrets and the conning tower and over the armoured deck the more likely you are to disable that ship. We object most strongly to the fire of the big guns being interfered with by the use of smaller guns at the same time with all the smoke and mess that are engendered by them. The attention of the Observing Officers is distracted ; their sight is to a great extent obliterated, and even the theoretical result of the small guns is not worth the candle. . . . The ordinary six-inch gun in a battleship is, as regards torpedo-boat attack, of just as much use as a stick is to an old gentleman who is being snow-balled : it keeps his enemy at a respectful distance but still within the vulnerable range of the torpedo. In these days the locomotive torpedo can be fired at ranges at which it is absolutely impossible even to hope or think of hitting the Destroyer which fires the torpedoes at you. You may try to do it, but it is quite useless. Very well, then ; the six-inch gun does keep the Destroyer at a longer range than would be the case if the six-inch gun were not there, that's all. . . . Then the problem of speed has been touched upon. I quite see from one point of view that to lose two guns for an extra five-knot speed seems a great loss ; but there is one question which I should like to ask, and that is whether you would send out to sea a whole fleet, the whole strength of the nation, with no single ship of sufficient superior speed to pick up a particular ship of the enemy ? That is the point to rivet your attention upon. We must always in our Navy have ships of greatly superior speed to any one particular ship in the enemy's fleet, otherwise over the face of the sea you will have ships of the enemy roaming about that we cannot overhaul and that nothing can touch."

The above words were spoken by Admiral Bacon two and three-quarter years before Admiral von Spee and his fast Squadron were caught up and destroyed by the British fast Battle Cruisers, "Invincible" and "Inflexible." Admiral Bacon was a prophet! In other words, Admiral Bacon had Common Sense, and saw the Obvious.

It's difficult for a shore-going person to realise things obvious to the sailor. For instance : in the case of a Big Gun, if twice two is four, then twice four isn't eight, it's sixteen, and twice eight isn't sixteen, it's sixty-four ; that is to say, the bursting effect of a shell varies with the square. So the bigger the calibre of the gun the more immense is the desolating effect of the shell, and, incidentally, the longer the range at which you hit the enemy.

The projectile of the 20-inch gun that was ready to be made for H.M.S. "Incomparable" weighed *over two tons*, and the gun itself weighed 200 *tons*. Such a projectile, associated with a Howitzer, may effect vast changes in both Sea and Land War, because of the awful and immense craters such shell explosions would effect.

To illustrate the frightful devastating effect of such huge shell I will tell a story that I heard from a great friend of mine, a Japanese Admiral. He was a Lieutenant at the time of the Chino-Japanese War. The Chinese vessels mounted very heavy guns. One of their shells burst on the side of the Japanese ship in which my friend was. The Captain sent him down off the bridge to see what had happened, as the ship tottered under the effect of this shell. When he got down on the gun deck, he saw, as it were, the whole side of the ship open to the sea, and not a vestige of any of the crew could he see. They had all been blown to pieces. The only thing he rescued was the uniform cap of his friend, the Lieutenant who was in charge of that division of guns, blown up overhead between the beams. The huge rope mantlets that acted as splinter nettings hung between the guns had utterly disappeared and were resolved into tooth powder ! (so he described it).

I digress here with an anecdote that comes to my mind and which greatly impressed me with the extraordinary humility of the Japanese mind. I had remonstrated with my Japanese friend as to Admiral Togo not having been suitably rewarded for his wonderful victory over the Russian Admiral Rozhdestvensky. He replied : " Sir, Admiral Togo has received the Second Class of the Order of the Golden Kite ! " We should have made him a Duke straight off ! Togo was made a Count afterwards, but not all at once—for fear, I suppose, of giving him a swelled head. He was a great man, Togo ; he was extremely diffident about accepting the English Order of Merit, and even then he wore the Order the wrong way out, so that the inscription " For Merit " should not be seen. The Mikado asked him, after the

great battle, to bring to him the bravest man in the
Fleet ; the Mikado expecting to see a Japanese of some
sort. I am told that Admiral Togo brought Admiral
Pakenham, who was alongside him during the action.
I quite believe it ; but I have always been too shy to
ask my friend if it was true. All I know is that I never
read better Despatches anywhere than those of Admiral
Pakenham.

Somewhat is said in my " Memories " of the un-
mistakable astoundingness of huge bursting charges
in the shell of big guns. (I should be sorry to limit the
effects to even Geometrical Progression !) I don't
think Science has as yet more than mathematically
investigated the amazing quality of Detonation.. Here is
a picture (see opposite p. 176) of only eighteen inch gun
shells, such as the Battle Cruiser " Furious " was
designed and built to fire. Her guns with their enormous
shells were built to make it impossible for the Germans
to prevent the Russian Millions from landing on the
Pomeranian Coast ! In this connection I append a
rough sketch by Oscar Parkes of a twenty-inch gun
ship (see opposite). The sketch will offend the
critical eye of my very talented friend, Sir Eustace
Tennyson d'Eyncourt, but it's good enough for shoregoing
people to give them the idea of what, but for the prodigious development of Air-craft, would have been as great
a New Departure as was the " Dreadnought." The shells
of the " Incomparable " fired from her twenty-inch
guns would each have weighed over two tons ! Imagine
two tons being hurled by each of these guns to a height

Lord Fisher's design:
1,000 feet long.
Six 20-in guns.

H.M.S. "Dreadnought"
526 feet long.
Ten 12-in guns.

Stem to stern "Dreadnought's"
bows would reach this point

Full Broadside of Fisher's design (A)
"Dreadnought" (B)

LORD FISHER'S PROPOSED SHIP, H.M.S. "INCOMPARABLE," SHOWN ALONGSIDE H.M.S. "DREADNOUGHT."

Reproduced by courtesy of "The Graphic"

above the summit of the Matterhorn, or any other mountain you like to take, and bursting on its reaching the ground far out of human sight, but yet with exact accuracy as to where it should fall, causing in its explosion a crater somewhat like that of Vesuvius or Mount Etna, and consequently you can then easily imagine the German Army fleeing for its life from Pomerania to Berlin. The " Furious " (and all her breed) was not built for Salvoes ! They were built for Berlin, and that's why they drew so little water and were built so fragile, so as to weigh as little as possible, and so go faster.

It is very silly indeed to build vessels of War so strong as to last a hundred years. They are obsolete in less than ten years. But the Navy is just one mass of Tories ! In the old days a Sailing Line of Battleship never became obsolete ; the winds of Heaven remained as in the days of Noah. I staggered one Old Admiral by telling him that it blew twice as hard now as when he was at sea ; he couldn't go head-to-wind in his day with sails only, now with the wind forty miles against you you can go forty miles dead against it, and therefore the wind is equal to eighty miles an hour. He didn't quite take it in. I heard one First Sea Lord say to the Second Sea Lord, when scandalised at seeing in a new ship a bathroom for the midshipmen, that he never washed when he went to sea and he didn't see why the midshipmen should now ! But what most upset him was that the seat of the water-closet was mahogany French-polished, instead of good old oak holystoned every morning and so always nice and damp to sit on. (Another improvement is unmentionable !)

I must not leave this chapter without expressing my unbounded delight in having to do business with so splendid a man as Major A. G. Hadcock, the Head of the Ordnance Department at the Elswick Works, who fought out single-handed all the difficulties connected with the inception of the eighteen-inch and the twenty-inch guns of the " Furious " and " Incomparable." I have another friend of the same calibre, who has consistently been in the forefront of the Battle for the adoption of the biggest possible gun that could be constructed—Admiral Sir Sydney Eardley-Wilmot ; he was also the most efficient Chief of the Munitions Department of the Admiralty. When I was gasping with Hadcock over a 20-inch gun, Wilmot had a 22-inch gun ! I really felt small (quite unusual with me !). Now I hope no one is going to quote this line when they review this book :—" Some men grow great, others only swell."

# CHAPTER XIV

WHEN I was ". sore let and hindered " in the days of my youth as a young Lieutenant, a cordial hand was always held out to me by Commodore Goodenough. He was killed by the South Sea Islanders with a poisoned arrow. Being on intimate terms with him, I sent him, in 1868, a reasoned statement proving conclusively that masts and sails were damned as the motive power of warships.

(As a parenthesis I here insert the fact that so late as 1896 a distinguished Admiral, on full pay and in active employment, put forward a solemn declaration that unless sixteen sailing vessels were built for the instruction of the Officers and men of the Navy the fighting efficiency of the Fleet would go to the devil.)

Commodore Goodenough was so impressed by my memorandum that he had a multitude of copies printed and circulated, with the result that they were all burnt and I was damned, and I got a very good talking to by the First Sea Lord. I hadn't the courage of those fine old boys—Bishops Latimer and Ridley—and ran away from the stake. Besides, I wanted to get on. I felt

my day had not yet come. Years after, I commanded
the " Inflexible," still with masts and sails. She had
every sort of wonderful contrivance in engines, electricity,
etc.; but however well we did with them we were accorded
no credit. The sails had as much effect upon her in a
gale of wind as a fly would have on a hippopotamus in
producing any movement. However, we shifted topsails
in three minutes and a half and the Admiral wrote home
to say the " Inflexible " was the best ship in the Fleet.
Ultimately the masts and sails were taken out of
her.

It was not till I was Director of Naval Ordnance that
wooden boarding pikes were done away with. I had a
good look round, at the time, to see if there were any
bows and arrows left.

What my retrograde enemies perfectly detested was
being called " the bow and arrow party." When later
they fought against me about speed being the first
desideratum, the only way I bowled them over was by
designating them as " the Snail and Tortoise party."
It was always the same lot. They wanted to put on so
much armour to make themselves safe in battle that
their ideal became like one of the Spithead Forts—it
could hardly move, it had so much armour on. The
great principle of fighting is simplicity, but the way a
ship used to be built was that you put into her everybody's fad and everybody's gun, and she sank in the
water so much through the weight of all these different
fads that she became a tortoise ! The greatest possible
speed with the biggest practicable gun was, up to the

time of aircraft, the acme of sea fighting. Now, there is only one word—" Submersible."

But to proceed with another Prediction :

The second prediction followed naturally from the first. With machinery being dictated to us as the motive power instead of sails, officers and men would have to become Engineers, and discipline would be better, and so you would not require to have Marines to shoot the sailors in case of mutiny. Now this does sound curious, but again it is so obvious. When the sails were the motive power, the best Petty Officers—that is to say, the smartest of the seamen—got their positions, not by good conduct, but by their temerity aloft, and the man who hauled out the weather-earing in reefing topsails in a gale of wind and balanced himself on his stomach on a topsail yard, with the ship in a mountainous sea, was a man you had to have in a leading position, whatever his conduct was. But once the sails were done away with and there was no going aloft, then the whole ship's company became what may be called " good conduct " men, and could be Marines, or, if you liked to call them so, Sailors. One plan I had was to do away with the sailors ; and another plan I had was to do away with Marines. I plumped for the sailors, though I loved the Marines.

In December, 1868, I predicted and patented a sympathetic exploder for submarine mines. In the last year of the war this very invention proved to be the most deadly of all species of submarine mines.

Quite a different sort of prediction occurs in a letter

# RECORDS

I wrote to Sir Maurice Hankey in 1910, and of which he reminded me in the following letter :

LETTER FROM SIR M. HANKEY, K.C.B. (SECRETARY TO THE WAR CABINET).

OFFICES OF THE WAR CABINET,
2, WHITEHALL GARDENS, S.W.
*May 28th*, 1917.

MY DEAR LORD FISHER,

I am sending your letter along to my wife and asking her to write to you and send both a copy of your letter to me in 1910 about Mr. Asquith's leaving office in November, 1916,[1] and also to write to you about your prophecy of war with Germany beginning in 1914, and Sir John Jellicoe being in command of the Grand Fleet when war broke out.

I have the clearest recollection of the incident. My wife and I had been down to you for a week-end to Kilverstone. You had persuaded us not to go up by the early train on the Monday, and you took us to the rose-garden, where there was a sundial with a charming and interesting inscription. You linked one arm through my wife's and the other through mine, and walked us round and round the paths, and it was walking thus that you made the extraordinary prophecy—

" *The War will come in* 1914, *and Jellicoe will command the Grand Fleet.*"

I remember that my practical mind revolted against the prophecy, and I pressed you for reasons. You then told us that the Kiel Canal, according to experts whom you had assembled five or six years before to examine this

---

[1] This was said in 1910, and Mr. Asquith did leave office as here predicted, in November, 1916, six years afterwards! And Sir John Jellicoe took command of the Grand Fleet forty-eight hours before war was declared, and the war with Germany did break out as predicted in 1914!

question, could not be enlarged for the passage of the new German Dreadnoughts before 1914, and that Germany, though bent on war, would not risk it until this date. As regards Jellicoe, you explained how you yourself had so cast his professional career in such directions as to train him for the post, and, after a brief horoscope of his normal prospects of promotion, you indicated your intention of watching over his career— as you actually did.

All this remains vividly in my mind, and I believe in that of my wife, but, as I am not going home for a few days, she shall give you her unbiassed account.

The calculation itself was an interesting one, but what strikes me now as more remarkable is the " flair " with which you forecasted with certainty the state of mind of the German Emperor and his advisers, and their intention to go to war the first moment they dared.   .   .   .

No more now.

In haste,

Yours ever,

(Signed)　　M. P. A. HANKEY.

The grounds for my prophecies are stated elsewhere. I won't repeat them here. They really weren't predictions ; they were certainties.

I remark in passing that what the sundial said was :—

" Forsitan Ultima."

By the way, I was called a sundial once by a vituperative woman whom I didn't know ; she wrote a letter abusing me as an optimist, and sent these lines :—

> " There he stands amidst the flowers,
> Counting only sunny hours,
> Heeding neither rain nor mist,
> That brazen-faced old optimist."

215

Another woman (but I knew her) in sending me some lovely roses to crown the event of a then recent success, sent also some beautiful lines likewise of her own making. She regretted that I preferred a crown of thorns to a crown of the thornless roses she sent me. The rose she alluded to is called " Zephyrine Drouhin," and, to me, it is astounding that it is so unknown. It is absolutely the only absolute thornless rose ; it has absolutely the sweetest scent of any rose ; it is absolutely the most glorious coloured of all roses ; it blooms more than any rose ; it requires no pruning, and costs less than any rose. I planted these roses when I left the Admiralty in 1910. Somebody told the Naval Attaché at Rome, not knowing that he knew me, that I had taken to planting roses, and his remark was : " They'll d—d well have to grow ! " He had served many years with me.

# CHAPTER XV

## THE BALTIC PROJECT

*Note.*—This paper was submitted for my consideration by Sir Julian Corbett, in the early autumn of 1914.

FROM the shape the war has now taken, it is to be assumed that Germany is trusting for success to a repetition of the methods of Frederick the Great in the Seven Years' War. Not only are the conditions of the present war closely analogous—the main difference being that Great Britain and Austria have changed places—but during the last 15 years the German Great General Staff have been producing an elaborate study of these campaigns.

Broadly stated, Frederick's original plan in that war was to meet the hostile coalition with a sudden offensive against Saxony, precisely as the Germans began with France. When that offensive failed, Frederick fell back on a defensive plan under which he used his interior position to deliver violent attacks beyond each of his frontiers successively. By this means he was able for seven years to hold his own against odds practically identical with those which now confront Germany ; and in the end, though he made none of the conquests he

217

expected, he was able to secure peace on the basis of the *status quo ante* and materially to enhance his position in Europe.

In the present war, so far as it has gone, the same methods promise the same result. Owing to her excellent communications, Germany has been able to employ Frederick's methods with even greater success than he did ; and at present there seems no certain prospect of the Allies being able to overcome them soon enough to ensure that exhaustion will not sap the vigour and cohesion of the coalition.

The only new condition in favour of the Allies is that the Command of the Sea is now against Germany, and it is possible that its mere passive pressure may avail to bring her to a state of hopeless exhaustion from which we were able to save Frederick in the earlier war. If it is believed that this passive pressure can achieve the desired result within a reasonable time, then there is no reason for changing our present scheme of naval operations. If, on the other hand, we have no sufficient promise of our passive attitude effecting what is required to turn the scale, then it may be well to consider the possibility of bringing our Command of the Sea to bear more actively.

We have only to go back again to the Seven Years' War to find a means of doing this, which, *if feasible under modern conditions*, would promise success as surely as it did in the eighteenth century.

Though Frederick's method succeeded, it was once brought within an ace of failure. From the first he knew that the weak point of his system was his northern frontier.

*He knew that a blow in force from the Baltic could at any time paralyse his power of striking right and left, and it was in dread of this from Russia that he began by pressing us so hard to provide him with a covering fleet in that sea.*

Owing to our world-wide preoccupations we were never able to provide such a fleet, and the result was that at the end of 1761 the Russians were able to seize the port of Colberg, occupy the greater part of Pomerania, and winter there in preparation for the decisive campaign in the following spring. Frederick's view of his danger is typified in the story that he now took to carrying a phial of poison in his pocket. Owing, however, to the sudden death of the Czarina in the winter the fatal campaign was never fought. Russia made peace and Prussia was saved.

So critical an episode in the early history of Prussia cannot be without an abiding influence in Berlin. Indeed, it is not too much to say that in a country where military thought tends to dominate naval plans, *the main value of the German Fleet must be its ability to keep the command of the Baltic so far in dispute that hostile invasion across it is impossible.*

*If then it is considered necessary to adopt a more drastic war plan than that we are now pursuing, and to seek to revive the fatal stroke of* 1761, *it is for consideration whether we are able to break down the situation which the German fleet has set up. Are we, in short, in a position to occupy the Baltic in such strength as to enable an adequate*

*Russian army to land in the spring on the coast of Pomerania within striking distance of Berlin or so as to threaten the German communications eastward?*

The first and most obvious difficulty attending such an operation is that it would require the whole of our battle force, and we could not at the same time occupy the North Sea effectively. We should, therefore, lie open to the menace of a counterstroke which might at any time force us to withdraw from the Baltic ; and the only means of preventing this—since the western exit of the Kiel Canal cannot be blocked—

*would be to sow the North Sea with mines on such a scale that naval operations in it would become impossible.*

The objections to such an expedient, both moral and practical, are, of course, very great. The chief moral objection is offence to neutrals. But it is to be observed that they are already suffering severely from the open-sea mining which the Germans inaugurated, and it is possible that, could they be persuaded that carrying the system of open-sea mining to its logical conclusion would expedite the end of the present intolerable conditions, they might be induced to adopt an attitude ot acquiescence. The actual attitude of the northern neutral Powers looks at any rate as if they would be glad to acquiesce in any measure which promised them freedom from their increasing apprehension of Germany's intentions. Sweden, at any rate, who would, after Holland, be the greatest sufferer, has recently been ominously reminded of the days when Napoleon forced her into war with us against her will.

In this connection it may also be observed that where one belligerent departs from the rules of civilised warfare, it is open to the other to take one of two courses. He may secure a moral advantage by refusing to follow a bad lead, or he may seek a physical advantage by forcing the enemy's crime to its utmost consequences. *By the half measures we have adopted hitherto in regard to open-sea mines, we are enjoying neither the one advantage nor the other.*

On the general idea of breaking up the German war plan by operations in the Baltic, it may be recalled that it is not new to us. It was attempted—but a little too late—during Napoleon's Friedland-Eylau campaign. It was again projected in 1854, when our operations in the Great War after Trafalgar, and particularly in the Peninsula, were still living memories. In that year we sent a Fleet into the Baltic with the idea of covering the landing of a French force within striking distance of Petrograd, which was to act in combination with the Prussian army ; but as Prussia held back, the idea was never carried out. Still, the mere presence of our Fleet—giving colour to the menace—did avail to keep a very large proportion of the Russian strength away from the Crimea, and so materially hastened the successful conclusion of the war.

On this analogy, it is for consideration whether, even if the suggested operation is not feasible, a menace of carrying it out—concerted with Russia—might not avail seriously to disturb German equilibrium and force her to desperate expedients, even to hazarding a Fleet action or to alienating entirely the Scandinavian Powers by drastic measures of precaution.

The risks, of course, must be serious ; but unless we are fairly sure that the passive pressure of our Fleet is really bringing Germany to a state of exhaustion, *risks must be taken to use our command of the Sea with greater energy* ; or, so far as the actual situation promises, we can expect no better issue for the present war than that which the continental coalition was forced to accept in the Seven Years' War.

*Lord Fisher to Mr. Lloyd George.*

36, BERKELEY SQUARE,
LONDON,
*March* 28th, 1917.

DEAR PRIME MINISTER,

I hardly liked to go further with my remarks this morning, recognising how very valuable your time is, but I would have liked to have added how appalling it is that the Germans may now be about to deal a deadly blow to Russia by sending a large German Force by sea from Kiel to take St. Petersburg (which, as the Russian Prime Minister, Stolypin, told me, is the Key of Russia ! All is concentrated there !). And here we are with our Fleet passive and unable to frustrate this German Sea attack on Russia. All this due to the grievous faulty Naval strategy of not adopting the Baltic Project put before Mr. Asquith in association with the scheme for the British Army advancing along the Belgian Coast, by which we should have re-captured Antwerp, and there would have been no German submarine menace such as now is. An Armada of 612 vessels was constructed to carry out this policy, thanks to your splendid

222

approval of the cost when you were Chancellor of the Exchequer.

I. Our Naval Strategy has been unimaginative.

II. Our shipbuilding Policy has been futile, inasmuch as it has not coped with the German Submarine Menace.

III. Our Naval Intelligence of the enemy's doings is good for nothing. For it is impossible to conceive there would have been apathy at the Admiralty had it been known how the Germans were building submarines in such numbers—3 a week, Sir John Jellicoe told us at the War Cabinet. I say 5 a week.

Yours, etc.,

(Signed) FISHER.

28/3/17.

I append a couple of extracts from Memoranda made by me in 1902, when I was Commander-in-Chief of the Mediterranean Fleet.

" Here we see 5,000 of these offensive floating mines laid down off Port Arthur, covering a wider space than the English Channel, and we, so far, have none, nor any vessel yet fitted ! What a scandal ! For a purpose unnecessary to be detailed here, it is absolutely obligatory for us to have these mines instantly for war against Germany. They are an imperative strategic necessity, and must be got at once."

### AUTOMATIC DROPPING MINES FOR OCEAN USE.

" The question of the use of these mines as an adjunct to a Battle Fleet in a Fleet action has not been put forward so strongly as desirable as compared with their use for preventing ingress or egress to a port. They can be used with facility in the open sea in depths up to 150 fathoms. There is no question that they could be em-

ployed with immense effect to protect the rear of a
retreating Fleet. This type of mine is quite different to
the blockade mine. They are offensive mines. Is it
wise, indeed is it prudent not to acquaint ourselves, by
exhaustive trials, what the possibility of such a weapon
may be, and how it may be counteracted ? "

# CHAPTER XVI

## SCAPA FLOW.

AGES before the War, but after I became First Sea Lord on Trafalgar Day, 1904, I was sitting locked up in a secluded room that I had mis-appropriated at the Admiralty, looking at a chart of the North Sea, and playing with a pair of compasses, when these thoughts came into my mind ! " Those d—d Germans, if dear old Tirpitz is only far-seeing enough, will multiply means of ' dishing ' a blockade by making the life of surface ships near the coast line a burden to them by submarines and destroyers. (At this time the Germans had only one submarine, and she a failure !) Also, as their radius of action grows through the marvellous oil engine, and ' internal combustion ' changes the face of sea war, we must have our British Fleet so placed at such a distance from hostile attack that our Force off the Enemy's Coast will cut off his marauders at daylight in the morning on their marauding return." I put that safe distance for the British Fleet on my compasses and swept a circle, and behold it came to a large inland land-locked sheet of water, but there was no name to it on the chart and no soundings in it put on the chart. I sent for the Hydrographer, and pointing to the spot, I said : " Bring me the large scale chart. What's its name ? " He didn't know. He would find out.

He was a d—d long time away, and I rang the bell twice and sent him word each time that I was getting angry !

When he turned up, he said it hadn't been properly surveyed, and he believed it was called Scapa Flow ! So up went a surveying ship about an hour afterwards, and discovered, though the current raged through the Pentland Firth at sometimes 14 knots, yet inside this huge secluded basin it was comparatively a stagnant pool ! Wasn't that another proof that we are the ten lost tribes of Israel ? And the Fleet went there forty-eight hours before the War, and a German in the German Fleet wrote to his father to say how it had been intended to torpedo the British Fleet, but it had left unexpectedly sooner for this Northern " Unknown ! " Also, he said in his letter that Jellicoe's appointment as Admiralissimo was very painful to them as they knew of his extreme skill in the British Naval Manœuvres of 1913. Also, thirdly, he added to his Papa that it was a d—d nuisance we had bagged the two Turkish Dreadnoughts in the Tyne the very day they were ready to start, as they belonged to Germany !

The mention of Jellicoe reminds me of Yamamoto saying to me that, just before their War with Russia, he had superseded a splendid Admiral loved by his Fleet, because Togo was " just a little better ! ! ! "

The superseded man was his own *protégé*, and Togo wasn't. No wonder these Japanese fight!

Prince Fushishima, the Mikado's brother, told me of 4,000 of a special company of the bluest blood in Japan, of whom all except four were killed in action or died of wounds—only nine were invalided for sickness. However, I remarked to him we were braver than those 4,000 Japanese, because their religion is they go to Heaven if they die for their country, and we are not so sure! He agreed with me, and gave me a lovely present.

## A PRE-WAR PROPHECY.

On December the 3rd, 1908, when I was First Sea Lord of the Admiralty, I hazarded a prophecy (but, of course, I was only doing the obvious!) that should we be led by our anti-Democratic tendencies in High Places, and by Secret Treaties and by Compromising Attendances of Great Military Officers at the French Manœuvres at Nancy, into a sort of tacit pledge to France to land a British Army in France in a war against Germany, then would come the biggest blow to England she would ever have experienced — not a defeat, *because we never succumb*—but a deadly blow to our economic resources and by the relegation of the British Navy into a " Subsidiary Service." I said in 1908 (and told King Edward so) that the German Emperor would, in such a case, order his generals " to fight neither with small nor great," but only with the English and wipe them out! So has it

come to pass, as regards the Emperor giving these orders and his having this desire !

The original English Expeditionary Force was but a drop in the Ocean as compared with the German and French millions of soldiers, and the value, *though not the gallantry* of its exploits, has been greatly over-rated. It was a very long time indeed before the British Army held any considerable portion of the fighting line in France, and instead of being on the seashore, in touch with the British Fleet and with easy access to England, the British Expeditionary Force was by French directions and because of French susceptibilities, stationed far away from the sea, and sandwiched between French troops. We have always been giving in to the susceptibilities of others and having none of our own ! The whole war illustrates this statement. The Naval situation in the Mediterranean perhaps exemplifies this more than any other instance !

Had the French maintained the defensive in 1915, it is unquestionable that it would have been the Germans and not the French who would have suffered the bloody losses in the regions of Artois and the Champagne.

*We built up a great Army, but we wrecked our ship-building.* We ought to have equipped Russia before we equipped our own Armies, for, had we done so, the Russians would never have sustained the appalling losses they did in pitting pikes against rifles and machine-guns. This was the real reason of the Russian Catastrophe— the appalling casualties and the inability of the old *régime* to supply armaments on the modern scale. Had another policy been pursued and the British Fleet, with its enormous supremacy, cleared the Baltic of the German Navy and landed a Russian Army on the Pomeranian Coast, then the War would have been won in 1915 ! Also, as I pointed out in November, 1914, to Lord Kitchener, we ought to have given Bulgaria all she asked of us. When later we offered her these same terms she refused us with derisive laughter !

There was no difficulty in all this, but we were pusillanimous and we procrastinated.

*We did not equip Russia !* WE DID NOT SOW THE NORTH SEA WITH THOUSANDS UPON THOUSANDS OF MINES, as I advocated in the Autumn of 1914, and I bought eight of the fastest ships in the world to lay them down ! This sowing of the North Sea with a multitude of mines would automatically have established a Complete Blockade ! Again, we did not foster Agriculture, and we almost ceased building Merchant Ships, and robbed our building yards and machine shops of the most skilled artisans and mechanics in the world to become " cannon fodder " ! But a wave of unthinking Militarism swept over the country and submerged the Government, and we were in May, 1918, hard put to it to bring the American Army across the Atlantic as we were so short of shipping.

It needs not a Soldier to realise that had the British Expeditionary Force of 160,000 men been landed at Antwerp by the British Fleet in August, 1914 (instead of its occupying a small sector in the midst of the French Army in France), that the War would certainly have ended in 1915. This, in conjunction with the seizure of the Baltic by the British Fleet and the landing of a Russian Army on the Pomeranian Coast would have smashed the Germans. All this was foreshadowed in 1908, and the German Emperor kindly gave me the credit as the Instigator of the Idea so deadly to Germany.

## The " Monstrous " Cruisers so Derided in Parliament

*Note.*—When I came to the Admiralty as First Sea Lord in October, 1914—three months after the War had begun—I obtained the very cordial concurrence and help of Mr. Churchill and Mr. Lloyd George (Chancellor of the Exchequer) in an unparalleled building programme of 612 vessels of types necessary for a Big Offensive in Northern Waters (*the decisive theatre of the War*). Coal-burning Battleships then under construction were re-designed to burn oil, with great increase of their efficiency and speed, and the last two of these eight Battleships were scrapped (the " Renown " and " Repulse "), and, together with three new vessels—the " Courageous," " Glorious," and " Furious "—were arranged to have immense speed, heavy guns and unprecedented light draught of water, thus enabling them to fulfil the very work described in this letter below of absolutely disposing of hostile light cruisers and following them into shallow waters. They were also meant for service in the Baltic.

Ever since their production became known, Naval critics in both Houses of Parliament (quite ignorant of new Naval strategical and tactical requirements) have consistently crabbed these new mighty Engines of War as the emanations of a sick brain, " *senile and autocratic !* " Hence the value of the following letter from an eye-witness of high rank :

# THE NAVY IN THE WAR

### To Lord Fisher from a Naval Officer

*December 12th, 1917.*

DEAR LORD FISHER,

In the late action in the Heligoland Bight the only heavy ships which could get up with the enemy were the " Repulse," " Courageous " and " Glorious " (the " Renown " and " Furious " were elsewhere).[1] They very nearly brought off an important " coup ! " Without them our light cruisers would not have had a " look in," or perhaps would have been " done in ! " When public speakers desired to decry the work of the Board of which you were a Member in 1914 and 1915, and particularly that part of the work for which you were so personally responsible as this new type of heavy ship, no condemnation was too heavy to heap on your design !

It is a pleasure to me, therefore, to be able to let you know that they have fully justified your anticipation of their success.

I trust you are quite well and will believe me,

Yours sincerely,

————.

### Lord Fisher to a Friend.

*August 22nd, 1917.*

MY BELOVED FRIEND,

I am scanning the dark horizon for some faint glimmer of the end of the War. Not a sign of a glimmer ! So far as the Germans are concerned, there is indisputable authority for stating that Germany is equal to a seven years' war ! Are we ? So far, alas ! we have had no Nelson, no Napoleon, no Pitt ! The one only " substantial victory " of ours in the War (and, as Nelson wished, it

[1] These are the five Battle Cruisers built on my return to the Admiralty in 1914–1915.

was not a Victory—it was Annihilation !) was the destruction of Admiral von Spee's Armada off the Falkland Islands. . . . And the above accomplished under the sole direction of a Septuagenarian First Sea Lord, who was thought mad for denuding the Grand Fleet of our fastest Battle Cruisers to send them 14,000 miles on a supposed wild goose chase. . . . And how I was execrated for inventing the Battle Cruisers ! ' Monstrous Cruisers," they called them ! To this day such asses of this kidney calumniate them, and their still more wonderful successors, the "Repulse," "Renown," "Furious," "Glorious," and "Courageous." How would they have saved England without these Fast Battle Cruisers ? . . . And yet, dear friend, what comes to the Author of the Scene ?

The words of Montaigne !

> " Qui de nous n'a sa ' terre promise,'
> Son jour d'extase,
> Et sa fin en exil ? "

Yours, etc.,

(Signed)  FISHER.

*Note.*—Much talk of a recent *mot* at a great dinner-table, where society's hatred of Lord Fisher was freely canvassed, and his retirement (in May 1915) much applauded. " I did not know," remarked a statesman, " that Mr. Pitt ever put Lord Nelson on the retired list."

### THE DREADNOUGHT BATTLE CRUISER.

The following imaginary dialogue I composed in 1904 to illustrate the text that " Cruisers without high speed and protection are absolutely useless " :—

" The 'Venus,' an Armoured Cruiser, is approaching her own Fleet at full speed !

" Admiral signals to 'Venus' : ' What have you seen ? '

" ' Venus ' replies : ' Four funnels hull down.'

" Admiral : ' Well, what was behind ? '

" ' Venus ' replies : ' Cannot say ; she must have four knots more speed than I had, and would have caught me in three hours, so I had to close you at full speed.'

" Admiral's logical reply : ' You had better pay your ship off and turn over to something that is some good ; you are simply a device for wasting 400 men ! ' "

The deduction is :

## ARMOUR IS VISION.

So we got out the " Dreadnought " Battle Cruiser on that basis, and also to fulfil that great Nelsonic idea of having a Squadron of very fast ships to bring on an Action, or overtake and lame a retreating foe. And in the great war this fast " Dreadnought " Battle Cruiser carried off all the honours. She sank the " Blücher " and others, and also Admiral von Spee at the Falkland Islands.

But the *sine qua non* in these great Ships must ever be that they carry the Biggest Possible Gun. It was for this reason that the 18-in. gun was introduced in the Autumn of 1914[1] and put on board the new Battle Cruiser

---

[1] This 18-in. gun was ordered by me without any of the usual preliminary trials or any reference to any Gunnery Experts whatever. The credit of its great success is due to Major Hadcock, Head of the Elswick Ordnance Manufacturing Department, who also designed the 20-in. gun for the fast Battleship Type which was to have been built had I remained at the Admiralty in May, 1915.

A model of this 20-in. gun Battle Cruiser of 35 knots speed, was got out before I left the Admiralty—three days more they would have started building.

"Furious"; and indeed all was completely arranged for 20-in. guns being placed in the succeeding proposed Battle Cruisers of immense speed and very light draft of water and *possessing the special merit of exceeding rapid construction.*

Alas! those in authority went back on it! It was precisely the same argument that made these same retrograde Lot's wives go back from oil to coal. Coal, they said, was good enough and was so safe! Lot's wife thought of her toasted muffins. Notice now especially that if a man is five per cent. before his time he may possibly be accounted a Genius! but if this same poor devil goes ten per cent. better, then he's voted a Crank. Above that percentage, he is stark staring Mad.

(N.B.—I have gone through all these percentages!)

### THE WAY TO VICTORY.

*Lord Fisher to the Prime Minister.*

HOUSE OF LORDS,
*June 12th, 1917.*

MY DEAR PRIME MINISTER,

In November, 1914, Sir John French came specially from France to attend the War Council to consider a proposal put forward by the Admiralty that the British Army should advance along the sea shore flanked by the British Fleet. Had this proposal been given effect to, the German Submarine Menace would have been deprived of much of its strength, and many Enemy Air Raids on our coast would have been far more difficult. The considerations which made me urge this proposal at that time have continuously grown stronger, and to-day I feel it my duty to press upon you the vital necessity of a joint Naval and Military operation of this kind. I do not feel justified in arguing the Military advantages which are, however, so obvious as to be patent to the whole world, nor the political advantage of getting in touch with Holland along the Scheldt, but solely from a Naval point of view the enterprise is one that ought to be undertaken with all our powers without further delay. The present occasion is peculiarly favourable, as we can call upon the support of the whole American Fleet.

Yours truly,

(Signed)  FISHER.

36, BERKELEY SQUARE,
LONDON,
*July 11th,* 1917.

MY DEAR PRIME MINISTER,

In putting before your urgent notice the following two propositions, I have consulted no one, and seen no experts. It is the emanation of my own brain.

Owing to two years of departmental apathy and inconceivable strategical as well as tactical blunders, we are wrongly raided in the air, and being ruined under water.

I remember a very famous speech of yours where you pointed out that we had been fourteen times " Too Late ! "

This letter is to persuade you against two more " Too lates " :

(1) The Air :
   You want two ideas carried out :
   (*a*) A multitude of bombing aircraft made like Ford cars (so therefore very expeditiously obtained thereby).
   (*b*) The other type of aircraft constantly improving to get better fighting qualities.
   The Air is going to win the War owing to the sad and grievous other neglects.

235

(2) The Water :

Here we have a very simple proposition. Now that America has joined us, we have a simply overwhelming sea preponderance !
Are you not going to do anything with this ?

Make the German Fleet fight, and you win the war !

How can you make the German Fleet fight ? By undertaking on a huge scale, with an immense Armada of special rapidly-built craft, an operation that threatens the German Fleet's existence !

That operation, on the basis in my mind, is one absolutely sure of success, because the force employed is so gigantic as to be negligible of fools.

If you sweep away the German Fleet, you sweep away all else and end the War, as then you have the Baltic clear and a straight run of some 90 miles only from the Pomeranian Coast to Berlin, and it is the Russian Army we want to enter Berlin, not the English or French.

Yours truly,<br>
(Signed)  FISHER.

*Lord Fisher to a Friend.*

*February 28th,* 1918.

MY DEAR FRIEND, . . .

Quite recently we lost a golden opportunity of wrecking the residue of the German Fleet and wrecking the Kiel Canal, when the main German Fleet went to Riga with the German army embarked in a huge fleet of transports and so requiring all the Destroyers and Submarines of Germany to protect it.

Well, in reply to your question, this is what I would do now :

I would carry out the policy enunciated in the Print on the Baltic Project which was submitted early in the war[1] and again reverted to in my letter to the Prime Minister, dated June 2nd, 1916. Sow the North Sea with mines

[1] See Chapter XV.

as thick as the leaves in Vallombrosa! That blocks
effectually the Kiel Canal, if continued laying of these
mines is always perpetually going on with damnable
pertinacity! Then I guarantee to force a passage into
the Baltic in combination with a great Military co-
operation, but that co-operation must not be the co-
operation of the Walcheren Expedition!

> " Lord Chatham with his sword drawn
> Was waiting for Sir Richard Strachan,
> Sir Richard, longing to be at 'em !
> Was waiting for the Earl of Chatham ! "

It has got to be chiefly a Naval Job! And the Army
will be landed by the Navy! The Navy will guarantee
landing the Army on the Coast of Pomerania and elsewhere. Three feints, any of which can be turned into
a Reality.

Further in detail I won't go, but I can guarantee success.

Have I ever failed yet? It's an egotistical question,
but I never have!

What a d—d fool I should be to brag now if I wasn't
certain!

Yours, etc.,

(Signed) FISHER.

P.S.—I have heard some Idiots say that the Baltic
Sea is now impregnable because of German mines in
it. No earthly System of mines can possibly avoid
being destroyed. We can get into the Baltic whenever
we like to do so. I guarantee it.

" SOW THE NORTH SEA WITH MINES."

(Written in November, 1914).

The German policy of laying mines has resulted in
denying our access to their harbours ; has hampered

our Submarines in their attempts to penetrate into German waters ; and we have lost the latest type of " Dreadnought " (" Audacious ") and many other war vessels and over 70 merchant vessels of various sizes.

As we have only laid a patch of mines off Ostend (whose position we have notified), the Germans have free access to our coasts to lay fresh mines and to carry out raids and bombardments.

We have had, to our own immense disadvantage in holding up our coastwise traffic, to extinguish the navigation lights on our East Coast, so as to impede German ships laying mines. At times we have had completely to stop our traffic on the East Coast because of German mines ; and the risk is so great that freights in some cases have advanced 75 per cent.—quite apart from shortness of tonnage.

The Germans have laid mines off the North of Ireland, and may further hamper movements of shipping in the Atlantic.

The German mine-laying policy has so hindered the movements of the British Fleet, by necessitating wide detours, that to deal with a raid such as the recent Hartlepool affair involves enormous risks, while at the same time the German Fleet can navigate to our coast with the utmost speed and the utmost confidence. They know that we have laid no mines, and the position, of course, of their own mines is accurately charted by them—indeed we know this as a fact. Our Fleet, on the contrary, has to confine its movements to deep water, or slowly to grope its way behind mine-sweeping vessels.

*There is no option but to adopt an offensive mine-laying policy.*

It is unfortunate, however, that we have only 4,900 mines at present available. On February 1st (together with 1,000 mines from Russia) we shall have 9,110, and on March 1st we shall have 11,100 mines. This number, however, is quite inadequate, but every effort is being made to get more. Also FAST Mine-Layers are being procured, as the present ones are very slow and their coal supply very small. So at present we can only go very slow in mine-laying ; but carefully selected positions can be proceeded with.

We must certainly look forward to a big extension of German mine-laying in the Bristol Channel and English Channel and elsewhere, in view of Admiral Tirpitz's recent statements in regard to attacking our commerce.

Neutral vessels now pick up Pilots at the German island of Sylt, and take goods unimpeded to German ports— ostensibly carrying cotton, but more probably copper, etc., and thus circumventing our economic pressure.[1] *This would be at once stopped effectually by a mine-laying policy.*

Nor could any German vessels get out to sea at speed as at present ; they would have to go slow, preceded by mine-sweeping vessels, and so would be exposed to attack by our Submarines.

[1] The Foreign Office would not permit an efficient blockade, and the outrageous release of vessels carrying war-helping cargoes caused intense dissatisfaction in the fleet. No vessels ever passed our chain of Cruisers without detention and examination.

# RECORDS

## A BIRTHDAY LETTER

*Lord Fisher to a Friend.*

*January 25th*, 1918.

MY DEAR FRIEND,

A letter to-day on my birthday from an eminent Engineer, cheers me up by saying that never has France been so vigorously governed as she is now by her present Prime Minister, Clemenceau, and that he is my age, 77.

The Conduct of the War, both by Sea and Land, has been perilously effete and wanting in Imagination and Audacity since May, 1915.

I know these words of mine give you the stomach-ache, but so did Jeremiah the Jews when he kept on telling them in his chapter v., verse 31 :

> " The prophets prophesy falsely,
> And the priests [the unfit] bear rule by their means,
> And my people love to have it so,
> And what will ye do in the end thereof ? "

(Why ! Send for Jephthah !)
" And Jephthah said unto the elders of Gilead " (who came supplicating, asking him to come back as their captain)

> " Did ye not hate me and expel me ?
> And why are ye come unto me now when ye are in distress ? "

And the elders of Gilead said unto Jephthah :

> " We turn again to thee now, that thou mayest go with us and fight ! "

By Sea, when the German Fleet took the German Army to Riga, we had a wonderful sure certainty of destroying the German Fleet and the Kiel Canal, but

240

THE SUBMARINE MONITOR M 1, which lately returned from a successful cruise in the Mediterranean. She is designed to fight above or below water. She carries a 12-inch gun firing an 850-lb. shell, which can be discharged when only the muzzle of the gun is above water.

we let it slip because there were risks. (As if war could be conducted without risks !) Considered Rashness in war is Prudence, and Prudence in war is usually a synonym for imbecility !

Observe the Mediterranean ! The whole Sea Power of France and Italy is collected in the Mediterranean to fight the puny Austrian Fleet, but they haven't fought it. Not only that, but hundreds of vessels of the English Navy are perforce out in the Mediterranean to aid them ; and yet the German ships, " Goeben " and " Breslau," known to be fast, powerful and efficient, emerge from the Dardanelles with impunity and massacre two of our Monitors—never meant to be out there and totally unfitted for such service—and two obsolete British Destroyers have to put up a fight ! But God intervened and sent the " Goeben " and " Breslau " on top of mines. It was thus the act of God and not the act of our Sea Fools that kept these two powerful German ships from going to the coast of Syria, where they would have played Hell with Allenby and our Palestine Army.

We have pandered to our Allies from the very beginning of the War, and yet practically we find most of the money and have found four million soldiers, and a thousand millions sterling lent to Russia have been lent in vain.

You know as well as I do that our Expeditionary Force should have been sent in August, 1914, to Antwerp and not to France ; we should then have held the Belgian Coast and the Scheldt, but this was too tame—we were all singing :

"Malbrook s'en va-t'en guerre ! "

The Baltic Project was scoffed at, though it had the impregnable sanction of Frederick the Great, and the project was turned down in November, 1914 ; and now the Germans, because of their possession of the Baltic as a German lake, are going to annex all the Islands they want that command Russia and Sweden, and the Russian Fleet, with its splendid " Dreadnoughts " and Destroyers disappear and eight British Submarines have been sunk. Ichabod !

Yours truly,<br>FISHER.

THE GERMAN SUBMARINE MENACE.

*Lord Fisher to a Friend.*

*March 2nd,* 1918.

MY DEAR " MR. FAITHFUL,"

You write anxious to have some connected statement in regard to the whole history of the German Submarine Menace.

Now, the first observation thereon is the oft-repeated indisputable statement that no private person whatever can hope to fight successfully any Public Department. So even if you had the most conclusive evidence of effete apathy such as at first characterised the dealing with this German Submarine Menace, yet you would to the World at large be completely refuted by a rejoinder in Parliament of departmental facts. Nevertheless here is a bit of Naval History.

In December, 1915, the Prime Minister (Mr. Asquith) unexpectedly came up to me in the Lobby of the House of Commons, and said he was anxious to consult me about Naval affairs, and he would take an early opportunity of seeing me ! However, he must have been put off this for I never saw him. A month afterwards I pressed him in writing to see Sir John Jellicoe in regard to the paucity both of suitable apparatus and of suitable measures to cope with the German Submarine Menace ; after much opposition the Prime Minister himself sent for Sir John Jellicoe and he appeared before the War Council. This is my Memorandum at that time, dated February 7th, 1916 :

242

## MEMORANDUM.

" I have just heard that, notwithstanding the opposition to it, Sir John Jellicoe will attend the War Council at 11.30 a.m. next Friday. That he may have strength and power to overcome all ' the wiles of the Devil ' is my fervent prayer.

" That there has been signal failure since May, 1915, to continue the Great Push previous to that date of building fast Destroyers, fast Submarines, Mine Sweepers and small Craft generally is absolutely indisputable.

" Above all, it was criminal folly and inexcusable on the part of the Admiralty to allow skilled workmen (20,000 of them) to be taken away from shipyards. Also it was inexcusable and weak to give up the Admiralty command of steel and other shipbuilding materials.

" Kitchener instantly cancelled the order to take men from the shipyards when it was attempted by his subordinates while I was First Sea Lord. He saw the folly of it !

" Again, deferring the shipbuilding that was in progress was fatuous. I saw myself two fast Monitors (each of them a thousand tons advanced) from which all the workmen had been called off. A few months afterwards there was feverish and wasteful haste to complete them. So was it with the five fast big Battle Cruisers of very light draught of water. All similarly delayed.

" Well ! Jellicoe, a ' No Talker,' at the War Council was opposed to a mass of ' All Talkers,' so he did not make a good fight ; but when he got back to the Grand Fleet at Scapa Flow he remembered himself and wrote a most excellent Memorandum, which put himself right.

" However, a wordy war is no use ; nothing but a cataclysm will stop our ' Facilis descensus Averni.' "

We must by some political miracle swallow up Korah, Dathan and Abiram and have a fresh lot. In Parliament we have nothing but the *suggestio falsi* and the *suppressio veri*! A little bit of truth skilfully disguised:

> " A truth that's told with bad intent,
> Beats any lie you can invent."

In reply to your question with reference to Mr. Bonar Law's corrected statement in Hansard, the Printer's date at the bottom of the Submarine Paper,[1] sent to the Prime Minister and First Lord of the Admiralty is January, 1914, seven months before the War.

Yours always,

FISHER.

*Lord Fisher to Sir Maurice Hankey, K.C.B., Secretary to the War Cabinet.*

19, ST. JAMES'S SQUARE.

MY DEAR HANKEY,

In reply to your inquiry, my five points of peace (as regards Sea war only) are :

(1) The German High Sea Fleet to be delivered up intact.
(2) Ditto, every German Submarine.
(3) Ditto, Heligoland.
(4) Ditto, the two flanking islands of Sylt and Borkum.
(5) No spot of German Territory in the wide world to be permitted ! It would infallibly be a Submarine Base.

Yours,

(Signed) FISHER,

*October 21st, 1918.*
(Trafalgar Day).

See Chapter XI.

Why we were not as relentless in carrying out our Peace requirements at Sea as on Land is positively incomprehensible.

The German Fleet was not turned over and was afterwards sunk at pleasure by the German crews. I don't feel at all sure that every German submarine, complete and incomplete, was handed over. Every oil engine ought to have been cleared out of Germany. Through some extraordinary chain of reasoning, absolutely incomprehensible, the three Islands of Heligoland, Sylt and Borkum were not claimed and occupied. In view of the prodigious development of Aircraft it was imperative that these Islands should be in the possession of England.

All this to me is absolutely astounding. The British Fleet won the War, and the British Fleet didn't get a single thing it ought to have, excepting the everlasting stigma amongst our Allies, of being fools, in allowing the German Fleet to be sunk under our noses, because we mistook the Germans for gentlemen.

### The Miracle of the Peace

(*that took place at the* 11*th hour of the* 11*th day of the* 11*th Month !*) only equalled by the Destruction of Sennacherib's Army, on the night described in the 25th verse of the 19th chapter of Second Book of Kings ! The heading of the chapter is " *An Angel slayeth the Assyrians.*"

" That night the Angel of the Lord went forth . . . in the morning behold they were all dead corpses ! "

# RECORDS

A Cabinet Minister, in an article (after the Armistice) in a newspaper, stated that the Allies were at their last gasp when the Armistice occurred as it did as a Miracle! for Marshal Foch had been foiled on the strategic flank by the inability of the American Army to advance and the unavoidable consequences of want of experience in a new Army (*immense but inexperienced— they were slaughtered in hecatombs and died like flies!*) and so the American advance on the Verdun flank was held up, and Haig therefore had to batter away instead (and well he did it!). And though the British Army entered Mons, yet the German Army was efficient, was undemoralised, and had immense lines of resistance in its rear before reaching the Rhine! There was no Waterloo, no Sedan, no Trafalgar (though there could have been one on October 21st, 1918, for the German Naval Mutiny was known! Sir E. Geddes said so in a Mansion House Speech on November 9th, 1918). There was no Napoleon—no Nelson! but " The Angel of the Lord went forth. . . ."


*Lord Fisher to a Friend.*

*March 27th, 1918.*

My Dear Blank,

It has been a most disastrous war for one simple reason—that our Navy, with a sea supremacy quite unexampled in the history of the world (we are five times stronger than the enemy) has been relegated into being a " Subsidiary Service!". . .

# THE NAVY IN THE WAR

What *crashes* we have had ·

Tirpitz—Sunk.
Joffre—Stranded.
Kitchener—Drowned.
Lord French— ⎫
Lord Jellicoe— ⎬Made Viscounts.
Lord Devonport— ⎭
Fisher—Marooned.
Sir W. Robertson—The " Eastern Command " in
    Timbuctoo.
Bethmann-Hollweg— ⎫
Asquith— ⎬Torpedoed.

Heaven bless you ! I am here walking 10 miles a day !
and eating my heart out !

And a host of minor prophets promoted. (We don't
shoot now ! we promote !)

Yours, etc.,

(Signed) FISHER.

27/3/18.


*To Lord Fisher from an Admirer.*

*21st November,* 1918.

DEAR LORD FISHER,

We are just back after taking part in the most
wonderful episode of the war, and my heart is very full,
and I feel that the extraordinary surrender of the Flower
of the German Fleet is so much due to your marvellous
work and insight—in giving England the Fleet she has
—that I must write you !

I suppose the world will never again see such a sight
—a line of 14 heavy, modern, capital ships, with their
guns fore and aft in securing position, in perfect order
and keeping good station, quietly giving themselves up
without a blow or a murmur. Surely such a humiliating

247

and ignominious end could never have been even thought of in all history past or present.

Had I been in a private ship I would have used every endeavour to get you up to see the final fulfilment of your life's work. As it is, I can't think it was very gracious of the authorities not to have ensured your presence. But history will give you your due.

Forgive this effusion, and please don't bother to answer it. But *I* realise that to-day's victory was yours, and it is iniquitous that you were not here to see it.

Your affectionate and devoted admirer,

————.

*To Lord Fisher from Admiral Moresby.*

FAREHAM,
*July 9th*, 1918.

DEAR OLD FRIEND,

Just a line. One of our " Article writing " Admirals sent me one of them on the progress of the war ! Your name was not mentioned, nor your services alluded to ! I returned it, saying it was the play without Hamlet. You might be wrong, or despised, but you could not be *ignored*. With our Navy revolutionised, Osborne created, obsolete cruisers scrapped, naval base shifted from Portland to Rosyth, Dreadnoughts and Battle Cruisers invented, Falkland Islands victory, and so on, he might as well talk of Rome without Cæsar. He replied and said you were an Enigma, and that covered it all ! There is some truth in this, for such are all born leaders of men, from our Master, the greatest Enigma of all (who made thee thyself, who gave thee power to do these things), down to all who can see what is going on on the other side of the hill. . . .

Yours ever,
(Signed)  J. MORESBY.

# POSTSCRIPT

LAST night, in finishing off the examination of several boxes of old papers, I came across a forgotten letter written a fortnight after the Battle of Trafalgar from the " Dreadnought " (which ship participated in the Battle). On mentioning it I was told there was a " Dreadnought " in the Navy at the time of Henry VIII. I think one of the Docks at Portsmouth dates from that time, and the " Dreadnought " may have been docked in it. I love the delicious little touch at the end of this letter where everyone seals their letters with black wax in memory of Nelson, and the prayer and poetry are lovely. And where his acquaintance in Collingwood's Ship " had been shortened by the Hand of Death," and

> " Roll softly ye Waves,
> Blow gently ye Winds

O'er the bosom of the deep where the bodies of the Heroes rest, until the Great Day, when all that are in their grave shall hear the Voice of the Son of God, when thou O Sea! shall give up thy dead to Life Immortal, and thou O Britain be grateful to thy defenders ! that the Widows and Orphans of thy deceased Warriors be precious in thy sight—Soothe their sorrows, alleviate their distresses and provide for their wants by anticipating their wishes."

(The Straits of Gibraltar the writer spells " *Streights*.") He adds " Our splendid Success has been dearly bought. Our gallant Chief is dead. In the arms of Victory fell the greatest Hero that ever any age or Nation ever produced."

# APPENDIX I

# APPENDIX I

LORD FISHER'S GREAT NAVAL REFORMS

*By* W. T. STEAD

" He being dead yet speaketh."—*Hebrews* xi. 4.

[The following account of Lord Fisher's Naval Reforms is extracted from *The Review of Reviews* for February, 1910.]

I BRIEFLY summarise Lord Fisher's four great reforms :

1. The introduction of the nucleus crew system.

2. The redistribution of the fleets in accordance with modern requirements.

3. The elimination of inefficient fighting vessels from the Active List of the Navy.

4. The introduction of the all-big-gun type of battle-ship and battleship-cruiser.

To these four cardinal achievements must be added the system of common entry and training for all executive officers and the institution and development of the Naval War College and the Naval War Staff.

By the nucleus crew system all our available ships of war are ready for instant mobilisation. From two-fifths to three-fifths of their complement, including all the expert and specialist ratings, are on board, so that they are familiar with the ship and her armament. The rest of the crew is held in constant readiness to come on board. Fisher once aired, in after-dinner talk, the daring idea that the time would come when the First Lord of the Admiralty would be supreme over the War Office, and would, as in the days of the Commonwealth, fill up deficiencies in ships' crews by levies from the territorial forces. Landsmen can serve guns as well as sailors.

The second great revolution was necessitated by the alteration in the centre of international gravity occasioned by the growth of the German Navy. Formerly the Mediterranean Fleet ranked first in importance. Now the Home Fleet concentrates in its four divisions all the best fighting ships we possess. It is hardly too much to say, as M. Hanotaux publicly declared, that Admiral Fisher had, by concentration and redistribution, magnified our fighting naval strength by an amount unparalleled in a hundred years. That the fighting efficiency of the Fleet has been doubled under Fisher's *régime* is to understate the facts. To say it has been trebled would hardly be over the mark. And what is the most marvellous thing of all is that this enormous increase of efficiency was achieved not only without any increase of the estimates, but in spite of a reduction which amounted to nearly five millions sterling—three and a half millions actual and one and a half millions automatic increase checked.

This great economy was largely achieved by the scrapping of ships too weak to fight and too slow to run away.

# APPENDIX I

One hundred and fifty obsolete and useless ships were removed from the effective list ; some were sold, others were broken up, while a third class were kept in store for contingencies. They were lame ducks, all useless in war, costly in peace, consuming stores, wasting the time of officers and men. The obsolete ships were replaced on foreign stations by vessels which could either fight or fly. . . .

Of the introduction of the " Dreadnought " and super-" Dreadnoughts " I have already spoken.

Apart from the above matters of high policy, a number of other reforms or advances have been made during the past five years which are beyond all criticism. Opinions may differ as to the details of some of these services, but there is no dispute as to their immense contribution to the fighting efficiency of the Navy. Some of these may be thus briefly enumerated :

1. Complete reorganisation of the dockyards. [6,000 redundant workmen discharged.]

2. Improved system of refits of ships, and limitation of number of vessels absent at one time from any fleet for repair.

3. Introduction of the Royal Fleet Reserve, composed only of ratings who have served for a period of years in the active service.

4. Improvements of Royal Naval Reserve, by enforcing periodical training on board modern commissioned ships in place of obsolete hulks or shore batteries.

5. Establishment and extension of Royal Naval Volunteer Reserve.

6. The establishment of a service of offensive mines and mine-laying vessels.

7. The introduction of vessels for defensive mine-sweeping in harbours and on the open sea.

8. A complete organisation of the service of auxiliary vessels for the fleets in war.

9. The development of submarines, and the equipment of submarine bases and all the necessary auxiliaries.

10. The proper organisation of the Destroyer Flotillas, with their essential auxiliaries.

11. The enormous development of wireless telegraphy afloat, the equipment of powerful shore stations round the coast and at the Admiralty, and the introduction of a special corps of operators.

12. The experimental stage of aerial navigation entered upon.

13. The foundation of the Royal Naval War College and its development.

14. The establishment of Signal Schools at each port.

15. The establishment of a Navigation School.

16. Enormous advances in the Gunnery training and efficiency of the Fleet.

17. Great improvements in torpedoes and in the torpedo training.

18. The introduction of a naval education and training for Engine Room Artificers.

19. The introduction of the new rating of Mechanician for the Stoker Class for engine-driving duties.

20. Complete reorganisation of the arrangements for mobilisation, whereby every officer and man is always

detailed by name for his ship on mobilisation, and the mobilisation of the whole fleet can be effected in a few hours.

21. The introduction of a complete system of intelligence of trade movements throughout the world.

22. The stores of the Fleet put on a modern basis both in the storehouses ashore and those carried in the ships themselves—recognising the far different conditions now obtaining to those of sailing-ship days of long voyages, necessitating larger supplies being carried, and modern conditions of production and supply enabling stores on distant stations and at home being rapidly replenished. Some millions sterling were economised in this way with increased efficiency, as the Fleet was supplied with up-to-date articles ; the only thing that gained by the age of the old system was the rum.

23. The provision of repair ships, distilling plant, and attendant auxiliaries to all fleets, and the preparation of plans elaborated in a confidential handbook providing for all the auxiliary vessels required in war.

In addition to all the above reforms great improvements have been made in the conditions of service of officers and men, all tending to increase contentment and thereby advance efficiency. Some of these are as follows :

1. The introduction of two-year commissions, in place of three years and often four [so that men were not so long away from their homes and the crews of ships did not get stale].

2. Increases of pay to many grades of both officers

257                              s

and men—as regards Commanders, the only increase since the rank was introduced.

3. Ship's Bands provided by the Service, and a School of Music established, and foreign musicians abolished.

4. The long-standing grievances of the men with regard to their victualling removed. Improvements in cooking. Bakeries fitted on board ships.

5. The Canteen system recognised and taken under Admiralty control, and the old abuses abolished.

6. The clothing system reformed, and much expense saved to the men.

7. Great improvements effected in the position of Petty Officers.

8. An educational test instituted for advancement to Petty Officer.

9. Increase of pension granted to Chief Petty Officers.

10. Allotment stoppages abolished.

11. Allowances paid to men in lieu of victuals when on leave.

12. Promotions from the ranks to Commissioned Officer introduced.

13. Warrant rank introduced for the telegraphist, stoker, ship's steward, writer, ship's police, and ship's cook classes.

I print the foregoing from a return drawn up by an expert familiar with details of the Service. To the general reader they will be chiefly interesting as suggesting the immense and multifarious labours of Admiral Fisher. It is not surprising that he found it necessary to start work every morning at four o'clock.

# APPENDIX II

# APPENDIX II

*Born January 25, 1841, at Rambodde, Ceylon.*

Son of Captain William Fisher, 78th Highlanders, A.D.C. to the Governor of Ceylon, and Sophia, daughter of A. Lambe, of New Bond Street, and granddaughter of Alderman Boydell. His godmother was Lady Wilmot Horton, wife of the Governor of Ceylon ; and his godfather Sir Robert Arbuthnot, Commanding the Forces in Ceylon.

*Entered the Royal Navy, June 13, 1854.*

Received a nomination for the Navy from Admiral Sir William Parker, the last of Nelson's Captains. Joined his first ship, the " Victory," at Portsmouth, on July 12, 1854. The " Victory " was also the last ship to fly his flag as an Admiral, October 20, 1904.

Served in Russian War, in Baltic (Medal) in " Calcutta " 84 guns.

Served in the China War, 1856–60, including the capture of Canton and Peiho Forts. (China Medal, Canton and Taku Clasps.) Given command of a small vessel by Admiral Sir James Hope, Commander-in-Chief, the " Coromandel," of which he was acting Captain at the age of 19.

Also served in " Highflyer," Captain Shadwell ; " Chesapeake," Captain Hilles ; and " Furious," Captain Oliver Jones. Returned home in 1861 from the China Station.

*Lieutenant, November 4, 1860.*

In passing for Lieutenant, he won the Beaufort Testimonial ; and was advanced to Mate on January 25, 1860, and confirmed as Lieutenant within eleven months.

# RECORDS

*March* 28, 1863.

Appointed to H.M.S. " Warrior," Captain the Hon. A. A. Cochrane, the first seagoing ironclad, for gunnery duties. Served in her for three and a half years.

*November* 3, 1866.

Appointed to the Staff of H.M.S. " Excellent," gunnery schoolship, Portsmouth, Captain Arthur W. A. Hood.

*August* 2, 1869.

Promoted to Commander, and appointed to the China flagship.

*September* 19, 1872.

On returning from China in H.M.S. " Ocean," was appointed to " Excellent " for Torpedo Service. Started the " Vernon " as a Torpedo Schoolship. Visited Fiume to arrange for the purchase of the Whitehead Torpedo.

*October* 30, 1874.

Promoted to Captain, and re-appointed to " Excellent " for torpedo service and instructional duties, remaining until 1876.

*November* 16, 1876.

Appointed for special service in " Hercules," flagship of Vice-Admiral the Hon. Sir James Drummond, Commander-in-Chief, Mediterranean.

*March* 15, 1877.

Appointed Flag-Captain to Admiral Sir A. Cooper-Key, Commander-in-Chief, North American Station, in the " Bellerophon."

*June* 7, 1878.

Appointed Flag-Captain to Admiral Sir A. Cooper-Key, Commanding the Particular Service Squadron, in the " Hercules."

# APPENDIX II

### *January* 1, 1879.

Appointed in command of the " Pallas," corvette, on Mediterranean Station, returning home in July. President of a Committee for the revision of the " Gunnery Manual of the Fleet."

### *September* 25, 1879.

Appointed Flag-Captain to Vice-Admiral Sir Leopold M'Clintock, Commander-in-Chief, North American Station, in the " Northampton."

### *January* 18, 1881.

Appointed to command the " Inflexible," the largest ship in the Navy.

### *July* 11, 1882.

Took part in the bombardment of Alexandria. Afterwards landed with the Naval Brigade at Alexandria. Arranged for the first " armoured train," and commanded it in various skirmishes with the enemy.

### *August* 14, 1882.

Awarded the C.B. for service at Alexandria ; also Egyptian Medal, with Alexandria Clasp ; Khedive's Bronze Star ; Order of Osmanieh, 3rd Class ; etc.

### *November* 9, 1882.

Invalided home through illness contracted on active service.

### *April* 6, 1883.

Appointed in command of " Excellent," gunnery schoolship.

### 1884.

Collaborated with Mr. W. T. Stead in the production of " The Truth About the Navy," resulting in increased Navy Estimates and the opening of a new era in the provision of an adequate Fleet.

# RECORDS

*November* 1, 1886.

Appointed Director of Naval Ordnance, occupying this post four and a half years. Carried out the transfer of the control of naval ordnance from the War Office to the Admiralty.

*August* 2, 1890.

Promoted to Rear-Admiral.

*May* 21, 1891.

Appointed Admiral-Superintendent of Portsmouth Dockyard. Expedited the completion of the " Royal Sovereign," first of a new type of battleships. Acted as host when the French Squadron under Admiral Gervais visited the Dockyard, 1891.

*February* 1, 1892.

Appointed Third Sea Lord and Controller of the Navy, and served in the administrations of Lord George Hamilton, Earl Spencer, and Mr· G. J. Goschen as First Lords ; and Admirals Sir A. Hood, Sir A. H. Hoskins and Sir F. W. Richards as First Sea Lords. During this period the firm stand of the Admiralty Board brought about the resignation of Mr. Gladstone, March 3, 1894.

*May* 26, 1894.

Appointed K.C.B.

*May* 8, 1896.

Promoted to Vice-Admiral.

*August* 24, 1897.

Hoisted his flag in H.M.S. " Renown " as Commander-in-Chief, North American Station.

1899.

Attended the first Hague Peace Conference as Naval Delegate.

# APPENDIX II

Appointed Commander-in-Chief, Mediterranean Station, with his flag in the " Renown," remaining in this post until June 2nd, 1902. Admiral Lord Beresford, Second-in-Command, says of this period in his " Memoirs " : " While Vice-Admiral Sir John Fisher was Commander-in-Chief of the Mediterranean Fleet, he greatly improved its fighting efficiency. As a result of his representations, the stocks of coal at Malta and Gibraltar were increased, the torpedo flotillas were strengthened, and the new breakwaters at Malta were begun. Some of Sir John Fisher's reforms are confidential ; but among his achievements which became common knowledge, the following are notable : From a 12-knot Fleet with breakdowns, he made a 15-knot Fleet without breakdowns ; introduced long range target practice, and instituted the Challenge Cup for heavy gun shooting ; instituted various war practices for officers and men ; invited, with excellent results, officers to formulate their opinions upon cruising and battle formation ; drew up complete instructions for torpedo flotillas ; exercised cruisers in towing destroyers and battleships in towing one another, thereby proving the utility of the device for saving coal in an emergency ; and generally carried into execution Fleet exercises based, not on tradition, but on the probabilities of war."

1900.

Received from the Sultan of Turkey the 1st Class of the Order of Osmanieh.

*November* 2, 1901.

Promoted to Admiral.

*June* 5, 1902.

Returned to the Admiralty as Second Sea Lord, remaining until August 31, 1903, with Lord Selborne, First Lord, and Admiral Lord Walter Kerr, First Sea Lord.

*June* 26, 1902.

Appointed G.C.B. in the Coronation Honours List.

265

# RECORDS

*December* 25, 1902.

Launched new scheme of naval entry and education for officers, with training colleges at Osborne and Dartmouth.

*May* 2, 1903.

Made his first public speech at the Royal Academy Banquet.

*August* 31, 1903.

Appointed Commander-in-Chief at Portsmouth, in order to supervise personally the inauguration of his new education scheme at Osborne College. Also energetically promoted the formation and development of the first British submarine flotilla.

*November* 7, 1903.

Appointed member of Committee with Lord Esher and Colonel Sir George Clarke (Lord Sydenham) to reorganise the War Office on the lines of the Admiralty Board.

*October* 21, 1904.

Appointed First Sea Lord in Lord Selborne's administration, and held this office for five years and three months, the period of his greatest activity and his preparation for a war with Germany. Some of the more notable of his many reforms are dealt with in his " Memories."

Also appointed, October 21, 1904, First and Principal Naval Aide-de-Camp to King Edward VII.

*December* 6, 1904.

Admiralty Memorandum on the Distribution of the Fleet, introducing nucleus crew system for ships in reserve, and withdrawing obsolete craft from foreign stations.

*January*, 1905.

Committee appointed to inquire into the reorganisation of the dockyards.

# APPENDIX II

*March 6, 1905.*

Appointment of Rear-Admiral Percy Scott to newly-created post of Inspector of Target Practice. By this and other means, including the service of Captain J. R. Jellicoe as Director of Naval Ordnance, the marksmanship of the Navy was vastly improved.

*December 4, 1905.*

Awarded the Order of Merit, and promoted by Special Order in Council to be an additional Admiral of the Fleet, thus giving him five more years on the active list in order to carry out his policy.

*February 10, 1906.*

Launch of the " Dreadnought," the first all-big-gun and turbine-driven battleship, as recommended by the Admiralty Committee on Design presided over by the First Sea Lord (Sir John Fisher).

*November, 1906.*

Establishment of the Naval War College at Portsmouth.

*January, 1907.*

Institution of a service of Fleet Auxiliaries—ammunition and store ships, distilling and hospital ships, fleet repair ships, fishing trawlers as, mine sweepers, etc., etc., etc., etc.,

*March, 1907.*

Creation of a new Home Fleet, with the " Dreadnought " as flagship for service in the North Sea.

*August, 1907.*

New scheme of advancement and pay of naval ranks and ratings introduced.

# RECORDS

*September*, 1907.

Establishment of a wireless telegraphy branch, and installation erected on the Admiralty building.

*November* 9, 1907.

Speech at the Lord Mayor's Banquet, assuring his countrymen that they could sleep quietly in their beds, and not be disturbed by invasion bogeys.

*June*, 1908.

Visited Reval with King Edward and Queen Alexandra on their visit to the Tsar of Russia. Awarded G.C.V.O. on the conclusion of this cruise.

*June* 17, 1908.

Created honorary LL.D. of Cambridge University.

*June*, 1909.

Entertained delegates to Imperial Press Conference at a review of the Fleet at Spithead, and a display of submarines, etc.

*December* 7, 1909.

Raised to the peerage as Baron Fisher of Kilverstone, in the County of Norfolk, after the manor bequeathed to his only son by the late Mr. Josiah Vavasseur, C.B.

*January* 25, 1910.

Retired from office of First Sea Lord, and was succeeded by Admiral of the Fleet Sir Arthur Wilson, but remained a member of the Committee of Imperial Defence. Recording his retirement in the First Lord's Memorandum, dated March 4, 1910, Mr. Reginald McKenna said : " The measures which are associated with his name and have been adopted by several successive Governments will prove of far-reaching and lasting benefit to the Naval Service and the country."

# APPENDIX II

*March* 10, 1910.

Took the oath and his seat in the House of Lords.

*May* 24, 1912.

Visited at Naples by Mr. Churchill (the new First Lord) and Mr. Asquith (Prime Minister).

*July* 30, 1912.

Appointed Chairman of the Royal Commission on Oil Fuel and Oil Engines for the Navy.

*September* 7, 1914.

Appointed Honorary Colonel of the First Naval Brigade, Royal Naval Division.

*October* 30, 1914.

Recalled to the Admiralty as First Sea Lord.

*December* 8, 1914.

Victory of Admiral Sir Doveton Sturdee over Admiral Count von Spee, due to the prompt dispatch from England of two battle-cruisers immediately on receipt of the news of the Coronel disaster. This was the most decisive battle of the war, the German force being practically annihilated.

*January* 24, 1915.

Action of Sir David Beatty off the Dogger Bank, and sinking of the " Blücher "—another striking success of the battle-cruiser design.

*May* 15, 1915.

Resignation as First Sea Lord over the Dardanelles question.

*July* 5, 1915.

Appointed Chairman of the Board of Invention and Research.

269

# RECORDS

*November* 16, 1915.

First speech in House of Lords, in reference to Mr. Churchill's speech on the previous day, following the latter's resignation from Cabinet.

*March* 21, 1917.

Second speech in House of Lords, declaring his refusal to discuss Dardanelles report during the war.

Awarded the Grand Cordon, with Paulownia, of the Japanese Order of the Rising Sun.

*May* 5, 1919.

Speech at the luncheon to Mr. Josephus Daniels, U.S. Naval Secretary.

*October* 21 (Trafalgar Day) 1919.

Publication of "Memories."

*December* 8 (Falkland Islands Day) 1919.

Publication of "Records."

# INDEX

# INDEX

## A

Action, 45

Adams, John Couch, 21

Admiralty House, Portsmouth, King Edward's visit to, 24, 25

Admiralty policy: replies to criticisms, 98 *et seq.*

Alcester, Lord, 30

Alderson, General, 54

Alexandria, bombardment of, 63, 256

Allan, Sir William, 88

Allenby, Lord, 241

American advance on Verdun, 246

Animated biscuits, 8

Arabi Pasha, 30

Arbuthnot, Sir Robert, 261

Archbishop and the pack of cards, the, 32

Armoured trains, institution of, 30

Ascension, the, 45

Asquith, Rt. Hon. H. H., 65, 179, 194, 214, 222, 242, 247, 269

Augé, M., 59

Automatic dropping mines for ocean use, 223–224

Aylesford, Lord, 3

## B

Bacon, Admiral Sir Reginald, 128, 181; on the big gun, 204–206

Baker, Mrs., Lord Fisher's cook, 26; invited to Buckingham Palace by King Edward, *ibid.*

Balfour, Rt. Hon. A. J., 56, 65, 98

Balliol College, Oxford, 2

Baltic project, the, 217 *et seq.*, 236, 241

Battle hymn of the American Republic, the, 77, 78

Beatty, Earl, 269

Beaufort Testimonial, won by Lord Fisher, 255

Beaumont, Admiral Sir Lewis, 30

Beilby, Sir George, 66

Benbow, Sir Henry, letter of, to Lord Fisher, 171

Beresford, Admiral Lord Charles, on training of officers and men for the Navy, 167–170; 260

Bethmann-Hollweg, Herr von, 247

Bible, the, and other reflections, 38 *et seq.*; Wyclif's translation, 43; Tyndale's, *ibid.*; Coverdale's, 44; Authorised, *ibid.*; Revised, *ibid.*; Cranmer's "Great Bible," *ibid.*

Big gun, the, 204 *et seq.*

Birthday Honours List a serial novel, 73

Black, Dr. Hugh, 38, 39, 77

Boar, Mr., 128

Board of Invention and Research, 193, 269

# INDEX

# INDEX

# INDEX

# INDEX

Lightning Source UK Ltd.
Milton Keynes UK
UKHW02n0951221018
330967UK00009B/794/P